URBAN

ENVIRONMENTAL

POLICY ANALYSIS

URBAN

ENVIRONMENTAL

POLICY ANALYSIS

HEATHER E. CAMPBELL AND ELIZABETH A. CORLEY

Routledge
Taylor & Francis Group

LONDON AND NEW YORK

First published 2012 by M.E. Sharpe

Published 2015 by Routledge
2 Park Square, Milton Park, Abingdon, Oxon OX14 4RN
711 Third Avenue, New York, NY 10017, USA

Routledge is an imprint of the Taylor & Francis Group, an informa business

Library of Congress Cataloging-in-Publication Data

Campbell, Heather E., 1961–
  Urban environmental policy analysis / by Heather E. Campbell and Elizabeth A. Corley.
    p. cm.
  Includes bibliographical references and index.
  ISBN 978-0-7656-2429-1 (hardcover : alk. paper)
  1. Urban ecology (Sociology) 2. Environmental policy. 3. City planning—Environmental
aspects. I. Corley, Elizabeth A., 1972– II. Title.

HT241.C357 2012
307.76—dc23   2011030529

ISBN 13: 9780765624307 (pbk)
ISBN 13: 9780765624291 (hbk)

Heather E. Campbell dedicates this book to
Her Parents, for teaching her to love learning,
Dr. John Mendeloff, for teaching her to love public policy analysis, and
Her Family, for being so supportive during the endgame

Elizabeth A. Corley dedicates this book to
Her Parents

Contents

Introduction xi

Part I: A Model and Policy Tools for the Urban Environment 1

1. An Environmental Policy System Framework for the City...........................3
  Modeling the City's Physical System...7
  The Social System..11
  The Policy Process 15
  An Overview of the City System 19
  The Purpose of the System Model 21

2. Policy-Analytic Concepts for the Urban Environment 25
  Private Goods 25
  Public Goods, Rivalry, Excludability, and Congestion 26
  Marketable Public Goods and Legal and Physical Excludability 33
  Common Pool Resources (CPRs) and the Tragedy of the Commons 35
  Externalities..41
  Recapitulation Regarding Public Goods 43
  The Right Amount of Pollution Is Rarely No Pollution..................................44
  The Law of Unintended Consequences..45
  The Fallacy of Sunk Costs 46
  How to Use the Information from This Chapter 47
  Discussion Questions 47
  Notes...49
  References 49

3. Useful Policy Instruments for Correcting Market Failures.......................51
  Some Useful Policy Instruments 52

Generic Solutions for Pure Private Goods 52
Information Problems...57
Generic Solutions for Marketable Public/Toll Goods 58
Generic Solutions for CPRs 61
Generic Solutions for Pure Public Goods 68
Congestion and Externalities..70
Excess Risk 72
Conclusion...73
Discussion Questions 75
Recommended Website 75

4. **Benefit-Cost Analysis**...78
The Basic Idea of Benefit-Cost Analysis...78
Three Important Issues in Formal BCA: Monetization,
    Standing, and Time...80
Standing: Whose Costs and Benefits Should Be Counted?.............80
Monetization..84
Taking into Account Externalities 101
Plug-In Shadow Prices 110
Other Issues That Are Likely to Arise in BCAs of
    Urban Environmental Policy 110
Sensitivity Analysis 114
Conclusion...114
Discussion Question and Exercises..116
Recommended Websites...116

**Part II: Bridging Policy, Politics, Economics, Ecology, Media,
and Communication**...121

5. **Integrating Policy, Ecosystem Management, and
Environmental Media** 123
Ecosystem Management..124
Adaptive Management 129
The Holistic Consideration of Air, Water, and Land
    Within the Conceptual Model 131
Checklists for Administrators 134
Conclusion...137

Part III: Environmental Media and Environmental Justice 139

6. **Air**..141
Interactions Between Air, Water, Land..141
Key Ecological Issues 142
Key Social Issues 145

Policy Tools in the Air Context 149
Conclusion and Checklist for Administrators 159

7. **Water** 163
Interactions 164
Key Ecological Issues 167
Key Social Issues and Policy Tools in the Water Context..........170
Conclusion and Checklist for Administrators 186
Recommended Websites..190

8. **Land**..195
Land Use in the Urban Environment..195
Trends in Urban Land Use 196
Key Ecological Issues 197
Key Social Issues 205
Policy Tools in the Land Context..208
Conclusion and Checklist for Administrators 211

9. **Environmental Justice**..215
The EJ Debate 215
Does Environmental Injustice Matter?..219
What Should Analysts Do About EJ?...221
Conclusion...225
Recommended Websites..226

Part IV: Communicating About Environmental Policy 231

10. **Learning from Citizens: Public Participation in Environmental Policy**
    By Nicholas L. Cain...233
Recent Trends in Public Participation 234
Benefits, Limits, and Cautions: Is It Worth the Effort?................238
Tools for Public Participation..238
Conclusion...251
Recommended Websites..253
References 253

11. **Creative, Democratic Methods for Teaching and Learning
    from Citizens**..257
Use Excellent Graphics 258
Reimagine Graphical Concepts..262
Consider Policy Games 262

Use Cutting-Edge Technology to Present Decision-Making
Data Creatively 274
Apply Several Creative Methods to Legitimation: Use an SVR 275
Conclusion 281
Notes 282
References 282

12. Conclusion 285
Take a Holistic Approach to Environmental Policy 285
Use Adaptive, Flexible, and Inclusive Management 287
Consider Interactions Between Environmental Media 287
Make Contextual and Ethical Use of Policy Tools 287
Summary 290
Note 291
References 291

Index 293
About the Authors 311

Introduction

For a variety of reasons, the city has become a central figure in environmental policy. One reason is a general rise in the importance of cities. Another reason is the growth in global urbanization under way in the early part of the twenty-first century. A third reason, at least in the United States, is because of the "new federalism" and the abrogation of certain environmental policy responsibilities by the national government, along with failures of many subnational states to step in and fill the gap. Due to the rise of global urbanization, the majority of people worldwide now live in cities; therefore, cities do and will generate a significant portion of human-caused pollution (United ScienceDaily, 2007; Nations Information Service, 2004). For all these reasons, it makes sense to focus on cities in attempts to improve global environmental health. There is an old saying: If you want to hunt ducks, go where the ducks are. When it comes to environmental change, cities are where the ducks are.

Another reason to focus on the local level, as one scholar has argued, is that "local governments exist at a level in which there is personal contact between government actors and the regulated parties, which can create powerful social norms;" local government, then, may be an ideal arena for environmental control (Flatt, 2007, 2). Significant research in the cooperation literature indicates that personal contact enhances cooperation (Orbell, van de Kragt, and Dawes, 1988; Ostrom, Walker, and Gardner, 1992), and, among governmental units, cities may be most suited to creating personal contacts. Furthermore, cities themselves have chosen to accept significant burdens of environmental policy, as certain endorsements at the 75th annual meeting of U.S. mayors indicate (U.S. Conference of Mayors, 2007, for example, 164–168).

This book is intended to assist administrators and other decision makers as they focus on the importance of environmental policy within the context of the city. Its aim is to help current and future urban decision makers, administrators, and analysts consider the many and interrelated issues of urban environmental policy, with the goal of improving the quality of both policy and administrative decisions.

Some portions of this chapter were first published in H.E. Campbell, "A Comparative Framework for Analyzing Urban Environmental Policy," *Journal of Comparative Policy Analysis*, 12, 4 (2010), 373–394. Used with permission.

The authors do this by:

- illustrating a systems-based model of the city that provides a holistic view of environmental media (land, air, and water) and highlights the extent to which environmental policy decisions are intertwined with the Natural, Built, and Social systems of the city;
- introducing basic and environment-specific policy-analytic models, methods, and tools;
- presenting and discussing specific environmental policy puzzles that will confront cities; and
- presenting methods for understanding and educating public opinions around urban environmental policy.

Throughout this book, examples from cities around the world are given to help clarify the relationship between ideas and their application, and to introduce people in one city, region, or country to ideas from others.

This book can help those at higher levels of the decision-making chain, as well. Clearly, supranational-, national- and state-level decision makers need to understand and affect city environmental policy and outcomes. A crucial factor in modern pollution is that "the paradigmatic modern environmental harm is anything but local. It is generally trans-boundary harm caused by products or processes in a national or international market, whose profits are far removed from their harms" (Flatt, 2007, 4). The concentration of human populations within cities means that there will also be a concentration of environmental harm there—and those same environmental harms will emanate from the affected cities. So, while cities themselves need to work on urban environmental issues, work at all other levels of government is also warranted.

As the history of urban planning explicates, this is not a new situation for cities (see, for example, Daniels, 2009). In the introduction to a special 100th-anniversary issue of the *Journal of the American Planning Association*, Birch and Silver (2009) point out that, even in the first 1909 meeting of the National Conference on City Planning, the environment was a major concern; later, "the passage of national antipollution legislation (for example, the Clean Air and Clean Water Acts) similarly resulted from environmental abuses first seen in cities" (119). Today, however, cities have become linchpins in sustainability practices.

Fortunately, there is evidence that we may have reached a point where citizens worldwide are prepared to act. As reported by World Public Opinion, a 2007 survey performed by GlobeScan and the Program on International Policy Attitudes (PIPA) for the BBC World Service asked 22,000 people in 21 countries— both industrialized and developing—about their beliefs regarding human activity, climate change, and what should be done to alleviate problems in the future. "Large majorities . . . believe that . . . strong action must be taken, sooner rather than later, in developing as well as developed countries. . . . In 13 of 21 [of the] countries [polled], at least twice as many call for 'major steps starting very soon' as those concluding that 'modest steps over the coming years' will suffice" (World Public Opinion, 2007). Respondents were residents of Canada, the United States, Mexico, Brazil, Chile, Spain, Italy, France, Germany, Russia, Great Britain, Turkey, Egypt, Nigeria, Kenya, South Korea, China, Australia, Philippines, Indonesia, and India, with urbanized individuals the only ones polled in some countries. Perhaps the president of GlobeScan summed up the results best: "The strength of these findings makes it difficult to imagine a more supportive public opinion environment for national leaders to commit to climate action" (World Public Opinion, 2007).

This book is directed toward policymakers and practitioners in particular, rather than general citizens. The evidence amassed in these pages shows that worldwide environmental problems are sufficiently complex and interwoven to warrant systemic solutions. As Thomas L. Friedman (2007) bluntly puts it, "To Save Energy, Change Leaders, Not Light Bulbs." We hope this book can help change leaders by giving them a clearer understanding and better policy tools to help approach the complex problems—including the political problems—inherent in urban environmental policy.

Friedman's (2007) points are apparently embedded in a belief in human-caused, or anthropogenic, climate change; however, to use and benefit from this book, readers need not share this view—a firm belief that your city has environmental issues that need addressing will suffice. We do not wish to derail interest in this book and its tools by focusing excessively on the huge debate regarding anthropogenic climate change (the hypothesis that the planet is entering a warmer age due to human effects on the global system linked to the massive natural experiment caused by the Industrial Revolution and the exhalation of vast quantities of carbon dioxide [CO_2] into the atmosphere). We strongly believe there is sufficient evidence in favor of human-caused change to accept the hypothesis for now, but we want to make it clear that the value of this book does not hinge on a shared acceptance of this theory.

As noted at the Conference on Climate Change and Higher Education in Arizona ("Preparing Our Students for a Changing World"), we know Earth's climate will change—whether due to human behavior or not (Crow, 2007). Daniel Sarewitz made a similar point in his discussion of the importance of social adaptation: "Adaptation has been portrayed as a sort of selling out, because it accepts that the future will be different from the present. . . . The future will be different from the present no matter what, so to not adapt is to consign millions to death and disruption" (2007). We know that cities will need to grapple with environmental change on the local level, even if not on the global level. Therefore, we need to have policy and administrative systems that adapt and respond to these changes. Since humans are increasingly concentrated in cities, we specifically need urban policies that adapt and respond to the challenges ahead.

"To Save Energy, Change Leaders, Not Light Bulbs"

People often ask: I want to get greener, what should I do?
. . . Choose the right leaders. It is so much more important to change your leaders than to change your light bulbs.
    Why? Because leaders write the rules, set the standards and offer the tax incentives that drive market behavior across a whole city, state or country.

Source: Friedman, 2007.

THE IMPORTANCE OF THE RISE OF URBANIZATION

As Exhibit I.1 indicates, the rise of urbanization is an important feature that affects the futures of both industrialized and developing countries. There are at least two reasons why city decision makers should be concerned: One is idealistic and focuses on the good of the populace; the other is instrumental. At least in the United States, residents are highly mobile, and cities must compete for companies and workers and the tax dollars they generate. If resident dissatisfaction is high enough, residents with resources will leave and go to another city where conditions are better. Some evidence suggests this mobility will continue to rise worldwide, particularly among people whose high economic status generates a disproportionate percentage of tax dollars. In addition, levels of pollution will have an impact on the health and satisfaction of those who remain, impacting the stresses and demands on all city services.

Exhibit I.1

The Importance of Urbanization

Today urbanization is a dominant demographic trend and an important component of land-transformation processes worldwide. [In 2000] slightly less than half of the world's population now resides in cities, but this proportion is projected to rise to 61 percent in the next 30 years (UN, 1997a). The Developed nations have more highly urbanized populations; for example, close to 80 percent of the U.S. population is urban. However, projections for the twenty-first century indicate that the largest cities, and the largest growth in city size, will occur in developing nations. Between 1980 and 2030, the percentage of the urban population on the African continent will double from 27 percent to 54 percent (UN Population Division, 1997a). Urbanization trends of the past century also show a dramatic rise in the size of cities: Over 300 cities have more than 1 million inhabitants, and 16 "megacities" have populations exceeding 10 million (UN Population Division, 1997b). Urbanization interacts with global change in important ways. For example, although urban areas account for only 2 percent of Earth's land surface, they produce 78 percent of greenhouse gases, thus contributing to global climate change. Cities also play a central role in alteration of global biogeochemical cycles, changes in biodiversity due to habitat fragmentation and exotic species, and changes in land use and cover far beyond the city's boundaries. . . .

The growing impact of urban areas on the face of the earth is reason enough to study them. An even more compelling argument for understanding how cities work in an ecological sense is the fact that humans live in them and must depend on proper management to maintain an acceptable quality of life for the foreseeable future.

Source: Grimm et al., 2000. Used with permission.

Though it may seem extreme to worry about our own civilization at this point, history shows that some past urban environmental systems became so degraded as to be destroyed:

> Among the more severe human-induced environmental impacts are those associated with ancient urban societies, whose dense populations, rising rates of consumption, and agricultural intensification led to regional degradation so extreme that cities were abandoned and the productive potential of entire civilizations was undermined to the point of ruin. Archaeology has documented repeated examples of such impacts. (Grimm et al., 2000, 572)

Though it is clear that our ability to manage the impact of concentrated human population has improved vastly, the continued human concentration in both the developed and lesser developed world, in some instances in cities of sizes never before seen, means that we must continue to manage these effects. Even if areas are not so severely degraded as to require abandonment, without careful attention to waste processes, cities can become unpleasant and unhealthy places to live.

There are at least two other reasons to focus attention on urban environmental policy. One is that in some cases cities have made more progress toward sustainability than national governments (Devuyst with Hens and De Lannoy, 2001). Examples of successful city endeavors can help cities learn from each other. Second, Chapter 28 of Agenda 21, a United Nations action plan focusing on sustainability (sometimes called the Rio Agenda), places special emphasis on "local governments" (as cited by Devuyst with Hens and De Lannoy, 2001). Especially in Europe, with the creation of the Charter of European Cities & Towns Towards Sustainability, also known as the Aalborg Charter (European Commission, 1994), many cities have begun the process of improving their sustainability within a participative governance process (Devuyst with Hens and De Lannoy, 2001). As suggested earlier, citizens may feel more connected to city government than to higher levels of government, and this may inspire a greater willingness to act at the local level.

THE IMPORTANCE OF A POLICY-ANALYTIC PERSPECTIVE

Roseland (2001) maintains that the earlier literature on "eco-cities" had "much inspiration but relatively little guidance" (92) for practitioners who wished to apply these "concepts to the communities where they work and live" (92). The author organizes more recent green literature on cities (see Table I.1) by the "backgrounds, world views, or orientations of the people who generally participate in each type of literature" (Roseland, 2001, 93). There are two factors of particular interest in Roseland's organization of categories: one is his claim that only "occasional academics" (94) work in the practitioner literature; the other is his failure to mention policy analysts in any of his categories.

Though academic policy analysts have done much work in environmental policy, and while the field of policy analysis targets practitioners, there has been little

Table I.1

Categories in the Green Literature on Cities

Designers	Practitioners	Visionaries	Activists
The costs of sprawl	Sustainable urban development	Sustainable communities	Green cities
Sustainability by design	Sustainable cities Local sustainability initiatives	Community self-reliance	Eco-cities Eco-communities

Source: Roseland, 2001.

drawing together of the policy-analytic framework and approach in a pragmatic format for coping with the environmental problems of cities. This book begins to fill that gap.

THE PLAN OF THIS BOOK

In order to cover many topics useful to successful urban environmental policy analysis and administration, this book is organized as follows:

- Chapter 1 presents a graphical framework of the city as an interlinked set of three systems: the Natural System, the Concretion System, and the Social System. Because of the government sector's importance to environmental policy, particular attention is given to this subset of the Social System.
- Chapters 2 and 3 are closely tied. The former presents basic concepts in the field of policy analysis that are useful in thinking about policy problems and their solutions; it concentrates on attributes of goods (products and services) that allow us to analyze their potentially problematic elements. Chapter 3 looks at the general classes of policy solutions that may be useful to urban environmental policy in particular.
- Chapter 4 offers an introduction to Benefit-Cost Analysis, a key tool in policy analysis, with special emphasis on topics that are useful for urban environmental policy.
- Chapter 5 provides tools for integrating the information contained in Chapters 1 through 4 when performing your own analysis. It also serves as a bridge to the next sections.
- Chapters 6 through 9 inform the reader about ecological and other contexts of urban environmental policy concern, including not only land, water, and air, but also environmental justice.
- The last section, composed of Chapters 10 and 11, discusses methods for understanding public opinions and educating the public to engage more effectively in democratic governance regarding urban environmental policy issues. Topics include standard methods such as surveys, charettes (design exercises), focus groups, and town hall meetings, as well as less traditional

methods such as games, contingent valuation method, and structured value referenda.
- Chapter 12 concludes with a review of the main themes of the book.

Throughout, as appropriate, the material is leavened with case materials relevant to theory and/or practice in cities throughout the world.

WHAT THIS BOOK DOES NOT DO

This book does not attempt to tell you what policies to adopt in your city. In urban environmental policy, one size rarely fits all. Those policies suitable for your city depend on the particular problems to be addressed, the prevailing culture of the city, the powers of the government, city-specific demographics, potential interactions between environmental media, the range of citizen opinions, and a host of other factors. Here we wish to give you the tools to think analytically, creatively, and holistically about urban environmental policy.

There are broader, activist-inspired social movements throughout the world to create cities that are *fully* sustainable—environmentally, socially, culturally, and in terms of net energy analysis. Examples include the World Health Organization (WHO) Healthy Cities project and C. Maser's 1997 book *Sustainable Community Development* (both mentioned in Devuyst with Hens and De Lannoy, 2001). Maser (1997) argues that a truly sustainable city arises "as a community-directed process of development based on: a) transcendent human values of love, trust, respect, wonder, humility, and compassion; b) active learning, which is a balance between the intellect and intuition, between the abstract and the concrete, between action and reflection; c) sharing that is generated through communication, cooperation, and coordination . . . " and so on through "g) a shared societal vision that is grounded in long-term sustainability, both culturally and environmentally" (explicated in Devuyst with Hens and De Lannoy, 2001, 22). WHO argues that "a healthy city in the future would have a clean, safe, high-quality physical environment, and would operate within its ecosystem. . . . The community would be strong, mutually supportive, and non-exploitative . . . and its people would have a strong sense of connectedness with their biological and cultural heritage, as well as with other groups and individuals within the city" (explicated in Devuyst with Hens and De Lannoy, 2001, 28). Some of these movements are categorized under the term "eco-cities." Without in any way denying the desirability of such comprehensive goals, this book focuses more narrowly on improving the process and outcomes of urban environmental policies in their most generally understood sense—policies focusing on the pollution generated by and environmental amenities affected by humans in urban environments.

This book incorporates the assumption that policy processes and outcomes occur within a generally democratic city governance structure—one in which residents have relative freedom to live and work where they want, and policymakers must and do care about the opinions of the residents. While there are many indications that the world may rapidly become a far less desirable human habitat, we believe that the political process and system—at least within the U.S. setting—is unlikely to make the utopian leap in one go. Instead, by applying "the art of the possible," we can help decision makers achieve more incremental improvements that have a greater likelihood of success. A central tenet of policy analysis is the idea that one should not let the perfect be the enemy of the good—that is, it is better to work toward a likely improvement than to spurn smaller-scale improvements and hold out for an unlikely "perfect" solution. This is why this book only makes steps toward sustainability.

CONCLUSION

The purpose of this book is to help cities navigate the route to sustainability. With environmental progress and education, eventually we may be able to achieve the broadest goals of sustainability; before that can happen, though, we need to improve the unsustainable environmental load our cities now generate and help emerging cities avoid the same problems other cities have created. This book seeks to help with the good, since we don't believe the perfect is possible.

ACKNOWLEDGMENTS

We would like to acknowledge Felipe Ruiz Acosta, for artistic depictions of the system model; Nick Cain, for writing Chapter 10 and for contributions to Chapter 7; Jeffrey Callen, for research assistance; Alan Campbell and Patricia Campbell, for editing far above the call of duty; Brett Close, for comments on Chapter 2; Brandon Dabling, for significant research assistance, and especially for the management of the permissions process and the formatting; Michael Davidson, for comments on Chapter 7; Janet Denhardt and Robert Denhardt, for help with the enterprise of publishing a book; Adam Eckerd, for comments and contributions to Chapter 9; Dietram Scheufele for comments and feedback; Louise Shaler, for her wonderful global water-news summaries; Robin Sobotta, for comments and contributions to Chapter 9; Josh Tasoff, for discussions of market failure; Fern Tiger of Fern Tiger Associates, for contributions to Chapter 11; Carol Tschudi, for comments on Chapter 4; Michael Tschudi, for quick and terrific maps and line figures; Clara Tschudi-Campbell, for comments on Chapter 1; Alexis Vaughn, for comments on Chapter 2; and Ellen Williams for comments and feedback.

REFERENCES

Birch, E.L., and C. Silver. 2009. One hundred years of city planning's enduring and evolving connections. *Journal of the American Planning Association*, 75, 2, 113–122.

Crow, M. 2007. Preparing our students for a changing world. Speech delivered at the Conference on Climate Change and Higher Education in Arizona, Tempe, AZ, September 27.

Daniels, T. L. 2009. A trail across time: American environmental planning from city beautiful to sustainability. *Journal of the American Planning Association*, 75, 2, 178–192.

Devuyst, D., with L. Hens and W. De Lannoy (eds.). 2001. *How Green Is the City? Sustainability Assessment and the Management of Urban Environments.* New York: Columbia University Press.

European Commission. 1994. Charter of European cities & towns towards sustainability. Approved by the participants at the European Conference on Sustainable Cities & Towns, Aalborg, Denmark, May 27. http://ec.europa.eu/environment/urban/pdf/aalborg_charter.pdf (accessed March 10, 2011).

Flatt, V.B. 2007. Act locally, affect globally: How the structure of local government makes it the best arena for engagement and work with the private sector to control environmental harms. Social Science Research Network (SSRN), August. http://papers.ssrn.com/sol3/papers.cfm?abstract_id=1002664.

Friedman, T.L. 2007. To save energy, change leaders, not light bulbs. *Arizona Republic*, October 23, p. B5.

Grimm, N.B., J.M. Grove, S.T.A. Pickett, and C.L. Redman. 2000. Integrated approaches to long-term studies of urban ecological systems. *BioScience*, 50, 7 (July), 571–584.

Maser, C. 1997. *Sustainable Community Development: Principles and Concepts*. Delray Beach, FL: St. Lucie Press. As cited in Devuyst with Hens and De Lannoy, 2001.

Orbell, J.M., A. van de Kragt, and R.M. Dawes. 1988. Explaining discussion-induced cooperation. *Journal of Personality and Social Psychology*, 54, 5, 811–819.

Ostrom, E., J. Walker, and R. Gardner. 1992. Covenants with and without a sword: Self-governance is possible. *American Political Science Review*, 86, 2, 404–417.

Roseland, M. 2001. The eco-approach to sustainable development in urban areas. In *How Green Is the City?* ed. D. Devuyst with L. Hens and W. De Lannoy. New York: Columbia University Press.

Sarewitz, D. 2007. In the News. *ASU Insight*, 27, 33 (April 20), 3.

ScienceDaily. 2007. World population becomes more urban than rural. *Science News*, May 25. http://www.sciencedaily.com/releases/2007/05/070525000642.htm (accessed January 31, 2010).

United Nations Information Service. 2004. UN report says world urban population of 3 billion today expected to reach 5 billion by 2030. UNIS Vienna, March 25. http://www.unis.unvienna.org/unis/pressrels/2004/pop899.html (accessed January 31, 2010).

United Nations Population Division. 1997a. Urban and rural areas, 1950–2030. 1996 revision. New York: United Nations.

———. 1997b. Urban agglomerations, 1950–2015. 1996 revision. New York: United Nations.

U.S. Conference of Mayors. 2007. The United States Conference of Mayors 75th Anniversary, 1932–2007. Adopted resolutions, June. http://www.usmayors.org/75thAnnualMeeting/resolutions_full.pdf (accessed September 10, 2007).

World Public Opinion. 2007. Developed and developing countries agree: Action needed on global warming. BBC World Service poll, September 24. http:/www.worldpublicopinion.org/incl/print-able_version.php?pnt=412 (accessed September 27, 2007).

URBAN

ENVIRONMENTAL

POLICY ANALYSIS

Part I

A Model and Policy Tools for the Urban Environment

1 An Environmental Policy System Framework for the City

When beginning to think about urban environmental policy, the task can seem overwhelming. Just envisioning the urban system is difficult. A city incorporates infrastructure, including transportation modes (for example, public roads, private roads, bridges, railroads, airports, and ferries); water, sewer, and gas pipes and water treatment plants; electricity generating stations and the distribution grid; wire-based and wireless communication structures; street lighting, including traffic lights; public buildings; private buildings; and a vast stock of signs. A city also includes a complex aggregation of institutions—the embodiment of government and laws—including the organizations that allow for policing, firefighting, education, recreation services, zoning, and the collection and disposal of waste. Clearly, the list could go on, and the enumerated items can overlap and interact. Additionally, they defy tidy aggregation with private elements such as gated communities and private schools.

Thinking about environmental issues is an equally complex task. Urban environmental issues may encompass anything from the effects on air quality and human health of heavy dust raised during construction, to the effects on and interaction of non-native species with native species, to tradeoffs between water and urban heat—if we reduce lawns, we will save water, but will we increase urban heat-island effects?

Because of the complexity of each of these topics, it is useful to have a model, or mental framework, for thinking about urban environmental policy. Such a framework is a simplification of reality that focuses the analyst's attention solely on those specific factors important to the task at hand.

This chapter presents a new, graphical, systems-based framework model designed to help researchers and decision makers understand the extent to which environmental policy decisions are intertwined with the natural, built, and social systems of the city. Such a framework can provide a mental checklist to help reduce the likelihood of neglecting key elements of urban environmental issues. Use of the term "graphical" indicates that this new framework is primarily pictorial and conceptual, and is not

A version of this chapter was published as H.E. Campbell, "A Comparative Framework for Analyzing Urban Environmental Policy," *Journal of Comparative Policy Analysis,* 12, 4 (2010), 373–394. Used with permission. Special thanks to Felipe Ruiz Acosta, who produced the figures in this chapter.

A *model* is a simplification of reality for a specific analytic purpose. The interior designer's model of an airplane's seats, rugs, and overhead bins is as valid as the aerospace engineer's fuselage model used for testing lift and stresses—but each is valid as a completely different simplification of the same object for a different purpose. At least in the social sciences, we currently are far from having some type of unified theory that can explain all phenomena. Like the interior designer and the engineer, we select models that can help us with our tasks.

described with a set of equations. Similarly, it is "systems-based" because it is inspired by systems thinking—including concepts of sources, sinks, feedback, etc.—but it is not expressed as a computer-based dynamic model. The framework is designed as both a teaching tool and an analysis tool, especially to serve those who are now or will become urban policymakers and administrators throughout the world as they struggle with issues of sustainability, arguably the most important challenge of our age (Heffernon, Welch, and Melnick, 2007).

In this book, we simplify the urban environmental policy framework by depicting the city as three different layers that interact with each other. Our goal is to maintain a holistic view of urban environmental policy analysis and help readers learn how the policy and governmental aspects can affect the other pieces of the urban environmental system.

We call the three layers the "Natural" System, the "Concretion" System, and the "Social" System. Together the Natural and Concretion Systems form the Physical System. A key element of the Social System is the Governmental Subsystem. All of the layers are part of "an interconnected system held together by flows of energy, water, people, ideas, and materials" (Gober, 2006, 9). Each of these layers is explained in detail later but introduced briefly in the next few paragraphs.

The Natural System is that part of the city that is provided by nature. The Natural layer is the biogeophysical system that the city is placed upon and within; it includes the physical geography of the space, the plants and animals that inhabit it, and the climate, especially temperatures and precipitation. Generally, these are attributes that nature supplies to the city. Though all of these are affected by human occupation, they also serve as constraints on urbanization.

The Concretion layer encompasses the physical parts of the city that are or have been created by humans. The Concretion System represents the physical elements that people place upon and within the Natural layer. They include buildings and roads, public works, utility systems, mines, and dumps. If all the people suddenly left the city, the concretions would still be there. These elements are affected by the Natural layer, and also affect it, not only in very visible ways—such as via dams—but also in less obvious ways, such as by affecting patterns of movement and habitation of plants and animals. Use of the term "concretion" (House, 1973) is intended to remind the analyst that the physical structure of the city builds up over time, like the layers of a seashell, and that newer concretions may lie upon older ones.

The Social layer includes the social institutions that humans create. In this context, an "institution" is not a physical place, but a social organization (Ostrom, 2005). An institution can include something like a club or a bureaucracy, but it can also include laws (for example, the U.S. Constitution is an institution) or even social norms. Thus, the city's economy is an institution (a form of social organization), as are neighborhoods, neighborhood associations, religious congregations, firms, and nonprofit organizations (also called nongovernmental organizations, or NGOs). Both the Natural and Concretion layers affect the Social layer—and vice versa.

It is fairly easy to see how the Natural and Concretion layers affect each other and how the Social and Concretion layers affect each other. Floods, hurricanes, and tornadoes remind us that the Natural System affects the Social System. Ensconced in our own cultures, it can be more challenging to see how the Social System affects the Natural System, yet our cultural assumptions and habits definitely affect the Natural System.

What is culture? In its most basic sense, it is defined as a "way of life, lifestyle; customs, traditions, heritage, habits, ways, mores, values" (Oxford American Dictionaries, 2005). However, significant social science research on culture may provide additional illumination. Ostrom (2005, 27) notes, "The term *culture* is frequently applied to the values shared within a community. Culture affects the mental models that participants in a situation may share" (emphasis in original). In their book *Risk and Culture*, which focuses on the perception of environmental risk, Douglas and Wildavsky (1982, 8) argue that the perception of environmental risk is inextricably embedded in culture: "Our guiding assumptions are that any form of society produces its own selected view of the natural environment." They define culture as a "set of shared values and supporting social institutions" (1982, 8). Culture varies from city to city, from nation to nation, from religion to religion. Our habits, ways of life, traditions, mental models, and so on affect how we interact with nature.

> What is culture? A "way of life, lifestyle; customs, traditions, heritage, habits, ways, mores, values" (Oxford American Dictionaries, 2005). Culture varies from city to city, from nation to nation, from religion to religion. Our customs, way of life, traditions, etc. affect how we interact with nature.

Case 1.1 and Case 1.2 demonstrate the influence of culture (part of the Social System) on the Natural System. The "environmental services" we ask of nature depend on attributes of our society. Under current conditions, Case 1.1 could not arise in, for example, the United States. Case 1.2, on the other hand, is possible only in a society with significant use of toilet paper and condoms. There are parts of the world where toilet paper is not routinely used, and condoms were illegal, for example, in Ireland until the 1970s (Collier, 2007, 171). Depending on your "mental models," one use of the river may appear strange while the other appears normal (though "normal" and "desirable" are not necessarily the same).

———■ **Case 1.1** ■———

An Example of the Effect of the Social System on the Natural System—Rivers in Indian Cities

Statues of Hindu God Causing River Pollution

New commercially made idols used in the Hindu festival Ganesh Caturthi are releasing toxic dyes into India's waterways, spurring a campaign to return to traditional, natural materials.

[In Surat, an Indian city of about 3.8 million people, it was estimated that more than 26,000 Ganesh idols made from a paste-like form of calcium sulfate known as plaster of Paris were submerged in the Tapi River in September 2009. The statues were coated with paints containing mercury, cadmium, lead, and carbon, all of which are hazardous (TNN 2009).]

Ganesh Statues Causing Trouble

The "Ganesh Chaturthi" festival celebrates the birthday of the elephant god Ganesh, and is held during the beginning of August or September every year according to the Hindu calendar. The festivities end with the immersion of thousands of large Ganesh statues into bodies of water [throughout India].

The growing crowds honoring Ganesh have attracted commercial vendors offering brightly colored statues that may look appealing but are threatening India's waterways, according to environmentalists.

Traditionally, the idols were made with natural ingredients such as mud, clay and vegetable-based dyes. But the commercialization of the holiday has spawned a proliferation of bigger and brighter idols made out of plaster of Paris and painted with toxic chemical dyes, according to the Kalpavriksh environment action group, which is campaigning to make the festival more environmentally sensitive.

"This festival brings together thousands of people, but in modern times is also contributing to serious environmental pollution," the Kalpavriksh group says, thanks to new commercial Ganesh statues "painted using toxic chemical dyes to make them bright and attractive to buyers."

The toxic materials are poisoning water bodies, harming plants and fish, and sickening those who drink the water downstream. "The immersion of idols made out of chemical materials causes significant water pollution," the group says, also citing problems with the festival's crowds and noise.

Source: findingDulcinea.com, 2008. Used with permission.

Also within the Social layer is the Governmental Subsystem. Democratic governments receive their power from the people, but they also serve as constraints on the people and thus on both the Social and Concretion layers. Though government need not always act in a coercive manner, among social institutions its particular feature is the legitimate power to coerce compliance.[1] Government serves as the "watchman."

■———— **Case 1.2** ————■

An Example of the Effects of a Different Social System on the Natural System—A River in Two U.S. Cities

Urban Renewal—Efforts to Reduce Mississippi River Pollution

A racing shell speeds by. A car clatters overhead. Streetlights on the frail black arch of the old Lake Street bridge wink off as the city awakens. Graffiti advises me to Spit on Authority. This is the Mississippi River between Minneapolis and St. Paul [the Twin Cities]. . . .

This section of river was once too polluted to support [much] life. Thirty years ago a Minnesota Department of Natural Resources fisheries crew found a mere seven species of fish in a stretch that should have produced dozens; bacteria was robbing the river of oxygen as it broke down raw and partially treated sewage. One biologist reported that the surveyors' nets were "so filled with toilet paper and condoms they had to go home." Winona State University professor Calvin Fremling found that despite their abundance on the river from northern Iowa to St. Louis, mayflies were conspicuously absent from the Twin Cities down to Lake Pepin.

Source: Breining, 1994. Used with permission.

Though it will not always coerce, the fact that it can is one key to its importance. Governmental coercion is not unconstrained, since legitimate governments are themselves constrained by law and social norms, and ultimately governments may be overthrown.

As the boxed definition of a model suggests, we are not claiming that this is the only available model of the city. Instead, we introduce this model as one that can help us focus on the different elements of the city that are most relevant to urban environmental policy. In particular, it is important that we emphasize the Governmental Subsystem within the Social layer and analyze it at some length; for our purposes, it is the government that serves as the primary lever for accomplishing public policy.

MODELING THE CITY'S PHYSICAL SYSTEM

Our pictorial model of the city is shown in several figures, features boxes, arrows, and clouds. Figure 1.1 defines these symbols. As is standard in systems models, boxes indicate major systems or subsystems of the model, and arrows indicate flows. Thus, the arrows between the Natural System box and the Concretion System box (shown in Figure 1.2) indicate that resources and constraints flow between these two systems: they affect each other. Clouds indicate "sources" and "sinks." Sources and sinks are locations outside the modeled system from which flows come and to which flows go. Use of the cloud symbol indicates that these sources and sinks are not directly dealt

Figure 1.1 **Symbols Used in System Models**

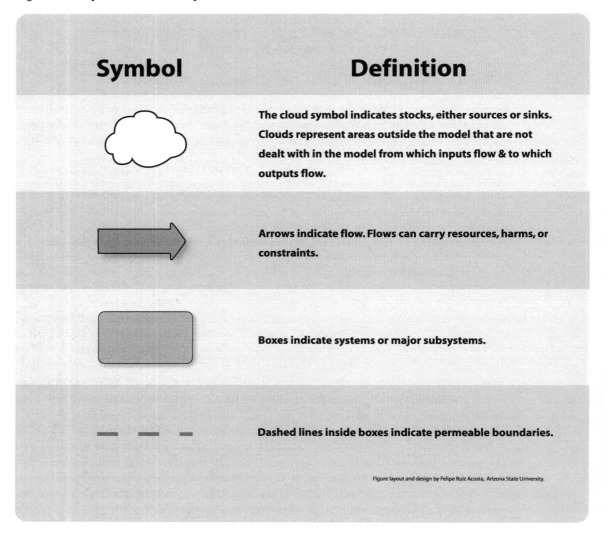

Symbol	Definition
	The cloud symbol indicates stocks, either sources or sinks. Clouds represent areas outside the model that are not dealt with in the model from which inputs flow & to which outputs flow.
	Arrows indicate flow. Flows can carry resources, harms, or constraints.
	Boxes indicate systems or major subsystems.
	Dashed lines inside boxes indicate permeable boundaries.

Figure layout and design by Felipe Ruiz Acosta, Arizona State University.

with by the model—they are cloudy to us. Here, the modeled system is the city, so these clouds remind us that resources and constraints can come from outside the city and can leave the city. In our model, we also use a dashed line to indicate a permeable interface between subsystems of the model. Throughout the system figures (Figures 1.2, 1.3, and 1.5), you will see symbols inside system and subsystem boxes. These symbols are intended to remind you of many of the elements that are involved in the city system, though they are not exhaustive.

Figure 1.2 shows a model of the Physical System of the city, incorporating both the Natural System and the Concretion System. Note that the natural and human-made physical systems of the city are tightly coupled. Each changes and constrains the other.

Figure 1.2   **The Physical System of the City**

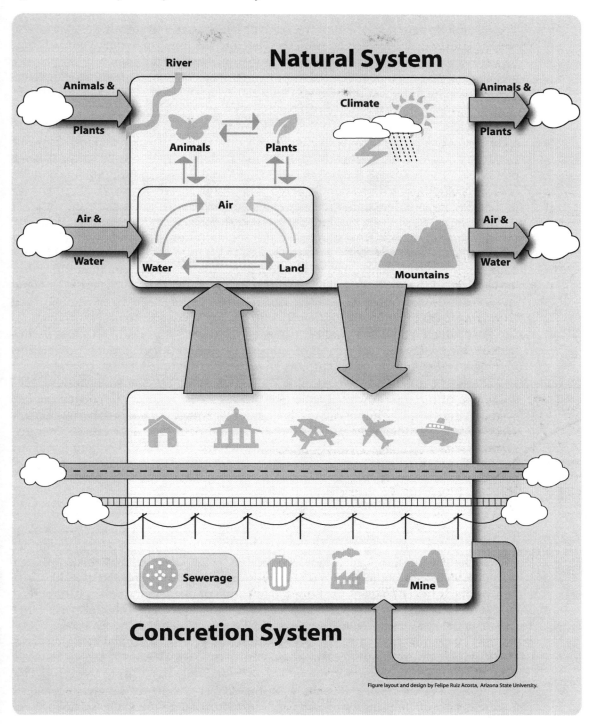

Figure layout and design by Felipe Ruiz Acosta, Arizona State University.

THE NATURAL SYSTEM OF THE CITY

The Natural System (top of Figure 1.2) provides resources and amenities to the city, as well as constraints. Physical constraints related to the city's geography are indicated by the river and mountain symbols in the figure (these do not represent all possible geophysical barriers but are reminders of them). Such constraints affect, though do not fully determine, the form of the city. The weather symbol reminds us that the climate is also an important part of the city's Natural System.

Air, water, and land inextricably interact in the Natural System, but they are not fully contained within the city. Air and water flow into the system and also flow out. Land may flow into the system through dust or erosion (via air or water) or volcanism; otherwise, land flows are minor. Air, water, and land flows can bring in or take away resources or pollution. For example, rivers whose sources are far away can bring water to the city, and aquifers under the city can be depleted by users outside the city.

The Natural System also includes plants and animals, including bacteria. While we focus primarily on modeling humans in the Social System, it is important to keep in mind that all living things are part of the Natural System and cannot survive without it. Animals are not stationary; they flow into and out of the city system. Plants also flow into and out of the system, carried by wind, water, and animals. These flows of plants and animals can have positive or negative consequences for the city. For example, West Nile virus–carrying mosquitoes that fly into the city cause health problems that may need to be dealt with by public health agencies. On the other hand, birds that fly into the city during their annual migration may please residents and attract bird-watching tourists—and eat mosquitoes! (Illinois Department of Public Health, 2007).

The cloud symbols at the beginning of animal, plant, air, and water inflows, and at the end of their outflows, indicate that their sources or sinks are outside the city system. However, it is important to remember that sources or sinks that exist outside a city's system can be brought into the system via purchase, annexation, intergovernmental arrangements, or other means. In other words, the city's boundaries are not fixed over time.

THE CONCRETION SYSTEM OF THE CITY

The shape and form of the Concretion System (bottom of Figure 1.2) are influenced by the form of the Natural System, and also directly affect it. These two systems interact with each other in significant ways, as indicated by the large arrows connecting them in the figure. For example, land is often re-formed in development, and the addition of impervious surfaces changes the flow and retention of precipitated water. Cities create concentrated waste, and that waste affects the air, land, and water. Cities also use water, and that affects water through-flows and outflows.

The Concretion System shows a feedback loop because existing concretions constrain (though do not determine) the development of new concretions. Here, outcomes from the Concretion System of the model affect not only the Natural System but the Concretion System itself. Depending on the city site, existing concretions can be hundreds or even thousands of years old. Some old concretions, such as cathedrals or parks, provide benefits to the city, while others, such as toxic waste dumps, impose

Feedback is "the modification or control of a process or system by its results or effects" (Oxford American Dictionaries, 2005). In a system model, a feedback loop, a curving arrow coming out of a system and returning to the same system, models this concept.

costs. Depending on the city's history, there may be leftover concretions, such as abandoned mines, that at one time provided resources but are now hazards.

Transportation and utility networks are examples of concretions that contribute flows. Transportation occurs via land, air, and water, with transportation concretions including airports, roads, railways, and piers. Reminders of these types of concretions are the road, railroad, telephone, airplane, and boat symbols.

Transportation networks not only facilitate movement within the city but allow things and people to move into and out of the city. Inflows and outflows along the transportation network will contain things that are both good and bad for the city. For example, transportation networks carry goods and people, but they also carry flows of plants and nonhuman animals, with consequences such as those described in the examples involving birds and mosquitoes. Moreover, the concentration of transportation generates noise and air pollution. Because of the inextricable links between land, water, and air—indicated in the Natural System diagram—airborne pollutants inevitably end up involving the land and water, as well. Utility networks allow for the flow of energy, information, and water, all of which are crucial to the city. Because the city creates concentrated waste streams, utility networks also include sewerage systems and waste dumps.

The Concretion layer also affects the plants and animals of the Natural System directly. Concretion changes the hospitality of an area to plants and animals, making the area less hospitable to some and more hospitable to others. Thus, the biological patterns of the Natural System are changed by the city. For example, quagga mussels, native to Eastern Europe and "the scourge of [U.S.] Western waters," are spread by boats and by the water distribution system itself. They affect the hospitality of the waters to other plants and animals (McKinnon, 2008).

THE SOCIAL SYSTEM

Figure 1.3 depicts the city's Social System. Elements of the Social System (shown at the top of the figure) can be thought of as varying along a spectrum of how private or public they are; some elements are more private and individual, while others are more public, group-oriented, and joint. The vertical arrow on the left side of the figure is not a standard systems-model arrow. Instead, it indicates a qualitative difference between that which is private and that which is public. The extent of the difference is determined by each society's culture, as are many other features of the Social System. As with the elements included in the Natural System figure, the pictorial representations of social elements included in the figure are not exclusive. Specific "cloud source" arrows are not

Figure 1.3 **The Social System of the City**

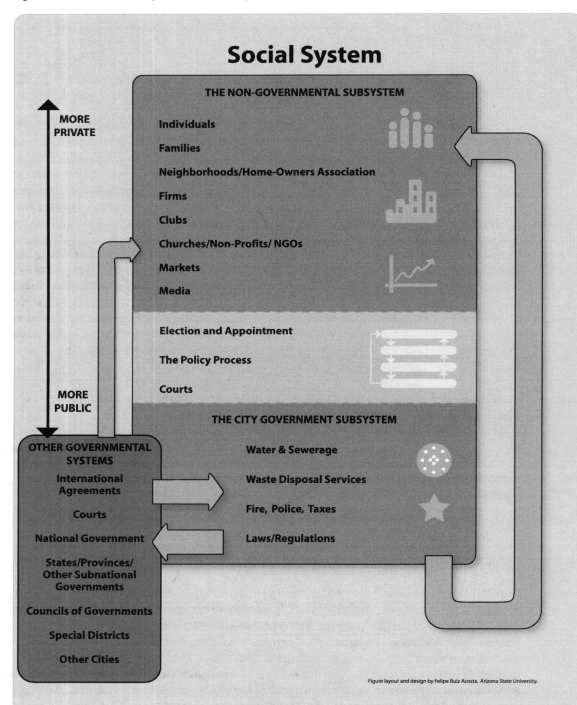

shown in the Social System because the flows of trade, ideas, culture, and knowledge come into the Social System largely through the Concretion System.

As indicated above, the Governmental Subsystem is modeled as a large portion of the Social System but is clearly an element of it rather than a separate entity. Its size in the diagram indicates its importance for our task—urban environmental policy—and is not intended to indicate what percentage of the city's Social System is governmental (which, in any event, will vary, especially based on the country in which the city is located).

Note that the Governmental Subsystem is divided from the Nongovernmental Subsystem portion of the Social System by a permeable barrier (indicated by the dashed lines) within which the terms "Election and Appointment," "The Policy Process," and "Courts" have been placed. Again, the Governmental Subsystem is clearly part of the Social System. However, access to the Governmental Subsystem from the other elements of the Social System is not direct: It is mediated by the election and appointment of public officials, by the court system, and by the Policy Process itself.

The representation of the Social System and the Governmental Subsystem is designed to be useful across many different cities. One reason the barrier shown is permeable is because its exact location will vary. In some cities, for example, the press is actually part of the government; in others, unions may have a quasi-governmental role; the importance of NGOs will vary across cities; and, in certain cases, markets may not be entirely separate from government. As indicated by Ng (2007), some differences may be more or less systematic across regions of the world. The following example refers to East Asia:

> Most conceptualizations on the governance of sustainable development are based on Western democratic contexts with a market-based economy and an active citizenry. Capacity in fostering partnerships and consensus building among different stakeholders is often identified as an essential quality in implementing sustainable development. The four East Asian cities discussed . . . are fundamentally different: they all have a "strong" government exerting major direct or indirect influences on market sectors that are at varying stages of development and their civil societies are relatively immature, if not inactive. (Ng, 2007, 351)

In this quote, Ng points out some systematic differences between cities in Western democracies and East Asia. The intent is that the model of the Social System is sufficiently flexible to allow its use in either of these contexts, as well as in others.

A large arrow feeds from the City Government Subsystem back into the Social System, reminding us that governmental actions are not the end of the social process; rather, they function as an important element that feeds back into the Social System and affects it. In particular, the government seeks to affect the behavior of the other elements of the Social System. Notice that the Governmental Subsystem can exert influence on any or all of the elements of the Social System, from the behavior of the individual or family to the behavior of entire markets or even to the behavior of other governmental units. In Case 1.3, a governmental entity uses its understanding of its own cultural context to influence individual behavior and thereby improve the environment. Case 1.4 provides an example of government affecting whole organizations, some of them governmental. These cases illustrate the importance of culture: The solution presented in Case 1.3 is useful only in

---

■———— **Case 1.3** ————■

Government Policy Affecting Individual Behavior to Improve the Environment

Tossing Copper, Silver Coins in Rivers May Help Reduce Water Pollution (India)

The Hindu practice of tossing coins into rivers as religious offerings may turn out to be a way of purifying contaminated water, agreed a group of environmentalists and social activists at the International River Festival in Bandrabhan, Madhya Pradesh, India.

Replacing a regular coin with one made of a combination of copper and silver—which is believed to stop cell division—could check the reproduction of bacteria. Anil Dave of Narmada Samagra, the organizers of the festival, announced that the [Government of India's] Indian Institute of Technology in Roorkee would mint thousands of Rs [rupees] 2 and Rs 5 coins and offer them on the banks of the Narmada River.

Source: Ghatwai, 2008.

■———— **Case 1.4** ————■

Government Policy Affecting Organization Behavior to Improve the Environment

Urban Renewal—Efforts to Reduce Mississippi River Pollution

In recent years . . . improvements to the Twin Cities' sewer system have reduced pollution and increased dissolved oxygen. During a recent fisheries survey, workers netted 25 walleyes and more than 170 saugers in a single lift; the fish stuck from the net "like quills from a porcupine." Mayflies flew so thick one summer night that state road crews plowed a foot-deep layer of insect bodies from river bridges.

In 1988, 72 miles of the Twin Cities stretch was designated a national river and recreation area. The National Park Service is working with local governments to beef up zoning and establish a green corridor to protect the river's banks.

Source: Breining, 1994. Used with permission.

---

countries where masses of people throw coins into the river, and the solution presented in Case 1.4 is useful only in societies with highly evolved regulatory organizations.

In Figure 1.3, the arrow from the Other Governmental Systems box coming into the Social System should also be noted. As mentioned earlier, the city exists within a network of other governments, and those other governments influence, and at times constrain, the city's actions. Other governments may act directly on the city government, but they can act directly on the nongovernmental elements of the Social System as well—from individuals to clubs, from markets to media.

THE POLICY PROCESS

As shown in Figure 1.3, the Policy Process serves as a mediator between the government and the rest of the Social System. It is the interface between the governmental and nongovernmental parts of society. The area of the model that contains "Election and Appointment," "The Policy Process," and "Courts" is shown as permeable on both sides—both the Governmental Subsystem and the Nongovernmental Subsystem, through their various elements (some of which are indicated), influence and are influenced by this interface between government and the rest of the city's Social System.

It is important for the urban environmental policy analyst or administrator to have a firm grasp of the Policy Process, especially the various stages involved in the process, in order to understand where she or he is most likely to exert the greatest influence. Figure 1.4 shows a model of the Policy Process. Also called the "stages" or "policy cycle" model, this model is quite common in the policy literature, and some variant of it can be found in many sources (see, for example, Birkland, 2005, and Dye, 1998). However, many depictions are essentially one-way processes, except for a single feedback loop created by Policy Evaluation affecting Problem Identification. The model we present here is more realistic in presenting various feedbacks and cycles that often occur in the Policy Process. It is also worthwhile for administrators and analysts to remember that the policy cycle is not the only cycle that affects them. Business cycles (growth versus recession), election cycles (election versus nonelection years), and weather cycles (drought versus flood versus seasonal conditions) can also affect urban environmental policy (Heffernon, Welch, and Melnick, 2007).

In considering Figure 1.4, first note the dashed lines on the top and bottom of the central diagram. These lines, which mimic the dashed lines in Figure 1.3, remind us that the Policy Process occurs within the Social System and is permeable to both to the Nongovernmental and Governmental Subsystems. In important ways, the Policy Process is actually the conduit that allows policy demands and policy outcomes to flow back and forth between the general and governmental portions of the Social System. Elected and appointed governmental officials are important participants—often the most important participants—in the Policy Process. Courts frequently serve a key oversight or gatekeeper role. In addition, it is worth noting that the news media, though not part of the official Policy Process, can exert significant influence, particularly during the Problem Identification stage of policymaking. For this reason, the media are shown in Figure 1.3 right next to the dashed line separating the Nongovernmental Subsystem from the Policy Process. As mentioned earlier, in some societies the media may be part of the governmental system; if so, their location within the diagram should be changed.

A process is a pattern of activities, and the Policy Process is a general pattern of activities that occurs in society to transform "problems"—situations that the society determines need to be addressed—into policies that are expected (at least by some

Figure 1.4 **The Policy Process Within the Framework**

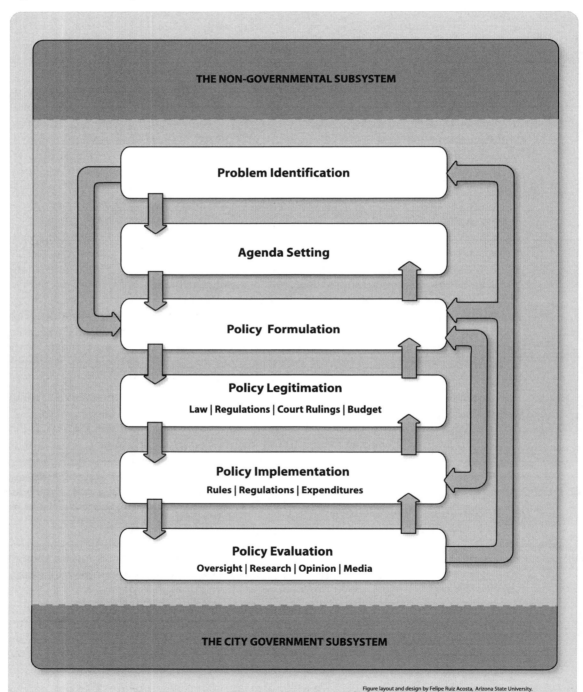

Figure layout and design by Felipe Ruiz Acosta, Arizona State University.

elements of society) to address those problems. The following section explains the main activities of the Policy Process, how they are interlinked, and at what point policy analysis is most likely to provide useful input.

PROBLEM IDENTIFICATION STAGE

Every society is defined by a variety of attributes and characteristics, all of which may be thought of as floating in a sort of social-system soup. Some of these attributes will be seen as problematic under given circumstances that vary across time and place. For governments to focus attention on specific problems, usually either a large number of people or powerful people must identify them as particularly important.

Some of these "problems" earn their name after earlier attempts to solve them have failed. This interaction explains the arrow between the Policy Evaluation box and the Problem Identification box. Policy analysis may be important during Problem Identification, for example by providing evidence that something is or is not a key concern.

AGENDA-SETTING STAGE

Before any problem can be addressed by the Governmental Subsystem, it must reach a governmental agenda. Generally, there are many more problems than there are resources (including attention) available to deal with them. Governmental decision makers—elected or appointed, depending upon the type of issue—must determine that a specific problem is sufficiently important to warrant placement on the agenda. Though placement on the official agenda does not ensure policy outcomes, it is an important step in the process: Problem identification alone is insufficient. In some places, items make it onto the agenda only through the direct action of government officials, but in others they may also arrive there via the initiative or proposition process. The many different official agendas include the legislature's agenda, a court's docket, a ballot, a regulatory review panel's meeting agenda, and the like.

Referenda, initiatives, and *propositions* are procedures that allow for more direct democracy than the representative democracy we most often see in modern industrialized nations. Referenda are generated by elected officials in a process whereby officials *refer* issues to the people for their vote. Initiatives and propositions are initiated outside the official government, for example by individuals, grassroots organizations, or firms, and then voted on by the people.

POLICY FORMULATION STAGE

Once a problem reaches the agenda, a policy must be formulated if there is to be a policy outcome. It is not sufficient, for example, for the government to decide to "do something about the problem of vehicular tailpipe emissions." A specific policy response must be developed in order to reach a desired outcome. Detailed questions must be answered. In the aforementioned example, would the policy cover all vehicles, or only commercial vehicles? Would it cover all engine types, or might diesel engines be exempt? How often would vehicles need to be checked for compliance? What entities would have the right to certify that a vehicle meets the requirements? What types of emissions would be tested, and at what levels?

Determining the particulars of possible policy responses to a socially identified problem occurs during the Policy Formulation stage. Sometimes, as indicated by the arrows on the diagram flowing from the Problem Identification box to the Policy Formulation box, policy solutions are formulated before a problem ever reaches the official agenda. This is particularly true in the case of citizen initiatives or propositions. Policy entrepreneurs, both inside and outside government, may formulate policy solutions that they then try to move onto the agenda (Kingdon, 2003), which explains further the arrow from Problem Identification to Policy Formulation and the arrow flowing back from Policy Formulation into Agenda Setting.

Policy analysis can be very important during the Policy Formulation phase, either in helping to design policies, or else in analyzing the likely outcomes of different policies so as to advise decision makers regarding efficacy.

POLICY LEGITIMATION STAGE

Suppose a problem reaches an official agenda and a policy is formulated to deal with that problem. In nations that observe the rule of law (meaning the law is preeminent and restricts arbitrary uses of power), such a policy cannot be implemented without appropriate legitimation. Depending on the circumstances, legitimation can be achieved in various ways, including through a vote of the electorate, a vote of representatives, the creation of regulations by legitimate regulatory entities, or a court ruling. Even if a policy is formulated before it reaches the official agenda, the legitimation process may require additional formulation. For example, a bill may be amended in committee, or a regulation may go through several hearings and revisions before its final form is chosen. This is why the arrows indicate the possibility of a looping cycle between legitimation and formulation. In the latter case, this portion of legitimation will occur in agencies, directed by administrators, rather than in a legislative body such as the city council.

POLICY IMPLEMENTATION STAGE

Once a policy has been legitimated, it must be implemented. In the past, implementation was generally accomplished via governmental agency or bureau. In the last decade or two, however, it may increasingly result from some type of agreement between a governmental unit and the private or nonprofit/NGO sector, or by contracting with the private sector. The field of public administration deals primarily with this stage of the Policy Process. Though often ignored in process models, Policy Implementation generally involves additional formulation because legislation and other forms of legitimation usually do not cover all the details necessary for implementation. This is the reason for the arrow from the Implementation box to the Formulation box.

Policy analysis can provide useful input during this stage, including information needed to choose and adjust implementation details that have not been covered by the officially legitimated formulation of policy. Administrators are crucial at this stage.

POLICY EVALUATION STAGE   — Full cycle + adjust Problem ID and Formation

process
eval -
review
implementation
process

summative
post
completion

Policy Evaluation may be performed on policies while they are in process (sometimes called Process Evaluation if it focuses on evaluating the implementation process itself) or after a policy is completed (sometimes called Summative Evaluation). Evaluation can occur through formal analysis, which is usually performed by government officials, by the courts, by contract researchers, by academics, or by members of think tanks. Evaluation can also stem from informal analysis—that is, in the arena of public opinion. Quite often, evaluation is reported by the news media or even made by members of the media (for example, in editorials). Information from all types of Policy Evaluation is fed back into the Policy Process. As shown in Figure 1.4, evaluation can feed into the Policy Formulation as well as Problem Identification stages.

great impact

→ Policy analysis can have important effects on the Policy Evaluation phase, but it is only one of many elements influencing evaluation outcomes. Other key factors such as public opinion, which itself may or may not be influenced by formal policy analysis, figure into the picture. Analysts often believe that formal analysis should determine policy outcomes, but it seldom does so on its own. If analysts fail to understand that formal policy analysis is only one voice in society's evaluation, they are likely to feel great disappointment in their jobs.

AN OVERVIEW OF THE CITY SYSTEM

Physical = Natural + Built

Up to this point, the Physical System, composed of the Natural and Concretion Systems, and the Social System of the city, consisting of Other Governmental Systems and the Nongovernmental and Governmental Subsystems, have been shown separately. Let's take a moment to consider how all of the city systems fit together and interact. Figure 1.5 shows a color version of the integrated model of the city system.

There are some important things to notice about this overview, the first being that the city is most certainly not a closed system. The city exists within a web of relationships to other cities and to areas/units/entities/systems that contain it or overlap it—including (but not limited to) metropolitan areas, regions, watersheds, migration routes, states, countries, and even the world. The inflows from cloud symbols and the outflows to cloud symbols that are connected to each element of the system remind us of this very important fact. Since our focus is urban environmental policy analysis, the city is the unit of analysis, but the fact that it is linked to other systems is very important and must not be forgotten. This is especially true because, as mentioned earlier, the official and practical boundaries of the city change over time and can be changed as a matter of policy. Additional land can be acquired, or intergovernmental agreements can be made. Suppose, for instance, that a city has insufficient water for its projected growth. It could purchase land that includes additional water sources, or

Figure 1.5 **An Overview of the City System**

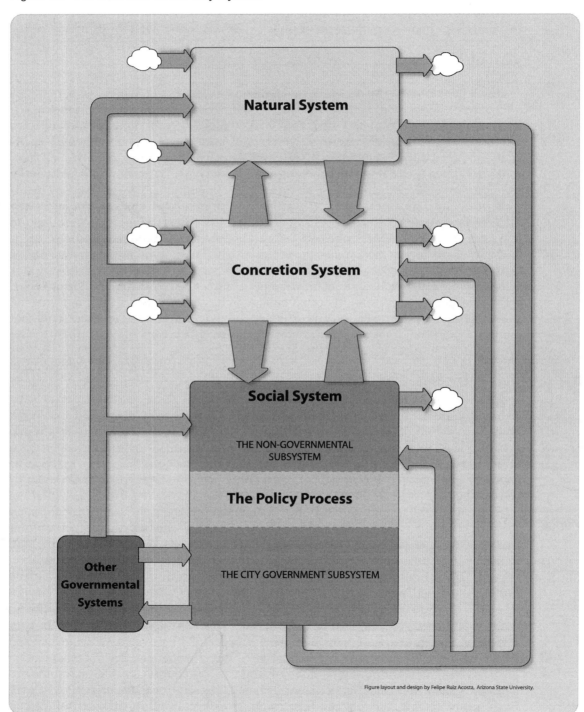

Natural System

Concretion System

Social System

THE NON-GOVERNMENTAL
SUBSYSTEM

The Policy Process

THE CITY GOVERNMENT SUBSYSTEM

Other
Governmental
Systems

Figure layout and design by Felipe Ruiz Acosta, Arizona State University.

it might make an arrangement to buy water from another governmental entity (another city, a tribal government, or another state with water to spare).

Second, though it is analytically useful to think of the Natural, Concretion, Social, and Other Governmental Systems separately, they are all inextricably linked—though to greater and lesser degrees. The Natural System provides amenities and constraints to the Concretion System, and the Concretion System also changes the Natural System. Similarly, the Concretion System affects the Social System, which itself affects the Concretion System. The Social System has direct effects on the Natural System, for the attributes of the Social System—partially determined by culture—determine the types of demands that the society places on nature. The Governmental Subsystem may have direct effects on the Social System, the Concretion System (for example, through zoning or direct building), and the Natural System. The flow from the Other Governmental Systems reminds us that, in most cases, cities operate within larger government structures and have only limited authority and autonomy granted to them by higher levels of government. Among the important links from a city to other systems, this constraint from above can be quite significant. Though the Natural System can have a direct influence on the Governmental Subsystem—such as when Hurricane Katrina destroyed governmental communications systems and buildings—usually the Natural System has only an indirect influence on the Governmental Subsystem. Typically, Natural System influences on the Governmental Subsystem are filtered through the Nongovernmental Subsystem via direct effects on social elements and via the society's perceptions of the current state versus the desirable state of the Natural System.

Third, notice that the figure retains important elements of the Social System. For example, the dashed lines again remind us that the Policy Process is the interface between the Governmental Subsystem and the rest of society. It is retained in the overview diagram because it is the specific locus of policy decision.

THE PURPOSE OF THE SYSTEM MODEL

The purpose of the system framework of the city as we have developed and presented it here is threefold. First, it captures key elements for urban environmental policymaking in a simplified structure that administrators, analysts, students, and others can use to think through urban environmental policy questions. It helps us explicate important elements of the urban environmental policy system and relationships between those elements. Grimm, Grove, Pickett, and Redman (2000) explain: "Humans dominate Earth's ecosystem. . . . Therefore, humans must be integrated into models for a complete understanding of extant ecological systems." The model presented responds to this request in a policy-relevant way. A unique feature of the framework is its thorough integration of the governmental and policy systems into the ecological system.

Second, the framework is designed to be general enough to be used across nations, and even across regions of the world that have systematically different sociocultural and governmental systems.

Third, urban environmental policy administrators and analysts can use this representation as a mental checklist to help them think through all the effects of proposed

■———— **Case 1.5** ————■

An Example Using the Urban Environmental Policy System Framework

Suppose a Drought Is Causing Subsidence in Your City

Suppose that you, working in government, are faced with an urban environmental problem. This problem has been identified by the news media, and your office is receiving multiple communications about it each day. Let's assume the problem is that your city is in a drought. Therefore, excess groundwater is being withdrawn, and cracks are appearing in buildings and land. This situation is now your problem, because your boss has asked you to come up with a suitable policy response. How can the framework developed here help you with that task?

Look at the system diagrams, and use them to help analyze the problem. This problem originates in both the Natural System and the Social System. It is caused not only by the drought (part of the Natural System) but also by the excessive use of groundwater by the Social System (use that exceeds sustainability). It is perceived as a problem by members of the Social System primarily because of its effects on the Concretion System (people are worried about the effect of ground fissures on concretions), and also because of the potential for harm to the Concretion System spreading to the Social System. Some members of the Social System may also be concerned about the direct effects on the Natural System (aquifer depletion affects plants, surface water, and thus animals, which may diminish natural beauty). Tracing the factors of the problem in this way lets us identify where the problem originated and where the effects of concern are. The problem originated in the Natural and Social Systems, and the outcomes of concern are located in the Concretion, Social, and perhaps Natural Systems.

As a policy analyst, you probably cannot stop the drought itself. But you can design policies to fix the Concretion System; note, however, that this solution will be temporary unless the underlying problem is fixed. In this case, then, the concretion nexus is where problems are apparent, but it is not a primary source for solutions.

You might create policies that directly address the Social System's excessive use of groundwater. What are ways to do this? Society could cut back on water use overall, leading to decreased use of groundwater. Potential policies could act on different parts of the Social System. For example, you could try to create policies that cause individuals and households to use less water, you could try to get firms and other organizations to use less water, and/or you could change policies so that the government uses less water.

Another approach involves thinking outside the Governmental Subsystem box and considering a change in the city's mix of water sources: This might be achieved by expanding the city to encompass other water sources or by negotiating with other entities to receive water from other sources they control. By increasing the use of non-groundwater sources of water, use of groundwater would decline. A quick look at the figures indicates that you could ask a higher level of government to act to solve this problem.

Once you develop the general form of your proposed policy, you turn to Figure 1.4 to see how your proposal must work its way through the policy process. On what formal agenda must it appear? Are there past evaluations that might help in its formulation?

Case 1.5 *(continued)*

Who must legitimate it? What agency is best suited to implementing it? In addition, since you know that the current problem is primarily observed in the Concretion System, you know that this is a good place to look for evidence after your proposed policy is ready for evaluation. Has the rate of complaints about cracking declined?

As illustrated by this example, use of the urban environmental policy system framework presented here gives you an organized way to think about

- where a policy problem arises,
- where the problem is observed,
- where solutions can be found,
- what steps must be completed for the policy to be implemented, and
- how you can evaluate policy success.

policies. Case 1.5 gives an example of this type of use, which can guide action-oriented policy analysis to consider where an environmental problem arises, where it is observed, how it can be solved, and what parts of the Policy Process need to be activated to bring a solution to fruition. The system framework is used throughout this book to explicate points and to highlight how different areas of urban environmental policy concern fit into the city system.

The next three chapters introduce some key concepts in policy analysis and eco-system management. Following that, this conceptual model and those key concepts are applied to specific urban environmental policy areas.

NOTE

1. Historically, churches and male heads of household were also able to coerce legitimately; in most modern states, the ability of churches to coerce is significantly limited and, in advanced societies, heads of households may only coerce children—and even that power is limited.

REFERENCES

Birkland, T.A. 2005. *An Introduction to the Policy Process: Theories, Concepts, and Models of Public Policy Making*, 2d ed. Armonk, NY: M.E. Sharpe.

Breining, Greg. 1994. Urban renewal—efforts to reduce Mississippi River pollution. *Sierra*, July-August. http://findarticles.com/p/articles/mi_m1525/is_n4_v79/ai_15518158/?tag=content;col1 (accessed February 28, 2010).

Collier, A. 2007. *The Humble Little Condom: A History*. Amherst, NY: Prometheus Books.

Douglas, M., and A. Wildavsky. 1982. *Risk and Culture: An Essay on the Selection of Technical and Environmental Dangers*. Berkeley: University of California Press.

Dye, T.R. 1998. *Understanding Public Policy*, 9th ed. Upper Saddle River, NJ: Prentice Hall.

findingDulcinea staff. 2008. Statues of Hindu god causing river pollution. findingDulcinea, August 21. http://www.findingdulcinea.com/news/international/Aug-08/Hindu-Elephant-Statues-Causing-River-Pollution.html (accessed September 8, 2009).

Ghatwai, M. 2008. Tossing copper, silver coins in rivers may help reduce water pollution. Indian

Express, February 27. http://www.indianexpress.com/news/tossing-copper-silver-coins-in-rivers-may-h/277479/. Summary obtained from L. Shaler, *Global Water News Watch* (College of Science, University of Arizona), March 3, 2008.

Gober, P. 2006. *Metropolitan Phoenix: Place Making and Community Building in the Desert.* Philadelphia: University of Pennsylvania Press.

Grimm, N.B., J.M. Grove, S.T.A. Pickett, and C.L. Redman. 2000. Integrated approaches to long-term studies of urban ecological systems. *BioScience*, 50, 7 (July), 571–584.

Heffernon, R., N. Welch, and R. Melnick. 2007. *Sustainability for Arizona: The Issue of Our Age.* Tempe, AZ: Morrison Institute for Public Policy, School of Public Affairs, College of Public Programs, Arizona State University.

House, P. 1973. *The Urban Environmental System: Modeling for Research, Policy-Making, and Education.* Beverly Hills, CA: Sage.

Illinois Department of Public Health. 2007. *IDPH Health Beat: Mosquitoes.* April 25. http://www.idph. state.il.us/public/hb/hbmosquito.htm (accessed February 27, 2010).

Kingdon, J.W. 2003. *Agendas, Alternatives, and Public Policies,* 2nd ed. New York: Longman.

McKinnon, S. 2008. Lakes brace for mussel invasion: Officials urge boaters to fight foreign quagga. *Arizona Republic*, September 8. http://www.azcentral.com/news/articles/2008/09/08/20080908lakes-quaggas0908.html (accessed September 17, 2008).

Ng, M.K. 2007a. Introduction: Sustainable development and governance in East Asian world cities. *Journal of Comparative Policy Analysis*, 9, 4 (December), 317–320. http://www.informaworld.com/smpp/section?content=a787316304&fulltext=713240928 (accessed February 28, 2010).

———. 2007b. Governance for sustainability in East Asian global cities. *Journal of Comparative Policy Analysis,* 9, 4, 351–381.

Ostrom, E. 2005. *Understanding Institutional Diversity.* Princeton, NJ: Princeton University Press.

———. 2009. Institutional analysis and development: Micro. Syllabus for POLS Y673, Indiana University, Bloomington, August 26. http://www.indiana.edu/~workshop/courses/Y673/y673_fall_2009. pdf (accessed February 2009).

Oxford American Dictionaries. 2005. Version 1.0.2 [electronic]. Cupertino, CA: Apple Computer, s.v. "culture."

TNN. 2009. A day after Ganesh visarjan: Riverbank littered with broken idols. *Times of India*, September 4. http://timesofindia.indiatimes.com/city/surat/A-day-after-Ganesh-visarjan-Riverbank-littered-with-broken-idols/articleshow/4973599.cms (accessed February 27, 2009).

2 Policy-Analytic Concepts for the Urban Environment

As of 2012, the field of policy analysis is new as social science disciplines go. Whereas the study of politics is thousands of years old, the study of economics many hundreds of years old, and the study of public administration more than a hundred years old, the study of policy analysis, as such, is only decades old. Yet, since its development, the field has drawn together and developed a set of useful concepts into a policy tool-kit. These concepts were drawn from all of the above-named fields and have much to contribute to improved governance. This chapter, along with Chapters 3 and 4, focuses on those policy-analytic concepts that are particularly relevant to the study of urban environmental policy. Chapter 2 focuses on the concept of public goods and also presents many related concepts, including the Tragedy of the Commons, externalities, and the problem of the free rider. Chapter 3 discusses policy instruments (tools government can use), including regulation, taxation, privatization, suasion, and others. Chapter 4 presents an introduction to Benefit-Cost Analysis (BCA), both a useful tool and a central paradigm in policy-analytic thinking.

The concepts introduced in this chapter are particularly useful in helping an analyst or administrator quickly classify many urban environmental issues and understand (1) how they are likely to arise and (2) what kinds of harm they are likely to do to the social good. The next chapter is useful in thinking through what types of solutions might help alleviate environmental problems. The concepts introduced in Chapters 2, 3, and 4 are well integrated into the policy field broadly and are useful outside the specific area of urban environmental policy as well as within it.

PRIVATE GOODS

The "goods"—meaning, "things we consume"—that most of us routinely think about are private goods: the clothes we wear and the food we eat, for example. For these goods, ownership is clear, and there is little benefit or cost to others that stems from your consumption decisions. Yes, the crunching of your apple could be annoying to the person next to you, or someone might not like the way your pants look, but these effects are minor and fairly random; others might like the smell of your apple or love the look of your pants.

PUBLIC GOODS, RIVALRY, EXCLUDABILITY, AND CONGESTION

> In the policy analysis tool kit, *public goods* are classified by their characteristics, not by whether they are provided by public entities (like government).

Public goods are quite different. There are several types of public goods, but for all public goods—to a greater or lesser extent—ownership is unclear, and there are systematic costs or benefits to multiple people. We elaborate on the characteristic of unclear ownership (classified as "nonexcludability"), and the characteristic of shared costs or benefits (called "nonrivalry" or "non-rivalrousness"). Its opposite, "rivalry," is sometimes called "subtractability" (Heikkila, 2004).

Pollution is a classic public good.[1] If construction creates dust pollution, perhaps including Valley Fever viruses,[2] who owns that pollution? Ownership is unclear, and yet all of the people who live or work downwind from the construction are affected by the dust, and all of those downwind systematically bear costs from the dust. Even though those with asthma, those who catch Valley Fever, young children, and elderly folks tend to be more harmed, all people downwind will receive some harm.

Please note that the terms "public good" and "private good" do not imply that the one is provided by the government and the other by companies. Private goods may be provided by government, and public goods may be provided by private entities. For example, the government may distribute cheese or milk to low-income people, even though food is a pure private good; on the flip side, a homeowners' association may provide a park, which is a type of public good. In this context, the terms have to do with characteristics of the goods themselves rather than their means of provision, as we explain in following sections.

The standard models that economists use assume that all goods exchanged in the market are pure private goods. You have probably heard of the famous Invisible Hand, which is often invoked by U.S. politicians. The Invisible Hand Theorem (it is a theorem because it can be proved mathematically to be true under certain conditions) was first identified by the Scottish economist and social philosopher Adam Smith in his famous *An Inquiry into the Nature and Causes of the Wealth of Nations* (usually known simply as *The Wealth of Nations* [1776/2003]). According to the theorem, natural market behavior involving voluntary exchange will lead to the best possible outcome for society—"best" being defined as the outcome that maximizes the total benefit to society, or the "efficient" outcome. Under this scenario, there can be no role for government to improve the market (or society more generally) other than to enforce private property rights to ensure that exchange really is voluntary. In a world of pure private goods and strictly voluntary exchange, government intervention will actually cause harm by decreasing social benefits.

The following is the famous passage that refers to the Invisible Hand. The described result has become known as the Invisible Hand Theorem.

> Every individual necessarily labors to render the annual revenue of the society as great as he can. He generally indeed neither intends to promote the public interest, nor knows how much he is promoting it. . . . He intends only his own gain, and he is in this, as in many other cases, led by an invisible hand to promote an end which was not part of his intention. . . . By pursuing his own interest he frequently promotes that of the society more effectually than when he really intends to promote it.

Source: Smith, 1776.
Note: Please excuse the seemingly sexist language. Smith was writing in the eighteenth century—a time when society shared the social fiction that "he" and "man" referred to all humans, regardless of gender.

To reiterate, the caveat here is that even in an "invisible hand world" the enforcement of private property rights is required."

This "best possible outcome for society" is called "efficiency," or "Pareto efficiency."[3] A situation is defined as Pareto efficient if no one can be made better off without someone else being made worse off. It may be unclear why this is an efficient or desirable point until the definition is turned around: If someone *can* be made better off without making anyone else worse off, then we are not using all social resources to their maximum benefit, and we should do so.

Proving the Invisible Hand Theorem requires the assumption that all goods exchanged are private goods. When goods are public goods, the natural working of the market is very unlikely to maximize the benefit to society. In fact, in certain situations, the unconstrained market—the unconstrained exercise of voluntary exchange—may destroy society's benefit. Therefore, in the case of public goods, the government has the opportunity to improve the workings of the market, thus improving society's benefit and economic efficiency.

When considering the environment, much of the focus is on goods that are, in some way, public goods. It is useful for the environmental policy analyst or administrator to be able to identify the nature of environmental goods as well as what ways they are public rather than private. There are several different types of public goods, as explained in the sections that follow. Each one exhibits its own type of "market failure"—the way that a natural market, a market of voluntary exchange, will fail to maximize social benefit. The ability to classify each situation quickly, so as to understand what type of market failure to expect, can be quite useful. As elaborated in the next chapter, such classification allows for more immediate insights into potential solutions.

Market failure is a term used to indicate that a naturally occurring market will not operate efficiently to provide the maximum social benefit. Generally, *only markets for pure private goods* can be assumed to provide efficient outcomes.

PURE PUBLIC GOODS

Pure public goods are both *nonrival* and *nonexcludable.*

To understand pure public goods, it is useful first to analyze their opposites: pure private goods. As mentioned earlier, when dealing with pure private goods, ownership is clear. Also, there is little cost or benefit to others of your consumption decision, because only one person at a time can consume a pure private good. The first characteristic is known as "excludability." A private good is said to be excludable because the owner can decide whether to exclude others from participation in the good. That is, only you get to decide who wears your pants or who gets to bite your apple. The fact that only one person at a time can enjoy each unit of the good is referred to as rivalrousness or rivalry.

People sometimes think that rivalry and excludability are one and the same. A simple example will show that these really are different concepts. Suppose that I am listening to music on my computer while I type this. I have the *right* and *ability* of exclusion—I can decide who may or may not listen to my music, and I can prevent others from listening by using headphones. But the music itself is nonrival—more than one person *can* listen to the music at the same time. This is quite different from the example of the apple. We cannot both enjoy the same bite of apple, yet we can both enjoy the same byte of music.

Pure public goods are the exact opposite of pure private goods: they are both nonexcludable and nonrival. An ultimate pure public good is the ozone layer. It is nonexcludable—you can't choose who can and cannot use the ozone layer—and it is nonrival—all the people, plants, and animals on Earth are consuming the same ozone layer at the same time. To further explain the concept of nonrivalrousness, Birkland discusses nonrival goods as "indivisible . . . because they cannot be divided into parts for individuals to consume" (2005, 67). This idea certainly fits the example of the ozone layer.

When a good is *excludable*, some can be excluded from participating in the good. When a good is *rival*, only one person at a time can consume the same (unit of the) good.

Table 2.1 presents the beginnings of a taxonomy of goods, based on their rivalry and excludability. So far we have discussed only pure private goods and pure public goods, but later we will fill in the remaining spaces. Still, even without the other types of goods labeled, the taxonomy shows you that there must be two other types of public goods—one resulting from the fact that ownership cannot be controlled, and the other based on the fact that consumption can be shared.

When goods are nonexcludable, they cannot be priced—that is, some entrepreneur can't put a price on them and sell them. This is problematic because, if a price can't be charged, then a naturally occurring market is very unlikely to provide the good. In a land of voluntary exchange, you generally won't trade something valuable for something that you can use for free on your own. Thus, most purely nonexcludable

Table 2.1

Developing a Taxonomy of Types of Goods

	Excludable	Nonexcludable
Rival	Pure private goods	
Nonrival		Pure public goods

Source: Table inspired by Weimer and Vining, 1992, 46.

goods are provided either by nature (like the ozone layer), by the government, or by nonprofit organizations (which are also known internationally as NGOs).

Another problem accompanies the lack of ability to price: It has been recognized throughout both the policy and economics literature that free things tend to be over-consumed. If a good is free, people naturally will respond to the market signal and use the good up to the point where it has zero value to them. In a world of voluntary exchange, you will not exchange $10 for something unless you get at least $10 of benefit from that thing. But, if the transaction costs you nothing, you will consume a good until the benefit to you of that consumption is very low—zero or almost zero.

So, one problem with pure public goods is that they typically will not be provided by naturally arising markets—that is, by the type of markets the Invisible Hand Theorem assumes. When nature provides pure public goods, they generally will be overcon-sumed, meaning they are consumed to the point of zero value to the individual, even though their value to society is not zero. If nature provides enough of the good for everyone to consume as much as he or she wants at zero price, then we do not have a problem. However, as our planet has become more populated, and as populations have become more concentrated, such a scenario has become more unlikely. The indigenous peoples of North America took all the bison they wanted at a price of zero, sometimes even wasting parts of the kill. However, there were enough bison available so this didn't matter. Once the number of settlers increased and their technology became advanced enough for people to shoot buffalo out of a train (enjoying this hunting to the point of zero value to themselves), the bison became nearly extinct.

It is important to note that there is a difference between the *price* of something and its *cost*. The price of shooting the bison may have been nearly zero, but the cost to society of their slaughter rose as the number of bison diminished.

It is important to make a distinction between the *price* of something and its *cost*. The *price* is what people pay—the price charged. The *cost* is the actual value of all the resources used to create the good.

For social efficiency, *the price must equal the "marginal cost,"* which is the cost of the last one of the good produced. In any case where the price does not equal the marginal cost, a naturally occurring market will be inefficient.

■──── **Case 2.1** ────■

Hunting the Passenger Pigeon in the Early American Frontier (New York)

"See, cousin Bess! See, 'Duke, the pigeon roosts of the south have broken up! They are growing more thick every instant. Here is a flock that the eye cannot see the end of. . . ."

The houses and the signs of life apparent in the village drove the alarmed birds from the direct line of their flight, toward the mountains, along the sides and near the bases of which they were glancing in dense masses, equally wonderful by the rapidity of their motion and their incredible numbers.

. . . The reports of the firearms became rapid, whole volleys rising from the plain, as flocks of more than ordinary numbers darted over the opening, shadowing the field like a cloud; and then the light smoke of a single piece would issue from among the leafless bushes on the mountain, as death was hurled on the retreat of the affrighted birds, who were rising from a volley, in a vain effort to escape. Arrows and missiles of every kind were in the midst of the flocks; and so numerous were the birds, and so low did they take their flight, that even long poles in the hands of those on the sides of the mountain were used to strike them to the earth.

. . . None pretended to collect the game, which lay scattered over the fields in such profusion as to cover the very ground with fluttering victims.

. . . Among the sportsmen was Billy Kirby, who, armed with an old musket, was loading, and without even looking into the air, was firing and shouting as his victims fell even on his own person.

Source: Cooper, 1823/1964, 233–235.

As shown by the aforementioned example and as Case 2.1 illustrates, this is not a problem that exists only among urbanized people who are out of touch with nature. The excerpt from *The Pioneers* (1823/1964) in Case 2.1 takes place in the late eighteenth century. Here, James Fenimore Cooper (author of *The Last of the Mohicans* [1826] and *The Deerslayer* [1841]) writes about New York State when it was a barely settled wilderness. As you may know, the passenger pigeon eventually became extinct.

CONGESTION

The example of the bison also highlights the concept of congestion in understanding public goods and environmental policy. Sometimes a good is said to be "nonrival to the point of congestion." A common example of such a good is a bridge. A bridge is nonrival because many people can consume the same bridge at the same time. Furthermore, there is essentially no cost to one person of another's using the bridge—that is, up until the point of congestion. Once the bridge becomes congested, adding another person increases the crossing time for everyone on the bridge, which imposes a cost on each person, and thus a social cost.

This concept of the change in cost of use of a nonrival good is very important, because it affects how the good should be priced for social efficiency. If the *cost* of

---

■———— **Case 2.2** ————■

Congestion Pricing in the City of London

A basic economic principle is that consumers should pay directly for the costs they impose as an incentive to use resources efficiently. Urban traffic congestion is often cited as an example: if road space is unpriced traffic volumes will increase until congestion limits further growth. For decades economists have recommended road congestion pricing (special tolls for driving on congested roadways) as a way to encourage more efficient use of the transport system, and address congestion and pollution problems providing net benefits to society. . . .

In recent years a few cities have implemented various forms of congestion pricing, including Singapore, Orange County, [California] (State Route 91), and the cities of Trondheim, Oslo, and Bergen in Norway, but proponents have been frustrated at the political resistance congestion pricing faced in other major cities. . . .

Since February 2003 the city of London has charged a fee for driving private automobiles in its central area during weekdays as a way to reduce traffic congestion and raise revenues to fund transport improvements. This has significantly reduced traffic congestion, improved bus and taxi service, and generates substantial revenues. Public acceptance has grown, and there is now support to expand the program to other parts of London and other cities in the U.K. This is the first congestion pricing program in a major European city, and its success suggests that congestion pricing may become more politically feasible elsewhere. . . .

How the Program Works

Since 17 February 2003 motorists driving in central London on weekdays between 7:00 am and 6:30 pm are required to pay £5, increasing to £8 in July 2005. There are some exemptions, including motorcycles, licensed taxis, vehicles used by disabled people, some alternative fuel vehicles, buses and emergency vehicles. Area residents receive a 90 percent discount for their vehicles. The charging area is indicated by roadside signs and symbols painted on the roadway. . . . Approximately 110,000 motorists per day pay the charge. . . .

Source: Litman, 2006, 1. Used with permission.

---

consumption is (essentially) zero, then the *price* of consumption should be zero in order to induce the proper amount of consumption for the greatest good of the society. However, if the cost of consumption is positive, then the price needs to reflect that cost. Otherwise, as in the cases of the bison and the pigeons, the good will be over-consumed. This line of thinking gives rise to the concept of "congestion pricing"—pricing differently for a good under conditions of congestion. See Case 2.2 for an example of the use of congestion pricing in the city of London.

Many environmental policy problems arise simply because of congestion. In cases where few people live along a large river, it doesn't matter if people dump small amounts of waste into it. The cost of this action is essentially zero for people downstream and for the plants and animals in the river (don't forget that animals also emit waste into the river), and all share in the nonrival use of the river's water. However, once the area around the river becomes congested, the increased dumping of waste into it imposes true costs on those downstream, as well as on river inhabitants and the society more broadly. The river

Figure 2.1 **Thinking of Excludability and Rivalry as Continuums**

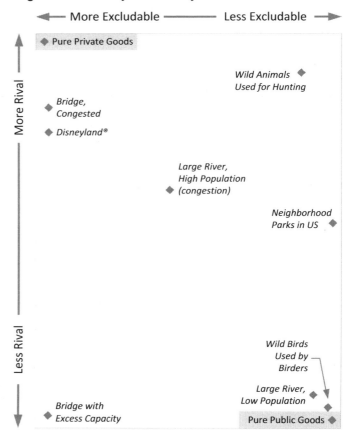

Source: Adapted from Levy, 1995, 84. Used with permission.

moves from a point of nonrivalrousness toward rivalrousness in the sense that many people are still using the same river, but now their uses impose costs on the other users.

John Levy (1995) introduces the idea of conceptualizing rivalry and excludability along continuums rather than in either/or binary categories (as in Table 2.1). Figure 2.1 shows this different conceptualization. If we think of rivalry as having different levels along a continuum, then we could (theoretically) measure how rivalrous something is along the continuum based on the cost that any one use imposes on other users. The higher the cost of an additional use, the more rival the congested good has become. Both the continuous and the binary ways of thinking about whether a good is rival or excludable are useful. The binary method illustrated in Table 2.1 allows us to categorize goods and their market failures. The spatial method illustrated in Figure 2.1 shows that some goods are more rival than others, and that circumstances—such as congestion, technology, or law—can change the extent to which a good is more or less rival or excludable. Though the nature of the good affects the attributes of rivalry and excludability, these attributes are not completely fixed.

Table 2.2

Adding to a Taxonomy of Types of Goods

	Excludable	Nonexcludable
Rival	Pure private goods	
Nonrival	Marketable public or toll goods	Pure public goods

MARKETABLE PUBLIC GOODS AND LEGAL AND PHYSICAL EXCLUDABILITY

> *Marketable public goods*, also called *toll goods*, are *nonrival* but are *excludable*. Thus, a toll or price can be charged for these goods, and entrepreneurs may provide them.

The example of the bridge also introduces the concept of a "marketable public good," also called a "toll good." Marketable public goods belong in the lower left quadrant of Table 2.1, as shown in Table 2.2. A marketable public good is excludable. This is important because it means that there can be a price and thus a market for such a good. However, unlike a pure private good, a marketable public good is nonrival (to the point of congestion). The marketable public good can be provided by a naturally occurring market: the entrepreneur will be induced to do so because she or he can charge a price and make a profit. Because the good is nonrival, though, in order to induce the proper amount of consumption for the good of society, it should be provided free to the point of congestion and priced only when congestion occurs. Of course, entrepreneurs will not want to give away their expensively developed toll goods; they will want to charge for them and make money. Therefore, entrepreneurs will usually provide too little of a marketable public good. Historically, there have been times and places where bridges and even roads were developed by private entrepreneurs who then charged tolls. It may be the fact that entrepreneurs often undersupply toll goods that explains the adoption, over time, of their provision by governments rather than entrepreneurs.

LEGAL AND PHYSICAL EXCLUDABILITY MAY BE DIFFERENT

This example also raises the point that, when considering the concept of excludability, it is important to note that there is sometimes a distinction between legal and physical excludability. As indicated earlier in the music example, for full excludability, someone must have both the *right* and *ability* of exclusion. For some goods, there may be a conflict between their legal classification as excludable or not, and their physical attribute of excludability. Often, students who have spent most of their lives in the southwestern United States will argue that roads and bridges are not, in fact, excludable. This is because, in the Southwest, roads and bridges are not usually subject to exclusion. There has been a social decision to turn something that is excludable in a *physical* sense (for example, a bridge) into a *legally* nonexcludable good. Excluding cars from a bridge is quite easy, since there are only very specific access points at the bridge's ends. In many cases, users are not excluded from publicly provided bridges and roads; instead, a price of zero is charged. On the other hand, in some portions of the United States (especially in the East and in the Denver and San Francisco areas of the West), bridges and sometimes roads are constituted under legal excludability and tolls are charged to use them.

Returning to Levy's (1995) conceptualization of rivalry and excludability as existing along a continuum, we can think of the level of a good's excludability as moving along the continuum based on law and enforcement. The higher the penalty for violating legal excludability, and the greater the likelihood of getting caught, the greater the level of excludability. The level of excludability can also be a matter of custom: Americans almost never pick flowers from another's front yard, not because there is any particular enforcement of exclusion, but as a matter of custom.

Look again at Figure 2.1, and note that an uncongested bridge is shown in the lower left-hand corner of the rivalry-excludability space. This positioning says that an uncongested bridge is not very rival but is very excludable. However, consider a specific bridge, such as the Mill Avenue Bridge in Tempe, Arizona: *Legally* this bridge is not excludable—a decision has been made *not* to charge a toll for crossing this bridge. Thus, this specific bridge could be placed in Table 2.2's space farther right—that is, closer to the pure public good's location—indicating that it is both nonrival and legally nonexcludable.

Whether a good is physically and/or legally excludable can go the other way, as well. For example, the Grand Canyon National Park is legally excludable. Fees are charged for private vehicles and also for people entering on foot, bicycle, or motorcycle (National Park Service, 2011). However, the Grand Canyon is not really physically excludable. The park includes over a million acres of land (more than 4,900 square kilometers), and the river length of the canyon is over 270 miles (almost 450 kilometers) (National Park Service, 2009). Clearly, it would take an army of rangers to keep people out of the Grand Canyon, and the U.S. National Park Service does not post such an army there. When a good is not physically excludable but is legally excludable, it can be expected that some people will violate the law (consider the copyright problems the music industry is currently experiencing, or rates of illegal immigration through the world). However, in situations where (1) social norms strongly support the legal determination of excludability, (2) the populace is law-abiding, (3) there is a high probability of violators being caught, or (4) the cost to individuals of obeying the law is low, most people will abide by legally created excludability even when it does not perfectly match physical excludability.

Marketable public goods are usually provided by people, rather than by nature. As the bridge example suggests, they may be very important to urban areas. Infrastructural elements are often by their very nature toll goods, even when societies choose not to charge tolls.

COMMON POOL RESOURCES (CPRs) AND THE TRAGEDY OF THE COMMONS

As you have likely guessed from Table 2.2, the fourth type of good is not excludable but is rival in consumption. These goods are called "common pool resources," "common property resources," or "CPRs." CPRs are not excludable (at least up to the point of congestion) but are rival in consumption. Sometimes CPRs are called "free" goods, but this is a misleading locution since, while the price to consume the good may be zero, the cost of consumption often is not. CPRs are very relevant to environmental policy, since they are often provided by nature and thus are key parts of what people think of as "the environment."

Adequate provision/protection of CPRs can be complicated because many CPRs are not stationary in space and their movement does not respect political boundaries. Consider, for example, monarch butterflies, which travel up to 2,000 miles (over 3,200 kilometers) from Mexico to the United States or to Canada, thus migrating across many different political boundaries (Pacific Grove Museum of Natural History, n.d.). Suppose that your city decides to make monarch butterflies a protected species; this will have little effect if people in other cities along the migration route gather the butterflies or kill their caterpillars.

Common pool resources are also called *common property resources* and are often referred to as *CPRs*. They are *rival*, but not *excludable*. They are usually supplied by nature and are frequently overconsumed in high-population situations.

Georges Bank was an enormously rich Atlantic fishery that overlapped the boundaries of U.S. and Canadian coastal waters; fish swam between political jurisdictions. Unfortunately, "overfishing on a massive scale brought many fish populations, including cod, haddock, and halibut, to the brink of commercial extinction" (American Museum of Natural History, 1998). Free-swimming ocean fish are classic CPRs. They are (physically) nonexcludable, but rival in consumption: If you catch and keep a fish, I cannot catch it. The sad story of Georges Bank is a common one for CPRs. As with the bison discussed earlier, part of the reason for overfishing Georges Bank was a change in technology (American Museum of Natural History, 1998). In low-population, simple-technology situations, overfishing Georges Bank or destroying bison herds were both nearly impossible, but as technology and levels of demand change, the sustainability of CPRs also changes.

CPRs are not always animals. Another example of a CPR is the Ogallala Aquifer, an enormous underground water source (see Figure 2.2). Even though the Ogallala Aquifer does not move around in the same way that butterflies, bison, or fish do, it still presents a governance problem: it underlies parts of Wyoming, South Dakota,

Figure 2.2 **The Ogallala Aquifer Is Overlain by Eight U.S. States**

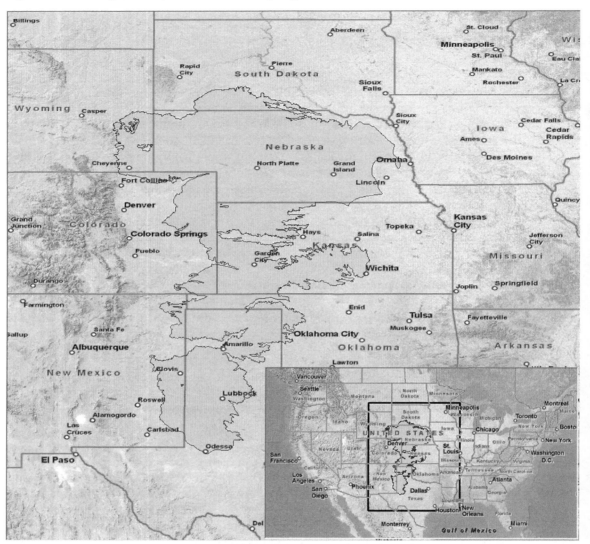

Source: Map produced by Michael K. Tschudi. Used with permission.

Nebraska, Colorado, Kansas, New Mexico, Oklahoma, and Texas (North Plains Groundwater Conservation District). Clearly, one state's consumption of the aquifer can have an impact on the consumption of other states. In fact, even though it is fully contained within the United States, the Ogallala Aquifer is being depleted: It "is in a state of overdraft owing to the current rate of water use. If withdrawals continue unabated, the aquifer could be depleted in only a few decades" (Water Encyclopedia, 2007). Adding to policy difficulties, in some cases those whose properties do not lie above underground CPRs may access them via diagonal drilling.

Within the context of CPRs, people may replace the term *rivalrous* with the term *subtractable*. As indicated in Figure 2.2, some CPRs may be nonrival in certain uses (such as birds for bird-watching), but when they are subtracted from the common pool (as in hunting) they are rival.

TRAGEDY OF THE COMMONS

Closely related to the concept of CPRs is the concept of the Tragedy of the Commons. This idea was first brought into general awareness in 1968 by the ecologist, author, and biology professor Garrett Hardin, who first used the term in a speech that was then published in the prestigious journal *Science*. Key portions of his speech are reproduced here. Interestingly, the most famous passage appears in a subsection entitled "Tragedy of *Freedom* in a Commons" (Hardin, 1968; emphasis added).

> The tragedy of the commons develops in this way. Picture a pasture open to all. It is to be expected that each herdsman will try to keep as many cattle as possible on the commons. Such an arrangement may work reasonably satisfactorily for centuries because tribal wars, poaching, and disease keep the numbers of both man and beast well below the carrying capacity of the land. Finally, however, comes the day of reckoning, that is, the day when the long-desired goal of social stability becomes a reality. At this point, the inherent logic of the commons remorselessly generates tragedy.
>
> As a rational being, each herdsman seeks to maximize his gain. Explicitly or implicitly, more or less consciously, he asks, "What is the utility to me of adding one more animal to my herd?" This utility has one negative and one positive component.
>
> 1) The positive component is a function of the increment of one animal. Since the herdsman receives all the proceeds from the sale of the additional animal, the positive utility is nearly +1.
>
> 2) The negative component is a function of the additional overgrazing created by one more animal. Since, however, the effects of overgrazing are shared by all the herdsmen, the negative utility for any particular decision-making herdsman is only a fraction of −1.
>
> Adding together the component partial utilities, the rational herdsman concludes that the only sensible course for him to pursue is to add another animal to his herd. And another; and another. . . . But this is the conclusion reached by each and every rational herdsman sharing a commons. Therein is the tragedy. Each man is locked into a system that compels him to increase his herd without limit—in a world that is limited. Ruin is the destination toward which all men rush, each pursuing his own best interest in a society that believes in the freedom of the commons. Freedom in a commons brings ruin to all. . . .
>
> In a reverse way, the tragedy of the commons reappears in problems of pollution. Here it is not a question of taking something out of the commons, but of putting something in—sewage, or chemical, radioactive, and heat wastes into water; noxious and dangerous fumes into the air, and distracting and unpleasant advertising signs into the line of sight. The calculations of utility are much the same as before. The rational man finds that his share of

the cost of the wastes he discharges into the commons is less than the cost of purifying his wastes before releasing them. Since this is true for everyone, we are locked into a system of "fouling our own nest," so long as we behave only as independent, rational, free-enterprises. (Hardin, 1968. Used with permission.)

As indicated by the passage on pollution, the idea of the Tragedy of the Commons is applicable not only to CPRs (the common pasturage is a CPR) but also to pure public goods (such as the air we breathe).

SOLUTIONS TO THE TRAGEDY OF THE COMMONS

In the time since Hardin, policy analysts have considered solutions to the Tragedy of the Commons. Hardin (1968) himself proposed what is frequently called "mutual coercion mutually agreed upon," a measure that societies often use. To continue with the example of the common pasture, how would mutual coercion work? The community that shares the pasturage would determine a suitable number of animals to pasture on the common, allocating shares to each herder, and then agree to post a guard—sometimes called the watchman—who would prevent every herder from pasturing more than his or her allotment. In the box below Jared Diamond (2004) gives a current example of mutual coercion mutually agreed upon. Mutual coercion mutually agreed upon can succeed in preventing the Tragedy of the Commons, but it can be difficult to use when CPRs or pure public goods cross political/legal boundaries.

In addition, "transactions costs" can make such solutions difficult in large groups. In theory, bargaining could lead to efficient solutions to the Tragedy of the Commons or other public goods failures. But the more parties who have to bargain, the higher the costs of bargaining. Likewise, the more parties who have to agree to a bargain, the more incentive for various types of strategic behavior, including greatly overstating what is necessary to make one feel compensated for any losses.

Another identified solution to the Tragedy of the Commons is privatization. If a single owner could take over the "common" and make it private, the single owner would be unlikely to overgraze the pasture because the calculus that Hardin describes (above) would change, and the owner would receive not only the benefits, but also bear all of the costs of grazing decisions. Case 2.3 gives a historical example of changing ownership so that something that was once held in common was instead held privately.

The remaining solution to the tragedy of the commons is for the consumers to recognize their common interests and to design, obey, and enforce prudent harvesting quotas themselves.... A good example:... Montana water rights for irrigation.... Nowadays the ranchers mostly obey the water commissioner whom they themselves elect.

Source: Diamond, 2004, 429.

■———— **Case 2.3** ————■

A Historical Example of Turning a Common into a Private:
The Enclosure Movement

Historically, in England and other parts of Europe, it was in fact the case that certain tracts of land were held in common. In England during the eighteenth and nineteenth centuries, many of these commons were "enclosed"—meaning that they were changed from common property to private property—via acts of Parliament. Some contemporaneous commentators argued that open fields were highly inefficient (Kain, Chapman, and Oliver, 1995, 3–4), and some modern scholars argue that the purpose of enclosure was to increase agricultural efficiency:

> Robert Allen develops the view expressed by Jim Yelling that old open field rents were generally below the marginal productivity of the land and concludes that enclosure offered the means by which this extra income could be diverted to the landlord. (Kain, Chapman, and Oliver, 1995, 2; see also *Encyclopaedia Britannica*, 1984, Vol. III, 886)

Kain, Chapman, and Oliver (1995) review historical evidence that many commons were, in fact, heading toward destruction and tragedy (see especially p. 5). Enclosure, however, "was greatly resisted by the peasantry and was disastrous for small landholders and landless peasants" (*Encyclopaedia Britannica*, 1984, Vol. III, 886).

While privatization of a common can increase the efficiency of its use, it is important to remember that it can also greatly change the distribution of wealth among users. If a common that belonged to many is assigned to a single owner, that single owner will now reap, in a concentrated way, the benefits that before were shared. This was so much the case in England that some scholars have declared the enclosure movement to have been "'a plain enough case of class robbery'" (Kain, Chapman, and Oliver 1995, 2).

Sources: Encyclopaedia Britannica, 1984; Information from Kain, Chapman, and Oliver, 1995.

What's the difference between a CPR and a pure public good? A CPR is rival in consumption, so it can be used up. A pure public good is nonrival in consumption, so it can't be used up. Note that a good can switch from being a pure public good to being a CPR in the event of congestion. This is one way to think about what has happened to the ozone layer.

A third solution is to have a higher level of government enforce CPR-preserving behavior. For example, in *2001: A Space Odyssey* (1968), Arthur C. Clark proposes higher-level coercion leading to the public good of world peace. As explicated in the novel (and shown in the Stanley Kubrick film of the same title, though not explained), the world is at peace because it is encircled by nuclear warheads

■———— **Case 2.4** ————■

The Power of Higher-Level Coercion in the Protection of a CPR

Tensions mounted from the escalating demand for water from SRP [Salt River Project, an Arizona utility], municipalities, and farmers. By 1980, the state was consuming almost five million acre feet of water a year, twice the annual renewable supply. Even with the Central Arizona Project [CAP] coming online in the mid-1980s, there still would be a deficit, assuming prevailing levels of consumption. Land subsidence resulted in damaged roads and building foundations in many parts of the valley. Groundwater depletion also caused aquifer compaction, a reduction in overall storage space, and a decline in water quality. Cities understood that continued growth would require groundwater conservation, but knew that they consumed only 5 percent of the state's water supply. The major concessions to maintain growth and avoid an environmental disaster would need to come from the farmers who used 89 percent of the state's water supply.

Resolution of this problem signaled a shift in the balance of power from farmers who controlled a large majority of the state's water to cities that housed 80 percent of the state's population and voters. Early efforts to mediate the dispute revealed deep-seated suspicion and distrust on all sides. The cities and mines accused the farmers of being water monopolists. Farmers felt that cities and mines were openly hostile to agriculture, and they preferred the status quo. Despite these differences, the momentum for groundwater reform was strong as urban growth eventually would be curtailed by water shortages.

In February 1977, President Jimmy Carter proposed to cancel the funding of 19 Western water projects, including CAP. In November 1977, a 25-member commission was set up to study the problem of groundwater depletion and draft a proposed law. At the crux of the debate was whether farmers' right to use groundwater was a property right or, as the cities and mines argued, a public resource governed by the same rules as surface water. *Secretary of the Interior Cecil Andres warned that he would not allocate CAP water until Arizona passed a groundwater bill.* Moreover, allocations had to be made in 1980 to keep the CAP on schedule. Secretary Andres visited Phoenix in October 1979 and declared in no uncertain terms: no groundwater code, no CAP.

Then-Governor Bruce Babbitt assembled stakeholders, including leaders of the legislature and representatives from cities, mines, and agriculture. This so-called "rump group" met in private for hundreds of hours. Babbitt was able to broker a delicate compromise among the three powerful antagonists (cities, farmers, and the mines), first because he was a skilled negotiator and knew a great deal about western waters issues, and second, *because there was simply no choice but to settle if the state was to continue to grow.* The state legislature passed the Groundwater Management Act on June 11, 1980, and the governor signed the bill the next day. Because it was passed by an 80 percent majority, the Act went into effect immediately. . . . The Ford Foundation named this Act one of the nation's ten most innovative programs in state and local government.

Source: Gober, 2006; emphas is added. Used with permission.

controlled by an authority higher than any single country. If any country attacks another, the aggressor country will be destroyed. Case 2.4 illustrates such a case using the example of underground water—a clear CPR—in the arid southwestern United States. In Case 2.4, the federal government and Cecil Andres served as the higher level of government that forced the users of the common to cooperate for its preservation.

The Nobel Prize–winning economist Elinor Ostrom and her colleagues have spent considerable time determining the conditions under which the Tragedy of the Commons will *not* occur, even without government intervention. Their work is impressive and fascinating, but much of its results imply that preventing a Tragedy of the Commons without government intervention usually requires that *small groups* share the common, which makes it less relevant to high-population *urban* environmental policy.

EXTERNALITIES

Environmental policy analysts also often use the concept of the "externality." Externalities can be either positive or negative (meaning either good or bad), though people tend to focus more on negative ones, particularly in environmental policy. As we mentioned earlier, pollution is a pure public good. However, pollution can also be classified as an externality. This understanding helps introduce the following definition: an externality exists when there is an actual item that can be bought or sold in the market but that inevitably (at least under current technology) creates—as part of either its production or consumption—a public good as well. Thus, steel is a private good that can be bought and sold in markets, but it cannot be produced without producing pollution, a pure public good. Thus, pollution is a negative externality of steel production.

Externalities can be positive as well. For example, if you receive a vaccine against a contagious disease, the vaccine produces a positive externality in consumption. The vaccine itself is a private good—it is rival (if you get that unit of vaccine, I cannot also get it) and excludable (vaccine producers can restrict sale of the vaccine to only those who pay the price). But your consumption of the vaccine produces a pure public good that is positive: everyone around you receives a nonexcludable, nonrival benefit of reduced risk of contracting the disease you have been vaccinated against.

> The *externality* situation occurs when production or consumption of a private good also produces a public good; the public good is *external* to the marketplace transaction, affecting those who are neither sellers nor buyers of the private good. Externalities can be either *positive* or *negative*.

Though environmentalists tend to focus more on negative externalities—perhaps because it is seen as more unfair to "force" people to consume something bad against their wills than to "force" them to consume something good—positive externalities also can be relevant to both environmental policy and urban policy. For example, sup-

Exhibit 2.1

Positive and Negative Externalities of Open Space in Residential Areas

Weicher and Zerbst (1973) look at single-family dwellings in Columbus, Ohio, surrounding five neighborhood parks. They use dummy variables for whether a house is adjacent to and faces a park, backs to a park, or is adjacent to and faces an area of heavy recreational use or a park building. Their results suggest that [the] price is higher if the house faces a park, all else being equal, but lower if it either backs to a park or is across from a heavily used park or park building. More recent studies with a broader focus continue to pick up this negative effect on properties located next to busy urban and suburban parks. (McConnell and Walls, 2005, 10)

Especially in the context of much other evidence that people value open space, we can infer that a busy park provides negative externalities (such as noise and lights) to nearby residents, even though the open space without much use, such as "greenways, forests, and other natural areas in urban locations" (McConnell and Walls, 2005, 64), provides measurable positive externalities.

Source: McConnell and Walls, 2005.

pose that you plant a tree. The tree itself is rival (if you buy it, I cannot) and excludable (you can plant it in your backyard and keep others from enjoying it). However, the tree's effects on the air benefit the environment in ways that are purely public. The tree has positive externalities. Exhibit 2.1 illustrates that open space such as parks can have both positive and negative externalities.

When a good has positive externalities, it will tend to be underconsumed compared to the social optimum. This is because the person (in this case, you) who purchases the good (the tree) generally takes into account only his or her individual benefit from it. Thus, you will not be willing to pay the full value of the good, because you will not gain the benefit that accrues to others, nor take this into account in the decision as to how much you value the good and therefore how much you are willing to pay. The price of a good cannot be higher than people's willingness to pay for it; if it is, it will not sell and the price must be lowered. Additionally, producers will not produce a good if they do not make a profit on its production. Since consumers will undervalue goods with positive externalities, the price will be too low, and too little will be created and used.

Supply + demand

Naturally occurring markets will produce *too little of goods with positive externalities* and *too much of goods with negative externalities.*

Similarly, goods with negative externalities will be overproduced. Producers decide how much to produce based on how much people are willing to pay for the good and how much it costs them to produce it. However, the external effects are not considered as costs to the producer. The producer, then, will perceive production costs as lower than they really are to society overall, produce too much, and sell at too low a price that doesn't take into account the full social costs of production.

FREE RIDERS

The concept of the "free rider" is also part of the constellation of concepts surrounding public goods. Free riders are particularly relevant to externalities. A free rider is a person (or organization) who seeks to share in the benefit of some type of public good without sharing in the costs of its production. It is important to note that, because people have different tastes, some people truly may not value a given public good or positive externality and as a result would not want to contribute to its production. Technically, then, these people are not free riders. However, consider someone who values a park near his/her house, but doesn't want to pay for any of its upkeep. That person is a free rider (if he or she gets away with it).

The tendency of humans to free ride—particularly in situations where there are a large number of people sharing in the public good—complicates the provision of public goods including positive externalities, and also the protection of CPRs.

RECAPITULATION REGARDING PUBLIC GOODS

Private goods are both rival and excludable, while pure public goods are neither. "Impure" (or mixed) public goods include CPRs, which are rival in consumption but nonexcludable, and marketable public goods, which are excludable but nonrival in consumption. All three types of public goods—pure, marketable, and common pool—are directly relevant to urban environmental policy and administration because urban and environmental policy are often directly concerned with goods of one or all of these types.

Table 2.3 presents the completed taxonomy of good types, ordered by rivalrousness and excludability, and also explains whether each type of good is likely to be provided by naturally occurring markets or not, what type of market failure will occur (for example, will the good be underproduced? overconsumed?), and what the appropriate role of government might be. Of course, the statements in Table 2.3 are simplifications and generalizations, but they are useful during policy analysis. This taxonomy provides a quick means of analyzing and understanding many situations, even when encountered for the first time.

Several related concepts that are central to the policy-analytic approach to urban environmental policy and its administration have been introduced in this chapter, especially including congestion, legal versus physical excludability, the Tragedy of the Commons, free riders, and externalities.

Before leaving the discussion of such general policy-analytic concepts, it is important to explain (1) why achieving zero levels of pollution is almost never the right policy decision, (2) the Law of Unintended Consequences, and (3) the Fallacy of Sunk Costs.

Table 2.3

A Taxonomy of Types of Goods, Their Likely Provision, Their Usual Market Failures, and Appropriate Roles for Government

	Excludable	Nonexcludable
Rival	**Pure private goods** Absent other failure (e.g., monopoly), naturally occurring markets will provide the right amount. Government should stay out, except to enforce property rights.	**Common pool resources (CPRs)** Rarely provided by markets. Often provided by nature. Often overconsumed and destroyed in high-population situations. Government can improve social welfare by reducing consumption.
Nonrival	**Marketable public goods** (Toll goods) Entrepreneurs will provide these goods but will charge too much for them (absent congestion), so too little will be consumed. Only government or nonprofits/NGOs will supply for free. Absent congestion, government can improve social welfare by increasing consumption (perhaps by increasing production or through subsidization).	**Pure public goods** (Including externalities) Good ones are rarely provided by markets, usually supplied by nature, government, or NGOs. Good ones are typically underproduced, bad ones overproduced. Government can improve social welfare by increasing production of good ones and reducing production of bad ones.

THE RIGHT AMOUNT OF POLLUTION IS RARELY NO POLLUTION

Sometimes, in their zeal to return the world to a more beautiful, healthier, cleaner state, people are tempted to believe that the right amount of pollution—that is, the amount that would maximize social benefit—is no pollution. In almost every case, this is incorrect. Of course, it is impossible for humans (or any animal) to live upon Earth without creating pollution. However, even excluding this basic and inconvenient point, the fact is that most pollution is created in the process of creating something else that we value. Most pollution is an externality and, as defined above, externalities are generated in the production of something else—and this other thing is valued by society or it would not be produced and sold. While people's decisions about the amount of that "something else" to consume should take into account the full social costs of its externalities, only in the most extreme cases will it be true that the cost of the negative externalities will fully overwhelm the benefit of the primary good.

Though rare, there have been goods that had such severe negative externalities that their production—and thereby their pollution—was reduced to zero. At one time, DDT was a widely used pesticide in the United States. However, in June of 1972, "William D. Ruckelshaus, Administrator of the Environmental Protection Agency, issued an order finally cancelling nearly all remaining Federal registrations of DDT products. Public health, quarantine, and a few minor crop uses were excepted. . . . Ruckelshaus said he was convinced that the continued massive use of DDT posed unacceptable risks to the environment and potential harm to human health" (U.S. Environmental Protection Agency, 1972).

But, consider electricity production, which is almost always joined with pollution of some type. While we might wish to reduce electricity consumption to reduce pollution, energy is so valuable that we will not give it up in order to eliminate its pollution. Life involves tradeoffs. At this point, if we gave up electricity, we would cause more harm to people than its pollution causes. Similarly, in many cases, while we should reduce consumption of pollution-causing goods, we should not reduce it to zero.

THE LAW OF UNINTENDED CONSEQUENCES

The Law of Unintended Consequences is conceptually simple, yet very important. Throughout the study of policy, analysts often have found that a policy intended to have one effect frequently also has unintended effects. Exhibit 2.2 provides a simple illustration of this point.

Exhibit 2.2 illustrates more than one point. First, the congestion pricing caused some people to behave as free riders (literally as well as figuratively!) by driving in the heart of London during congested times without paying the congestion fee. This caused the unintended consequence of a new crime: theft of license plates. Second, the London congestion pricing case illustrates that unintended consequences are not always negative: Though the cameras were installed in order to allow efficient enforcement of the congestion pricing plan, they also improved antiterrorism policing. Third, the case provides a warning that unintended consequences, if sufficiently severe, can threaten an otherwise successful policy.

◼━━━━━━━━━◼

Exhibit 2.2

Unintended Consequences of Congestion Pricing in London

London's Congestion Fee Begets Pinched Plates (United Kingdom)

This city's congestion pricing for drivers is heralded around the world for reducing traffic and pollution (Sheth, 2007).

[But] there's an unintended consequence. License plate counterfeiting and thefts are increasing. . . . Traffic cameras enforce congestion fees in London. A computer matches plates and registrations and sends bills to the home address. If you get a cloned plate you ride for free (Kramer, 2007).

Police are under pressure to come up with solutions because they don't want to scrap the cameras. The citywide network of traffic, pedestrian and congestion charge has proved critical in tracking bigger crime such as the terrorist attacks in July 2005 and subsequent bombing attempts (Sheth, 2007).

Sources: Sheth, 2007, and Kramer, 2007.

◼━━━━━━━━━◼

In order to minimize the likelihood of unanticipated consequences, analysts should be careful to think through how incentives have changed with a change in policy. With congestion pricing, something that was free now has a price. This creates an incentive for people to avoid the price. All else equal, when a good's price goes up, people consume less of that good (the intended consequence was a decrease in driving levels in central London). However, it is also true that some people will become free riders, and some will engage in criminal acts in order to free ride. There can also be unintended border effects—neighborhoods next to the congestion pricing area might find a huge increase in the number of cars parked in their neighborhoods; if such parking increases were unintended, this might cause demand for a new policy to correct the problem.

> *The Law of Unintended Consequences:* Policy changes will result in outcomes other than those that are the focus of the policy. To reduce problems from this law, think through how the new policy has changed incentives and how people—both criminal and law-abiding—might change their behaviors in response.

The Fallacy of Sunk Costs

The Fallacy of Sunk Costs is also quite simple, but powerful. Unfortunately, it tends to be ignored, especially in the political realm. Basically, it says that it is a fallacy to consider past resource expenditures when determining whether a policy should be pursued. The most appropriate analogy we have seen is from Levy (1995), who points out that the best route to your destination is determined by where you are right now, not by how you got to where you are. Similarly, whether a policy is worth pursuing or not has to do with the resources needed *from this point on* to achieve it, along with the benefit that will be gained from its pursuit. If the benefits do not exceed the costs, then the resources used up to this point are irrelevant—as they are if the benefits do exceed the costs from this point forward.

> *The Fallacy of Sunk Costs* occurs when people throw good money after bad. Past resource expenditures are irrelevant when deciding whether to spend future resources in order to achieve a policy goal.

Unfortunately, politicians often act as if the fact that resources have been spent means that more resources must be spent until we get at least some good out of those resources already spent. This approach causes social waste. The past resources are *sunk*—they have been used, and this cannot be changed—but the resources we spend in the future should be used in a way that provides social benefit. The concept of the Fallacy of Sunk Costs exists in folk wisdom, as indicated by the saying, "Don't throw good money after bad."

HOW TO USE THE INFORMATION FROM THIS CHAPTER

This chapter introduces many concepts used by policy analysts as they think about policy. Those introduced here are specifically useful to urban environmental policy analysts. To get the best use from these concepts, you need to train yourself to think about them whenever you encounter a new policy problem. You might want to get in the habit of asking yourself the following questions:

- What type of good is under consideration? Pure private, pure public, marketable, CPR? If the answer to this question isn't immediately apparent, think about rivalry and excludability.
  - Is congestion relevant?
  - Is this a Tragedy of the Commons?
  - Is the public good at issue an externality?

As explicated in the next chapter, understanding the answer to these questions will help you understand what general types of policy interventions are likely to be successful.

As you consider policy solutions, be sure to keep in mind the Fallacy of Sunk Costs; remember, as well, that what matters is resource expenditures going forward and whether they are likely to exceed benefits gained from a policy change. Also be prepared to explain this concept to some who might think they must keep spending on an old policy in order "make good" on past effort.

Finally, think about the Law of Unintended Consequences, and try to anticipate unintended consequences of proposed policy solutions. Keep in mind that people have a natural tendency to become free riders, and some are even willing to engage in illegal behavior. In some societies, corruption is a norm. Though thinking explicitly about the unintended consequences of a policy does not guarantee that you will think of all of them, making it a habit to do so can help reduce undesirable unintended outcomes and aid in the realization of ancillary benefits of policy change.

At the end of Chapter 1, we used a case, Case 1.5, to illustrate how an analyst might use the System Model developed in the chapter. We end Chapter 2 by revisiting that case (in Case 2.5), using some of the concepts presented in this chapter. Case 2.5 shows how you can use this chapter's concepts in your own policy thinking.

DISCUSSION QUESTIONS

1. In Figure 2.1, what type of good are "Wild Animals Used for Hunting"? What type are "Wild Birds Used by Birders"? ("Birders" are bird-watchers.) What makes them different types of goods?
2. For Table 2.1, explain one good that belongs in each quadrant. Briefly explain your answers, using the concepts of rivalry and excludability.
3. Give an example from the book of a good that is nonrival to the point of congestion. Give an example of a good that is *not* in this chapter that is nonrival to the point of congestion.

■———— **Case 2.5** ————■

Using Public Goods Concepts

Revisiting Case 1.5 with New Concepts: Suppose a Drought Is Causing Subsidence in Your City

What types of goods are involved in the case of the drought that is causing subsidence in your city?

Rain is a common pool resource (CPR): it is provided by nature, it is rival in consumption, and it is nonexcludable. Rain falls where it will; we have neither the legal nor the physical ability to exclude some from its benefits (or harms). We say it is rival in consumption because specific rain that is consumed by one is not available for consumption by another.

An aquifer is also a CPR. Again, it is supplied by nature, it is difficult to exclude consumers (especially if more than one legal/political jurisdiction lies above it), but the water within it is rival in consumption (that is, it is subtractable).

Since CPRs are generally overconsumed (as noted in Table 2.3), we should expect that both rain and water in aquifers will be overconsumed. With rain less available, we can expect greater overconsumption of the aquifer than before because these goods are close substitutes, especially for outdoor water uses. Here, the drought combined with the current population and its demands has caused the aquifer to become congested. We also should realize that a Tragedy of the Commons is quite possible if we do not intervene. In fact, subsidence shows that we are already experiencing some Tragedy of the Commons.

However, the water distribution system used in most modern cities moves water from the "less excludable" side of the spectrum, as illustrated in Figure 2.1, to the "more excludable" side. In modern urban settings, most people don't dig a well to get their water; they purchase it from a water provider (often a city), and it is delivered via pipes to their dwellings. As mentioned earlier, if a good is excludable, then a price can be charged. As discussed further in the next chapter, increasing prices can reduce consumption, so understanding the nature of the good helps us realize one possible solution to this policy problem (more solutions are discussed in Chapter 3).

The material in Chapter 2 also indicates that we can expect free riders and unintended consequences. How might free riders behave and how might the unintended consequences manifest themselves? Free riders might engage in water theft, an unintended consequence (parallel to the free-rider plate-theft behavior in the city of London). We also might observe increased numbers of wells drilled in the city. Water theft might sound unlikely to you, but it currently exists (as just one example, the town of Purcellville, Virginia, USA, has an entire page on its website devoted to water theft, at http://www. purcellvilleva.com/index.aspx?NID=247. During the 2008 drought in Georgia—during which restrictions were placed on outdoor watering—some homeowners had wells dug on their properties (CBS News, October 23, 2007). This unintended behavior was a benefit to well-diggers, but not helpful to successful water management during the severe drought.

The analysis in the previous chapter (Case 1.5) also indicates that problems from excessive use of the aquifer show up in the Concretion layer. Harm to the Concretion

Case 2.5 *(continued)*

layer can be seen as a negative externality of excessive aquifer consumption. Individual buildings are generally pure private goods that have specific owners who can be expected to fix them. But people who overconsume water are unlikely to consider the external costs of their consumption decisions on those whose structures are damaged—they think the water is free or near-free and ignore its true costs. In addition, what about the other parts of the Concretion layer such as the streets? Given standard social arrangements, these are often legally pure public goods, and therefore they are very unlikely to be fixed except by the direct intervention of government.

Thus, using policy concepts introduced in this chapter, we can

- understand what attributes of the aquifer lead to its overuse,
- gain insight into one possible solution,
- gain insight into possible unintended consequences of that solution (water theft and new wells), and
- understand that even once we've solved the water-use problem, we will still be faced with another policy problem to solve—damage to pure public goods in the Concretion layer.

NOTES

1. Though the term "goods" simply means things produced and consumed, sometimes "goods" that are bad are referred to as "bads," so we could also say that pollution is a classic public bad.

2. According to the Mayo Clinic website, in Southern California and the American Southwest, dust may contain spores of "the lung disease, valley fever, known medically as coccidioidomycosis, or cocci" (2006). Construction activities, or wind alone, can lift the spores into the air, where they are readily breathed in. "Valley fever can cause fever, chest pain and coughing, among other symptoms. Most people who inhale the valley fever fungus have few, if any, problems. But some, especially pregnant women, people with weakened immune systems, and those of Asian, Hispanic and African descent may develop a serious or even fatal illness" (Mayo Clinic, 2006).

3. Pareto efficiency is named after the French-Italian economist Vilfredo Pareto.

REFERENCES

American Museum of Natural History. 1998. Will the fish return? How gear and greed emptied Georges Bank. http://www.amnh.org/sciencebulletins/biobulletin/biobulletin/story1208.html (accessed September 19, 2007).
Birkland, T.A. 2005. *An Introduction to the Policy Process: Theories, Concepts, and Models of Public Policy Making*, 2d ed. Armonk, NY: M.E. Sharpe.
CBS News Video. 2007. Panic rising in Georgia. October 23. http://www.cbsnews.com/video/watch/?id=3395746n (accessed August 22, 2011).
Clark, A.C. 1968. *2001: A Space Odyssey*. New York: New American Library.
Cooper, J.F. [1823] 1964. *The Pioneers*. With an afterword by Robert E. Spiller. New York: Signet, 1964.
Diamond, J. 2004. *Collapse: How Societies Choose to Fail or Succeed*. New York: Viking.
Encyclopaedia Britannica. 1984. Vol. III. Chicago, IL: University of Chicago Press, s.v. "enclosure."
Gober, P. 2006. *Metropolitan Phoenix: Place Making and Community Building in the Desert*. Philadelphia, PA: University of Pennsylvania Press.

Hardin, G. 1968. The tragedy of the commons. *Science*, December 13. http://www.garretthardinsociety.org/articles/art_tragedy_of_the_commons.html (accessed September 21, 2007).

Heikkila, T. 2004. Institutional boundaries and common-pool resource management: A comparative analysis of water management programs in California. *Journal of Policy Analysis and Management*, 23, 1, 97–117.

Kain, R.J.P., J. Chapman, and R.R. Oliver. 1995. *The Enclosure Maps of England and Wales, 1595–1918*. Cambridge, UK: Cambridge University Press. http://assets.cambridge.org/97805218/27713/excerpt/9780521827713_excerpt.pdf.

Kramer, M. 2007. Congestion pricing flaw: Cloned license plates. http://keepnycfree.com/media/files/2007-11-27_Cloned_License_Plates_(WCBS-TV).pdf (accessed 22 August, 2011).

Levy, J.M. 1995. *Essential Microeconomics for Public Policy Analysis*. Westport, CT: Praeger.

Litman, T. 2006. *London Congestion Pricing: Implications for Other Cities*. Victoria, BC, Canada: Victoria Transport Policy Institute. http://www.vtpi.org/london.pdf.

Mayo Clinic staff. 2006. Valley fever: Definition. MayoClinic.com. http://www.mayoclinic.com/health/valley-fever/DS00695 (accessed September 12, 2007).

McConnell, V., and M. Walls. 2005. The value of open space: Evidence from studies of nonmarket benefits. Report prepared by Resources for the Future, Washington, DC, January. http://www.rff.org/Documents/RFF-REPORT-Open Spaces.pdf.

National Park Service. 2009. Grand Canyon: How big is it? http://www.nps.gov/grca/faqs.htm#big. (accessed September 19, 2007).

———. 2011. Grand Canyon: Fees & reservations. http://www.nps.gov/grca/planyourvisit/fees-reservations.htm (accessed September 19, 2007).

Pacific Grove Museum of Natural History. n.d. Monarch Grove Sanctuary: The migration phenomenon. http://www.pgmuseum.org/ (accessed September 19, 2007).

Sheth, N. 2007. London's congestion fee begets pinched plates. *Wall Street Journal,* November 2, B1–B2.

Smith, Adam. [1776] 2003. *The Wealth of Nations*. New York: Bantam Classics, 2003.

Town of Purcellville, Virginia. 2006–2008. Water theft. http://www.purcellvilleva.com/index.asp?NID=247 (October 1, 2008).

U.S. Environmental Protection Agency. 1972. DDT ban takes effect. Press release, December 31. http://www.epa.gov/aboutepa/history/topics/ddt/01.html (accessed March 10, 2011).

Water Encyclopedia. 2007. Ogallala Aquifer. http://waterencyclopedia.com/Oc-Po/Ogallala-Aquifer.html (accessed September 25, 2007).

Weicher, J. and R. Zerbst. 1973. Externalities of neighborhood parks: An empirical investigation. *Land Economics*, 49, 99–105.

Weimer, D.L., and A.R. Vining. 1992. *Policy Analysis: Concepts and Practice*, 2d ed. Englewood Cliffs, NJ: Prentice Hall.

3 | Useful Policy Instruments for Correcting Market Failures

In Chapter 1, we stress that government is the primary lever in urban environmental policy. We also mention that, although government may not always use it, one of its key attributes is its ability to coerce compliance. In Chapter 3, we present different ways in which government can act to make policy change, including, but not limited to, coercive means. This chapter develops a tool kit of general ideas regarding ways to achieve policy outcomes. These standard methods can be applied to particular policy areas, and examples are given throughout. The focus in this chapter is on governmental instruments that are particularly useful in urban environmental policy. Other works (see, for example, Bardach, 2009; Birkland, 2005; Salamon, 2002; Weimer and Vining, 1999) provide broader discussions of generic policy instruments.

In this chapter, we organize the discussion of governmental policy instruments by types of market failures, most of which were delineated in Chapter 2. In this way, we hope analysts and administrators can think through policies more directly and quickly to address specific types of failure that they have identified. Table 3.1 begins the presentation by listing types of market problems matched with solutions. Next, solutions are described and illustrated in more detail. The intent is not to cover every possible policy instrument that could be useful in a particular case, but to focus on those that most clearly fit the failure in the urban environmental policy context. In some cases, you may want to consider using a solution in one box for a problem in another; likewise, you may find additional ideas for solutions in the scholarly literature or in agency reports from other jurisdictions—or even in other units of your own jurisdiction.

In terms of the Policy Process model presented in Chapter 1, understanding generic policy solutions is most directly relevant in the Policy Formulation stage. However, it can also be used during the Evaluation stage, when a specific solution can be compared to the attributes of the policy situation under consideration to understand if the solution's policy instruments are well suited to the policy domain. In addition, generic policy solutions may be utilized during the politics of the Legitimation stage to argue that a specific policy's chosen tools are or are not appropriate.

SOME USEFUL POLICY INSTRUMENTS

For quick reference, Table 3.1 (page 54–55) joins policy concerns with useful solutions. The following discussion is categorized by market and types of goods as listed in the table.

GENERIC SOLUTIONS FOR PURE PRIVATE GOODS

If your analysis indicates that a new policy will affect a pure private good, unless there are other market failures or important distributional concerns, the appropriate policy recommendation is to free the market—that is, to remove government intervention other than the standard enforcement of law.

In private-good circumstances, government intervention cannot be efficiency enhancing and may actually reduce social welfare significantly. Even if some concept of equity is the primary justification for government intervention, decision makers should proceed with caution. A common urban policy example is rent control, which is often justified on equity grounds. However, much research indicates that rent control harms overall social welfare and often helps the well-off more than the putatively targeted groups (see, for example, MIT Center for Real Estate).

MONOPOLIES AND NATURAL MONOPOLIES

Economists say that there are four main types of market failure: missing markets (which can include public goods and externalities), market power, asymmetric information, and human cognition problems (Tasoff, personal communication). Monopoly, natural monopoly, and monopsony are all problems of market power. "Natural monopoly" is the most relevant to urban environmental policy, so it is emphasized here.

Natural monopolies may be of relevance in urban environmental policy analysis because many utilities—such as water, sewerage, and electricity—are provided by natural monopolies. The concept of a natural monopoly is reasonably straightforward, though the solution to it is not. A natural monopoly is also called a "declining-cost industry." For most firms, while average costs fall over some range of production, these costs rise throughout the range of market demand. In a natural monopoly, this is not the case. Instead, throughout the range of total demand for the good in a specific market, average costs are declining (or perhaps are flat). This is usually caused by very high initial costs of production—high costs before any of the good can be produced—followed by very low marginal costs. As an example, a citywide water distribution network is very expensive, but in many cases each unit of water itself is inexpensive—and it doesn't matter if a residence will receive a single unit of water or many. Either way, the pipe must be laid at a certain fixed cost. Because of the fact that average costs are declining over the entire range of demand, a firm that can supply more of the product than its competitors can charge a lower price (because the average costs that it must cover are, in fact, lower) and drive its competitors out of the business. However, once the successful firm drives out all the lower-amount/higher-cost suppliers, it will tend to act like any other monopolist and supply too little compared to the social optimum, while charging an excessive price. Furthermore, there is an additional element of social cost if natural monopolies compete with one another. Again, consider the case of water supply. Suppose that two water companies compete with each other; if they lay duplicate pipe, social waste has occurred.

Each solution to natural monopoly has potential drawbacks. Until the 1980s, direct regulation of the successful firm(s) to enforce greater provision at lower prices was the standard American solution. A benefit of this system is that distributional issues can also be regulated; for example, the regulated firm can be required to offer a "lifeline" rate to low-income customers. A problem with this system is that it is difficult for regulators to gather sufficient information to regulate price and quantity at an optimal—or even near-optimal—level. The information asymmetries between the regulated firm and the regulatory agency are great and quite difficult for the agency to overcome. Because firms generally must be compensated for capital investment (at least under U.S. law), historically there have been cases of firms wasting social resources through overcapitalization. Averch and Johnson (1962) were the first to identify this problem.

Information asymmetry exists when one party to a transaction understands more about the true attributes of the good to be exchanged than another. It is a violation of assumptions of the perfectly competitive market, and therefore the Invisible Hand Theorem may not hold when information asymmetry is present.

Until the 1980s, the standard European solution was government ownership of the natural monopoly. This solution is still practiced in many parts of the world, including (in some cases) the United States. For example, a city's water is often provided by a city-owned water company. This solution allows pricing or other provisions to be targeted toward specific social goals. The problem with this solution is that the government monopoly—feeling little-to-no external pressures of either competition or regulatory oversight—has few incentives to innovate and even fewer to keep costs appropriate. Whether reduced innovation matters or not depends on the good. In the 1980s and 1990s, it became clear to many countries that innovation in telecommunications services was imperative; innovation in water supply, for example, may be less urgent.

Also, to the extent that political pressure affects a government monopoly, prices may be kept too low. This can be of particular concern if changes in social costs require significant increases in pricing. In Tucson, Arizona, in the 1970s, it became necessary for the city's utility to raise water rates. "Business accused the council of being anti-growth while residents gathered signatures to recall the council. At a special election that fall, every council member who voted for the price increase was voted out of office" (Walton, 2010). This event resonated throughout Arizona for more than a decade, reducing politicians' willingness to raise water prices.

Table 3.1

Market Failures and Some Useful Solutions

Market, Good, and Failure Types	Analysis and Useful Solutions *Approaches*
Pure Private Goods	
No other market failure	There is no justification for government intervention except to maintain property rights and for equity/fairness/distributional concerns. For efficiency, free the market!
With monopoly or natural monopoly	Markets acting alone will supply too little, and monopolists will usually gain monopoly "rent" (excess profits). In some cases, there may be sufficient demand elasticity (e.g., through close substitutes) that no intervention is needed. Otherwise, solutions include: • Directly regulating the market to enforce greater provision at lower prices • Auctioning or contracting the market to require greater supply and/or lower prices • Direct government provision to supplement supply • For natural monopoly, a combined strategy of monopoly ownership of the infrastructure and competitive provision of what is carried
With monopsony	Monopsony (the case in which the buyer has market power) can lead to exploitive pay for inputs, especially labor (where "exploitive" means below marginal benefit) • Mandate minimum wages (or other prices) at marginal benefit to the organization with monopsony power • Provide protection to unions (or other combinations) so that they can counter monopsony power • Subsidize suppliers of inputs
Information Problems	• Require information provision through regulation • Subsidize information provision • Provide information directly • If the information problem is an inability to correctly assess risk, a solution may be to mandate, provide, or subsidize insurance
Toll/ Marketable Public/Toll Goods	In some cases, demand is sufficiently elastic (e.g., through many close substitutes) that losses are minimal and intervention is not necessary. In other cases, options are: • Direct provision (e.g., of roads, bridges) • Contracting for additional provision • Subsidies to providers so that they will provide more
Common Pool/Property Resources (CPRs)	
Quantities are adequate to meet all demand even at a price of zero (0) with continued flows of the good	No intervention is required, but monitoring should occur since this can change rapidly.
Small groups use the CPR	• Small groups may be able to negotiate suitable responses without government action • Government can serve as an "honest broker" to assist in negotiations
CPR is fixed in space and some appropriate governmental unit contains the CPR	• Regulate to limit use via quotas, which can be assigned using a first-come, first-served basis; lotteries; auctions; or other methods • Regulation with pricing to limit use • Serve as the watchman—enforce limits

(continued)

Table 3.1 *(continued)*

Market, Good, and Failure Types	Useful solutions *Approaches*
	• Conversion to private ownership: Temporary, via auctions or contracts; Permanent (auctions are recommended so that society can share the value; Other methods, such as incumbency, may be considered for fairness)
	• Suasion/education
CPR is fixed in space, but multiple governmental units overlap the CPR	• Intergovernmental agreements
	• Change boundaries of governmental units or create a new one so that a single appropriate governmental unit contains the CPR (such "appropriate units" can be special districts if they have sufficient power of monitoring and enforcement)
CPR is mobile	• Intergovernmental agreements
	• Create a governmental unit that contains the range of the mobile CPR (such units may need to be "supra-governmental" such as Councils of Governments)
	• Seek key points in time or space where regulation may be especially effective
	• Enforce

Pure Public Goods

Small groups
- Small groups may be able to negotiate creation of good ones and amelioration of bad ones
- Government can serve as an "honest broker" to facilitate agreements
- Suasion

Large groups
- Directly provide goods
- Subsidize provision of goods
- Tax provision of bads
- Enforce
- Suasion/education

Congestion Problems

Reduce congestion through:
- Pricing/taxing
- Quotas
- Changing ownership

Externalities
- Tax negative externalities
- Subsidize positive externalities
- Regulate amounts
- Enforce
- Create tradable permits
- Directly provide goods with positive externalities
- Suasion/education

Excess Risk

If risk is too widespread within a population, insurance firms may not be able to adequately diversify the risk and will not provide adequate insurance:
- Provide insurance to consumers or insurers
- Facilitate or mandate the creation of a risk pool by many insurers
- Directly reduce risk
- Tax risk-creating behavior
- Subsidize risk-reducing behavior
- Regulate risky behavior

A possible solution to the problem of government supply is that government may own the high-cost infrastructure, but not the competitive good that is distributed through it. For example, the city could own the water distribution system, but customers might purchase water from independent suppliers that pay to use the distribution network. In this way, the naturally monopolistic distribution network would be owned by government, but prices for the distributed good would still be subject to competitive pressures. If water became more expensive, the water suppliers would charge more, but the costs of the monopolistic city infrastructure would not be affected. When considering a good as crucial to life as water, the downside of such a scenario is that, since water is absolutely necessary, cities and citizens may not be willing to allow its provision to be driven solely by the market. In the case of water, this unwillingness may be exacerbated because some believe that access to water is a basic human right, and therefore water, in particular, should not be subject to the market and the profit motive. In fact, in July of 2010, the United Nations General Assembly asserted: "Safe and clean drinking water and sanitation is a fundamental human right" (Seshan, 2010). Free water is not a good solution to this belief, however, since goods with a price of zero will be overconsumed.

Another option for the provision of natural monopoly goods is to auction off or contract out provision to a single firm. Though a single winner will hold the natural monopoly, competition will occur during the auctioning or contracting event. The competition of the auction or the contracting process increases the chances that costs and prices will be closer to the (lower) social optimum, and the contract can be written to require social goals such as lifeline rates. There are two potential problems with such a solution: (1) Especially if the firm that wins the contract or auction underbid (either intentionally or unintentionally), it is likely to degrade the quality of provision unless the contract includes quality requirements; (2) Frequently such contracts are inflexible for their duration, which can lead either to windfall profits for the contract-holder, or else to excess hardship and losses for the contract-holder. Such contracts should be designed with care and expert advice.

At this point, you may be wondering why these options are recommended at all, since each one includes associated problems. In general, government intervenes when the market acting on its own cannot provide a good at the right level. This means that socially desirable provision is complex. As you will see, there is rarely a perfect solution—just some solutions that are better than others. And policy can be better designed and implemented if analysts and administrators are aware of the pitfalls of recommended solutions. We intend in this chapter to give you a suite of good solutions along with their potential weaknesses. Forewarned is forearmed, and you should always be on the lookout for unintended consequences.

MONOPSONY

"Monopsony," which is listed in Table 3.1 for completeness, can be a type of market failure even for private goods. Most people know about monopoly—it occurs when one organization dominates the market for selling a good—but many have not heard of monopsony. Monopsony occurs when one organization dominates the market for purchasing (instead of selling) a good. Usually the good in question is a production input, and this includes specialized labor. The professional sports organizations in the United States, among them the National Football League, exercise monopsony power over their "workers" (the team members) who have very specialized talents (Sharp, Register, and Grimes, 2007).

There are cases in which government exercises monopsony power. For example, suppose a person wants to work as an aerospace engineer developing fighter planes. In the United States, such a person can only work legally in that capacity as an employee of the U.S. government (or of American firms that work for the U.S. government under specialized government contracts). In that case, the U.S. government or its agent has monopsony power in the hiring of fighter-plane engineers. In the monopsony case, the organization with monopsony power (for example, the U.S. government hiring fighter-plane engineers) will tend to purchase or hire too little of the input and pay too little for it.

Monopsony is not likely to be of particular importance in urban environmental policy analysis, but it can be useful for all policy analysts and administrators to re-member that government may engage in monopsony failings.

INFORMATION PROBLEMS

One of the assumptions of the perfectly competitive market mentioned in Chapter 2 is known as "perfect information." This term is a bit misleading, however. It doesn't mean that everyone in the market has to be like a god, knowing all that is now or has been or will be. Instead, it means that all parties to a transaction have basically the same information about the good, correctly understanding prices and important attributes of the good under consideration.

Information problems can occur if one party to the transaction knows less about some important element of the good than does the other (for example, if producers know, but consumers do not, that a car will explode upon impact). As defined on page 53, this is called "information asymmetry." A second possible information failure oc-curs when no party to the transaction understands important attributes (for example, in the early days of coal-fired plants, no one understood the health impacts of the coal smoke). Research is a solution to this problem, and government can perform research or encourage it through subsidization. Third, information problems can occur if for some reason people cannot correctly assess the risks involved in a transaction (for example, due to human cognition problems).

In urban environmental policy analysis, the last point is an especially likely infor-mation problem because many environmental factors involve complex, technical as-sessments of risk. Many studies have shown that humans have difficulty in correctly assessing risk, especially risk that is low and builds over time (Szalavitz, 2008, 1). In 2010, an analysis of the "exposure of cooks at night markets in Taiwan" to "polycyclic aromatic hydrocarbons" (PAHs)[1] formed by food cooking found that "at all typical food stalls in night markets [but one] . . . the excess lifetime cancer risk (ELCR) of cooks are beyond the acceptable target risk range of 10(–6) to 10(–4) for occupational work-ers set by USEPA" (Zhao, Yu, and Lin, 2010). Even knowing that this finding means that their added risk of cancer from holding this job is greater than .0001—and that the U.S. Environmental Protection Agency considers this an unacceptable level of added risk—may not be very useful to the Taiwanese night-market cooks.

A standard solution to information problems is "information provision," which, as indicated in Table 3.1, can be accomplished in a number of ways, including by regulation requiring information provision, by direct governmental provision, or by subsidization of provision. When the problem of risk-understanding is particularly high, insurance to protect people from the misunderstood risk can be a solution. In the example of the Taiwanese cooks, how might these different options play out?

1. The city government could require that the employers post signs explaining that inhaling cooking fumes increases cancer risks. This would require monitoring to ensure that the employers complied.
2. Alternatively, the city could subsidize employers to inform workers, perhaps by providing them with signs, or reimbursing them for sign expenditures. Again, the government would need to monitor to make sure that the signs were actually posted.
3. The government could itself provide the information through a public information campaign. There could be signs on buses and radio announcements warning workers of this risk. As is frequently the case, rather than providing the public service announcement itself, the government could contract with a private organization (for-profit or nonprofit) to perform the public information campaign.
4. The city could provide (or contract) training programs to help owners or workers learn best practices for dealing with the dangerous cooking pollutants.
5. If it turns out that workers cannot correctly understand the information about risks of the cooking fumes, and so they accept more risk than is socially optimal, the government could induce (through one of the means listed in the table) provision of insurance against the eventual cancers that the night-market cooks will incur.

Information provision can be a solution beyond problems that are specifically information-based. You may notice that Table 3.1 includes "suasion/education" as a policy solution to various failures such as CPRs. Suasion (persuasion) or education efforts must include information provision. Again, solutions may be interchangeable: One solution that is particularly useful for one type of market problem may also be useful for others. Therefore, Exhibit 3.1 discusses information provision as a form of suasion, and Exhibit 3.2 shows an example of such use.

Suasion is the term used in to indicate persuasion or education as opposed to some other form of governmental compulsion.

GENERIC SOLUTIONS FOR MARKETABLE PUBLIC/TOLL GOODS

As noted in Table 3.1, the problem of a marketable or toll good is not always sufficient to necessitate government intervention. For example, movie theaters are marketable

Exhibit 3.1

Using Information as Suasion

The norm of carbon neutrality has spread remarkably in recent years, but anecdotal information suggests that it has yet to spread beyond those who adhere to pro-environmental abstract norms. Given the timing and magnitude of the short- and long-term emissions reduction targets, the carbon-neutrality norm will need to spread not only among those who ascribe to environmental norms but also to those who do not. This Part examines how policymakers can use the regulatory regime to push the emerging carbon-neutrality norm toward a tipping point without propagandizing. As a general matter, policymakers can do so by requiring that agencies collect and disseminate accurate information about the consequences of individual carbon emissions and the steps that individuals can take to mitigate those consequences. Although many past informational efforts have been ineffective, in prior times of crisis—such as the scrap drives of World War II—government has engaged in successful efforts to persuade individuals to act by providing information about the effects of behavior. The costs and benefits of the measures proposed in this Part will require careful analysis, but many of these measures have the potential to deliver emissions reductions more quickly and at lower costs than many of the traditional measures (Vandenbergh, 2007, 152).

To address this information deficit, public information campaigns will need to reflect a sophisticated understanding of how information is received, processed, and used by individuals. For example, the National Research Council has suggested that information is more likely to generate behavior change if it is understandable, attracts attention, stays in the memory, is provided at times and places that are close to the point of decisionmaking, and is provided by a trustworthy source (Brewer and Sterns, 2005, 155).

Source: Vandenbergh and Steinemann, 2007.

---

public goods. People can be excluded, but the good itself (the showing of the movie) is nonrival in consumption to the point of congestion. At least in the industrialized world, we do not find governments providing or subsidizing movie theaters, and it can be expected that the social losses from movie theaters are small. First, because building a movie theater is not particularly expensive, we should expect to see a lot of them; such competition tends to increase supply and reduce price. Second, the demand for movies in theaters is quite "price-elastic," especially with the growth

> Goods can be *substitutes* or *complements* for other goods. *Substitutes* are just what they sound like—they are goods that can substitute for another if prices rise too high or availability declines. *Complements* are goods that people tend to consume together; bread and butter are complementary goods.

Exhibit 3.2

**Part of an Air Quality Brochure from a
Hamilton County, Ohio, Anti-Idling Campaign**

Have You Ever Left Your Car Running While . . .

- waiting to pick someone up?
- running errands?
- sitting at the drive-through?

If you said "yes" to any of these questions, you've idled your car. Idling means leaving a vehicle's engine running when it is parked or not in use.

Idling happens without much thought. Many people idle their cars because they think it's easy, convenient and efficient.

But that's wrong! Idling is harmful to our air quality, our health, our cars and our wallets!

How Idling Affects Air Quality

- Cars are the number one source of air pollution in the Greater Cincinnati area. Like driving, idling releases emissions into the air. Unlike driving, idling is unnecessary.
- Car exhaust contains: nitrogen oxides (NOx), volatile organic compounds (VOCs), particulate matter (PM), carbon monoxide (CO) and carbon dioxide (CO_2).
- An hour of automobile idling burns approximately 1/5 of a gallon of gas and releases nearly 4 pounds of CO_2 into the air. Excessive amounts of CO_2 in the atmosphere can increase global warming.
- An idling car needlessly releases these pollutants into the air. Reducing idling is an easy way to reduce vehicle emissions.

How Idling Affects Your Health

The pollutants found in exhaust not only affect our environment, they also affect our health. PM is the name for tiny particles, such as soot, dust and dirt, found in the air. When inhaled, these small particles travel deep into the lungs and sometimes into the bloodstream. Inhaling PM can:

- aggravate asthma,
- cause coughing or difficult breathing,
- decrease lung function,
- exacerbate cardiovascular problems and
- lead to chronic bronchitis.

CO slows the delivery of oxygen to the body's organs and tissues. Exposure to CO aggravates heart disease and can cause headaches and visual impairment.

Children are especially sensitive to the effects of air pollution because they breathe more quickly and take in more air than adults.

Children spend more time outdoors than adults, which further increases their exposure to vehicle emissions and air pollution.

Acronym Guide: NOx: Nitrogen Oxides, VOCs: Volatile Organic Compounds, PM: Particulate Matter, CO: Carbon Monoxide, CO_2: Carbon Dioxide

Source: Hamilton County Environmental Services' Air Quality Management Division.

in close substitutes, including free television, cable television, satellite television, movies on DVDs, movies downloaded online, etc. Third, rather than suffer empty theaters, movie houses often charge much lower prices at low-demand times of day, increasing the likelihood that, at least at these times, the prices of movies are close to the socially optimal price. Fourth, movies in theaters are not considered necessities.

Marketable public goods can be of relevance to urban environmental policy analysis. As we mention elsewhere in this book, roads and bridges are marketable public goods, and they are also key features of the Concretion System. An inadequate supply of roads and bridges can exacerbate urban environmental problems; if motorized vehicles idle in congestion, they create more pollution than if those same vehicles travel smoothly to their destinations (Hamilton County, Ohio). Since bridges serve as bottlenecks, it may be that inadequate bridge capacity can be an urban environmental problem. It is also worth noting that public utility infrastructure, such as the water distribution system mentioned earlier, is also a key feature of the Concretion System of the city and can be thought of as a marketable public good. If the utility infrastructure is not properly maintained, it too can lead to urban environmental problems. For instance, inadequate maintenance of the distribution system can cause leaking and water waste. Improper maintenance of a water treatment system can result in excess chemicals in the air and ground.

In the event that a marketable public good is of social concern, useful solutions include direct provision by government, contracting for provision, or subsidies to providers so that they will provide more and charge a lower price. Though vouchers to users could also serve as a solution, in the case of marketable public goods it is usually more administratively feasible to subsidize providers and provision rather than to subsidize users. This is because the marketable good is often fixed in space, but the users are not. Furthermore, there will be fewer providers than users. Administrative feasibility should also be considered as part of social efficiency. If a solution cannot be effectively administered, it is more likely to fail.

GENERIC SOLUTIONS FOR CPRs

As detailed in Chapter 2, CPRs are directly relevant to urban environmental policy analysis. In some cases, nature provides a CPR in such amounts that even total demand when the good is free does not harmfully deplete it. In an earlier chapter, for example, we discussed Native American Indians' ancestral use of bison as such a case. However, changes in human taste, population, or technology can rapidly affect whether a CPR is sustainable at full (zero-price) demand, and nonhuman changes such as weather events can also affect the amount of a CPR and change its sustainability. So, if a CPR is valuable to society, it should be monitored even in cases where it is currently in great supply.

In some cases, the urban government may wish to monitor resources directly, but others may do the monitoring and the city can simply keep track of the results. In the United States, monitoring is done by divisions of the federal government (such as the U.S. Fish and Wildlife Service), as well as by state agencies (such as the Massachusetts Department of Fish and Game). Academics in many countries are interested in monitoring various CPRs, and they would probably be pleased to pass along their findings in exchange for heightened city government responsiveness to their concerns about the health of the CPR. Sometimes NGOs also monitor CPRs and make the information widely available.

CPRs AND SMALL GROUPS

As Elinor Ostrom and other members of the Workshop in Political Theory and Policy Analysis of Indiana University, Bloomington, have shown, small groups can be successful at maintaining a CPR without government intervention (works on this topic are too numerous to cite, but a good overview is presented in Ostrom, 1990). In some cases, the government can serve as an honest broker—one that has no personal gain from negotiations but seeks an outcome that benefits all involved—to help a small group reach and maintain a CPR-protection agreement. Exhibit 3.3 illustrates that while small groups can protect CPRs, brokers can help as well. In some cases, groups do not trust the government. You may have heard the mocking statement, "Hi, I'm from the government and I'm here to help!" Oftentimes, discriminated-against minorities and indigenous population groups have significant past experience that supports such distrust (see Chapter 9). In these cases, the city government could perhaps arrange for someone else—such as nongovernmental scientists—to serve as the honest brokers.

FIXED-IN-PLACE CPRs ENCOMPASSED BY A SINGLE GOVERNMENT

In the event that a CPR is fixed in place and a single governmental entity contains the CPR, and there are no extra-governmental entities that can pollute or otherwise damage the CPR, the management task is relatively simple—when compared to many other CPR situations, that is. A groundwater aquifer is an example of a stationary CPR. If a city fully controls the aquifer, then it need only resist political pressures to overdraw the aquifer (as in the Tucson case, mentioned earlier) and choose a management method to limit consumption to sustainable levels. As indicated in Table 3.1, methods include direct regulation via quotas, pricing, conversion of the CPR to private ownership, and suasion. If a direct regulatory method is chosen, enforcement is also recommended to avoid the risk of free riders who are willing to violate the law, destroying the common.

One possible tool of enforcement is the use of fines, which warrants consideration of the "theory of fines." If a fine is to serve as a successful deterrent, the expected value of the fine should be considered by the fining agency. The expected value of a fine is the amount of the fine multiplied by the probability of being caught. Thus, if the true social cost of failure to follow regulations is $100,000, and the likelihood that a firm will be caught violating the regulation is 0.1 (a 10-percent chance), the amount of the fine should be $1,000,000; that way, the expected value, equal to (0.1)($1,000,000), is equal to the true social cost and thereby provides an appropriate deterrent.

From an efficiency standpoint, price is a preferred regulatory option. It (1) is usually administratively simple and quite certain; (2) can send proper, behavior-changing

Exhibit 3.3

Historical Information about How Lobstermen Work Together to Protect a CPR, but Expert Information Can Help

All states and the federal government share a minimum legal size [for lobster catches], 3 1/4 inches carapace-length—from the eye socket to the beginning of the tail. A lobster caught at this size weighs about 1 1/4 lb. The minimum size for legal lobsters was increased in 1988 after scientists persuaded the lobstermen that at the size lobsters were being harvested, 90% of all lobsters were being captured before they'd had a chance to reproduce even once. They argued that only ten percent of the population could not continue to produce enough baby lobsters to keep the industry going for many more years. . . .

Any egg-bearing females must be released. Some female lobsters are "V-notched," that is, a triangular slice is cut from a tail flipper. This badge of motherhood is meant to keep them off the dinner table and in the breeding pool. Cutting the V-notch is a voluntary action on the part of conservation-minded lobstermen and the Department of Marine Resources. At the other end of the spectrum are lobster harvesters who scrub off the eggs from a female and remove any traces with bleach. Conscientious lobstermen and lobster police do not look kindly on these people. . . .

Maine lobstermen have traditionally protected their share of the resource through lobstering territories. In any port, they have an informal, often unspoken agreement about where each member of the fishing community may lay his traps. All the members of one community even lay their strings of traps in one direction, such as north to south, so they don't tangle their lines in someone else's gear. . . .

James Acheson, an anthropologist at the University of Maine, has studied Maine's closely-knit fishing communities for many years. He has found there is a hierarchy of fishermen, based on an individual's skill and family ties, which he calls "lobster gangs." The gangs claim and defend fishing territory, which not only ensures a continued livelihood for its members, but conserves the limited resources from overexploitation. (For more information, read *Lobster Gangs of Maine*, by James Acheson, 1988: University Press of New England, Hanover, NH.)

Source: Gulf of Maine Research Institute, 2001. Used with permission. GMRI notes that this information was correct as of the publication date, though some may be obsolete now.

signals as to the value of the CPR; and (3) affects all users. If the CPR is in danger only under peak-demand conditions, differential prices can be set for different times. An analysis by Campbell with Johnson and Larson (2004) compared different urban, residential water-conservation policies. Findings indicated that, even though the price-elasticity of demand for water is quite low, pricing was one of the most efficacious conservation policies. Because even small price increases are spread across the entire population, they can lead to large reductions in water use. The problem with a pricing solution, as suggested by the Tucson case, is that it may be politically infeasible.

Elasticity is an important concept and measure. The X-elasticity of Y—for example, the Price-elasticity of Demand—tells how responsive Y will be to changes in X. If the X-elasticity of Y is –2, then a 1 percent increase in X will result in a 2 percent decrease in Y. This is an *elastic* response. If the X-elasticity of Y is less than one in magnitude/absolute value, then it is termed *inelastic*.

If demand for a good is *price-elastic*, that means it is responsive to changes in price. Even if a firm has monopoly power, elastic demand decreases the equilibrium market price and increases the supply, all else equal. A good is more likely to be price-elastic if the market offers close substitutes for it.

Direct regulation via quotas is also generally certain and may be perceived as fairer than allocation through pricing (though, depending on how you define fairness, perception may not match reality). Quotas can be assigned in a number of ways, including limiting everyone to the same amount or using a first-come, first-served system until all use has been expended. Creating a lottery system—meaning the determination of who gains access to the quota depends on two factors: (1) who applies, and (2) the element of chance—is often perceived as fair. This method is used in the United States for some hunting quotas (see, for example, Minnesota Department of Natural Resources, 2011). Auctioning is often used if firms will be competing for the quota (for example, the right to run river rafting trips in a certain location). It can be used in other cases as well but may not be perceived as fair, since it gives the advantage to those with more wealth. However, a benefit of an auction is that the government gains income that can be used to help others in society, including those who did not win the auction (Weimer and Vining, 1999, chap. 1).

Regulation of CPRs can also be applied via "command-and-control," or direct behavioral regulation, often based on technology. Exhibit 3.4 gives an example of such regulation, which again tends to have the benefits of being widespread and generally certain and, like pricing, can be highly efficacious (Campbell, Johnson, and Larson, 2004).

When using regulatory methods, whether of quotas or command-and-control, enforcement is often important. There are people who will violate the law to free ride or to gain more than their share of a CPR. In many versions of Hardin's (1968) seminal story of the Tragedy of the Commons (quoted in Chapter 2), overgrazing occurs because some are willing to cheat on a community agreement, and one solution is to install a watchman. Though the history of lobstering excerpted in Exhibit 3.3 tells that small groups of lobstermen on islands have been able to manage the CPR effectively without government intervention, it also explains that some lobstermen cheat on even CPR-preserving agreements (Gulf of Maine Research Institute, 2001). There is also reason to believe that cheating is "contagious"—if people see others cheat and get away with it, they are more likely to do so themselves (see, for example, Hammond, 2000).

Exhibit 3.4

Direct Command-and-Control Regulation

Governor signs water-efficient toilet bill (California)

In Sacramento, California, [now former] Governor Arnold Schwarzenegger signed a bill that will require all new buildings to install water-efficient toilets and urinals. Beginning in 2010, 50 percent of all toilets sold in California will have to meet the new water-saving standards, increasing to 100 percent in 2014. Assembly-man John Laird of Santa Cruz said that AB 715 is the first piece of legislation of its kind in the nation and will yield savings of more than 8 billion gallons of water within ten years. There are currently at least 111 toilet models and 34 urinal models that use low-flush technology.

Source: San Francisco Business Times, 2007.

Another method for protecting a CPR is to convert it from "common" to "private." This option was discussed in Chapter 2. Belief in the efficiency of privatization is a principle of economics, but is also based on common sense—people are less likely to destroy a productive good if they bear the costs themselves; they will want to husband the wealth in their lifetimes, pass it to their heirs, or sell it at a high value. This method can be politically controversial, though not always. "Spectrum," or radio bandwidth, can be considered a CPR: it is hard to prevent people from using it, but the airwaves can become congested, making use impossible for all (i.e., if one bandwidth is in use, attempts by another to use that same bandwidth will result in interference for both). The United States has held spectrum auctions to great gain for the treasury and with little complaint from the populace, but this may be because private individuals don't have much demand for bandwidth—firms do. If a good has been used by the public, it is frequently the case that the public will find privatization offensive. It may be more acceptable if private rights to a CPR are issued as a temporary contract or concession, so that funds continue flowing to the public via the government. For example, the Liberian forest management system uses timber concessions (UNFAO), as do other countries.

CPRs may also be managed via suasion. This method may be in some sense the most democratic, but it also bears elements of uncertainty. As mentioned earlier, some people will behave as free riders, and if suasion is chosen as the only method, then punishment of free riders is not available to reduce their numbers. (Note, however, that suasion and sanctions can be combined.) Suasion campaigns are often popular; there have been "litterbug" campaigns in the United States since the 1950s (PennDot, n.d.) and Smokey the Bear (an anti-forest-fire symbol) has been around even longer. There is evidence that if people communicate, they are more likely to engage in coopera-tive behavior to provide a common good (Ostrom, Walker, and Gardiner, 1993), and Campbell with Johnson and Larson (2004) found that citizen education—especially face-to-face education—was an effective means of getting urban residential water consumers to reduce water consumption in Phoenix, Arizona. Public shaming, such as publishing in the newspaper the names of those who damage CPRs, can also be a suasion method. This was tried in Vietnam in 2008, where the deputy head of the Ho Chi Minh City Management Board of Industrial Zones and Export Processing Zones (Hepza) indicated that it was effective: "The enterprises all promised to settle the problems as soon as they can. Representatives of many enterprises on the list said that after their names were listed announced, their friends and partners called and criticized them for their activities. Several banks have announced they will not provide capital for polluters" (VietnamNews.biz, 2008).

CPRs Covered by Multiple Governments

If multiple governmental units have authority over a CPR, then the primary solutions are quite different from when it is controlled by a single governmental unit. One choice would be to create a special governmental unit that encompasses the entire CPR (whether mobile or immobile). An insight of institutional analysis is that CPR management is more efficient with such arrangements (Heikkila, 2004). The difficulty with such institution creation is that often the governmental units that currently share the CPR may not wish to give the CPR institution enough enforcement power. This is a common problem with regional councils of government (COGs) that seek to engage in multi-city planning for transit, environment, etc. The Great Lakes, straddling the U.S.-Canadian border, "are the largest surface freshwater system on the Earth. They contain about 84 percent of North America's surface fresh water and about 21 percent of the world's supply" (U.S. EPA, 2011). A Great Lakes Basin Compact created the Great Lakes Commission, but the commission can only collect and analyze data, recommend, consider, and publish reports, while the group of governments that participate (there are eight U.S. states surrounding the Great Lakes) "agrees to consider the action the Commission recommends" (Great Lakes Commission, 2003). Having the Great Lakes Commission is no doubt better than not having it—especially given that communication helps cooperation—but it relies on the goodwill of its members rather than its own power to protect the lakes.

Another option is to create intergovernmental agreements that in essence regulate or create quotas in the same way that individual use is regulated for CPRs in single-government contexts. As shown in Exhibit 3.5, in 2007 a National Research Council study recommended this approach for the Mississippi River. Exhibit 3.6 gives an example of a successful intergovernmental agreement to protect a CPR.

Mobile CPRs

Mobile CPRs (such as the monarch butterflies and passenger pigeons discussed in Chapter 2) may cross many governmental boundaries, presenting the same policy challenges discussed earlier in the subsection on CPRs covered by multiple governments.

Exhibit 3.5

NRC Urges Intergovernmental Agreement for a Major U.S. CPR

Study Urges U.S. to Better Protect River (United States)

A National Research Council study led by Professor David A. Dzombak of Carnegie Mellon University in Pittsburgh, Pennsylvania, concluded that the U.S. Environmental Protection Agency and the ten states sharing the Mississippi River needed to work harder at protecting its waters from pollution. The river, as a major traffic artery, is entitled to regular quality monitoring under the Clean Water Act, but its load of farm runoff (mainly fertilizers) now runs into the Gulf of Mexico in such quantities that oxygen-deprived "dead zones" appear every spring. The report stated that since no single program oversaw the entire river, the EPA ought to encourage better coordination among its four regional offices and between them and the states.

Source: Schmid, 2007.

Exhibit 3.6

Example of a Successful Intergovernmental Agreement

Sonoma on Track to Meet Water Conservation Target (California)

Sonoma County in California has drawn about 20 percent less water from the Russian River than it did last summer, said Pam Jeane of the Sonoma County Water Agency. She praised the conservation efforts of cities and towns, who saved far more water than the 15 percent cut ordered by the state in order to ensure that there would be enough streamflow for the autumn's salmon run. "They have really stepped up," said Jeane.

Source: Associated Press, 2007.

But even when they don't, they can present special problems for policy. Monitoring for violations in quotas for mobile CPRs is typically more difficult than monitoring associated with fixed CPRs, because there are more locations in which to violate the quota. One solution is to consult biologists or other appropriate experts to see if there are crucial points for monitoring. In this way, monitoring funds can be used more efficiently by focusing on specific locations or specific times. In the lobster example presented in Exhibit 3.3, it turned out that size was a crucial monitoring factor—lobsters needed to attain a sufficient size to breed—and female lobsters bearing eggs were also a crucial monitoring factor. Small and breeding lobsters will tend to appear in large numbers at certain times in the year. In Weimer and Vining's (1999) sample policy analysis (see Chapter 1) regarding the Canadian salmon fishery, it is pointed out that locations at the mouths of spawning streams are key points for monitoring the salmon CPR. These are examples of seeking "key points in time or space where regulation may be especially effective," as listed in Table 3.1

GENERIC SOLUTIONS FOR PURE PUBLIC GOODS

In some cases, nature provides a pure public good in such amounts that even total demand when it is free does not harmfully deplete the good. An example might be sunsets over the Rocky Mountains. However, even for public goods provided by nature, congestion is always a potential problem as the size of the planet's population continues to grow. For public goods that must be provided by human agency, as with CPRs, small groups may be able to negotiate suitable agreements and, again, government may be able to serve as an honest broker or arrange for an honest broker.

SUBSIDIZATION AND TAXATION

In large groups, it is very unlikely that people will come together to create a pure public good without some type of created incentive or coercion (the aforementioned "watchman"). Even when some of the pure public good is produced, it generally will be too little compared to the social optimum. One option is for the government (or a set of governments) to subsidize provision. Exhibit 3.7 suggests such subsidization for the pure public good of Earth's atmosphere. Lest Professor Hans Gersbach, the author of the excerpt in Exhibit 3.7, be accused of excessive pessimism—after all, some countries agreed to the Kyoto protocols while others did not, so one might assume those who agreed would follow through—it should be noted that many countries are not on target to meet their reduction agreements. In Canada, "emissions have gone up as much as 35 percent since 1990 because of continued increases in the exploitation of the country's oil resources, calling into question whether Canada can make its 5 percent reduction target," and, as of this report, Japan and Italy were among others who also were unlikely to meet their goals (Johnson, 2008).

The flip side of the subsidization coin is to tax the provision of public bads, and many people have argued for the taxation of greenhouse gas emissions.

DIRECT PROVISION

Typically, when dealing with pure public goods, the government provides the good directly, and free riding is prevented to a large extent by the coercive power of government to tax. A commonly presented example is national defense. It is a pure public good because, once a territory is defended, all members of the territory benefit from the same "unit" of defense. Clean air within a city is also a pure public good—and one of significant importance to urban environmental policy analysis and administration.

Exhibit 3.7

Subsidizing Provision of a Pure Public Good

The history since Kyoto suggests that the international coordination necessary for a serious effort at slowing climate change is nearly impossible to achieve. . . .

The problems with the Kyoto accord are clear to all. The developing world and the United States did not agree to join in CO_2 emissions reductions, and, as to the signatories, what will make them achieve their reduction targets?

It is easier either not to join or not to comply and let others do all the work of emissions reduction. That is the fundamental free-rider problem. Greenhouse gases disperse around the globe and burden everyone. One country's reductions burden it alone but benefit everyone. . . .

Imagine that the twenty largest industrial countries would be able to coordinate and agree to put a significant, though not extraordinary, amount of money into a fund. . . . Then, the countries agree to a constitution by which money will be paid out according to reductions in emissions: the Global Refunding System (GRS). If the system is set up properly, no further coordination is required, except in administering the system, measuring reductions and distributing money.

We won't need a global policeman to enforce significant reductions. Nations will choose to reduce on their own . . . (1–2).

Source: Gersbach, 2008. Used with permission.

Though city governments are less likely than higher levels of government to deal directly with pure public goods, they may deal with many that become so by law and custom. A public park, for example, though not technically a pure public good (a fence can be put around it to allow exclusion), may be a pure public good by law. Central Park in New York City is, by law, a pure public good. Anyone may enter it, and many people enjoy this same "unit" of park, including those who do not enter it physically but enjoy views of it; there is no exclusion, even of those who do not support it through their taxes. For pure public goods—whether in reality, such as a city's air, or by agreement, such as a city park—enforcement to prevent destruction is an important policy tool.

It should be noted, however, that even "direct" provision of a pure public good by government can be made by different organizational arrangements. The city government could engage in a public-private partnership, or a public-NGO partnership, or could contract out provision, etc. In fact, since 1998, Central Park has been jointly managed under terms of a contract between the city of New York and the Central Park Conservancy, a private organization (Central Park Conservancy, 2010). Management of the park is also supported by significant charitable contribution (Central Park Conservancy, 2010), reinforcing the point that, while there are free riders in the world, there are also those who will voluntarily contribute to the common good. The latter is one reason that "suasion including education" can be effective.

CONGESTION AND EXTERNALITIES

CONGESTION AS A NEGATIVE EXTERNALITY

Congestion and negative externalities are related because the policy problem with congestion is that it creates negative externalities.

1. When congestion endangers a CPR, a single person's consumption imposes costs on others who use the CPR in the present by increasing their costs of use (since increased scarcity of the CPR makes it more costly to use). Costs are imposed on those who would use the CPR in the future as well, either through increased scarcity or, in the case of collapse, because the CPR is not available at all.
2. With a toll or marketable public good, congestion often imposes negative externalities through the medium of time. Each new person added to a congested bridge imposes time costs on every other person on the bridge, but any individual probably considers only his or her time costs rather than the social sum of time costs.
3. A pure public good is nonrival in consumption—to the point of congestion. At low levels of use, a single factory, even if it is belching out smoke, is unlikely to harm the air in any significant way. But the air can become congested by many firms using it as a dumping ground, and then the value of the air to all is reduced. In fact, we can consider that sufficient congestion turns a pure public good into a CPR.

Congestion itself—which is just excess use—can be addressed through prices, taxes, quotas, or changes in ownership, as discussed in the sections on CPRs and marketable public goods. Reducing the congestion reduces its negative externalities.

> An entity is said to *internalize the externality* when its decision-making process fully takes into account all external costs or benefits of its actions. The most direct way to cause an entity to internalize the externality is to *tax* it at the level of the external costs or *subsidize* it at the level of external benefits.

EXTERNALITIES

In general, as mentioned in Chapter 2, externalities can be positive or negative, though people tend to focus more on the negative ones. Negative externalities are an important focus in urban environmental policy analysis, and some positive externalities should be, as well. Almost all pollution is a negative externality—an undesired by-product of the production and/or consumption of something that is desired. (If a volcano explodes, it causes air pollution that is not a negative externality but a pure public bad.)

Government can directly regulate the amount of production of a negative external-ity, but this command-and-control method has fallen out of favor in the policy field because it is less efficient than other methods. One of the more efficient methods is taxing production of the negative externality, which causes the firm to "internalize" the true social costs. This may well lead to changes in the production process; if so, overall social efficiency will usually be improved more than would be the case with simple rules about allowed amounts of emissions or required technologies of emissions control. Note, however, that analysts should consider the Law of Unintended Conse-quences and be careful that the new production process doesn't create new negative externalities that are even worse! Taxes are often controversial, and one difficult aspect of negative-externality taxes is that it can be hard to predict what level of emission reduction a specific tax will garner. In other words, reduction levels are less certain than with command-and-control regulation, though efficiency is more likely.

One concern with simple emission rules is that, while they seem fair because they are uniform, they may impose quite different costs on firms depending on differ-ences in production processes or inputs. For example, in the past, requirements to limit combustion products from coal could have quite different effects for U.S. firms, depending on whether they used harder western coal or softer southeastern coal; the two types produce different levels of certain pollutants such as sulfurs and also have different energy content (Union of Concerned Scientists, 2009). Another solution that imposes specific limits but is also more efficient is to allow tradable or auctionable permits. With such permits, firms that can reduce the negative externality at lower cost will reduce it below the average and then sell their extra permits to firms with higher costs. The good thing about such permits is that they can provide a given level of externality reduction at the least overall social cost. Depending on how they are set up, such permits can also give environmentalists the chance to purchase permits, retire them, and thus reduce the overall level of the pollutant. The bad thing about them is that they may result in much different externality levels by region or time period. Return to the example of coal: because coal is heavy and therefore expensive to transport, absent regulation, it is likely that southeastern companies tend to use southeastern coal, while western companies tend to use western coal. Allowing trad-able permits may provide the most overall efficient reduction of coal pollutants, but it is likely to lead to very different levels of pollution from coal in the two regions. This problem of "hot spots" is discussed further in later chapters.

If reductions of negative externalities are to be imposed, no matter what method is chosen, enforcement is likely to be required. Recently, some have argued for a type of semivoluntary regulation created by firms cooperating with the regulators to set up the regulatory regime. The expectation is that cooperative relationships between the regulator and the regulated will increase compliance and lead to better outcomes, but work by Kathryn Harrison suggests the reverse may be true (1995); therefore, these policy arrangements should be approached with caution.

Urban environmental policy analysts should also consider goods that create posi-tive externalities, such as parks or trees. Production of such goods can be subsidized through any of the variety of methods discussed above. Alternatively, the government could provide them directly or through various partnerships.

Suasion can also be used either to reduce negative externalities (such as litter) or to increase positive externalities. Arbor days—internationally celebrated holidays on which trees are planted and cared for (Arbor Day Foundation, n.d.)—can be considered a type of positive-externality suasion; they have led to the planting of millions of trees across many countries.

EXCESS RISK

Moral hazard is an economics term for a "lack of incentive to guard against risk where one is protected from its consequences, e.g., by insurance" (New Oxford American Dictionary, 2009). It implies the acceptance of more risk than one would ordinarily assume if one expected to pay all the costs oneself.

As we mention in Table 3.1 (see pages 54–55), if risk is too widespread within a population, insurance firms may feel that they cannot adequately diversify that risk, and so an appropriate market for insurance may not form. Such concerns are particularly relevant for urban environmental policy analysis and administration in the area of catastrophes such as floods, hurricanes, wildfires, earthquakes, and other natural disasters. Mandating or facilitating the creation of insurance is one possible solution. For example, the U.S. Federal Emergency Management Administration (FEMA) is a form of government insurance against natural disasters. Governments can also facilitate or mandate the creation of a private risk pool involving many insurers, thereby increasing risk diversification, but this may be beyond the powers of an urban government. Kunreuther et al. (2009) provide a detailed discussion of various risk-transfer methods. They argue, "The regulation of insurance companies and insurance markets plays a prominent role in the management of catastrophe risk" (26). However, a potential problem with risk-insurance schemes is that they create "moral hazard" for the insured. Because the insured will not bear the full cost of their decisions—say, to live on a cliff in an area subject to mudslides—they may accept more risk than is socially desirable.

Risk is not fixed, and another reasonable approach is to try to reduce risk to more socially desirable levels. Laws that require the separation of plant material and houses in areas with high wildfire risk or that forbid the use of flammable roofing materials focus on regulating risk reduction, as do coastal zoning laws that require certain types of building practices or that forbid residential building in certain areas (Kunreuther et al., 2009). In areas subject to flooding, governments could subsidize flood control or flood protection devices such as dry wells or floodwalls. The enormous seawalls of the Netherlands are examples of government provision of risk-reduction devices.

Alternatively, government could tax risky behaviors such as building in dangerous areas. A tax on risky behaviors can be especially justified if the funds are retained in an account that is then used to help those harmed by catastrophe. As always, government can try suasion, and, in catastrophe policy, suasion is often combined with other policy tools. The Saskatchewan, Canada, brochure, "What You Need to Know

Exhibit 3.8

Combining a Quota with a Fine-Like Price

The Irvine Model (California)

Irvine Ranch Water District [IRWD] in Orange County, California, pioneered a new model when it instituted an allocation-based rate structure in 1991.

Every household is given an allocation based on personal use needs of 55 gallons per person per day and lawn needs based on efficient watering. Customers can apply for an adjustment if there are more people in the house than the utility assumes. A base price is set for the allocation. If a household exceeds its allocated use, it is penalized with rates up to eight times higher than the base rate. On the other hand, if a household is water-frugal, it receives a discounted rate.

"Our water rates are the second lowest in our county," said Fiona Sanchez, IRWD's conservation manager. "Customers who use water efficiently are rewarded with low rates."

Not only are rates low, but use is low too. The average customer served by Irvine Ranch uses 52 percent less water per day than the average person served by other Orange County utilities. Efficient use helps to keep prices low by reducing the need to buy water imported from the Colorado River.

Source: Walton, 2010. Used with permission.

About Wildfire" describes a whole suite of policies and includes education and other suasion tactics (Government of Saskatchewan).

CONCLUSION

The purpose of this chapter is to give an overview of useful policy tools and link them to specific markets and types of goods. After defining the market circumstances surrounding a potential policy intervention, an analyst can turn to Table 3.1 for some quick ideas on suitable policy instruments. However, this table and the material herein are not exhaustive. As we have suggested before, policy analysts and administrators should be creative. Consider whether a policy recommended for one market circumstance may be useful in another, and try a combination of policies. Also consider your own administrative costs. Exhibit 3.8 shows a pricing method that combines a basic quota with a price so high as to be akin to a fine. And don't forget to look at suitable publications (whether articles or reports), because new ideas for policy solutions continue to emerge from both scholars and administrators.

Another factor that has been raised throughout this chapter is the method of provision. As indicated multiple times, there is more than one way to achieve a policy goal. Even "direct" government provision can be accomplished through public-private partnerships or contracting, instead of through more traditional provision by a govern-

■───────────────────────■

Exhibit 3.9

Thinking Beyond Suasion to Changing the Culture

The role of government is different in each phase of the transition [management] process. In the preparation phase, it must play the catalyst and director, with the emphasis on maintaining a wide playing field and organizing and stimulating discussions with other actors. In the take-off phase, other actors must actually be mobilized in the direction of the transition objective. Here and in the acceleration phase, the government has to stimulate learning processes about possible solutions. This can be achieved by drawing up an agenda, forming communal visions concerning what is desirable and possible, creating niches and anticipating the actor's interests: hence a role as stimulator. In the stabilization phase, the guidance is mainly orientated towards embedding, to prevent or contain backlashes and other negative effects: so a role as controller and consolidator (11).

Source: Rotmans, Kemp, and van Asselt, 2001. Used with permission.

■───────────────────────■

ment agency. As Salamon (2002) indicates, over the last couple of decades, at least in the United States, the way government does its business has been transformed; now it is not uncommon for government to serve as an overseer and contract-manager rather than as an actual provider. In addition to considering which policy tools are likely to improve social efficiency, analysts should consider

- the level of administrative efficiency available,
- how free riders or law breakers will affect the policy,
- whether unintended consequences are likely, and
- the question of local political feasibility.

Mention of political feasibility introduces the lesson that in many cases administrators and analysts should not just sit down alone and choose a policy tool. Instead, they should seek information from citizens. Techniques for doing so successfully are discussed in Chapters 10 and 11. Chapter 11, which focuses on educating citizens, also has much to contribute to any plan for suasion.

Before we close this chapter, it is worth considering another policy tool that has not yet been mentioned: long-term efforts to change culture. As briefly presented in Exhibit 3.9, Rotmans, Kemp, and van Asselt (2001) suggest that governments should engage in "transition management" to change social attitudes over a generation (which they define as twenty-five years). U.S. antismoking education efforts (combined with other techniques such as taxation) appear to have been able to create a dramatic change in social attitudes toward cigarette smoking in about that time. When the U.S. Surgeon General's first warning was issued in 1964, around 43 percent of the adult population in the United States smoked cigarettes, but by 1995 the proportion had dropped to about 23 percent (Womach, 2003), with majority opinion toward smoking becoming negative (McCarrier, 2003). If pursued with the same zeal, it is possible that attitudes toward various urban environmental goods or bads could be similarly transformed.

DISCUSSION QUESTIONS

1. Name other goods (not mentioned in this chapter) that you think may be natural monopolies. Explain why.
2. Using Table 3.1, decide what policy solutions you think are the most promising for the subsidence case provided in Chapters 1 and 2. Explain your reasoning.
3. Find a published estimate for a price-elasticity of demand that is relevant to urban environmental policy. Interpret it.

RECOMMENDED WEBSITE

Indiana University. 2008. Workshop in Political Theory and Policy Analysis. http://www.indiana.edu/~workshop/. From the website: The Workshop's teaching and research probes the inner workings of human institutions—structures of rules used to govern people and resources, in this usage—in order to better understand what works and what does not.

NOTE

1. PAHs "form from the incomplete combustion" of fuels such as coal and gasoline (USGS, 2010).

REFERENCES

Arbor Day Foundation. n.d. "Arbor Day." http://www.arborday.org/arborday/ (accessed January 29, 2011).

Associated Press. 2007. Sonoma on track to meet water conservation target. Summary obtained from L. Shaler, *Global Water News Watch* (University of Arizona), September 24.

Averch, H., and L.L. Johnson. 1962. Behavior of the firm under regulatory constraint. *American Economics Review*, 52, 5, 1052–1069.

Bardach, E. 2009. *A Practical Guide for Policy Analysis: The Eightfold Path to More Effective Problem Solving,* 3d ed. Washington, DC: CQ Press.

Birkland, T.A. 2005. *An Introduction to the Policy Process: Theories, Concepts, and Models of Public Policy Making*, 2d ed. Armonk, NY: M.E. Sharpe.

Brewer, G.D. and P.C. Sterns (eds.). 2005. *Decision Making for the Environment: Social and Behavioral Science Research Priorities*. Washington, DC. The National Academics Press.

Campbell, H.E., with R.M. Johnson, and E.H. Larson. 2004. Prices, devices, people, or rules: The relative effectiveness of policy instruments in water conservation. *Review of Policy Research*, 21, 5, 637–662.

Central Park Conservancy. 2010. The Official Website of Central Park: About the Central Park Conservancy. http://www.centralparknyc.org/about/ (accessed January 29, 2011).

Gersbach, H. 2008. A new way to address climate change: A global refunding system. *The Economists' Voice*, 5, 4, 1–4. http://www.bepress.com/ev/vol5/iss4/art2 (accessed January 27, 2011).

Government of Saskatchewan. n.d. What you need to know about wildfire. Department of the Environment. http://www.environment.gov.sk.ca/adx/aspx/adxGetMedia.aspx?DocID=832,785,242,94,88,Documents&MediaID=360&Filename=What+You+Need+to+Know+About+Wildfire.pdf&l=English (accessed January 29, 2011).

Great Lakes Commission. 2003. The Great Lakes Basin Compact. Great Lakes Commission/Commission des Grands Lacs. http://www.glc.org/about/glbc.html (accessed January 28, 2011).

Gulf of Maine Research Institute. 2001. Lobstering history. Gulf of Maine Research Institute. http://www.gma.org/lobsters/allaboutlobsters/lobsterhistory.html (accessed January 28, 2011).

Hamilton County, Ohio. n.d. Turn the key, be idle free: Southwest Ohio anti-idling campaign. Hamilton County Environmental Services (HCES) Air Quality Management Division, Cincinnati. http://www.hcdoes.org/airquality/pdf/Anti-Idling%20Brochure.pdf (accessed January 28, 2011).

Hammond, R. 2000. Endogenous transition dynamics in corruption: An agent-based computer model. Working Paper No. 19, December. Center on Social and Economic Dynamics, Brookings Institution, Washington, DC. http://www.brookings.edu/reports/2000/12corruption_hammond.aspx (accessed January 29, 2011).

Hardin, Garrett. 1968. The tragedy of the commons. *Science*, December 13. http://www.garretthardin-society.org/articles/art_tragedy_of_the_commons.html (accessed September 21, 2007).

Harrison, K. 1995. Is cooperation the answer? Canadian environmental enforcement in comparative context. *Journal of Policy Analysis and Management*, 14, 221–245.

Heikkila, T. 2004. Institutional boundaries and common-pool resource management: A comparative analysis of water management programs in California. *Journal of Policy Analysis and Management,* 23, 1, 97–117.

Johnson, T. 2008. G8's gradual move toward post-Kyoto climate change policy. Council on Foreign Relations, January 28. http://www.cfr.org/europerussia/g8s-gradual-move-toward-post-kyoto-climate-change-policy/p13640 (accessed January 28, 2011).

Kunreuther, H.C. and E.O. Michel-Kerjan, with N.A. Doherty, M.F. Grace, R.W. Klein, and M.V. Pauly. 2009. *At War with the Weather: Managing Large-Scale Risks in a New Era of Catastrophes.* Cambridge, MA: MIT Press.

McCarrier, K.P. 2003. Attitudes toward cigarette smoking and predictors of tobacco-related health perceptions in Arizona adults. Paper presented at the annual meeting of the American Association for Public Opinion Research. Sheraton Music City, Nashville, TN, August 16. http://www.allacademic.com/meta/p116292_index.html (accessed January 29, 2011).

Minnesota Department of Natural Resources. 2011. Hunting license lottery. Minnesota Department of Natural Resources Website. http://www.dnr.state.mn.us/licenses/lotteries/index.html (accessed January 28, 2011).

MIT Center for Real Estate. n.d. MIT researcher stands rent control assumption on its head. http://web.mit.edu/cre/news-archive/ncrentcontrol.html (accessed January 29, 2011).

New Oxford American Dictionary. 2005–2009. Version 2.1.3 [electronic]. Cupertino, CA: Apple, Inc., s.v. "moral hazard."

Ostrom, E. 1990. *Governing the Commons: The Evolution of Institutions for Collective Action.* Cambridge, UK: Cambridge University Press.

Ostrom, E., J. Walker, and R. Gardner. 1993. Covenants with and without a sword: Self-governance is possible. In *The Political Economy of Customs and Culture: Informal Solutions to the Commons Problem,* ed. T.L. Anderson and R.T. Simmons, 27–156. Lanham, MD: Rowman & Littlefield.

Pennsylvania Department of Transportation (PennDot). n.d. History of the Litter Bug and PennDot. http://www.dot.state.pa.us/Internet/pdKids.nsf/HistoryofLitterBugandPennDOT?OpenForm (accessed January 28, 2011).

Rotmans, J., R. Kemp, and M. van Asselt. 2001. More evolution than revolution: Transition management in public policy. *Foresight: The Journal of Futures Studies, Strategic Thinking, and Policy,* 3, 1, 15–31.

Salamon, L.M., ed. 2002. *The Tools of Government: A Guide to the New Governance.* New York: Oxford University Press.

San Francisco Business Times. 2007. Governor signs water-efficient toilet bill. October 12. http://www.bizjournals.com/sanfrancisco/stories/2007/10/08/daily54.html. Summary obtained from L. Shaler, *Global Water News Watch* (College of Science, University of Arizona), October 12, 2007.

Schmid, Randolph E. 2007. Study urges U.S. to better protect river. Summary obtained from L. Shaler, *Global Water News Watch* (University of Arizona), October 16.

Seshan, B. 2010. Water is a basic human right: UN. *International Business Times*, July 29. http://www.ibtimes.com/articles/39403/20100729/water-sanitation-human-right-united-nations-general-assembly-united-states-united-kingdom-australia.htm (accessed January 27, 2011).

Sharp, A., C. Register, and P. Grimes. 2007. *Economics of Social Issues*, 18th ed. Boston, MA: McGraw-Hill/Irwin.

Szalavitz, M. 2008. 10 ways we get the odds wrong. *Psychology Today*, January 1. http://www.psychologytoday.com/articles/200712/10-ways-we-get-the-odds-wrong (accessed January 27, 2011).

Tasoff, J. (PhD., University of California, Berkeley; presently assistant professor, Claremont Graduate University), in personal communication with author, March 2011.

Union of Concerned Scientists. 2009. How coal works. Union of Concerned Scientists briefing, Washington, D.C.. http://www.ucsusa.org/clean_energy/coalvswind/brief_coal.html (accessed January 29, 2011).

United Nations Food and Agriculture Organization (UNFAO). Law and regulations related to forestry in Liberia. Liberia Forest Initiative. http://www.fao.org/forestry/lfi/31586/en/ (accessed January 28, 2011).

U.S. Environmental Protection Agency. 2011. Great Lakes: Basic information. http://www.epa.gov/greatlakes/basicinfo.html (accessed 28 August 2011).

U.S. Geological Survey (USGS). 2010. Toxic substances hydrology program: Polynuclear aromatic hydrocarbons (PAHs) and/or polycyclic aromatic hydrocarbons (PAHs). U.S. Department of the Interior, August 10. http://toxics.usgs.gov/definitions/pah.html (accessed January 27, 2011).

Vandenbergh, M.P. and A.C. Steinemann. 2007. The carbon-neutral individual. *New York University Law Review*, 82; Vanderbilt Law & Economics Research Paper No. 07–29; Vanderbilt Public Law Research Paper No. 07–22. http://papers.ssrn.com/sol3/papers.cfm?abstract_id=1024159 (accessed March 11, 2011).

VietnamNews.biz. 2008. Hepza to make public the names of polluters. October 22. http://www.vietnamnews.biz/Hepza-to-make-public-the-names-of-polluters_177.html (accessed January 28, 2011).

Walton, B. 2010. U.S. urban residents cut water usage; utilities are forced to raise prices. Circle of Blue: Reporting the Global Water Crisis, April 19. http://www.circleofblue.org/waternews/2010/world/u-s-urban-residents-cut-water-usage-utilities-are-forced-to-raise-prices/ (accessed January 27, 2011).

Weimer, D., and A. Vining. 1999. *Policy Analysis: Concepts and Practice*, 3rd ed. Upper Saddle River, NJ: Prentice Hall.

Womach, J. 2003. U.S. tobacco production, consumption, and export trends. Report for Congress, Congressional Research Service of the Library of Congress, Washington, DC. http://www.nationalaglawcenter.org/assets/crs/RL30947.pdf (accessed January 29, 2011).

Zhao, P., K.P. Yu, and C.C. Lin. 2010. Risk assessment of inhalation exposure to polycyclic aromatic hydrocarbons in Taiwanese workers at night markets. National Center for Biotechnology Information, U.S. National Library of Medicine, National Institutes of Health, Bethesda, MD. http://www.ncbi.nlm.nih.gov/pubmed/20506023 (accessed January 27, 2011).

4 Benefit-Cost Analysis

Benefit-Cost Analysis (BCA), also known as Cost-Benefit Analysis (CBA), is one of the fundamental tools in the policy analyst's tool kit. In the United States, it has been used for more than 100 years, required of the U.S. Army Corps of Engineers since 1936 (Hanley and Spash, 1993), and required of federal agencies for more than two decades (Hahn and Sunstein, 2002). A watershed in its requirement was Executive Order 12866, which explicitly stated the philosophy that all regulation should consider costs and benefits of all regulatory alternatives and should select approaches that maximize net benefits (see Exhibit 4.1). Not only is BCA a useful analytic method, but its concepts are central to the way that policy analysts think about policy issues.

This chapter provides an introduction to BCA, explaining how to think through a benefit-cost problem and raising issues that focus specifically on elements relevant to urban environmental policy analysis. However, entire books have been written on the topic (see, for example, Boardman et al., 2006); therefore, if you need additional information, know that there are sources available to assist you. Some of the topics covered in this introduction, such as "existence value," are generally considered advanced topics, but they are discussed here because of their salience for urban environmental policy analysis in particular.

THE BASIC IDEA OF BENEFIT-COST ANALYSIS

The basic idea of Benefit-Cost Analysis is really simple—and quite old, too. As noted by Boardman et al. (2006, 1), Benjamin Franklin performed and advocated a type of BCA. In 1772, in a letter of advice to a friend, he clearly articulated the basics of BCA:

- Write down all the benefits of a course of action.
- Write down all the costs of a course of action.
- See whether costs or benefits dominate.
- If benefits dominate, engage in the course of action.
- If costs dominate, do not (Franklin, 1772).

Exhibit 4.1
Part of Executive Order 12866
(Issued by President William J. Clinton)

Section 1. Statement of Regulatory Philosophy and Principles. (a) The Regulatory Phi-losophy. Federal agencies should promulgate only such regulations as are required by law, are necessary to interpret the law, or are made necessary by compelling public need, such as material failures of private markets to protect or improve the health and safety of the public, the environment, or the well-being of the American people. In deciding whether and how to regulate, agencies should assess all costs and ben-efits of available regulatory alternatives, including the alternative of not regulating. Costs and benefits shall be understood to include both quantifiable measures (to the fullest extent that these can be usefully estimated) and qualitative measures of costs and benefits that are difficult to quantify, but nevertheless essential to consider. Further, in choosing among alternative regulatory approaches, agencies should select those approaches that maximize net benefits (including potential economic, environmental, public health and safety, and other advantages; distributive impact; and equity) unless a statute requires another regulatory approach.

Source: The White House, 1993.

Fundamentally, this is all there is to Benefit-Cost Analysis. Even when a formal BCA is not conducted, policy analysts consider this basic approach central to all that they do. However, since whole books are written on the topic, clearly, modern policy analysts go beyond Franklin's basic approach. To restate his advice for a modern-day BCA, we would say the following:

- Monetize all the social benefits of a policy that you can.
- Monetize all the social costs of a policy that you can.
- Subtract social costs from the social benefits to obtain the net benefits and see if they are positive; retain in their own units any benefits or costs that were not monetizable.
- If net benefits are positive, then the policy is potentially good for society overall and should be adopted.
- If net benefits are negative, then the policy reduces overall social welfare and should not be adopted.

This chapter presents some of the many issues involved in formal Benefit-Cost Analysis, and provides advice on how to deal with those issues.

To monetize is to attach a monetary value to costs and benefits of a policy.

In terms of the graphical system model presented in Chapter 1, BCA can be applied to any policy (either a past policy or a future policy) that affects any portion of the City System (Natural, Concretion, or Social). It is most likely to be used in the Problem Identification, Policy Formulation, or Policy Evaluation stages of the Policy Process.

THREE IMPORTANT ISSUES IN FORMAL BCA: MONETIZATION, STANDING, AND TIME

In formal BCA, not only must all the benefits and costs of a policy be determined but they also are usually monetized. "Monetization" is the term used by policy analysts to denote attaching a dollar value (or yen value, euro value, etc.) to costs and benefits. In some cases, this is quite simple: Some costs and benefits of a policy are bought and sold in properly functioning markets, and then the monetized cost or benefit is usually based on an observable market price. However, as indicated by the discussion in Chapter 2, many of the types of costs and benefits that we care about in urban environmental policy analysis—such as pure public goods and common pool resources (CPRs)—are not bought and sold in properly functioning markets. In such cases, it can be difficult to assign appropriate monetary values.

In formal BCA, it is imperative that all *social* benefits and costs—not just private or personal costs and benefits—are accounted for. This necessity leads to the question of *standing*. If it is society's costs and benefits that must be determined, then who is considered part of society? Who has standing such that his or her benefits or costs are cumulated in a BCA?

> *Standing* is the question of who is part of "society" for purposes of counting all of society's costs and benefits from a policy.

A third issue for BCA is the fact that costs and benefits of a policy do not appear all at one time. Consider the Golden Gate Bridge in San Francisco, or Tower Bridge in London. The Golden Gate Bridge took four years to build and was completed in 1937, and Tower Bridge took eight years to build and was completed in 1894. Any benefit-cost assessment of these bridges would need to take into account the fact that they entailed significant costs before any benefits were received, and yet they are still providing benefits generations after their completion. The following sections discuss these issues in more detail.

STANDING: WHOSE COSTS AND BENEFITS SHOULD BE COUNTED?

As indicated above, BCA is basically a method for adding up all the social benefits of a project, adding up all the social costs of the project, subtracting the costs from the benefits, and deciding to adopt the policy if benefits exceed the costs (that is if "net benefits" are positive). Yet, the issue of *whose* benefits and costs should be counted is not trivial, and there has been significant scholarly—and political—debate on this subject. Debate around inclusion for BCA purposes centers on three main topics:

- What geopolitical lines should be drawn to determine "society"?
- Should costs and benefits to criminals be included in the analysis?
- How should costs and benefits to future generations be treated?

GEOPOLITICAL LINES AND INCLUSION OR EXCLUSION

The BCA Rule: Ignore Geopolitical Boundaries

For those trained formally in Benefit-Cost Analysis, the question of where to draw lines of inclusion is answered very simply: include all those who bear any substantial costs or receive any substantial benefits, no matter where geopolitical boundaries exist. Thus, if the city of San Diego, California (a coastal city on the U.S.-Mexican border), is trying to decide whether or not to pursue a policy, it should consider benefits and costs to its own residents, as well as benefits and costs to those in Tijuana, Mexico (an adjacent city on the Mexican-U.S. border), and to residents of adjacent cities such as El Cajon, California. If the effects of the policy are felt as far away as Japan, those effects should also be included. To restate: In BCA, standing has nothing to do with geopolitical boundaries. All groups who otherwise have standing and receive costs and/or benefits should be included.

For certain types of urban environmental policies, geographic boundaries may determine who receives costs and benefits—for example, as discussed in Chapters 2 and 3, costs and benefits of a water policy may be confined to a certain watershed—but political boundaries do not always follow geography. Often, political boundaries are irrelevant to standing in BCA.

The Political Reality

Policy analysts, however, work within a political environment. The reality is that politicians and the political process often resist this simple definition of standing. Politicians and government organizations may be opposed to the idea that BCA should include the costs and benefits of people who neither vote nor pay taxes within their jurisdictions.

How should policy analysts deal with the difference between the political reality and the BCA prescription? We urge you to take the following path:

1. Try to persuade your manager that your BCA should include costs and benefits for all those affected.
2. However, if you cannot succeed, then do *two* BCAs: one that includes all social costs and benefits, and one that is limited to the costs and benefits of those within your political jurisdiction. This should not entail much more work, since the latter is a subset of the former.

In this way, you are obeying your organizational constraints while maintaining professional norms, and the comparison may have some persuasive power. But be aware that your manager may choose not to use the results from your inclusive analysis.

CRIMINALS

Though many people find this amazing, there are some economists who argue that Benefit-Cost Analysis should grant standing to criminals. In other words, the benefits to law-abiding citizens of a policy that reduces crime should be offset by the costs to criminals of this same policy. In more shocking terms, some analysts would argue that a policy that reduces rape should include as a cost the loss of "benefit" to the rapist (Trumbull, 1990).

Though, as discussed below, there are exceptions, in general we disagree with this position and argue that criminals should not have standing. As Trumbull (1990) argued so persuasively some time ago, generally BCA must recognize the social constraints that society has imposed. Criminal activity is, by definition, outside social constraints.

Criminals Usually Should Not Have Standing

A crucial foundation of BCA is the existence of a law-based society. In a society with no laws, BCA cannot make sense as a means of determining social policy. Thus, BCA should not grant standing to those who do not accede to the laws of the society that is seeking to create a common good. In essence, society has determined that criminals are antisocial—contrary to society, not part of society. As Stigler (1970, 527) asked, "What evidence is there that society sets a positive value upon the utility derived from a murder, rape, or arson? In fact, the society has branded the utility derived from such activities as [illegitimate]." Certainly, for major crimes such as felonies, within a society that conforms to the rule of law, whether to obey the law or to break it and pay the penalty is not seen as the same type of choice as whether to buy a soda and pay the price, or not to buy the soda and not to pay the price. Perhaps this type of choice can be seen as legitimate for minor infractions—you can choose whether to put money in the meter or accept the risk of paying the ticket—but choices with regard to felonies are not of that sort.

Trumbull (1990) points out the difference between tolerant and absolute social institutions. The illegality of theft, for example, is not tolerant:

> The important distinction is that the penalty under the absolute institution is not simply a price that is paid for the right to [break the law]. . . . Punishment does not imply retroactive consent. . . . The criminal laws are absolute, not tolerant, institutions . . . society has a purpose when it labels certain acts as criminal; the label communicates that these acts will not be tolerated or counted in the social weal. (212)

In addition, even if you disagree with the perspective above, it is important to remember that BCA is a subset of neoclassical microeconomics. Using the logic of neoclassical microeconomics, costs to criminals of a policy that prevents crime should generally be lower than the benefits to those who will no longer be affected by the crime. First, criminals did not value the stolen good enough to pay the market price for it. If they did, they would have bought it instead of stealing it. Thus, by the simple logic of microeconomics, the value of the good to those who bought it was higher than the value to those who stole it. Second, criminals often steal something in order to sell it (or sell parts of it), and in the process may damage the item, further reducing its value (Rhoads, 1985; Trumbull, 1990). The street value of a stolen good is lower than the legitimate market value of the good. This further demonstrates that the value of the good to the thief is lower than the value of the good to the original owner.

An economics joke goes like this: A young economist and an old economist are getting ready to cross the street when a Jaguar XK-E drives past. The young economist sighs. "Wow, I'd sure love to have one of those."
"Apparently not," replies the old economist.

This joke is funny to economists because one of the assumptions of neoclassical microeconomics is that people don't really have legitimate desire for something unless they are willing to pay the market price.

When Criminals Should Have Standing

There are three exceptions to the general principle that criminals should not have standing in BCA. First, sometimes a policy analysis is conducted to determine if a law should be changed (either to make something legal that is illegal, or to make something illegal that is currently legal). For example, one might perform a BCA to determine if marijuana should be made legal. In such cases, since the whole intent is to determine whether society would be better off with a change in legality status, those whose criminal status or behavior would change under the new law should have standing.

Second, though this is unlikely to be the case for an urban environmental policy, if the intent of a policy is to exert a positive impact on the criminal population's well-being, then their costs and benefits should be included. One example might be a policy to reduce prison overcrowding.

Third, it is important that BCA not become a tool that simply maintains the current social order. A scholar in our field once argued that too-close attention to the idea that BCA operates within the existing social structure would have resulted in policy analysts finding that slavery should be maintained. After all, the costs of eliminating slavery were very high to the slaveholders, and the benefits to those who freed slaves (other than by direct purchase) would not count since they were violating the law—a law that, in the United States under Supreme Court determination (see *Dred Scott v. Sandford,* 1856) was found to be absolute. Though it is not certain that this economic analysis is correct—because a BCA outcome would significantly depend on whether costs and benefits to slaves were included or not—the point is clear and important. When the social order encodes into law something that is against basic human rights or other ethical considerations, then that also must be considered in any Benefit-Cost Analysis.

It is often said that policy analysis has elements of both art and science. Like policy analysis in general, BCA has rules, but the analyst must also be thoughtful and nuanced in applying them. When determining whether to grant standing to those who violate laws, you should consider the issues raised in this section. To reiterate,

- generally, criminals do not have standing;
- however, the analyst must be careful that a concern with society's absolute institutions does not result in the analyst becoming the tool of an unjust system;
- if criminals do have standing, the benefits to the criminal are generally less than the costs to the victim; and
- when the purpose of the BCA is explicitly to consider a change in legality status, or specifically to provide benefits to criminals, then those who are now or will become criminals should have standing.

Fortunately, most BCA does not raise the difficult ethical issues that would be raised in an analysis of something like slavery. However, lesser ethical dilemmas may still be faced. Suppose that, in a traditional agrarian society, freeing up women's time from basic manual labor is valued by women but actually *dis*valued by men? This would present difficult analysis decisions.

FUTURE GENERATIONS

Another standing issue in BCA is the treatment of future generations. This issue is particularly important to urban environmental policy analysis, for in many cases urban policy and environmental policy involve trade-offs between the wishes and desires of present generations and those of future generations. Reducing the capacity of a city's aquifer may have little impact on current residents of the city, but it may prove to have a huge impact on those who will live in the city in the future.

The general principle in BCA is that people in future generations should have as much standing as people in the present generation. As we show later, however, this does not completely resolve the issue of how to treat the preferences of those in the future, because we do not know what their circumstances will be. For example, if the future will include a lot of wealth but few green spaces, we would assess the future benefit of an additional city park created now differently than we would if the future will be a world of significant poverty but lots of open space.

MONETIZATION

A key feature of BCA is the monetization of as many costs and benefits as practicable. In the case of goods and services that are bought and sold in properly functioning markets, this is fairly simple, for in BCA the "value" of something (whether cost or benefit) is the amount that people are willing to pay (WTP) for it, and, at the margin, this is the market price. However, as mentioned in earlier chapters, many of the things that are of interest to urban environmental policy analysts are not bought and sold in properly functioning markets because they are not pure private goods.

In this section, we move through different types of goods, explicating how to monetize their costs and benefits for use in BCA. As you will learn, some monetization methods involve sophisticated statistical or other methods that can be both difficult and time-consuming to apply. Yet we assert that even simple BCAs involving fairly basic estimates of social values can be of benefit to decision makers and administrators. As stated in Weimer and Vining (2009, xv), "Although CBA requires sometimes heroic efforts to monetize impacts as costs or benefits, applying it imposes a discipline on researchers to be comprehensive in comparing policies." The sophistication of a BCA should depend on the resources, including time, available to the analyst, and also on the expense and importance of the policy to be analyzed. Often, a simple, reasoned analysis will be informative.

Some critics of BCA are offended by the fact that estimates of costs and benefits may not be all-encompassing. This criticism is certainly accurate, but, as mentioned in the first chapter, the perfect should not be the enemy of the good. There is no method of social consideration that is all-encompassing. Even when performed in a back-of-the-envelope fashion, BCA provides useful information that political, administrative, and budgetary analyses do not.

AN EXAMPLE OF MONETIZATION

Suppose that you, as an urban environmental policy analyst, are asked to perform a BCA to see if it would be socially beneficial for your city to install a tennis court. This court would be installed on land that the city already owns but that is currently vacant, is not used for parking, and does not contain attractive or useful vegetation (such as trees). The proposed site is not near enough to any residences that sounds, parking, or lights will disturb residents. You should begin by considering all the costs of producing the tennis court.

Costs of the Tennis Court

The costs of the tennis court include:

1. the land on which it will be built
2. materials costs, including for the surface, fences, lights (if it is to be usable after dark), and windscreens (if needed)
3. labor costs
4. maintenance costs

Next, you need to assign monetary values to each of these costs.

1. The Land. It might be tempting to think that the cost of the land is zero because the city already owns it and the land is not in use. However, in BCA, the true cost of anything is its "opportunity cost"—the value that could be received in the next-best use. Therefore, even though the city would not have to pay for the land, its use still represents a social cost.

> In economics and BCA, the true cost of anything is its *opportunity cost*—the highest value of its other possible uses.

In general, land is for sale in a city, and the going market price usually represents the true opportunity cost of the land. However, land values differ drastically, depending on your city, and may differ significantly between areas of a single city, as well. In New York City, land costs could be as much as $2,300 per square foot, though the average price in 2006 was $366 per square foot (Federal Reserve Bank of New York, 2008). In contrast, in 2008, a 30,000-square-foot parcel sold for $30 per square foot in the city of Hemet, California (Schweizer, 2008). High variance in land costs requires that you use some type of local price rather than a national average price for vacant, buildable land.

If the land to be used were not vacant, you would also need to account for the cost of giving up its current use. For example, if it were currently used for parking, you could use the going price for parking in your city multiplied by the amount of use the parking lot currently gets.

2. Materials and *3. Labor Costs.* Private companies produce tennis courts, so it should be easy for you to find out the costs of their production. For example, information available on a commercial website in 2009 indicated that the standard size of a tennis court is 60 feet wide by 120 feet long, and the price to build it ranges from $22,000 to $55,000, depending on how much site work is needed, along with the choice of fencing, lighting, type of court surface, windscreens, etc. (Premier Tennis Courts Inc., 2003). With information about your own building site, you could narrow this estimate. There is no obvious, important market failure in the production of these inputs for producing your tennis court, so you can feel comfortable using the market price as an estimate of social cost, and such an estimate includes both labor and materials costs, so you do not need to figure these separately.

Again, it might be tempting to think that you need to use the wage-rate of the city workers who will build the tennis court (if it will be built by city workers rather than being contracted out, as is increasingly common). But, since BCA focuses on social costs, the true cost to society of construction work is the going market price for such labor, so the commercial bundling of materials and labor suffices for a cost estimate. This contention may seem untenable in situations where city workers are unionized and their wages are above the market wage. Technically, the opportunity cost of their labor is still the market wage, rather than the unionized wage, and the difference between them is what is called "monopoly rent" (Boardman et al., 1996). However, because city administrators care about budgetary costs, it may make sense for the BCA to include a range of costs for labor, using the going (competitive) market wage at the low end and the unionized (budgetary) wage at the other.

4. Maintenance Costs. Most physical infrastructure projects will require some type of maintenance. If nothing else, the tennis court will need trashcans and someone will need to empty them. Depending on your climate and chosen surface, it is also possible that the surface will need to be swept of leaves, rolled, etc. For example, clay courts require daily maintenance (essortment, 2002). In a real project, you would know what type of court is being considered—or perhaps part of the BCA is to estimate the tradeoffs between a more desirable surface that requires more maintenance, or a less desirable surface with lower maintenance costs. The goal of raising these issues here is to help you to think about the different types of costs that should be considered in an actual BCA.

Again, however, many of the costs of maintenance in this case can be determined from the private market. Many cities have private trash-haulage companies. Grounds maintenance certainly exists as a private industry. Based on rates from these private companies, you can project the social costs of maintenance.

TOTAL COSTS

Based on information about your specific project, suppose that the costs match those shown in Table 4.1.

Benefits of the Tennis Court

Once you have considered the costs of the policy, you also want to be sure to estimate the benefits. Usually, there are benefits to a proposed policy—whether they exceed the costs or not—or the policy would not be under serious consideration.

Clearly, there is one primary benefit of a municipal tennis court, and that is the pleasure and exercise of those who will use it. To compute benefits, you would need to know

    A. the number of players expected, and
    B. the benefit each player receives.

Again, you need to assign monetary values to the benefits.

A. The Number of Players Expected. In order to determine the social benefit of the tennis court, you must know how many people will use it. In other words, you must forecast use of the court. If your city already has a municipal court—or a city nearby or similar to yours does—this will make your forecasting task easier. However, you need to keep one thing in mind: How many people will play at the court will depend on the price to play. It is a law of economics that the higher the price, the lower the quantity demanded. If the proposed tennis court will function on a first-come, first-served basis, with no charge for use, then many more people will be likely to use it than if the price charged is $5 per player.

Though it will be inexact, if you can get a couple of different data points—for example, the number of daily tennis court users at a free or inexpensive local facility versus the number of daily users at a private, more expensive court—you can draw

Table 4.1

Costs of the Proposed Municipal Tennis Court

Cost category	Cost in dollars

Land
  Estimated as market price
  (70 ft. × 150 ft. at $20 per square foot)
	$210,000

Materials and labor Estimated as market price	$40,000
Maintenance (yearly) (Trash pickup and sweeping at $20 per month)	$240
Total cost	$250,240

a line between these two points to estimate likely use based on your situation.[1] Suppose, for instance, that a nearby town similar in size to yours charges $2 per player at its municipal tennis courts, while a private tennis club in your town charges $5 per player. The municipal facility gets 20 players per day (per court), while the private club gets 10 players per day per court. Again, this will be just an approximation, but you can estimate the relationship between price and demand by drawing a graph like that shown in Figure 4.1.

Though imperfect, this graph gives you a good way to "guesstimate" usage based on your city's pricing plans. From this illustration, it's reasonable to expect that you'll never get more than about 28 users per day, even if you charge nothing. You're unlikely to set a price higher than that at the private tennis club, so this also gives you reasonable guesses in the $1–$4 ranges you might possibly charge.

B. The Benefit Each Player Receives. Generally, we can consider that the benefit a player receives is a private benefit, so that benefit should be determined by the willingness to pay (WTP) of each player. If your proposed tennis court will charge a fee, then you can be sure that the benefit is at least the price paid. Strictly speaking, for the player who almost wasn't willing to pay, the benefit is the price paid. So, if you—like your neighboring town—will charge $2 per player, you can guess you'll get about 20 players per day, and the benefit will be at least $2(20) = $40 per day. Technically, this is a "lower-bound estimate" for the value of the court, because many players get more benefit than the price. In your analysis, you can note this is a lower-bound estimate.

It is a bit harder to estimate the benefit if access to your court will be free. However, since tennis courts exist and charge fees, we should be able to figure out a reasonable WTP for the good of playing tennis. For example, in September of 2009, the municipal Kiwanis Recreation Center in Tempe, Arizona, charged between $2 and $3.50 per player, depending on the type and level of play (City of Tempe, 2009). However, the CopperWynd resort in the nearby town of Scottsdale, Arizona, charged $5 per player (CopperWynd, 2009).

How can you know the true value to the people who will play at the proposed tennis court? Of course, you could figure this out using a survey, but a survey is probably not

Figure 4.1 **Approximate Price-Demand Trade-off for Tennis Court Use**

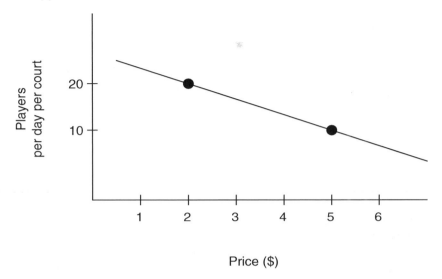

worth the cost and delay for a small project like this—it might well be for larger or riskier projects, though. (Chapter 10 discusses use of surveys and other opinion-gathering methods.) Additionally, you need to note that the municipal court may charge less than the full WTP, either because taxes offset some of the costs, or because the city considers that there is a public good in encouraging people to play tennis. Thus, when a price is set by government rather than by a market, it may underrepresent the true WTP.

To decide what price to use, you can choose one of the following:

- Use the range of prices and provide a range of possible benefits. This is kind of like a confidence interval—you can say you aren't sure of the true benefit, but it is between $2 and $5 per player.
- Use an average of the range of prices, for example, $3.88 (first taking the average of the two Kiwanis public fees and then averaging that with the private Copper Wynd fee).
- Consider the type of people who are likely to be playing in your particular location, and figure out if their WTP is likely to be closer to that charged at a resort hotel (where mostly well-off people play) or at a municipal court (where there is a broader range of household incomes represented). To a large extent, who plays at this tennis court will depend on who lives near to it, and you may have access to specific data (such as U.S. Census data) that provide information regarding the incomes of those nearby.

Suppose that your city will not charge anything for use of the proposed new tennis court, but there is another tennis court not very far away, and the people in the new court's proposed area are upper-middle-class. You might make the estimate shown in Table 4.2. Keep in mind that, based on this estimate, the city in question is in an

Table 4.2

Benefits of the Proposed Municipal Tennis Court

Benefit category	Benefits in dollars

Benefit to players
  Estimated as willingness to pay
  (20 players per day, $4 per player, 360 days per year)
	$28,800

Total Benefit	$28,800

Table 4.3

Net Benefits of the Proposed Tennis Court, First Year

Costs and benefits	Dollar values
Total benefits	$28,800
Total costs	−$250,240
Net Benefits	−$221,240

area with a mild climate; in Kansas, United States, or Moscow, Russia, people could not use an outdoor tennis court 360 days per year!

According to the net benefit rule of BCA, you now subtract total costs from total benefits to decide if the project is worthwhile, as shown in Table 4.3.

According to the benefit-cost principal, a project should be pursued if the benefits exceed the costs. Here, as estimated, they do not. "But wait!" you may say, "The tennis court will last far longer than just one year!" And you are correct: Estimation of the net benefits of the proposed court must take into account the fact that it will last for many years; thus, people will get benefits from it for many years. We deal with this time dimension of costs and benefits by discounting.

DISCOUNTING: TAKING INTO ACCOUNT STREAMS OF COSTS AND BENEFITS

As mentioned above with respect to San Francisco's Golden Gate Bridge and London's Tower Bridge, many urban environmental policy decisions have repercussions that last for many years, decades, or even centuries. In fact, many urban environmental policies can be thought of as public investments in the future.

How should analysts take into account this stream of benefits? Here, we could just add up all the benefits over the expected life of the court. According to the website used above, you should expect to resurface a tennis court every five to seven years (depending on use and weather). Suppose we expect our court's surface to last six years. Then, we could multiply benefits and ongoing costs (here, maintenance costs) times six years and reestimate our net benefits. Using the hypothetical values in Tables 4.1 and 4.2, this would result in benefits of $28,800(6) = $172,800 for the first six years of the court's existence. While the original land costs and the production of the court occur only in the first year, the maintenance costs occur over the entire six years, and so these would also need to be multiplied times six.

There is a problem with this procedure, however, and it results from basic human preferences: humans prefer things now to the same thing in the future. Would you rather have $5 now or $5 in a month? Would you rather save one life today or save one life in a year? Almost all people would prefer both the $5 and the saved life—indeed, any good thing—sooner rather than later, all else being equal. This truth is humorously expressed by the old cartoon character, Wimpy, who said, "I would gladly pay you Tuesday for a hamburger today." This is funny just because it is human nature to prefer the hamburger today—and the payment today! A payment in the future is not worth as much as a payment now.

Policy analysts take this truth into account through the process of "discounting." In discounting, just because humans prefer receiving good things now—and paying for them later—future costs and future benefits are monetized at *less* than their current value would be. Discounting is the mirror image of interest. In order for you to lend me money, meaning that you can't spend it now but will need to wait to spend it, I need to pay you interest to compensate you for the delayed benefit of the money. This is true even if you perceive absolutely no risk in making the loan to me and you expect no inflation.

The Discount Rate

In an economic or financial context, the term *real* means that a monetary value has been stripped of inflation. In this context, the opposite of *real* is *nominal*, where a nominal value includes inflation. Thus, a *real interest* or *discount rate* does not include any return for expected inflation.

Just as we can talk about the "interest rate," we can discuss the "discount rate." The proper discount rate is in some dispute, and different government agencies may mandate specific discount rates. For example, in 1991 the U.S. Environmental Protection Agency put forth some guidelines indicating that a 10 percent (real) discount rate "is most appropriate for environmental regulatory actions that have a relatively short time horizon" and that lower discount rates are suitable for "environmental regulatory activities that span several generations" (EPA, 2009); in January 2009, the U.S. Department of Health and Human Services, Centers for Medicare and Medicaid Services, issued a Benefit-Costs Analysis that used discount rates of 3 percent and 7 percent; The *Green Book* that guides public economic decision procedures in the United Kingdom uses a 3.5 percent discount rate (U.K. BIS, 2009). Exhibit 4.2 shows a U.S. Office of Management and Budget (OMB) directive on discount rates.

It is important to note the following:

- The *higher* the discount rate, the more we are valuing the present over the future.
- The *lower* the discount rate, the more we are valuing the future in relation to the present.

■--■

Exhibit 4.2

An OMB Discounting Directive

M–09–07   December 12, 2008

EXECUTIVE OFFICE OF THE PRESIDENT
THE DIRECTOR
OFFICE OF MANAGEMENT AND BUDGET
WASHINGTON, D.C. 20503

MEMORANDUM FOR THE HEADS OF DEPARTMENTS AND AGENCIES

FROM: Jim Nussle
          Director

SUBJECT: 2009 Discount Rates for OMB Circular No. A-94

On October 29, 1992, OMB issued a revision to OMB Circular No. A-94, "Guidelines and Discount Rates for Benefit-Cost Analysis of Federal Programs." The revision established new discount rate guidelines for use in benefit-cost and other types of economic analysis.

The revised Circular specifies certain discount rates that will be updated annually when the interest rate and inflation assumptions in the budget are changed. These discount rates are found in Appendix C of the revised Circular. The attachment to this memorandum is an update of Appendix C. It provides discount rates that will be in effect for the calendar year 2009.

The rates presented in Appendix C do not apply to regulatory analysis or benefit-cost analysis of public investment. They are to be used for lease-purchase and cost-effectiveness analysis, as specified in the Circular.

OMB Circular No. A-94

APPENDIX C
(Revised December 2008)

DISCOUNT RATES FOR COST-EFFECTIVENESS, LEASE PURCHASE,
AND RELATED ANALYSES

Effective Dates. This appendix is updated annually. This version of the appendix is valid for calendar year 2009. A copy of the updated appendix can be obtained in electronic form through the OMB home page at http://www.whitehouse.gov/omb/circulars/a094/a94_appx-c.html, the text of the main body of the Circular is found at http://www.whitehouse.gov/omb/circulars/a094/a094.html, and a table of past years' rates is located at http://www.whitehouse.gov/omb/circulars/a094/dischist-2009.pdf. Updates of the appendix are also available upon request from OMB's Office of Economic Policy (202–395–3381).

Nominal Discount Rates. A forecast of nominal or market interest rates for 2009 based on the economic assumptions for the Fiscal Year 2010 December Budget Baseline are presented below. These nominal rates are to be used for discounting nominal flows, which are often encountered in lease-purchase analysis.

**Nominal Interest Rates on Treasury Notes and Bonds
of Specified Maturities** (in percent)

3-Year	5-Year	7-Year	10-Year	20-Year	30-Year
2.7	3.3	3.7	4.2	4.7	4.5

Real Discount Rates. A forecast of real interest rates from which the inflation premium has been removed and based on the economic assumptions from the 2010 December Budget Baseline is

(continued)

Exhibit 4.2 *(continued)*

presented below. These real rates are to be used for discounting constant-dollar flows, as is often required in cost-effectiveness analysis.

Real Interest Rates on Treasury Notes and Bonds of Specified Maturities (in percent)

3-Year	5-Year	7-Year	10-Year	20-Year	30-Year
0.9	1.6	1.9	2.4	2.9	2.7

Analyses of programs with terms different from those presented above may use a linear interpolation. For example, a four-year project can be evaluated with a rate equal to the average of the three-year and five-year rates. Programs with durations longer than 30 years may use the 30-year interest rate.

Source: The White House, 2009.

■━━━━━━━━━━━━━━━━━━■

It is also important to note that, in some cases, the choice of the discount rate can determine whether or not a policy is estimated to have positive net benefits. Given these facts, you probably can believe that the choice of discount rate is contentious—both technically and politically. There are many ways to select a discount rate, and if this topic is important to you, you should do additional research on it. Even though none of the following approaches is uncontested, we list below some discount-rate guidelines that we recommend:

> The *social rate of time preference* is a society's preferred trade-off between current and future consumption.

1. The BCA discount rate should be a *real* discount rate, with benefits and costs estimated in real dollars. If for some reason benefits and costs are measured in nominal dollars, then the discount rate should also include inflation.
2. The BCA discount rate generally should be based on the "social rate of time preference" (which can vary across societies and time) rather than on the time-value of money. In other words, there is no particular reason that the social discount rate should match any easily observable interest rate for lending or borrowing money.
3. Because of item (2), public-goods policies with fairly long time horizons should have discount rates different from those with short time horizons; evidence shows that people's discount rate for the far future is different from that for the near future. As a rule of thumb, 50 years can be considered the break point between policies with "short" versus "long" time horizons (Boardman et al., 2006).
4. For policies with effects lasting less than 50 years, discount rates should be around 3.5 percent or less (note that 3.5 percent is the rate recommended in *The Green Book*). Sensitivity analysis can justify using levels as low as 1 percent and as high as 5 percent.

5. For policies with effects lasting more than 50 years (which can be the case for environmental policies and for large infrastructure policies), research supports the use of a time-declining discount rate. The best digest of the literature suggests using the rates in item (4) for the first 50 years, 2.5 percent for the next 50 years, 1.5 percent for the next 50 years, and 0.5 percent for the next 50 years (Boardman et al., 2006). Table 4.4 lays out these recommendations.

6. The choice of a discount rate is politically contentious, as those opposed to a policy will usually argue for a higher discount rate, while those in favor of a policy will usually argue for a lower discount rate. A way to evade this type of political dispute is to compute the "internal rate of return" (IRR), which is the discount rate that makes the net benefits of a project just equal to zero.

Table 4.4

Recommended Discount Rates for Different Time Periods

Time period	Recommended discount rate
0–50 years	3.5%
50–100 years	2.5%
100–150 years	1.5%
150–200 years	0.5%

Notes: The discount rates shown here are based on U.S. research on the social rate of time preference and are most likely to be useful for industrialized countries. The social rate of time preference is likely to be different across societies based on current wealth, meaning that less-developed countries may have different time preferences.

The discount rate should decline over time, so, to use this table correctly, the discount rate for a policy with effects lasting 100 years will be 3.5 percent for the first 50 years and 2.5 percent for the second 50 years, etc.

Of course, if you work for an organization that has a mandated discount rate, then you may have to use it; however, you can use these guidelines to check if the mandated discount rate is appropriate and, if it is not, use a more appropriate one and provide a range of values.

Some scholars argue that there is no ethical justification for discounting the costs and gains of future generations, but we find that position antithetical to the foundations of BCA and policy analysis. BCA is supposed to be based on the preferences of the *people*, rather than on the preferences of the *expert*. As indicated above, there is plenty of evidence that people prefer benefits now over the same benefit in the future, and so it is appropriate for BCA to discount future costs and benefits.

However, it should be noted that how you discount future costs and benefits does depend on what you think about the future. For example if you think people in the future will be richer than people today, then that suggests, all else being equal, use of a *higher* discount rate. Future benefits should be less valuable to us now if we know those in the future will have plenty of benefits.

On the other hand, unborn generations don't have any way to express their preferences. Future generations (and even current children to some extent) are poorly represented by the political process. Taking this into account implies use of a *lower* discount rate. If future generations don't have a voice in the political process, then their needs and desires are already discounted by the political process. The implication that discount rates should be lower for future generations is especially supported if you expect (1) that people in the future will be poorer, or (2) that they will lack some special benefits that we have now—such as special natural amenities that could be destroyed before those in the future have the chance to enjoy them. No one living now has a choice regarding whether to see huge flocks of passenger pigeons darkening the sky or whether to hear the call of the dodo. Due to light pollution, the magical pleasures of fireflies are already unavailable to many.

How to Use a Discount Rate

At this point, you may feel that you know everything about the discount rate except how to use it. Use of the discount rate is as conceptually simple as the use of an interest rate. An interest rate increases the value of a sum as it progresses into the future. The discount rate decreases the value of a sum as it progresses into the future. When we discount a stream of costs or benefits that are realized in the future, we compute what is known as their present values. To do this, we use the following formula:

Formula 1 $$\text{Present Value} = \sum \left[\frac{Monetized\ Value\ in\ Current\ Dollars_t}{(1+d)^{t-1}} \right]$$

where Σ (sigma) is the summation operator (summed over t),
d is equal to the discount rate, and
t indicates the time period.

To return to our proposed tennis court policy, if we expect the court to generate $28,800 in benefits per year for 6 years, then the present value (PV) of this stream of benefits is

Formula 2 $$\text{PV} = \sum \left[\frac{\$28,000}{(1+3.5\%)^{t-1}} \right] \quad \text{for } t = 6 \text{ years.}$$

Since 3.5 percent is equal to 0.035, this means that the present value is equal to

$$\sum \left[\frac{\$28,000}{1.035^{t-1}} \right] \quad \text{for } t = 6. \text{ This translates to the following.}$$

$PV = \$28,800/(1.035)^0 + \$28,800/(1.035)^1 + \$28,800/(1.035)^2 + \$28,800/(1.035)^3$
$\quad + \$28,800/(1.035)^4 + \$28,800/(1.035)^5$
$PV = \$28,800/1 + \$28,800/(1.035) + \$28,800/(1.0712) + \$28,800/(1.1087) +$
$\quad \$28,800/(1.1475) + \$28,800/(1.1877)$
$PV = \$28,800 + \$27,826.09 + \$26,885.74 + \$25,976.37 + \$25,098.04 + \$24,248.55$
$PV = \$158,834$

As you look at this set of present value calculations, there are a few things you should notice.

1. We don't discount benefits that we receive in the first year. The value of a benefit in the first year is the value of that benefit. Here, the value of $28,800 in the first year is $28,800.[2] Since a tennis court can be built very quickly, we don't need to worry that the first set of benefits cannot arrive right away. With a more complex project—such as a bridge—the first set of benefits might not arrive until several years have passed, in which case all benefits would need to be discounted. Suppose that in the first year of the project it is known that benefits will first become available five years from now—then your benefit discounting would start with $PV = Benefit/(1.035)^4$ and proceed from there.

2. Notice that the present value of a benefit that has the same value over several years into the future steadily declines over time. So, though we are assuming that the benefit players will receive is the same in each year, the calculated amount declines from $28,800 in the first year, to $27,826.09 in the second year, and to $24,248.55 in the sixth year. Again, this declining present value of benefits received in the future is based on human nature and on the human preference for a benefit now rather than the same benefit later.

3. Because of this decline over time in the value of a benefit received in the future, the present value of the tennis court is less than the value we got when we simply multiplied $28,800 by 6: $158,834 < $172,800. Noticing this provides a "smell test," meaning a check as to whether your computation seems about right. Your discounted value should always be less than you'd get simply by adding up the undiscounted values over the time period.

4. Though we usually expect inflation in the future, we did not inflate the value of the benefit stream. In BCA, you should generally use only real values, whether for costs, benefits, or the discount rate. If you do use inflated values for future streams of costs and benefits, then you must also inflate the discount rate. However, this is not recommended, because it adds another forecasting task and thus increases the uncertainty of your estimate. You are not likely to be able to forecast future inflation rates well.

Given the work involved in discounting the benefits of the tennis court over six years, you may be shuddering at the thought of the work involved in discounting a project that lasts for 100 years—or even 50. If so, you will be pleased to know that you do not need to perform these calculations yourself. Computer programs are available to do them for you. Excel, for example, can compute the present value of a stream of benefits or costs.

If we want to know the "*net* present value" (NPV) of the tennis court, we need to include (1) the costs and benefits that occur in the first year, (2) the benefits that occur for the five years after the first year, and (3) the costs that recur over the five years after the first year. In other words, we mustn't forget the maintenance costs (sweeping and trash pickup) that will be incurred by the city. Here we illustrate the use of Microsoft's computer program, Excel for computing the present value of the costs of the tennis court between development and resurfacing.

The first thing you want to do before using Excel to compute a present value is to look up the NPV function in the Help section. Programs change with each new version; therefore, while we can tell you how to use the NPV function *now*, at the time of this writing, that's no guarantee that it will still be how Excel's NPV function works at the time of reading. Go into Excel Help, type in NPV, and select NPV from the options. As you will find from the Help function, the NPV function in Excel requires the following arguments:

- NPV(rate, value1, value2, . . .), which can also be written as
- NPV(rate, cell1:lastcell)

However, you must also note that Excel uses a slightly different formula for discounting than the one just given:

Formula 3 $$NPV = \sum \left[\frac{Values}{(1+r)^i} \right]$$

The difference here is that they raise $(1 + r)$ to the power of "i" rather than to the power of "$t-1$." The difference between "t" and "i" is arbitrary, but the "-1" part is important. If you read the explanation, you will see that the Excel Help adds the following information:

> The NPV investment begins one period before the date of the value1 cash flow and ends with the last cash flow in the list. The NPV calculation is based on future cash flows. If your first cash flow occurs at the beginning of the first period, the first value must be added to the NPV result, not included in the values arguments. (Microsoft Office, 2004)

In other words, Excel's NPV function assumes that you will not receive any benefits in the first year—a reasonable assumption for complex projects, even though it is incorrect for our simple tennis court project. The excerpted paragraph explains that Excel will discount the very first entry (divide it by 1 plus the discount rate rather than leave it undivided, as will Formula 1 above), and that if you have values that should not be discounted, you will need to add them separately. Therefore, to use Excel to discount the tennis court's maintenance costs, do the following:

1. Type in your values, here 240 for 6 years:

	A
1	240
2	240
3	240
4	240
5	240
6	240
7	—

2. Pick a cell where you would like the discounted values to appear, then type in "=NPV(3.5 percent, A2:A6)" and hit Enter. (This command

assumes that you typed your values into the first six cells, cells A1 through A6). Note that you use A2 as your first cell in this command—rather than A1—because Excel's NPV command starts discounting with the very first cell entered. Once you hit Return, you should have the following value: $1,083.61.

3. Remember that this value is not the entire cost of maintenance over the first six years. You still need to add in the value for the first year. So, in the cell under your $1,083.61, type "=A7 + 240" and hit Return (this command assumes that you put your NPV command into cell A7). You should now have the value $1,323.61. This is the present value of six years of maintenance costs, starting in the first year and discounted over the next five years.

Now that you have discounted benefits and costs for the six years before you have to replace the tennis court's surface, you can produce the tennis court's complete net present value, as shown in Table 4.5. Looking at Table 4.5, note that the net benefits of the tennis court are still negative, but that taking into account the benefits over the next six years—even discounted—increases the net benefits so that they are less negative.

Table 4.5

Net Present Value of the Proposed Tennis Court, Six Years

Cost category	Cost in dollars
Land	
Estimated as market price	
(70 ft. × 150 ft. at $20 per square foot)	$210,000
Materials and labor	
Estimated as market price	$40,000
Maintenance (yearly, for six years)	
(Trash pickup and sweeping at $20 per month; for six years, discounted at 3.5%)	$1,083.61
Total Costs, Present Value	$251,083.61

Benefit category	Benefits in dollars
Benefit to players,	
Estimated as willingness to pay	
(20 players per day, $4 per player, 360 days per year; for six years, discounted at 3.5%)	$158,834
Total Benefits, Present Value	$158,834

Costs and benefits	Dollar values
Total Benefits	$158,834.00
Total Costs	−$251,083.61
Net Benefits	−$92,249.61

Making Sure to Include Benefits and Costs over the Entire Life of the Project

Is six years the entire useful life of the tennis court? We know that the tennis court's surface will need to be resurfaced six years after production, but our current BCA implies that, rather than resurfacing the court, at the end of six years the court will be closed. This is unlikely to occur. Instead, the city is likely to resurface the court and keep it available to players. This illustrates the importance of ensuring that a BCA covers all the years of costs and benefits that a policy will generate.

Suppose that the city is committed to keeping this tennis court open for at least 12 years, and suppose that it costs $5,000 to resurface a tennis court. Then, our stream of costs and benefits looks as presented in Table 4.6.

As you can see in Table 4.6, most costs are at the beginning of the policy, but then there are streams of costs and benefits that continue throughout the life of the project. This is quite common for public policies.

If the city plans to keep this tennis court in play for 12 years if it is built at all, then what is the present value of the net benefits of the proposed policy? Using Excel, we find that the tennis court has net benefits equal to $31,576.79. See Table 4.7 for more details of this calculation.

How to Compute the Internal Rate of Return

As mentioned above, the choice of the discount rate is contentious. One way to get around the contention is to compute the "internal rate of return," or the discount rate that makes net benefits become zero. To make our lives easier, Excel has an internal rate of return option, IRR. To use the IRR function, begin by consulting Excel's Help for IRR. Then (assuming the instructions are the same as they are as of this writing) pick a cell and enter "=IRR(values, guess)." The values used should be net benefit values such as those that appear in the third column of Table 4.7. You will enter the cell of the first value, such as C1, followed by a colon and the cell of the last value, such as C12. You aren't required to guess a value for the IRR, but Excel will work more quickly if you do. You can simply use some value greater than the discount rate you have chosen, which—assuming net benefits are positive—you know is less than the IRR (in the event that your first net benefits are negative, use a guess that is smaller than your chosen discount rate). For this example, the IRR is computed by Excel to be 6 percent.

As long as your decision maker believes that the appropriate social discount rate is less than 6 percent, then the proposed tennis court, with an expected life of 12 years, has positive net benefits and, under the basic decision rule of BCA, should be adopted.

In the event that you are comparing different, mutually exclusive policies—for example, suppose the land being considered for a tennis court is also being considered for a swimming pool—then you should select the policy with the highest net benefits. If you have multiple projects from which to choose—perhaps you can build two tennis courts or one tennis court and a Zen garden—but you also have a budget constraint, choose the combination of policies that meets the budget with the highest total net benefits (Stokey and Zeckhauser, 1978).

Table 4.6

(Undiscounted) Streams of Costs and Benefits If the Tennis Court Will Last 12 Years

Years	Categories	Benefits	Costs in dollars
Year 1	Land		$40,000
	Materials/Labor		$210,000
	Maintenance		$240
	Playing	$28,800	
Year 2	Maintenance		$240
	Playing	$28,800	
Year 3	Maintenance		$240
	Playing	$28,800	
Year 4	Maintenance		$240
	Playing	$28,800	
Year 5	Maintenance		$240
	Playing	$28,800	
Year 6	Maintenance		$240
	Playing	$28,800	
Year 7	Resurfacing		$5,000
	Maintenance		$240
	Playing	$28,800	
Year 8	Maintenance		$240
	Playing	$28,800	
Year 9	Maintenance		$240
	Playing	$28,800	
Year 10	Maintenance		$240
	Playing	$28,800	
Year 11	Maintenance		$240
	Playing	$28,800	
Year 12	Maintenance		$240
	Playing	$28,800	

Table 4.7

Net Benefits of the Tennis Court over 12 Years

Costs	Benefits	Net benefits in dollars (undiscounted)
$250,240	$28,800	−$221,440
240	28,800	28,560
240	28,800	28,560
240	28,800	28,560
240	28,800	28,560
240	28,800	28,560
5,240	28,800	23,560
240	28,800	28,560
240	28,800	28,560
240	28,800	28,560
240	28,800	28,560
240	28,800	28,560

Discounted Net Benefits, Years 2–12	$253,016.79
Net Benefits, Year 1	−$221,440.00
Total Present Value of Net Benefits	$31,576.79

Note: The present value of net benefits is positive, so society will be better off if the policy is adopted.

TAKING INTO ACCOUNT EXTERNALITIES

In general, as noted in Chapter 2, economists and policy analysts would argue that there is no justification for the government production of a purely private good. So, why might a city justifiably consider building a tennis court? Since the private market will charge a price, but many people use the same tennis court, it is a toll good/marketable public good, and so may be underproduced by the private market. Another way to think about this is that we might believe—especially in the industrialized world, where there is currently an epidemic of people who are overweight and in poor physical condition—that there is a positive externality of increasing exercise in our city. If citizens are healthier, they will contribute more and longer to society and demand less of society's resources in health care. Since BCA should include all social costs and benefits, if policymakers or analysts believe there are positive externalities, then those also need to be included in the benefit calculation. If the net benefits of a policy are positive even without the measurement of positive externalities, the analyst could list them at the end in their own units. See Table 4.8 for an example, and notice that giving up a bad thing (here, mortality) is a benefit. Also notice that retaining certain unmonetized benefits and costs is in keeping with the philosophy expressed in Executive Order 12866 (Exhibit 4.1).

On the other hand, the tennis court may provide negative externalities for those who live near it. For example, if the courts will be open after dark, the shining lights may disturb some residents' sleep. Under the rules of BCA, these negative externalities must also be included in the costs.

Let's consider possible negative externalities first. Suppose that a policy imposes negative externalities on some members of society. How do we include these in the BCA? In general, negative externalities, which partake of the nature of pure public goods attached to some good that is at least partly private, are not bought and sold in markets. However, as is generally the case in BCA, the key to monetization is to determine what nearby residents would be willing to pay to avoid the light pollution that the tennis court will cause. You could survey those residents who will be bothered and ask them how much the city would have to pay them to compensate them for the extra light, but a problem is that some people are prone to strategic behavior

---

Table 4.8

Net Benefits of the Tennis Court over 12 Years, Including Unmonetized Benefits

Discounted Monetized Net Benefits, Years 2–12	$253,016.79	
Monetized Net Benefits Year 1	−$221,440.00	
Unmonetized Benefits		Improved fitness and health; Reduced mortality
Total Present Value of Net Benefits	$31,576.79	+ Improved fitness and health; Reduced mortality

in such a situation and are likely to claim that they require more compensation than they really do. In addition, you might not have the time and resources available to conduct a survey before you complete the BCA.

The general solution to monetizing externalities and other goods not directly bought and sold in markets is to observe some behavior that lets you infer or *impute* a monetary value for the externality. For example, in the case of light from a tennis court, a fairly simple solution is for nearby residents to add thicker window coverings on the windows where the light leaks in. So, you could calculate the cost of adding new window coverings and thereby estimate the cost of the added light pollution. This type of estimate is called a "shadow price." Of course, some people may not find the added light troubling, in which case estimating the cost of the light in this way would probably present an "upper-bound estimate."

> A *shadow price* is an imputed, or assigned, price for something that does not have an efficient market price.

Once costs and benefits are no longer observable from market behavior and the analyst must rely on shadow prices, the certainty of estimation is reduced. All estimates or forecasts are uncertain; what is important is to be clear about which estimates or forecasts are especially uncertain and whether they are likely to be too high or too low. One rule of BCA is to make it clear when there is uncertainty about an estimate. So, you might add the expected cost of the light pollution to your analysis and indicate whether you expect that your estimate is high or low.

HEDONIC PRICING ANALYSIS

Another way to impute the value of externalities is to use hedonic pricing methods.[3] A "hedonic pricing model" is a particular type of empirical model of house or land prices: Rather than estimating house prices by the intersection of supply and demand, it analyzes them by desirable and undesirable attributes of the house itself and the neighborhood in which the house is located. Thus, the price of a house may be estimated based on its size, its age, how many bedrooms it has, how near it is to a beautiful park, how much noise it receives from the freeway, the quality of the neighborhood schools, and so on. Hedonic analysis can be used to estimate the cost of negative externalities such as airport noise (see, for example, Rahmatian and Cockerill, 2004) or the benefits of positive externalities such as open space. Opaluch and colleagues (1999) estimated that properties adjacent to open space in Southold, Long Island, New York, United States "had, on average, 12.8 percent higher value than similar properties located elsewhere" (King and Mazzotta, 2000). On the negative side, this same study found that "properties located within 20 meters of a major road had, on average, 16.2 percent lower per-acre value" (King and Mazzotta, 2000). In these cases, the hedonic models estimate the value of the positive externalities of open space and the negative externalities of major roads.

Estimating a hedonic model is quite time-consuming, since it requires detailed information about houses, their attributes, neighborhood attributes, and selling prices. In addition, estimating one correctly requires regression analysis (econometric) skills. For small projects such as the tennis court example, estimating a hedonic model is unlikely to be worthwhile. However, many hedonic studies already exist and are publically available, and it is possible that you could find one that provides a shadow price that you could use as part of your own analysis. For example, as of the time of this writing, typing "hedonic tennis" into Google brought up several references to articles providing hedonic-analysis-based estimates of the value of tennis courts.

ESTIMATING HEALTH BENEFITS

Suppose that your city will install a tennis court primarily in order to improve health and fitness. In general, estimating the value of positive externalities can be done in the same ways as estimating negative externalities. However, estimating benefits having to do with life, health, and quality of life—which often occur in environmental policy—is complex, and, as a result, some particular methods have been developed.

Value of Life

implicit (internal reasoning)   *explicit - showing how / rationale explaining*

When performing a Benefit-Cost Analysis of environmental policies (and even more for health and safety policies) it is often necessary to compute the value of a human life. Some people find this concept inherently repugnant, but the fact is that societies and political processes frequently make decisions about the value of a human life. Some of these are implicit, such as when a law that will save lives is deemed too expensive for passage. Some of these are explicit, such as in U.S. legal cases involving wrongful death, where the courts may make a determination that survivors should be compensated the value of the foregone earnings of the deceased (Feinberg, 2008). This is not only a Western reality: In Muslim sharia court, victims may be compensated with specific numbers of camels (Fernandes, 2009). Valuing and monetizing a human life in a BCA only makes our values explicit rather than allowing them to be implicit.

In performing policy analysis, we recommend five basic principles in the valuation of a human life.

1. In order to use social resources most effectively, we should be explicit in valuing human lives.
2. It should be noted that we are valuing *statistical lives*, not the lives of specific people.
3. To the greatest extent possible, the value of statistical lives should be determined by risk-money trade-offs that people make voluntarily.
4. Valuations of statistical lives should be the same for all people of the same age and with the same other risks in the same society.
5. In order to avoid political problems with assigning a value to statistical lives, it can be useful to report the cost per life saved of a policy rather than to assign a value of life and then report net benefits.

A *life-year* is one year of life saved for one person.

As stated above, the first principle is that we should be explicit in valuing human lives in order to use social resources more effectively. Suppose that you have two different policies: One can save 1,000 lives at a cost of $5,000 per life saved; the other can save 10 lives at a cost of $500,000 per life saved. You may notice that the total cost of these two options is exactly the same: $5,000,000. Given that governmental resources are always limited, most people would prefer, knowing no more, to save 1,000 lives for their expenditure of $5,000,000 rather than only 10. Explicitly understanding costs per lives saved allows societies to use their life-saving resources more efficiently—to save more lives rather than fewer.

Note that in the aforementioned example, we are talking just about "lives," not about the life of a specific person. In policy analysis broadly and BCA specifically, we are considering saving *statistical lives*, not identifiable people's lives. A mother may be willing to give all that she possesses, including her own life, to save the life of her baby; the people of Japan may consider that preserving the life of the emperor is worth much more than preserving anyone else's life. But in general, in a BCA, we are considering saving statistical lives—lives not of *specific* people, but of people we cannot identify whose *probability* of death will be lessened (or increased) by some policy or program. See Case 4.1 for a U.S. Environmental Protection Agency (EPA) discussion of this concept.

As an example, in the not-too-distant past in the United States, there were no seat belts in passenger automobiles. Then the U.S. government required that automakers conform to a set of Federal Motor Vehicle Safety Standards (FMVSS), including the addition of seat belts, and these added manufacturing costs. "In 2002, these technologies added an estimated $11,353,000,000 (in 2002 dollars) to the cost of new cars and LTVs [pickup trucks, sport utility vehicles and vans] over model years 1968–2002" (Kahane, 2004). However, a BCA would indicate that the more than $11.3 billion was money well spent, for it "saved an estimated 20,851 lives in the cars and LTVs on the road during that calendar year. That amounts to $544,482 per life saved in 2002" (Kahane, 2004). At least in highly developed societies, statistical lives are estimated to be worth more than $544,482, so the net benefits of the FMVSS are positive.

Compare this result to a recommended asbestos control policy for Canada, which was estimated to cost between $1,000,000 and $35,000,000 (in 1986 Canadian dollars) per life-*year* saved (Dewees and Daniels, 1986).[4] This means that the policy would cost something between U.S.$588,000 and $20 million in 1986 for each additional *year* of life gained from this program. (If the average person saved would live ten more years than without the program, the cost per *life* would be between $5.9 and $200 million). Would the proposed Canadian policy be worth it? To some extent, the answer to that question is a value judgment, but it is certain that Canada could save lives at a lower cost, even similar industrial-worker lives (Dewees and Daniels, 1986).

In 2008, something of a ruckus erupted when the EPA reduced the value of a statistical life used in its analyses. At that time, the new value was $6.9 million,

■———— Case 4.1 ————■

U.S. EPA Discussion of Valuing Life

What Does It Mean to Place a Value on Life?

The EPA does not place a dollar value on individual lives. Rather, when conducting a Benefit-Cost Analysis of new environmental policies, the agency uses estimates of how much people are willing to pay for small reductions in their risks of dying from adverse health conditions that may be caused by environmental pollution.

In the scientific literature, these estimates of willingness to pay for small reductions in mortality risks are often referred to as the "value of a statistical life." This is because these values are typically reported in units that match the aggregate dollar amount that a large group of people would be willing to pay for a reduction in their individual risks of dying a year, such that we would expect one fewer death among the group during that year on average.

This is best explained by way of an example. Suppose each person in a sample of 100,000 people were asked how much he or she would be willing to pay for a reduction in their individual risk of dying of 1 in 100,000, or 0.001 percent, over the next year. Since this reduction in risk would mean that we would expect one fewer death among the sample of 100,000 people over the next year on average, this is sometimes described as "one statistical life saved." Now suppose that the average response to this hypothetical question was $100. Then the total dollar amount that the group would be willing to pay to save one statistical life in a year would be $100 per person × 100,000 people, or $10 million. This is what is meant by the "value of a statistical life." Importantly, this is not an estimate of how much money any single individual or group would be willing to pay to prevent the certain death of any particular person.

Source: EPA, 2011.

a reduction of about $900,000 (Associated Press, 2008). The debate surrounding the decrease raises the general question of how one would decide the value of a statistical life to begin with. As with all other costs and benefits in BCA, the value of a life should be based on people's willingness to pay. For something like the value of a statistical life, this is usually determined through "revealed preferences" or through contingent valuation method (CVM). CVM is discussed in Chapter 10. People are said to reveal their preferences when they make trade-offs in market-based transactions.

The types of market decisions people make reveal information about their risk-money tradeoffs. For example, workers in higher-risk jobs may earn higher salaries than those in lower-risk jobs in the same industry. The risk-premium that is required for enough people to take the higher-risk jobs can reveal the value that people place on a statistical life. Let's suppose that there are two different types of construction jobs. One type pays $40,000 per year and the risk of death from this work is 1/10,000. The other type pays $45,000 per year and the risk of death from this work is 1/9,000. In this example, the workers with the riskier jobs accept an increased risk of death of 1/1000 and demand $5,000 to compensate them for this added risk. In this case, the revealed value of a statistical life is $5,000,000 $\left(\dfrac{\$5,000}{1/1,000} \right)$, or (Boardman et al., 2006).

Hedonic analysis methods, such as those discussed earlier in this chapter, are also revealed preference methods and can be used to estimate the value of a statistical life. Suppose that an analyst can estimate the house-price reductions that are due to some houses being near a polluting source that increases the risk of cancer; the analyst can then figure out revealed information about how much people require to be compensated for the increased risk of death from the cancer.

It is important to keep in mind that all revealed preference methods have weaknesses. The most important are that they assume two key things: (1) that the preferences of people who take the riskier jobs or live in the riskier areas are like the preferences of all people, and (2) that people fully understand the additional risk they are accepting. Both of these are problematic, and the latter assumption is often implausible due to a common inability to understand probabilistic risk fully.

Unless you have extensive additional training, you are unlikely to have the time and skills to develop useful revealed-preference estimates of values of a statistical life. Instead, you can use published estimates by experts, or you can use values selected by relevant government agencies. These are sometimes called "plug-in shadow prices." W. Kip Viscusi is an acknowledged expert on valuation-of-risks-to-life studies, so you might use some of his research (see, for example, 2010). Or, in the United States or similar industrialized countries, you might use EPA values when doing environmental policy analysis. As of the writing of this book, "EPA recommends that the central estimate of $7.4 million ($2006), updated to the year of the analysis, be used in all benefits analyses that seek to quantify mortality risk reduction benefits regardless of the age, income, or other population characteristics of the affected population" (U.S. EPA, 2011). "$2006" means that the base-year used for this dollar amount is 2006. In order to use the $7.4 million figure in later years, this amount must be inflated. So, in 2010 dollars, $7.4 million ($2006) is $8.03 million ($2010) (U.S. Department of Labor, n.d.). Inflation adjustment is typically done using the Consumer Price Index, and an adjustment calculator for U.S. dollar values is available from the U.S. Bureau of Labor Statistics (U.S. Department of Labor).

It seems clear that WTP for risk-reduction varies by society. For one thing, risk-reduction is generally a "normal good," meaning that, as incomes rise, quantity-demanded also rises. Thus, richer societies generally have higher estimated WTP for statistical lives. Second, even controlling for income, different societies value individual lives differently. Rafiq and colleagues (2010) published an overview of estimates of the value of a statistical life in developing countries. Their report centers on a 1999 study finding the value of a statistical life in Korea to be $0.5 million U.S. (Rafiq et al., 2010, 12). Inflated to $2010, this value is $0.84 million. Comparing this value with that of the EPA demonstrates that the revealed value of a statistical life can vary significantly by society. Values of statistical lives can also be expected to change over time. Since Korea, for example, has increased its wealth significantly since 1999, its value of a statistical life is likely to be higher today.

Item (4) of the five principles listed earlier states that the same value of a statistical life should be used for all people in the same society who are of the same age. The reason for the age caveat stems from evidence that people value the lives of young children more than they value the lives of others (see, for example, Viscusi, 2010). Hammitt and Haninger (2010) find that revealed "WTP to reduce risk to one's child is uniformly larger than to reduce risk to another adult or to oneself. Estimated values per statistical life are $6–10 million for adults and $12–15 million for children" (57).

Using the same value for all same-aged people in the same society is an equity issue. Though BCA is intended to increase social benefits overall—another way of saying that it is intended to increase social efficiency—it is also viewed as a process that can increase true representativeness. For a variety of reasons that we do not discuss here, political processes in representative democracies tend to overrepresent the goals of the relatively rich, well educated, and organized. BCA is only one input into the political process, but it can be a force against some of these known problems with representative democracy by representing the preferences of *all* members of the society, whether wealthy, organized, or not. Chapter 9 further discusses urban environmental equity issues.

> The *Kaldor-Hicks Criterion* is sometimes referred to as the *Kaldor-Hicks Compensation Principle* or the *Potentially Pareto Improving Criterion.*

In addition, the use of BCA is based on the Kaldor-Hicks Criterion. A BCA determines whether a society *could* be made better off by a policy. In order for it *actually* to be made better off, any losers must be compensated by the winners while leaving the winners better off. The Kaldor-Hicks principle argues that *potential* compensation— the ability for such compensation to occur—is sufficient. The use of this principle over many policies should, in general, make society better off, because winners and losers should be spread relatively equally over society. However, this is true only if certain groups are not consistently more likely to be winners (or losers) than others. Valuations of statistical lives that place higher value on those who work in higher-value occupations (as is often the case in court-ordered compensation and may be in insurance settlements) amplifies the problem of overrepresentation of the preferences of the wealthy. In general, the use of differential values for different classes of people within a society tends to codify social injustices into the BCA. For example, to the extent that labor markets result in discriminated-against groups earning less than other groups—and there is significant evidence that this has occurred in some times and places—valuing statistical lives based on earnings incorporates such discrimination. Interestingly, Kenneth Feinberg, who "managed the compensation funds for the Sept. 11, 2001 attacks," came to believe that it was unethical to place different values on the people who had died, though his training as a lawyer mandated this approach (Feinberg, 2008). In addition, such processes tend to value children *less* than many adults, since children are not yet employed in high-value jobs, nor can it be assumed they will be. Yet, this contradicts revealed preferences, as indicated earlier.

The EPA uses the same value of life for all, rather than using a different value based on one's employment. This is in keeping with what is currently considered best BCA practice. The EPA's decision to value the lives of all, no matter their age, at the same value is not in keeping with BCA best practices. This is probably the result of the great political outcry that occurred when, under the administration of George W. Bush, the EPA proposed to value the lives of those over 70 at less than younger lives (OMB Watch, 2003).

Clearly, the chosen value of a statistical life can cause political difficulty, as indicated by the uproar caused when the EPA dropped the value of a statistical life and proposed discounting the lives of those over 70. Thus, it can be sensible for an analyst to report a program's cost per statistical life saved rather than select a specific value for statistical lives and then compute whether net benefits are positive or negative. Using a cost per statistical life saved allows the political process to determine whether the cost is justified or not, rather than requiring the analyst to come up with a specific value that is likely to cause dispute.[5]

Though the Bush EPA's proposal to discount the lives of those over 70 was not well conceived, it is important to note that, based solely on people's preferences, lives saved often should be discounted over time. It seems clear that most people would rather save "a life" that will last for 10 years than to save "a life" that will last for only one more year, and they would rather save a life *now* than have to wait 10 years to save a life. This does imply that, on average, saving the lives of those 70 and above is worth less than, for example, saving the lives of those age 20 to 30. We expect that the 20-year-old life saved will last longer than the 70-year-old life saved. According to the U.S. Social Security Administration, as of 2006, a 20-year-old male could expect to live 56 more years on average, while a 70-year-old male could expect only about 13 more years (Social Security Online, 2006). However, there is no justification for discounting the lives only of those over 70. Instead, the value of a life saved should simply be adjusted for the number of years it is expected to last after it is saved, and this should be true no matter how old the person is.

Thus, adjustments for the value of a statistical life saved should depend not only on the expected ages of those saved, but also on the expectation of how much longer the statistical people will live even with the above policy in place. As stated in a publication of the Harvard Center for Risk Analysis, "If people who died because of air pollution would have soon died of other causes (for example, . . . people with cardiovascular disease) the value of prolonging their lives may be much smaller" (Harvard, 2001, 3). A policy that reduced the risk of death for a risky profession might very well result in a lower statistical value per life saved than one that reduced the risk of death for people over 70 who are not in a risky profession: In such a case, the 70-year-olds might have a longer life expectancy on average. There can be significant differences in how long life expectancy can be projected to last after an intervention, as well. For example, in 1998 chemotherapy for lung cancer resulted in only two more months of expected life, while chemotherapy for testicular cancer resulted in 107 months (almost nine years) of additional life expectancy (Harvard, 1998).

Quality-Adjusted Life Years

Another important issue to consider is the quality of the statistical life saved. Suppose a policy saves a statistical person's life, but that person is expected to remain in a coma for one year before dying. Compare this with another program that may save a statistical person's life and allow that person to live normally for one year. Complex issues involving the duration of a saved life, and the quality of a statistical person's life as well, lead to the concept of Quality-Adjusted Life Years, or QALYs. QALYs are sometimes referred to as Disability-Adjusted Life Years, or DALYs (Boardman et al., 2006), and a related concept is Quality-Adjusted Life Expectancy (Harvard, 1998). The concept of QALYs is often used in epidemiological analysis, and epidemiological analysis is often directly relevant to environmental policy analysis, so it is desirable for urban environmental policy analysts and administrators to understand them. "QALYs are used to measure an individual's future longevity and the quality of the individual's health during that time. . . . They are calculated by weighting the amount of time an individual will spend in each future 'health state' by an index that measures the 'health-related quality of life' in that state" (Harvard, 2003, 2). QALYs are developed using the contingent-valuation method or some related sophisticated survey methodology. As of 2010, the Tufts Medical Center for the Evaluation of Value and Risk in Health states that the most frequently cited acceptable cost per QALY is $50,000, though in practice, "health care innovations that cost less than $100,000/ QALY . . . are adopted" (Cost-Effectiveness Analysis Registry, n.d.).

Epidemiology is "the branch of medicine that deals with the incidence, distribution, and possible control of diseases and other factors relating to health" (New Oxford American Dictionary, 2009), as well as how diseases and other ailments spread through and affect populations.

As with value-of-a-statistical life calculations, estimating QALYs is complex and requires more training than you will gain from this book. However, you can use QALYs computed by others, and the Tufts Medical Center Cost-Effectiveness Registry provides valuable information on the concept (see Recommended Websites at the end of this chapter).

Other Health Benefits

Suppose that a policy will improve health rather than just reduce death. In this case, it is often fairly easy to estimate the benefit of the improved health by using the foregone/ avoided costs of treatment and the value of foregone activities during the illness. At a minimum, foregone activities from an illness include foregone workdays, which can be valued at the expected wage of workers who will be ill. For those who are not employed for pay, such as children or housewives/househusbands, it can be more difficult to estimate the value of their foregone activities, but attempts should still be made, or at least these costs should be kept in the analysis in their own units (as demonstrated for benefits in Table 4.8). The analyst should be creative. Consider that the market value of many tasks of housespouses can be approximated from market values (such as by using prices for cleaning services or for child care). Estimating the lost benefit of a foregone day of school attendance is difficult, but certainly we could argue that society values a school day at least at the level of local per-pupil expenditures per day. These are examples of other ways to find revealed preferences.

PLUG-IN SHADOW PRICES

In the preceding discussions of valuing life and health benefits, we mentioned the possibility of using values others have published rather than computing your own values for every BCA. Using plug-in shadow prices—publicly available shadow prices estimated by others—can increase the speed with which you are able to perform Benefit-Cost Analysis. Boardman and colleagues (2006) have a valuable chapter on plug-ins that explains their rationale for selecting the most justifiable values. They also discuss how you can use the economics and policy literature more broadly to find appropriate plug-in shadow prices for the value of time, life, QALYs, injuries, crime, etc.

We recommend the use of appropriate plug-ins—with two caveats. First, shadow prices change over time; make sure that you are using the most up-to-date values possible. Second, shadow prices change based on social, economic, and demographic characteristics; make sure that you are using shadow prices that are appropriate for your population. The latter caveat is of particular importance for those in lesser-developed countries (LDCs). You cannot expect that shadow prices for developed countries will be appropriate for LDCs.

OTHER ISSUES THAT ARE LIKELY TO ARISE IN BCAS OF URBAN ENVIRONMENTAL POLICY

EXISTENCE VALUE

In environmental policy, benefits may accrue to people who do not actually "consume" or even "use" a good in any meaningful sense. For example, it is possible for someone who never intends to visit the Great Wall of China, or Egypt's great pyramid of Cheops, or the Mayan pyramids at Chichen Itza to have a genuine willingness to pay for their preservation. Similarly, some people may value the existence of the snow leopard even if they never intend to hunt one or even see a real one. People can gain pleasure (or pain) just from the *existence* of something, and this is called "existence value."

Existence value can be particularly relevant in environmental policy because many environmental amenities are not used directly. From an analysis perspective, however, existence value is somewhat problematic, as it can be difficult to estimate; in the language used above, it is difficult to observe revealed preferences and to create shadow prices. If WTP is the measure, we nonetheless know that existence value is real, even if it is difficult to observe: We know, for example, that people donate funds to the Nature Conservancy so that it will buy and preserve land that donors may never see. Due to the problem of free riding, we expect that the total amount of such donations will be far below the level of actual existence value, but at least these sorts of donations provide concrete evidence of its reality.

Existence value is usually estimated through some sort of survey methodology (such as contingent valuation method, mentioned above and discussed in more detail in Chapter 10). Because existence value does not require any consumption of the good, the item from which someone gains existence value can be considered a pure public good in this context (Boardman et al., 2006). Therefore, many people can place some existence value on the same item, and the analyst cannot easily observe the value people are placing on it. In such cases, even a small amount of existence value per person can lead to large benefits for the item's continued existence. As of January 2011, there were about 6.9 billion people on Earth (U.S. Census, 2011). Suppose that 10 percent of those people gain some existence value from the presence of Antarctic penguins. Even if each of those people gains only 10 cents of benefit on average, then the existence value of Antarctic penguins is $69,000,000.

Because of the fact that existence values can be very high but simultaneously very difficult to observe, their use is controversial. Yet, the very basis of BCA requires their inclusion, if possible, since we have established that there can be true willingness to pay for pure existence value. To solve this conundrum, Boardman et al. (2006) recommend that, "whenever possible, costs and benefits should be presented with and without their inclusion to make clear how [existence values] affect net benefits" (229).

It is worth noting that existence value of the sort discussed here is at least conceptually different from the type of existence value society may receive from the continued presence of an indicator species. Because an indicator species alerts analysts to the state of an entire habitat, its existence value—to those who understand its importance—may take on the value of the entire habitat.

An *indicator species* is "an animal or plant species that can be used to infer conditions in a particular habitat" (New Oxford American Dictionary, 2009).

DOUBLE-COUNTING

One caution in the area of BCA is that analysts must be careful not to double-count either benefits or costs. If, as stated above, the existence value of an indicator species takes on the value of the entire habitat, then it would be unsuitable to count both the existence value of the indicator species *and* the value of other species in the habitat. This would be an instance of double-counting benefits.

For beginners, double-counting easily occurs when a policy involves transfers. In BCA, if something is a transfer, then it has no net benefit. The reason for this is simple and easily illustrated with an example: If I take $10 from you and give $10 to someone else, then your cost is $10 and the other person's benefit is $10 and the net benefits of this transaction—from the social perspective—are $0. For policy analysts, a salient point is that *taxes are transfers*. In taxation, the government takes money from some people and then spends those funds to create benefits for other people. So, returning to the tennis court example, the expenditure of $240 per month on maintenance personnel is a true social cost, but it would be double-counting costs if we *also* counted the loss of tax dollars to the taxpayer from this decision.

EMPLOYMENT AND MULTIPLIERS

Some policies under consideration in an urban environmental context will be large capital-improvement projects. For example, a metropolitan region might consider developing a light-rail system in order to reduce pollution from automobiles. When a policy or program can be viewed as an "economic development" project, the politics of analysis often change. There are two main types of pitfalls that can trip up the analyst in these types of settings: The first is the issue of the value of employment, and the second is the question of multipliers.

Employment: Benefit or Cost?

In many instances, urban boosters will argue that increased employment is a social benefit that should be included in BCAs. There are several problems with this claim. First, using workers who are already employed is a *cost* to the society, not a benefit. The true cost of any resource is its opportunity cost, or its cost in its next-best use. If workers are already employed, then using them for a new project takes them away from their next-best use, and the value of this should generally be represented by the market wage.

Now, suppose that workers are unemployed. Would hiring them represent a benefit? No, because the same principle applies. Using workers in one way—say for the light-rail project—prevents their use in another way. Even unemployed workers (those who do not yet have a job but wish to have one) do not have a value of $0 in their next-best use. Yes, their social cost is generally lower than the social cost of employed workers, but it is still above zero. Unemployed people may be performing useful labor at home, perhaps caring for children or yards or elderly parents; they may volunteer their services to churches or nonprofit organizations; or, even if they are doing nothing so clearly useful, people usually place some value on their own leisure time. Just reading a book or watching TV provides some benefit to the individual. In fact, the reality that people value their own "leisure" time (which, in economics, simply means time spent on unpaid activities) is captured by the concept of the "reservation wage." Each person has a reservation wage: a wage below which that person is unwilling to work for pay.

If your community has relatively full employment of the type of workers needed for the project under consideration, then the social cost of these workers is the going wage. If you have unemployment (beyond the natural rate of unemployment) for these workers, then their social costs will be lower than the going wage, but will not be zero. Estimating the social cost of their employment is difficult, however, and it is important to note that unless unemployment rates are very high, one cannot assume that most of those hired for the new project will have been unemployed—some will have been employed but will change jobs (Boardman et al., 2006). If you must estimate the cost of workers in a case where unemployment is above the full employment rate, you will need to do additional research or enlist the aid of an economist.[6] The most important point to remember is that hiring even unemployed workers is usually a social cost—not a social benefit as some will claim. Even when there are true social benefits from maintaining or creating jobs, they are often overestimated (Feser and Cassidy, 1996).

Full employment is the rate of unemployment that is consistent with no inflationary pressures due to wages. It varies over time and place depending on the demographics of the labor force, but in the United States it is usually on the order of a 3–5 percent unemployment rate. This is sometimes referred to as the *natural rate of unemployment*.

Multiplier Effects: Questionable in BCA

If hiring unemployed workers is not a direct social benefit, what about the multiplier effect of their wages? Perhaps that is a social benefit. The multiplier effect is a basic concept in economics. *New* expenditures (and especially new investment expenditures) have benefits that spread out through the society. Suppose, out of the blue, I were to give you $1,000. You probably would spend some of it and save some of it. The amount that you spent would go to others as profits, wages, etc., and they would spend part of what they received and save part of it, and so on. In addition, due to the fractional banking system, the amount that you saved would result in new loans of greater than the amount that you put into your savings account, and those new loans would also be spent and saved, and so on.

Multiplier effects do exist, but their use in BCA is questionable. There are several reasons for this (see Boardman et al., 2006, 124–125), but the most important one is very simple. Multiplier effects are usually secondary. In general, you want to focus your efforts on primary effects and ignore secondary effects—whether multipliers or others. This book is focused on urban environmental policy analysis, and so the expectation is that most of our readers will be working in an urban setting. This means that the time and resources available to you for performing BCA are likely to be limited. It is difficult enough to perform a high-quality BCA that focuses on the primary effects of a policy.

In some cases, levels of unemployment are so high that the primary goals of a policy are the employment effect and the multiplier effects of the new employment. In those cases, you will need to spend time on these issues; otherwise, they should usually be ignored, especially because "localized multiplier effects," which are likely to be of most interest to your city, "generally tend to be relatively small" (Boardman et al., 2006, 125).

SENSITIVITY ANALYSIS

When performing any type of analysis, it is a good idea to perform a "sensitivity analysis." "Sensitivity analysis is a way of acknowledging uncertainty about the values of important parameters. . . . [It] should be a component of almost *any* CBA" (Boardman et al., 1996, 187; emphasis in original). You may have noticed in earlier sections of this book that a benefit sometimes is referred to as being a "lower bound." For example, when discussing the benefits of the tennis court, we said: "So, if you . . . will charge $2 per player, you can guess you'll get about 20 players per day, and the benefit will be at least $2(20) = $40 per day. Technically, this is a 'lower-bound estimate' for the value of the court, because many players get more benefit than the price. In your analysis, you can note this is a lower-bound estimate." Similarly, when discussing the light pollution that the tennis court may cause, we stated: "you might add the expected cost of the light pollution to your analysis and indicate whether you expect that your estimate is high or low."

There are different ways to do sensitivity analysis. One way is to focus on one or two particular values that you may be uncertain about or that may be politically contentious. This category includes the value of a statistical life or the discount rate. To perform the sensitivity analysis, use a maximum reasonable value and a minimum reasonable value and see if the results change enough to create different implications about whether the policy has net benefits or net costs. Another way is to provide one estimate of net benefits using all the lower-bound values and another using the higher-bound values. These two situations provide a band of confidence around your total estimated net benefits. Noting as you go along whether your estimates are likely to be high or low will help with this latter type of analysis.

CONCLUSION

This chapter provides an overview of the basic technique of BCA and offers insight into issues that may be particularly relevant for BCAs of urban environmental policy. Case 4.2 gives an overview of the steps of a BCA and highlights some of the sticky issues.

Benefit-Cost Analysis can be difficult and time-consuming, especially in environmental policy. However, remember that BCA is a formal representation of the way that policy analysts think. Even when you don't have time or other resources for a formal BCA, keep in mind its basic principles: Do the benefits exceed the costs? What are all the costs and benefits to society? Who are all the groups and people that are affected? When will costs be incurred and benefits received? Even an informal BCA, which does not monetize all (or any) of the costs and benefits, can be illuminating and help us develop and choose better policies.

■———— **Case 4.2** ————■

Performing a BCA

1. List all the important benefits of a policy.
   - Foregone benefits are costs (giving up parking to get a tennis court is a cost).

2. List all the important costs of a policy.
   - Avoided costs are benefits (avoiding sick days is a benefit).

3. Remember that costs and benefits to *all* members of society are counted except those to *criminals* (unless the primary intent of the policy is to criminalize or decriminalize or otherwise directly affect criminals).
   - If your manager wants costs and benefits only for people within a particular region, plan to show both full costs and benefits and the requested subset.
   - Remember that "all members of society" includes future generations.

4. Double-check that you haven't double-counted.
   - Remember that transfers have no net benefits.
     ◦ Taxes are transfers.
   - If one benefit or cost is a subset of another, don't count them both.

5. Monetize all the benefits and costs that you can, and retain unmonetized benefits and costs in their own units.
   - For items that are bought and sold in markets, the costs and benefits can usually be determined based on market prices.
   - Workers' wages are a cost.
     ◦ In conditions of full employment, the cost of workers is the market wage.
       – If, however, city workers are paid above the market wage, you may need to include the budgetary cost.
     ◦ The cost of hiring the unemployed is below the market wage but above zero.
       – Remember that new projects are unlikely to hire only the unemployed.
   - Multiplier effects, like all secondary effects, usually should not be counted.
   - For things that are not bought and sold in markets, including pure public goods or externalities:
     ◦ when available, use plug-in shadow prices;
     ◦ use revealed preferences, such as via hedonic models or corrective purchases (such as buying thicker window coverings to block out light);
     ◦ for health effects, use costs of treatment and value of days;
     ◦ for lives, use accepted expert assessments of the value of a statistical life (such as the U.S. EPA's estimate) or compute cost per life saved.
       – If the quality or duration of lives saved is an issue, use QALYs.
       – Remember that revealed preferences in the U.S. indicate that children's lives are more highly valued than adults' lives.
       – Remember that equity concerns require that all lives of the same basic type (that is, of the same age, quality, and risk level) should be valued the same.

(continued)

Case 4.2 *(continued)*

    ◦ Use the Contingent Valuation Method or other sophisticated survey methods (see Chapter 10).
    ◦ Remember that the values placed on these things are likely to vary by society.

6. Determine when each cost and benefit will be received.

7. Discount all costs and benefits that will be received in the future, and/or compute the Internal Rate of Return (IRR).
   • Since discount rates can be politically contentious, it is a good idea to give a range of discount rates when they are used directly, or use the IRR.
   • Remember that discount rates decline in the long run (see Table 4.4).

8. Highlight all uncertainty in the BCA.
   • Perform sensitivity analysis.
   • If Existence Values are important to the analysis, show the different results when they are and are not included.

9. Remember to include all unmonetized costs and benefits in the final accounting.

10. If Net Benefits are positive, or if the cost per unmonetized benefit is reasonable for that type of benefit, recommend the policy.
   • If competing policies exist, recommend the one with highest net benefits.
   • If more than one policy is possible, recommend all with positive net benefits.
   • If more than one policy is possible but there is a budget constraint, recommend the combination of policies that meets the budget constraint and results in the highest net benefits.

DISCUSSION QUESTION AND EXERCISES

1. Go to the *Journal of Policy Analysis and Management*, vol. 11, no. 1 (1992), pp. 131–132, and read the scenario. Discuss what the principles of policy analysis indicate is the appropriate response to the question asked.
2. Using Excel or some similar program, compute the NPV of the stream of benefits for the tennis court.
3. Using Excel or some similar program, compute the IRR for the tennis court.

RECOMMENDED WEBSITES

King, D.M., and M.J. Mazzotta. 2000. Ecosystem Valuation. Funded by the U.S. Department of Agriculture National Resources Conservation Service and the National Oceanographic and Atmospheric Administration. http://www.ecosystemvaluation.

org/default.htm. From the website: "This website describes how economists value the beneficial ways that ecosystems affect people—ecosystem valuation."

Tufts Medical Center. 2010. Cost-Effectiveness Analysis Registry. The Center for the Evaluation of Value and Risk in Health, Institute for Clinical Research and Health Policy Studies. https://research.tufts-nemc.org/cear4/. From the website: "By browsing our interactive website, you can learn about the latest published cost-effectiveness analyses."

U.S. Department of Labor. n.d. CPI Inflation Calculator. Bureau of Labor Statistics. http://www.bls.gov/data/inflation_calculator.htm.

U.S. Environmental Protection Agency. 2011. Guidelines for Preparing Economic Analyses. National Center for Environmental Economics. http://yosemite.epa.gov/ee/epa/eed.nsf/webpages/Guidelines.html. From the website: "EPA's *Guidelines for Preparing Economic Analyses* establish a sound scientific framework for performing economic analyses of environmental regulations and policies."

NOTES

1. In cases where exact price-quantity trade-offs are key to the policy under consideration, someone trained in econometrics should perform a more sophisticated estimate of the demand curve. Alternatively, in some cases, published elasticities (defined in Chapter 3) can provide the needed information.

2. Remember from your algebra class that anything taken to the 0th power is equal to 1.

3. The word "hedonic" means "relating to or considered in terms of pleasant (or unpleasant) sensation" (New Oxford American Dictionary, 2009).

4. In 1986, the exchange rate between Canadian and U.S. dollars was approximately 1.7 Canadian dollars to one U.S. dollar (data360, 2011).

5. If an analyst reports the cost per life saved rather than net benefits, then technically the analysis is a Cost-Effectiveness Analysis, rather than a Benefit-Cost Analysis.

6. Be sure to consider pages 100–101 from Boardman et al. (2006).

REFERENCES

Associated Press. 2008. How to value life? EPA devalues its estimate. MSNBC.com, July 10. http://www.msnbc.msn.com/id/25626294/ (accessed January 4, 2011).

Bell, W.J., Jr., and L.W. Labaree, eds. 1956. *Mr. Franklin: A Selection from His Personal Letters*. New Haven, CT: Yale University Press.

Boardman, A.E., D.H. Greenberg, A.R. Vining and, D.L. Weimer. 1996. *Cost-Benefit Analysis: Concepts and Practice*. Upper Saddle River, NJ: Prentice Hall.

———. 2006. *Cost-Benefit Analysis: Concepts and Practice*, 3rd ed. Upper Saddle River, NJ: Pearson/Prentice Hall.

City of Tempe, Arizona. 2009. Adult impromptu tennis programs: Just drop in and play! http://www.tempe.gov/tennis/General%20Info/impromptu%20programs.htm (accessed September 16, 2009).

CopperWynd. 2009. Tennis lesson fees. http://copperwynd.com/Arizona-Tennis-Resorts/Arizona-Tennis-Fees.html (accessed September 16, 2009).

Cost-Effectiveness Analysis Registry. n.d. FAQ #6: What is the acceptable cost/QALY threshold? Center for the Evaluation of Value and Risk in Health, Institute for Clinical Research and Health Policy Studies, Tufts Medical Center. https://research.tufts-nemc.org/cear4/SearchingtheCEARegistry/FAQs.aspx (accessed January 6, 2011).

data360. 2011. Foreign exchange rate Canada/U.S. http://www.data360.org/dsg.aspx?Data_Set_Group_Id=60&page=2&count=100 (accessed January 4, 2011).

Dewees, D.N., and R.J. Daniels. 1986. The cost of protecting occupational health: The asbestos case. *Journal of Human Resources*, 21, 3 (Summer), 381–396.

essortment. 2002. Tennis information: Clay tennis court maintenance. http://www.essortment.com/hobbies/claytenniscour_sajt.htm (accessed September 16, 2009).

Federal Reserve Bank of New York, 2008. The price of land in the New York metropolitan area. *Current Issues in Economics and Finance: Second District Highlights*, 14, 3. By A. Haughwout, J. Orr, and D. Bedoll. http://www.newyorkfed.org/research/current_issues/ci14-3.html (accessed September 2, 2011).

Feinberg, K. 2008. What is the value of a human life? *This I Believe*, NPR, May 25. http://www.npr.org/templates/story/story.php?storyId=90760725 (accessed January 4, 2011).

Fernandes, E. 2009. Sharia law UK: Mail on Sunday gets exclusive access to a British Muslim court. MailOnline, July 4. http://www.dailymail.co.uk/news/article-1197478/Sharia-law-UK—How-Islam-dispensing-justice-side-British-courts.html (accessed January 4, 2011).

Feser, E.J., and G.D. Cassidy. 1996. Rethinking state rail policy: The benefits of rail preservation include more than jobs. *Policy Studies Journal*, 24, 1, 57–73.

Franklin, B. 1772. Benjamin Franklin's 1772 letter to Joseph Priestly. In *Mr. Franklin: A Selection from His Personal Letters*, ed. W.J. Bell, Jr., and L.W. Labaree. New Haven, CT: Yale University Press, 1956. http://www.procon.org/viewbackgroundresource.asp?resourceID=1474 (accessed August 1, 2009).

Hahn, R.W., and C.R. Sunstein. 2002. A new executive order for improving federal regulation? Deeper and wider cost-benefit analysis. John M. Olin Law & Economics Working Paper No. 150 (2d series), April. Available at SSRN: http://papers.ssrn.com/sol3/papers.cfm?abstract_id=309754.

Hammitt, J.K., and K. Haninger. 2010. Valuing fatal risks to children and adults: Effects of disease, latency, and risk aversion. *Journal of Risk and Uncertainty*, 40, 1, 57–83.

Hanley, N., and C.L. Spash. 1993. *Cost-Benefit Analysis and the Environment*. Cheltenham, UK: Edward Elgar.

Harvard Center for Risk Analysis. 1998. Gains in life expectancy from medical interventions. *Risk in Perspective*, 6, 8, 1–4.

———. 2001. The Mexico project. *Risk in Perspective*, 9, 1, 1–4.

———. 2003. Valuing health: Quality-adjusted life years or willingness to pay? *Risk in Perspective*, 11, 1, 1–6.

Haughwout, A., J. Orr, and D. Bedoll. 2008. The price of land in the New York metropolitan area. *Current Issues in Economics and Finance*, 14, 3, 1–7.

Kahane, C.J. 2004. Cost per life saved by the federal motor vehicle safety standards. NHTSA Report Number DOT HS 809 835, December. http://www.nhtsa.gov/cars/rules/regrev/evaluate/809835.html (accessed January 4, 2011).

King, D.M., and M.J. Mazzotta. 2000. Ecosystem Valuation Website: Methods, Section 3. http://www.ecosystemvaluation.org/hedonic_pricing.htm (accessed January 3, 2011).

Microsoft Office. 2004. Help: NPV, IRR. Microsoft® Excel® 2004 for Mac, Version 11.5. (accessed September 19, 2009).

New Oxford American Dictionary. 2009. Version 2.1.3 [electronic]. Cupertino, CA: Apple, Inc., s.v. "hedonic," "indicator species."

OMB Watch. 2003. EPA blasted for "senior death discount." May 16. http://www.ombwatch.org/node/1407 (accessed January 4, 2011).

Opaluch, J.J., T. Grigalunas, J. Diamantides, M. Mazzotta, R. Johnston, 1999. Recreational and resource economic values for the Peconic estuary system. Report prepared for the Peconic Estuary Program, Suffolk Country Department of Health Services, Riverhead, NY, by Economic Analysis, Inc. http://cfpub.epa.gov/si/si_public_record_Report.cfm?dirEntryID=85730.

Premier Tennis Courts, Inc. 2003. Frequently asked questions. http://www.premiertenniscourts.com/faqs.htm (accessed September 16, 2009).

Rafiq, M., M.K. Shah, S. Gul, and A.U. Rahman. 2010. On the value of statistical life and injury: A review. *European Journal of Economics, Finance and Administrative Sciences*, 25, 7–15.

Rahmatian, M., and L. Cockerill. 2004. Airport noise and residential housing valuation in Southern California: A hedonic pricing approach. *International Journal of Environmental Science & Technology*, 1, 1 (Spring), 17–25. http://www.ceers.org/ijest/issues/full/v1/n1/101003.pdf (accessed January 3, 2011).

Rhoads, S.E. 1985. Do economists overemphasize monetary benefits? *Public Administration Review*, 45 (November/December), 815–820.

Schweizer, A. 2008. Sales and leases: IHOP has purchased a 30,000-square-foot parcel of unimproved land located within Sanderson Plaza in Hemet for $900,000. *San Diego Business Journal*, September 8. http://www.entrepreneur.com/tradejournals/article/186688980.html (accessed August 31, 2009).

Social Security Online. 2006. Actuarial Publications: Period life table. http://www.ssa.gov/OACT/STATS/table4c6.html (accessed January 6, 2011).

Stigler, G.J. 1970. The optimal enforcement of laws. *Journal of Political Economy*, 78 (May/June), 526–536.

Stokey, E., and R. Zeckhauser. 1978. *A Primer for Policy Analysis*. New York: W.W. Norton.

Trumbull, W.N. 1990. Who has standing in cost-benefit analysis? *Journal of Policy Analysis and Management*, 9, 2, 201–218.

U.K. Department for Business, Innovation and Skills (U.K. BIS). 2009. Nuclear power generation cost benefit analysis. http://www.berr.gov.uk/files/file31938.pdf (accessed September 19, 2009).

U.S. Census Bureau. 2011. U.S. and world population clocks. http://www.census.gov/main/www/popclock.html (accessed January 6, 2011).

U.S. Department of Health and Human Services. 2009. Adjusted costs and benefits for versions 5010, D.0 and 3.0. January 30. http://www.cms.hhs.gov/TransactionCodeSetsStands/Downloads/5010 DocketAdjustedCostBenefit.pdf (accessed September 19, 2009).

U.S. Department of Labor. n.d. Tables and calculators by subject: CPI inflation calculator. Bureau of Labor Statistics. http://www.bls.gov/data/inflation_calculator.htm (accessed January 4, 2011).

U.S. Environmental Protection Agency (EPA). 2009. Regulatory economic analysis at the EPA: 2.6. EPA guidance. National Center for Environmental Economics. http://yosemite.epa.gov/ee/epalib/riaepa.nsf/8a8e79bebcf3a3a0852565a500501ed5/6fb916798827ac10852567570079530b?Open Document (accessed September 19, 2009).

———. 2011. Frequently asked questions on mortality risk valuation. National Center for Environmental Economics. http://yosemite.epa.gov/ee/epa/eed.nsf/pages/MortalityRiskValuation.html#means (accessed January 4, 2011).

Viscusi, W.K. 2010. The heterogeneity of the value of statistical life: Introduction and overview. *Journal of Risk and Uncertainty*, 40, 1, 1–13.

Weimer, D., and A. Vining. 2009. *Investing in the Disadvantaged: Assessing the Benefits and Costs of Social Policies*. Georgetown University Press.

The White House. 1993. Executive Order #12866: Regulatory Planning and Review. Office of the Press Secretary, September 30. http://govinfo.library.unt.edu/npr/library/direct/orders/2646.html.

———. 2009. Memorandum for the Heads of Departments and Agencies from Jim Nussle, Director, Regarding 2009 Discount Rates for OMB Circular No. A-94. http://www.whitehouse.gov/sites/default/files/omb/memoranda/2011/m11-12.pdf.

Part II

Bridging Policy, Politics, Economics, Ecology, Media, and Communication

5 | Integrating Policy, Ecosystem Management, and Environmental Media

In Chapter 1, we introduced a conceptual model of the urban environmental policy system. Then, in Chapters 2 through 4, we presented policy analysis tools of particular relevance to the urban environmental system. This chapter is a pivot point, turning attention from a purely policy-analytic perspective and toward an ecosystem-management perspective. The ecosystem-management perspective integrates the policy perspective with a holistic ecological view and a citizen-engagement focus. The chapters following this one (1) introduce ecological factors of the three major environmental media (air, water, and land); (2) address specific media-based challenges in the urban environmental context; and (3) address citizen-engagement methods. This chapter forecasts the importance of the chapters to come. Additionally, using a holistic conception of interactions between air, water, and land and between the Natural, Concretion, and Social Systems, we present checklists that assist the urban administrator in adopting an ecosystem-management approach.

The main conceptual model outlined in Chapter 1 introduces two layers of the Physical System: the Natural System and the Concretion System. Within a policy and governance context, we outline in this chapter some major approaches to the management of ecosystems that are relevant for these two systems. Our goal is to highlight key issues that are important for an administrator or analyst to consider when making policy decisions about interactions of the Natural System and the Concretion System with the Social System.

Chapter 5, then, serves as a bridge between our conceptual model and the dynamics of the Social System that address policy issues related to air, water, land, and natural resources and their interactions. We begin by exploring some of the existing literature on the concepts of *ecosystem management* and *adaptive management*—two areas of research and practice that strive to blend social, ecological, and economic systems into one holistic perspective focused on solving environmental problems.

Since the 1980s, ecosystem management and adaptive management have helped to draw science into the environmental policy process. The multifaceted nature of ecosystem management and adaptive management make them particularly relevant for our discussion of the linkages between the Physical System, the Social System, and environmental policy decisions. In the next two sections, we provide an overview of the concepts and explore how they have contributed to a more holistic view of environmental policy in the United States.

ECOSYSTEM MANAGEMENT

Over the past three decades, the relationship between ecology and public policy has changed because of the increasing role of scientific uncertainty in environmental policy-making (Ludwig, Mangel, and Haddad, 2001). While earlier policy questions might have been solved simply by looking at the scientific technicalities of the issue, recent environmental problems are often plagued by scientific uncertainty (for example, international climate change policy negotiations). Ludwig and colleagues (2001) argue that this increased role of scientific uncertainty in environmental policymaking requires that we reexamine the methods used in decision making. For example, when policymakers use scientific data to support their decision-making processes, they can no longer ignore social, political, or ethical issues. Within this new context, strong disciplinary boundaries are less useful because uncertain environmental policy problems span the natural sciences, engineering, economics, politics, and ethics. This interdisciplinary approach to environmental policy problems has led managers and administrators to the two related tools of ecosystem management and adaptive management.

DEFINITION OF ECOSYSTEM MANAGEMENT

While many scholars have debated the definition of ecosystem management, Grumbine (1994) provides a comprehensive overview of the term and how it has been used historically. We use his definition of the term as the anchor for our discussion of the concept. According to Grumbine, ecosystem management

> . . . integrates scientific knowledge of ecological relationships within a complex sociopolitical and values framework toward the general goal of protecting native ecosystem integrity over the long term. (31)

Keeping this explanation in mind, we can explore some of the recent policy findings in the area of ecosystem management and how they apply to environmental policy debates.

TRENDS AND PRINCIPLES OF ECOSYSTEM MANAGEMENT

Stakeholder Collaboration

There has been a relatively recent push in the environmental policy community to decentralize the management of resources and encourage stakeholder collaboration through ecosystem-management approaches (Steel and Weber, 2001). Yet, as Steel and Weber outline, these management processes must have the support of local citizens to be successful. In 1998, the researchers conducted a survey and concluded that the public is relatively well informed about ecosystem management, with over half of the respondents being at least moderately informed about the concept (Steel and Weber, 2001). However, despite the public's reasonable level of knowledge about ecosystem management, the survey respondents did not fully support the concept. For example, Steel and Weber (2001) found that citizens living in urban areas tend to be more supportive of ecosystem management than are citizens living in rural areas. Given this discrepancy in support, it can be important for administrators to think about the type of institutional structure for ecosystem-management practices that would receive support from both groups (for example, maybe a more grassroots effort or maybe a more decentralized effort to receive support from citizens living in rural areas). Ecosystem management efforts in the U.S. Pacific Northwest have received more support across a variety of stakeholder groups if they are both collaborative and decentralized; this is in contrast to management efforts that are noncollaborative and more centralized (Steel and Weber, 2001). One important lesson that we can take from the Steel and Weber study is that the way an ecosystem-management effort is institutionalized and implemented can be directly related to the level of citizen support it receives. Chapters 10 and 11 discuss some methods of institutionalizing citizen participation.

Following this thread of stakeholder engagement, natural resource agencies in the United States have adopted ecosystem-management principles as a way to increase stakeholder involvement in resource management (Koontz and Bodine, 2008). Ecosystem management, according to Koontz and Bodine, calls for "management based on stakeholder collaboration; interagency cooperation; integration of scientific, social, and economic information; preservation of ecological processes; and adaptive management" (2008, 60). Their outline fits well with Grumbine's (1994) definition but provides more details. Given that ecosystem management has such an integrative and collaborative focus, adoption of this approach by governmental agencies often signals that the agency is prioritizing both stakeholder involvement and a holistic perspective for environmental management. Yet, there are challenges to the implementation of ecosystem management at an agency level. After conducting a survey with employees and stakeholders at several U.S. natural resource agencies, Koontz and Bodine (2008) found that the most significant agency barriers to the implementation of ecosystem management are those related to integrating political, legal, and cultural issues—not scientific issues.

Another aspect of stakeholder collaboration that can be addressed through an ecosystem-management approach involves dealing with large-scale, transboundary environmental problems. Management of transboundary environmental issues (such as air pollution that drifts across city or state lines) can require collaboration among a variety of stakeholders as well as the different owners of private property (for example when the management area crosses private ownership boundaries) (Thompson, Anderson, and Johnson, 2004). Yet, as Thompson and colleagues discuss, using this approach to deal with transboundary issues is not always easy. Antitrust laws often hinder the collaborative process because they do not allow industries to participate fully in the collaboration and to share information.

So if this is a difficult process, how should administrators and analysts go about including stakeholders in ecosystem-management processes? Keough and Blahna

(2006) prepared a comprehensive review of the collaborative environmental management and ecosystem-management literature to identify eight key principles that managers should implement for successful collaborative ecosystem management. These eight principles consist of the following:

> integrated and balanced goals, inclusive public involvement, stakeholder influence, consensus group approach, collaborative stewardship, monitoring and adaptive management, multidisciplinary data, and economic incentives. (1373)

With respect to integrated and balanced goals, Keough and Blahna argue that managers need to pay particular attention to ecosystem-management goals as they relate to ecological, economic, and social outcomes. These three goals should be balanced, and no single component should be left out of the management plan. Second, all stakeholder groups (regardless of their characteristics) should be included in the public involvement phase of the project. Third, Keough and Blahna believe that managers should strive to incorporate stakeholder input into the management plan rather than just listening to stakeholders and ultimately disregarding their ideas. Fourth, the process of implementing an ecosystem-management plan is typically more successful if stakeholders are encouraged to meet together and develop a consensus-based approach to dealing with the environmental problems. Fifth, ecosystem-management processes have a higher chance of success if stakeholders are personally invested in the decisions that are made—and if they remain involved in future management decisions as they occur. Sixth, Keough and Blahna argue that stakeholders should agree to the active monitoring of environmental and social outcomes of the management approach so the effectiveness of the process can be evaluated. This point is also related to the seventh recommendation, which focuses on making sure that all types of data—ecological, economic, and social—are included in the monitoring process. Finally, Keough and Blahna suggest that the management plan should be designed to include economic incentives for a variety of stakeholders, including the public, local communities, and the agencies.

Inclusiveness and Engaging the Public

Several environmental policy scholars have explained how ecosystem-management principles represent a significant shift from the incremental and fragmented approach of engaging the public that has been encouraged by the National Environmental Policy Act (NEPA) of 1969 (Phillips and Randolph, 2000; Thrower, 2006). The original goal of NEPA was to take an interdisciplinary and systematic approach to linking scientific information with public involvement for environmental decision making. Yet, many social scientists have criticized the NEPA process and argued that it does not include the public early enough in the planning process. Phillips and Randolph (2000) contend that federal agencies can overcome some of the shortcomings of the NEPA process by incorporating ecosystem-management principles in their decision making.

Many natural resource agencies have adopted the concept of ecosystem management over the past three decades (Rigg, 2001) as a way to overcome the weaknesses of the NEPA process that Phillips and Randolph (2000) outlined. Since there is no single definition of ecosystem management that is used across all organizations, however, Rigg reports that these adoption efforts often have been disappointing; different organizations might apply different guidelines when they implement ecosystem-management strategies. We can take some important lessons about the role of public involvement in ecosystem management from Rigg's (2001) findings. Specifically, she demonstrates that the implementation of ecosystem management is often weakened by unsatisfactory communication between stakeholders and managers, uncertainty in budgets, uncertainty in scientific research, and a variety of policy requirements that can slow down the implementation process. The solution she suggests for managers is to "(1) build confidence and trust in the process, (2) acknowledge bias, (3) reconcile policy and funding constraints with long-term planning, (4) invest in scientific research, data collection, and monitoring capacity, and (5) explore the relationship between values and science" (78). Even though a holistic ecosystem-management approach to environmental problems does not solve the complex issue of public involvement in the policy process, one of the goals of this approach is to encourage stakeholder collaboration and involvement—and the explicit inclusion of the public as one of those stakeholder groups.

Dealing with Scientific Uncertainty and Incompleteness

One instance in which ecosystem management has been particularly useful for policy-makers is in the face of "issue incompleteness." Roe and Van Eeten (2001) distinguish the concept of (1) uncertainty from (2), complexity and (3) issue incompleteness. Even though some scientific policy issues might have all three of these characteristics, the authors describe how policy analysts should try to distinguish between these concepts when making decisions. They provide a guideline for making this distinction:

> Issues are uncertain when causal processes are unclear or not easily understood. Issues are complex when they are more numerous, varied and interrelated than before. Issues are incomplete when interrupted, postponed or left otherwise unfulfilled in important aspects. (111)

Roe and Van Eeten also note that, of the three concepts, issue incompleteness is the one most often ignored by policy analysts and theorists. Policymaking under the condition of issue incompleteness often requires interorganizational coordination—a concept that is studied more extensively in public administration than it is in policy analysis. From this work by Roe and Van Eeten, we can take the lesson that administrators and analysts should pay as much attention to issue incompleteness as they do to uncertainty and complexity—particularly in the case of environmental policy.

To address the concepts of issue uncertainty, complexity and incompleteness for environmental policy problems, analysts and administrators often need to gather the latest scientific data about the problem. Experts can provide scientific data about environmental problems for the policymaking process, but local knowledge from citizens can also be important for policymaking. Olsson and Folke (2001) stress the importance of including local ecological knowledge in natural resource management. They argue that "sustainable use of resources requires that management practices and institutions take into account the dynamics of the ecosystem" (85). As many environmental administrators know, local stakeholders often have substantial—and extremely useful—knowledge about the management of local resources. This knowledge can be helpful for ecological resilience if policymakers explicitly include it in their decision-making processes. Members of local communities frequently have unique scientific and/or social insights that should not be ignored when decisions are being made about resources within the community.

COMMON MISTAKES IN ECOSYSTEM MANAGEMENT

Environmental policy analysts and managers often find themselves repeating the same mistakes over and over as they tackle natural resource management and policy decisions. Folke and colleagues (2002) have outlined the two most common mistakes, both of which are linked with an insufficiently holistic approach to environmental policy. First, administrators and managers often erroneously assume that ecosystems respond to human intervention in a linear and predictable fashion; on the contrary, empirical evidence shows that because Social Systems and Natural Systems are coupled together, they behave in unpredictable and nonlinear ways. Second, the authors point to the mistaken assumption made by some administrators that Natural Systems can be managed in a vacuum, independent of Human and Social Systems; in reality, they cannot. The lesson from this work is that managers and administrators should embrace "flexible and open institutions and multilevel governance systems that allow for learning and increase adaptive capacity without foreclosing future development options" (Folke et al., 2002, 437). This is similar to the approach taken in adaptive management, which encourages experimentation with different policy tools combined with careful monitoring of their outcomes. We explain more about adaptive management later in this chapter.

BARRIERS AND OVERCOMING THEM

Choosing the "Appropriate" Institutional Design

As we have outlined so far, there are many challenges to implementing a holistic ecosystem-management approach for environmental policy problems. One of the most difficult challenges to overcome is the lack of awareness that administrators and analysts have about the institutional design issues surrounding ecosystem management (Imperial, 1999). According to Imperial (1999), exploring the role of institutional design in ecosystem management should help managers better understand the relationship between science and values during the decision-making process. Choosing the correct institutional design for the implementation of ecosystem management can play a large part in how successful the project is from ecological, political, and social perspectives. But what, exactly, is the "correct" or "appropriate" institutional design? Imperial (1999) defines a successful institutional design as the "right balance between federal (vertical) and local (horizontal) control in order to collectively achieve federal, state, and local objectives" (461). For example, some environmental policy issues are dealt with most effectively by using a decentralized and local institutional approach; others, however, require a more centralized governmental solution. We encourage you to think critically about your particular ecological, social, and political environment; it is unlikely that one institutional framework will be the best solution in all cases. Imperial concludes that "ecosystem-based management is as much a problem of 'governance' involving multiple organizations located at different levels of government as it is a question of science and designing effective policies for managing natural resources" (461).

Now that we have provided an overview of the concept of ecosystem management, we introduce the related topic of adaptive management, which is one tool that agencies or administrators can use to implement an ecosystem management approach.

ADAPTIVE MANAGEMENT

The term "adaptive management" was first coined in the 1970s by the Canadian ecologist C.S. Holling (1978). While there have been many interpretations of his definition within the ecology, economics, and policy communities since then, the concept generally describes an approach to managing ecosystems in a way that recognizes their complexity and dynamism. Consequently, the management of these systems should utilize flexible experiments that allow managers and scientists to react to changes in the ecological system by adapting their management and policy schemes. Given this, adaptive management can be particularly attractive in environmental policy cases that involve a considerable amount of scientific uncertainty (Umemoto and Suryanata, 2006).

Adaptive management is a process that involves incremental management steps; these steps are regularly evaluated to determine if the outcomes are desirable at various time intervals (Moir and Block, 2001). One of the strengths of this approach is that it is an iterative process with a strong feedback loop. As Moir and Block (2001) describe, if the outcomes of the intermediate management steps deviate from the desired scientific and policy outcomes, managers can adjust their activities at that time instead of waiting for the project to be finished. Thus, successful adaptive management requires the regular monitoring of outcomes and a modulated management response to those outcomes. One important point is that managers and administrators should not respond too rapidly, but rather focus on a longer-term cycle when they make decisions for adaptive management (Moir and Block, 2001)—that is, using a time frame that is similar to the ecosystem's dynamic cycle. If administrators or managers respond too quickly to short-term ecosystem outcomes, they might make decisions that are not optimal for the long-term management of the natural resource. Therefore, the Moir and Block (2001) vision of adaptive management requires a careful balancing act that is focused on both short-term outcomes and long-term goals.

How have adaptive management concepts been used by administrators and decision makers since the term was coined in the 1970s? Typically, policymakers and decision makers employ adaptive management to deal with scientific uncertainty about environmental problems (Walters, 2007). Walters defines the concept of adaptive management as the idea that "policy choices should be treated as deliberate, large-scale experiments; hence, policy choice should be treated at least partly as a problem of scientific experimental design" (Walters, 2007, 304). In this way, the concept of adaptive management explicitly links the three components of our model (Natural, Concretion, and Social) when dealing with natural resource policy issues.

Weaknesses of Adaptive Management

Despite the promise of adaptive management, sometimes these efforts fail. The difficulties are important to consider, particularly given how much time and money are required to successfully implement an adaptive management "experiment." Walters (2007) argues that failures are most often due to institutional problems—in particular, the unavailability of management resources for implementing the social/scientific experiment, hesitancy on the part of decision makers to embrace the uncertainty in the adaptive-management process, and a lack of strong leadership in carrying out the new vision for adaptive management.

Even though the benefits of adaptive management have been outlined by many scholars, Koontz and Thomas (2006) maintain that there is little evidence that this approach is better for the environment than more centralized management strategies. They believe the most important question of collaborative environmental management is, "To what extent does collaboration lead to improved environmental outcomes?" (111)—and they argue that the environmental policy community must ask whether adaptive-management processes lead to better outcomes for environmental quality than other methods, such as command-and-control regulations or market-based environmental policy tools. Since much of the previous research on policy outcomes of adaptive management has focused on social aspects of policy problems rather than scientific and environmental outcomes, Koontz and Thomas (2006) encourage analysts and administrators that implement adaptive management strategies to (1) require and support the monitoring of environmental policy outcomes, and (2) adopt standards for measuring environmental outcomes so data can be compared across cases.

Viewing the process from another angle, the question becomes, In what particular cases might adaptive management *not* provide the best policy solution? According to Roe and Van Eeten (2001), when there is a conflict "between rapid human population growth, increased resource extraction, and the rising demand for better environmental amenities" (195), then adaptive management might not be the best method. Additionally, the expensive nature of implementing an adaptive management approach means that it might not work well if an agency does not have the financial and time resources to successfully implement this type of scientific and policy experiment. To ensure improved ecosystem health, administrators should think about how to blend a variety of approaches to ecosystem management.

There are a variety of alternatives to an adaptive management approach. For example, Umemoto and Suryanata (2006) used the case of Hawaiian mariculture development to explore the role of informal social contracts in environmental policy decision making. When there are no formal institutions in place to implement adaptive-management goals, informal social contracts (supplemented by formal regulatory frameworks) can be a better option than adaptive management. Even though the planning field traditionally has not focused on informal social controls, they can be useful in environmental policy situations that involve scientific uncertainty and cultural diversity.

Mariculture is "the cultivation of fish or other marine life for food" (New Oxford American Dictionary, 2009).

So far in this chapter, we have introduced the definitions of ecosystem management and adaptive management and provided some guidelines from the literature on when they might be useful approaches for environmental policymaking. The most important take-home message of our discussion of ecosystem and adaptive management, however, is the focus on holistic management that both approaches adopt. To continue this theme and help link the Natural (ecological), Social, and Concretion Systems in a definitive way, we revisit our conceptual model and provide some checklists you might find useful as you incorporate this holistic view into your management and analysis decisions.

THE HOLISTIC CONSIDERATION OF AIR, WATER, AND LAND WITHIN THE CONCEPTUAL MODEL

Now that we have explored the definitions of adaptive management and ecosystem management—and how these techniques can link social and ecological systems for environmental policy—we revisit our system-based framework to explore how those linkages are important for the three environmental media that we cover in the next chapters: air, water, and land. The specific components that exist within the Physical System are laid out in Table 5.1.

Our goal here is threefold: (1) to outline the broad categories of plants, animals, and habitats that exist within the Natural System; (2) to link these categories with the Social and Concretion Systems; and (3) to generate checklists for analysts and administrators to use before making policy decisions that might have an impact on the urban environment. As noted in Chapter 1, our conceptual model assumes that interaction between systems—and within systems—occurs regularly. Using the checklists in Figures 5.1 through 5.3, combined with the information in Chapters 6, 7, and 8, analysts and administrators are more likely to achieve holistic urban environmental policy thinking that is in line with the philosophies of ecosystem management and adaptive management.

With respect to air as a resource, the Natural System components of the model include the ambient air we breathe, naturally occurring particulate matter, and any naturally occurring chemicals that have an impact on air quality (either positively or negatively). The components of the Concretion System include human-generated chemicals and human-generated particulate matter that impact air quality. As with water, the relevant policy issues for air focus largely on air pollution, human-health issues and ecosystem-health issues.

Regarding water as a natural resource, the components of the Natural System include surface water (such as lakes and rivers), groundwater, and existing aquatic habitats and ecosystems. On the other hand, the Concretion System components of the model include the water delivery system, the wastewater system, and any artificial bodies of water. From a water perspective, the key issues that local policymakers have to address within an urban environment include issues of water availability, water pol-

Table 5.1

Components of the Physical System

Ecological resource	Urban environmental issues	Components of the Natural System	Components of the Concretion System
Air	• Air pollution • Human health issues • Ecosystem health issues	• Ambient air • Naturally occurring particulate matter • Naturally occurring chemicals	• Human-generated particulate matter • Human-generated chemicals
Water	• Water availability • Water pollution • Human health issues • Ecosystem health issues	• Surface water • Groundwater • Aquatic habitats and ecosystems	• Water delivery system • Wastewater treatment system • Artificial bodies of water
Land	• Sprawl/land development Brownfields • Soil erosion • Ecosystem health issues	• Soil • Vegetation • Animals • Habitat and ecosystems on land • Humans	• Service infrastructure (e.g., electrical, water, trash, transportation, energy, and sanitation) • Buildings (including industrial, commercial, residential) • Transportation vehicles (e.g., cars, subway systems, buses, motorcycles)

lution, and human health. Water habitat health (suitability for nonhuman animals), though not yet a key issue, is becoming increasingly important as cities take a more comprehensive approach to sustainability.

To review our framework with respect to land resources, the general components of our model's Natural System include soil, vegetation, animals, habitat and ecosystems, and humans. These components often overlap with each other (for example, animals need habitat to survive) and across other components of the model (for example, humans are part of both the Natural System and the Social System). With respect to land, the Concretion System contains service infrastructure (for example, electrical, water, trash, transportation, other energy, and sewerage), buildings (including industrial, commercial, residential), and transportation vehicles (for example, cars, subway systems, buses, light rail systems, and motorcycles). The urban environmental issues that are relevant for local policymakers with respect to land as a natural resource include land development (also encompassing issues of sprawl), brownfields (contaminated sites), and soil erosion.

One point that should be apparent from Table 5.1 is that many of the policy-relevant issues for these three resources are related to either the *quantity* or *quality* of the natural resource: (1) how much of the resource is available for use, and (2) the environmental quality of those resources. Therefore, most of the policy alternatives that we explore for natural resources in an urban environment have to do with quantity and quality issues.

RELATIONSHIPS BETWEEN THE SOCIAL AND PHYSICAL COMPONENTS

When exploring the holistic philosophies of ecosystem management and adaptive management for environmental policymaking, it is important to consider the explicit relationships between the social and the physical components of our model (for example, the Natural and Concretion Systems). How are these systems linked? And why might those connections be important for administrators? Since this is not an environmental science text, we are most interested in exploring the physical components of the system only as they relate directly to the Social System. In Figure 1.3 (see Chapter 1), within the Social System we made a clear distinction between the range of players involved and how they vary on the public-private continuum. As you might remember, we outlined the most-private entities as beginning with individuals, families, neighborhoods, and firms. The list continued with attention on less-private entities such as clubs and churches. Even though our management of the Natural System from a policy perspective has an impact on all levels of players on this continuum, the entity that oversees that management (and determines the regulation of natural resources) is the governmental unit that is located at the bottom of the Social System schematic. Throughout the policy process, then, the government manages issues of resource quality and resource quantity for the urban environment. The actors in this policy process are outlined at the top of the Social System.

The Natural and Concretion Systems relate to the Social System through the policy process in varying ways. Different policy alternatives will likely have different positive and negative environmental impacts on the components of the Natural System and the components of the Concretion System. Even though we make policies within the Social System, we can implement and enforce urban environmental policies within the Natural, Concretion, or Social Systems—and usually policies affect some combination of all of these. Therefore, it is imperative that administrators and analysts think about the impacts of proposed policies on each system; in short, policymakers must take a holistic view rather than a fragmented one.

Let's consider an example to make this process clearer. Assume the state of Arizona has been asked by the U.S. Environmental Protection Agency to outline a State Implementation Plan (SIP) for achieving air quality standards that comply with the Clean Air Act. As part of the SIP, the Arizona Department of Environmental Quality (ADEQ) might propose stricter emissions standards for vehicles operating in the Phoenix metropolitan area (that is, a location where there are many on-road vehicles and significant air pollution problems associated with particulate matter and ozone levels). Before adopting stricter command-and-control standards, administrators and analysts would need to consider the impacts of the policy on the Social, Natural, and Concretion Systems. With respect to the Social System, individuals will be affected by this new policy because they will have to comply with stricter air emissions standards, which will place an additional financial burden on people who have older vehicles. (On average, older vehicles have been shown to produce the highest levels of air emissions.) This might also bring up an equity issue within the Social System, because people with older vehicles might be disproportionately less well off and therefore less able to pay for any repairs that might be required as a result of the new vehicle emissions standards. Another effect on the Social System is the positive benefit of additional repairs for firms that perform maintenance and testing of vehicles in the Phoenix area. So, while some entities within the Social System will benefit financially from the policy, others will be injured by it. As we know, however, any Benefit-Cost Analysis of this proposal does not have to address the issue of compensation between the winners and losers from the policy. In other words, the ADEQ would not be obliged to require that the winners (that is, maintenance companies) pay the losers (for example, individuals with higher-emitting vehicles); still, for reasons of efficiency, equity, and politics, it is important for analysts to consider all of the players within the Social System, as well as the potential impacts of the policy change on those groups.

A policy proposal like this one would also have impacts on the Natural and Concretion Systems. As we mentioned earlier, for air resources, the natural components of the system include ambient air, naturally occurring particulate matter, and naturally occurring chemicals. Components of the Concretion System include human-generated particulate matter and human-generated chemicals. Parts of each of these systems would be affected by stricter standards for vehicle emissions. The part of the Natural System that would receive the largest impact is ambient air, but analysts should still consider whether there would be any impacts on water and land. The parts of the Concretion System that would change with the policy would be a reduction in human-generated particulate matter and human-generated chemicals. A possible unintended consequence would be an increased rate of turnover in the fleet, possibly leading to more junked cars on the land. Since the policy would be proposed as part of a larger state-level compliance with federal air quality standards, one goal of the policy would be to reduce the emissions of air pollutions. Thus, the ambient air should become cleaner, particularly in the Phoenix metro area where the policy would be implemented, but it might improve air quality for areas downwind as well. As for the Concretion System, the adoption of the policy would reduce the amount of influx of human-generated particulate matter and chemicals into the environment from vehicles.

In order to think comprehensively about the impacts of this policy on the Social, Natural and Concretion Systems, an analyst should explore how the proposed policy would affect all components of the conceptual model, both positively and negatively. For this case, within the Social System, there are positive and negative financial impacts of the policy, and those are spread across different groups of people. As we have seen, however, the expected impacts on both the Natural System and the Concretion System are largely positive, with improvements in ambient air quality and a reduction in the emissions of human-generated chemicals and particulate matter. However, in keeping with adaptive-management practices, the program should include a monitoring system and incorporate a flexible design that can adapt to changes based on the latest findings. In this book, our goal is to stress the importance of considering the impacts of the proposed policy from a holistic perspective, because we believe that effects of policies on *all three* systems often are overlooked—or at least not often considered together by analysts and administrators.

CHECKLISTS FOR ADMINISTRATORS

Stepping back from this particular example, we next outline a set of checklists that can help analysts and administrators make holistic policy decisions about the urban environment—in other words, decisions that take into account the Natural, Concretion, and Social Systems as an integrated, interactive whole. These checklists can serve as guidelines for use of the policy tools presented earlier in this book and more richly described within the contexts of air, water, and land later in this book. Before a local decision maker employs a tool for policy change within the urban environment, he or she should go through this set of checklists to ensure that holistic consideration of the environmental issues has been made in advance.

First, Figure 5.1 provides a checklist for the Natural System that can be used by local decision makers as they evaluate the impacts of proposed policies on the components of the Natural System. Next, Figures 5.2 and 5.3 provide additional checklists for the Concretion System and the Social System, respectively. We encourage analysts to use these lists to think about possible policy options from a holistic perspective that includes an explicit focus on the feedback loops between the Natural, Concretion, and Social Systems, as outlined in our conceptual model. This is a necessary, though not sufficient, step toward ecosystem management.

Figure 5.1 **Checklist for the Natural System**

Which air, water, and land resources will be affected by the proposed policy?
____ Which natural resources will be positively impacted by the policy (with higher quantities of the resources or with improved quality of the resources)?
____ Which natural resources will be negatively impacted by the policy (with lower quantities of the resources or with decreased quality of the resources)?

Air Resources
____ How will the proposed policy impact ambient air quality, naturally occurring particulate matter in the air, and naturally occurring chemicals in the air?
____ Are there feasible ways that negative impacts can be mitigated?
____ Are there ways to expand any positive impacts on these air-based systems?

Water Resources
____ How will the proposed policy impact surface water, groundwater, and aquatic habitats and ecosystems?
____ Are there feasible ways that negative impacts can be mitigated?
____ Are there ways to expand any positive impacts on these water-based systems?

Land Resources
____ How will the proposed policy impact soil, vegetation, animals, land-based habitats and ecosystems, and human health?
____ Are there feasible ways that negative impacts can be mitigated?
____ Are there ways to expand any positive impacts on these land-based systems?

Policy Alternatives and Tools
____ What other policies or versions of the policy might feasibly improve the quality and quantity of land resources? Water resources? Air resources?
____ How does the choice of policy tools (covered in Chapter 3) impact the quality of land, water, and air natural resources?

Interactions
____ How might land, water, or air affect any of the other two?

Adaptive Management
____ Is the policy sufficiently flexible to allow for needed change?

Figure 5.2 **Checklist for the Concretion System**

Air
____ How will the proposed policy impact levels of human-generated particulate matter in the air and human-generated chemicals in the air?
____ Are there any feasible ways that negative impacts can be mitigated?
____ Are there ways to expand any positive impacts on these air-based systems?

Water
____ How will the proposed policy impact water delivery systems, wastewater treatment systems, and artificial bodies of water?
____ Are there any feasible ways that negative impacts can be mitigated?
____ Are there ways to expand any positive impacts on these water-based systems?

Land
____ How will the proposed policy impact service infrastructure, the built environment (e.g., office space, residential buildings), transportation systems, and planning (e.g., sprawl)?
____ Are there any feasible ways that negative impacts can be mitigated?
____ Are there ways to expand any positive impacts on these land-based systems?

Policy Alternatives and Tools
____ What other policies or versions of the policy might feasibly improve the quality of existing infrastructure in the urban environment?

Interactions
____ How might impacts in air, water, land, or affect any of the other two?

Adaptive Management
____ Is the policy sufficiently flexible to allow for needed change?

Figure 5.3 **Checklist for the Social System**

Equity Issues
____ Which groups would be most disadvantaged by the proposed policy?
____ Will discriminated-against minority groups be disproportionately disadvantaged? (Chapter 9)
____ Which groups would receive the most benefit from the proposed policy?
____ How does the choice of policy tools (Chapter 3) impact the outcome for various disadvantaged groups?
____ Is it likely that disadvantaged groups will be compensated by the groups that benefit from the proposed policy? If so, how? If not, is there a feasible way to encourage this type of activity?

Administrative Issues
____ Is the proposed policy administratively feasible?
____ Are there sufficient human resources to implement and enforce (if needed) the policy?
____ Are there sufficient resources for monitoring air-based, water-based, and land based systems?
____ Is the organization with administrative responsibility able to adapt as needed?

Political Issues
____ What is the landscape of political support and opposition for the proposed policy, including among citizens? (Chapter 10)
____ Are there ways to increase political support (for a desirable policy) or opposition (for an undesirable policy)? (Chapter 11)

Economic Issues
____ Are there sufficient financial resources to adopt and implement the policy?
____ Does the policy have positive net benefits?
____ How would the use of different economic policy tools yield support for alternative policies?

Interactions
____ Might changes in the Social System unexpectedly impact the Natural or Concretion Systems?

CONCLUSION

In Chapter 3, we outlined a series of generic policy instruments that are used regularly by analysts to choose between policy alternatives. Many of these tools are economic in nature. In Chapter 4, our discussion of Benefit-Cost Analysis emphasized the social-welfare-economic outcomes of policies that are being considered as alternatives. Yet, this chapter stresses our belief that there are additional considerations for urban environmental policymaking beyond economic analysis. Even though the economic analysis of policy alternatives often functions as the cornerstone for policy choices and decisions, we hope that our conceptual framework, the checklists presented in this chapter, and the information in the chapters to come help administrators and analysts consider holistically the impacts of proposed policies on the Natural System, the Concretion System, and the Social System.

REFERENCES

Folke, C. et al. 2002. Resilience and sustainable development: Building adaptive capacity in a world of transformations. *Ambio,* 31, 5, 437–440.

Grumbine, R.E. 1994. What is ecosystem management? *Conservation Biology*, 8, 1, 27–38.

Holling, C.S., ed. 1978. *Adaptive Environmental Assessment and Management.* New York: Wiley.

Imperial, M.T. 1999. Institutional analysis and ecosystem-based management: The institutional analysis and development framework. *Environmental Management*, 24, 4, 449–465.

Keough, H.L., and D.J. Blahna. 2006. Achieving integrative, collaborative ecosystem management. *Conservation Biology*, 20, 5, 1373–1382.

Koontz, T.M., and J. Bodine. 2008. Implementing ecosystem management in public agencies: Lessons from the U.S. Bureau of Land Management and the Forest Service. *Conservation Biology*, 22, 60–69.

Koontz, T.M., and C.W. Thomas. 2006. What do we know and need to know about the environmental outcomes of collaborative management? *Public Administration Review,* 66, 111–121.

Ludwig, D., M. Mangel, and B. Haddad. 2001. Ecology, conservation, and public policy. *Annual Review of Ecology and Systematics,* 32, 481–517.

Moir, W.H., and W.M. Block. 2001. Adaptive management on public lands in the United States: Commitment or rhetoric? *Environmental Management*, 28, 2, 141–148.

New Oxford American Dictionary. 2009. Version 2.1.3 [electronic]. Cupertino, CA: Apple, Inc., s.v. "mariculture."

Olsson, P., and C. Folke. 2001. Local ecological knowledge and institutional dynamics for ecosystem management: A study of Lake Racken Watershed, Sweden. *Ecosystems*, 4, 2, 85–104.

Phillips, C.G., and J. Randolph. 2000. The relationship of ecosystem management to NEPA and its goals. *Environmental Management*, 26, 1, 1–12.

Rigg, C.M. 2001. Orchestrating ecosystem management: Challenges and lessons from Sequoia National Forest. *Conservation Biology,* 15, 1, 78–90.

Roe, E., and M. Van Eeten. 2001. Threshold-based resource management: A framework for comprehensive ecosystem management. *Environmental Management*, 27, 2, 195–214.

Steel, B.S., and E. Weber. 2001. Ecosystem management, decentralization, and public opinion. *Global Environmental Change—Human and Policy Dimensions*, 11, 2, 119–131.

Thompson, J. R., Anderson, M.D., and Johnson, K.N. (2004). Ecosystem management across ownerships: the potential for collision with antitrust laws. *Conservation Biology*, 18(6), 1475–1481.

Thrower, J. 2006. Adaptive management and NEPA: How a nonequilibrium view of ecosystems mandates flexible regulation. *Ecology Law Quarterly*, 33, 3, 871–895.

Umemoto, K., and K. Suryanata. 2006. Technology, culture, and environmental uncertainty: Considering social contracts in adaptive management. *Journal of Planning Education and Research,* 25, 3, 264–274.

Walters, C.J. 2007. Is adaptive management helping to solve fisheries problems? *Ambio,* 36, 4, 304–307.

Part III

Environmental Media and Environmental Justice

6 Air

After introducing the holistic management approaches of ecosystem management and adaptive management in Chapter 5, we now turn to particular types of environmental media—such as air, water, and land—to explore the key ecological and social issues for each. In this chapter, we will focus on air; in Chapter 7, we focus on water; and in Chapter 8, we turn our discussion to land.

Air is a natural resource that we include as a component of the Natural and Concretion Systems of our model. When making important policy decisions, administrators should focus on the following aspects of air quality: ambient air quality, contamination by naturally occurring and human-made particulate matter, and contamination by naturally occurring and human-made chemicals in air. Improving air quality is clearly an important policy goal because poor air quality in an urban area can have a negative impact on human health, animal health, infrastructure, and vegetation.

Any discussion of air pollution, whether in this chapter, in the scholarly literature, or in deliberative bodies, involves a number of acronyms. Table 6.1 introduces several often-used acronyms used in this chapter and elsewhere. These acronyms are employed throughout this chapter, so please refer back to Table 6.1 if you need a definition of an acronym while reading.

INTERACTIONS BETWEEN AIR, WATER, AND LAND

As an administrator or analyst, it is particularly important to recognize the explicit connection between the three environmental media of air, water, and land that we discuss in this book. For example, air quality can have an impact on land use and land health; poor air quality can hinder the growth and survival of plants, animals, and humans that live on (and in) the land in urban areas. In fact, some urban regions have employed land-use restrictions as a way to control air quality. Ang-Olson and colleagues (2000) discussed a comprehensive overview of the techniques available to use land as an air quality control measure. In particular, they explain the role of land use in developing state implementation plans (SIPs) to reduce air pollution. For

Table 6.1

List of Acronyms for Chapter 6

Acronym	Full Name
CAA	Clean Air Act
CAAA	Clean Air Act Amendments
CO	Carbon Monoxide
CO_2	Carbon Dioxide
EPA	U.S. Environmental Protection Agency
NAAQS	National Ambient Air Quality Standards
NSR	New Source Review permitting program (EPA)
NO_2	Nitrogen Dioxide
NOx	Nitrogen Oxides
PM_{10}	Particles less than 10 micrometers in diameter
SIP	State Implementation Plan
SO_2	Sulfur Dioxide
SOx	Sulfur Oxides

example, transportation, land use, and air quality are often explicitly linked in SIPs to limit the development of new transportation systems in a region that is in noncompliance with air quality standards.

Another interaction between air, water, and land occurs through the use of land and water as a carbon sink for carbon dioxide pollution in the air. Carbon dioxide (CO_2) is a greenhouse gas that can be absorbed by water and land through two main mechanisms. The oceans can serve as a carbon-dioxide "sink" via mixing processes in the ocean that allow the water to absorb CO_2 from the atmosphere (McNeil, 2006). Plants and vegetation can serve as a carbon-dioxide sink through photosynthesis, which absorbs CO_2 and removes it from the air (Flugge and Schilizzi, 2005; Sartori et al., 2006; Sperow, Eve, and Paustian, 2003). This process of using water or vegetation to remove CO_2 from the air is called "carbon sequestration." Policymakers have an active interest in how this process can be used to reduce greenhouse gases and slow global warming. Natural scientists and social scientists alike have explored the practical application of carbon sequestration as a policy mechanism (Kennett, 2002; Kerr et al., 2003; Wilson et al., 2007).

KEY ECOLOGICAL ISSUES

For urban environmental policy administrators, the key ecological issues related to air quality are (1) the source of air pollutants, (2) the type of air pollutants, and (3) the impacts of the pollutants on the environment and human health. The Clean Air Act is the overarching regulation that guides most air quality–related policy decisions in the United States. This chapter provides a brief overview of the history of air pollution regulation (for a comprehensive overview, see Vig and Kraft, 2005). In addition, it explores some of the policy tools that are most commonly used for these air pollutants. The end of the chapter features checklists of important concepts for administrators and analysts.

In 1955, the Air Pollution Control Act was adopted as the first federal-level regulation that involved air pollution. Then, in 1963, the Clean Air Act (CAA) was the first federal regulation to focus explicitly on limiting air pollution. This legislation created the U.S. Public Health Service and authorized research on the control of air pollution. Several years later, along with a major shift in many environmental policies, Congress passed the Clean Air Act of 1970. This regulation led to the development of comprehensive state and federal regulations to control air pollution. After the establishment of the U.S. Environmental Protection Agency (EPA) in 1970, the agency was tasked with implementing the Clean Air Act of 1970.

Farrell and Lave (2004) provide a comprehensive overview of an EPA-sponsored study that outlines estimates of the annual health benefits of the 1970 CAA. Part of their study is a retrospective Benefit-Cost Analysis that demonstrates that nitrogen oxide (NOx) emissions dropped by 20 percent, lead emissions dropped by 99 percent, and other pollutant emissions dropped by percentages in between these numbers as a result of the 1970 CAA. They also report that the total costs of pollution control were around $0.5 trillion, while the total benefits were around $22.2 trillion. From both an economic and health perspective, the Clean Air Act of 1970 proved highly efficient and effective.

"EPA calls these pollutants 'criteria' air pollutants because it regulates them by developing human health-based and/or environmentally-based criteria (science-based guidelines) for setting permissible levels" (U.S. EPA, 2010).

The Clean Air Act was amended in 1977 and again in 1990. The 1990 amendments in particular led to more significant changes in U.S. air policy. One of the major shifts that resulted from the 1990 Clean Air Act Amendments (CAAA) was an expansion of the guidelines for attaining National Ambient Air Quality Standards (NAAQS). As a result of the 1990 amendments, the EPA was required to begin setting limits (with the NAAQS) for six "criteria air pollutants:" (1) particulate matter, (2) carbon monoxide, (3) sulfur oxides (SOx), (4) nitrogen oxides (NOx), (5) ground-level ozone, and (6) lead. In addition, the sources of these air pollutants were to be tracked and limited for both stationary sources (for example, smokestacks) and mobile sources (motor vehicles). If an area is identified as not being in attainment (that is, in nonattainment) for meeting the NAAQS for the six criteria pollutants, then officials in that region are required to submit a plan to the EPA outlining how the pollutants will be reduced to the required attainment levels. This concept goes back to the link between land use and air quality that we mentioned earlier. For example, if a region is in nonattainment for some portion of the NAAQS, administrators might choose to limit new transportation construction plans—or make other land-use changes—to try to limit air emissions and thus achieve attainment in the future.

One way that many states address air pollution nonattainment is by limiting air emissions from mobile sources like cars and trucks. State regulators often do this through an Inspection and Maintenance (I/M) testing program for vehicles. If you have had your car or truck tested for emissions before you were able to register it, then your state has implemented this type of I/M testing program. Such programs can be either "test-only" programs or "test-and-repair" (also called "garage-based") programs. In test-only programs, the testing facility is equipped to run the emissions test only; they cannot repair the vehicle if it fails the test. The test-and-repair or garage-based facilities are those that can run the emissions test and then actually repair the vehicle on-site if it fails the test. The EPA has struggled to determine which facility type is more effective at reducing emissions; "test-only" facilities are less likely to allow potential cheating behavior on the part of the test operators, while a local garage-based facility might record a "pass" for a failing vehicle owned by a regular customer if they think that it will ensure future business. Likewise, a garage might claim that a car was not in compliance in order to be paid for unnecessary work. Clearly, this is an issue of policy monitoring and enforcement, but state and federal officials have only limited resources to monitor testing stations.

To recap, the six pollutants that are the primary focus of the Clean Air Act—particulate matter, carbon monoxide, sulfur oxides, nitrogen oxides, ground-level ozone, and lead—gained their "dirty half-dozen" status because of their adverse affects on humans and the environment. Specifically, particulate matter has a negative impact on the health of the human lungs and heart. The source of these particles varies from smog to smoke and dust. The smaller particles (that is, those less than 10 micrometers in diameter, called "PM_{10}") are usually the most damaging because they can become lodged in a person's lungs or heart more easily than larger particles. Negative health effects include circulatory problems, asthma, and chronic bronchitis. Particulate matter can also damage the environment by contributing to acid rain, generating haze, and/or stressing the chemical and nutrient balance of a variety of ecosystem components.

Carbon monoxide (CO) is another of the criteria air pollutants that has negative health and environmental effects. A majority of the CO emissions come from mobile sources. Because CO bonds more readily to hemoglobin than oxygen does alone, these emissions can reduce the oxygen level in the heart and brain. They can also negatively impact the cardiovascular health of people with reduced heart capacity. From an environmental perspective, CO contributes to smog, which is particularly problematic in many urban areas.

The majority of sulfur dioxide (SO_2) emissions—number three on our list of air polluters—come from electricity generation and fossil-fuel combustion. SO_2 emissions can trigger breathing difficulties, cause respiratory illness, and significantly contribute to haze and reduced visibility. One of the most harmful aspects of SO_2 for human health and the environment is the way it interacts with other chemicals in the air. For example, acid rain forms when SO_2 emissions interact with nitrogen oxides in the air and the resulting chemicals become part of precipitation. Acid rain can disrupt the sensitive balance of crops, ecosystems, water bodies, and animal habitats, and it can damage parts of the Concretion System as well.

Nitrogen oxides represent the fourth of the six criteria air pollutants identified by the EPA. Major sources of NOx include mobile sources, electricity generation, and fossil-fuel combustion. Nitrous oxide (which is a member of the NOx family) is a greenhouse gas and therefore may contribute to global warming. Whether it interacts with SO_2 to generate acid rain or pollutes the environment without interaction, NOx pollution can lead to the deterioration of ecosystems, buildings, and water bodies, as well as plant and animal life. NOx particles also cause breathing and lung problems for humans. In addition, these chemicals can contribute to *eutrophication* in water bodies because of increased nitrogen loading. When NOx interacts with volatile organic compounds (VOCs) in the presence of sunlight, it forms ground-level ozone (another of the six criteria pollutants). Finally, NOx particles can contribute to the haze that lingers over many metropolitan areas, which in turn can contribute to a reduced quality of life for many people who live in the urban environment.

> *Eutrophication* can occur when large quantities of nutrients enter a lake or other body of water, typically from nonpoint-source runoff from fertilizers, sewage, or animal waste. The excessive nutrients cause plants and algae in the water to grow at a faster rate than they normally would. The ultimate decomposition of these plants in the water leads to a reduced dissolved oxygen level that can kill fish and other animals that depend on the oxygen in the water.

Ground-level ozone can cause breathing problems, chest pain, and a variety of lung problems for humans. This pollutant can also significantly damage the environment by making plants more sensitive to disease, reducing crop yields, and harming ecosystems.

The last criteria air pollutant is one that has been managed more effectively than the others over the past couple of decades: lead. Since mobile sources represent one of the major sources of lead in the air, the EPA's required phase-out of lead in gasoline has profoundly reduced the amount of this pollutant in the air. Despite this effort, lead emissions from nonroad (for example, construction) equipment and vehicles remain a problem. Additionally, humans can be exposed to lead in older homes through lead-based paint. Once it is ingested or inhaled, lead can compromise the immune system, the heart, the kidneys, the nervous system, and learning/developmental systems (especially in children). Fortunately, since the 1970s, we have also seen a reduction in exposure to lead through this source. Since lead accumulates in the environment, negative impacts on plants, animals, and ecosystems intensify over time.

KEY SOCIAL ISSUES

There are several key social issues that are important to the air quality component of our model. Some of the policy-relevant social aspects include

- diversity of stakeholder groups, and
- transboundary pollution issues.

It is imperative that city managers, analysts, and administrators recognize the complexity of the social component of air quality policy. As Mitchell (2005) describes, if we think about making policies within the context of sustainability, we must think about how to balance effectively the goals of economic well-being, environmental quality, and social equity. For air quality policy, this requires that analysts and administrators carefully identify stakeholder groups, think about transboundary issues for air pollution, and explore any inequities that are present (or might be present if they were to adopt a new policy).

Diversity of Stakeholder Groups

For air quality issues, the most common stakeholder groups include the following:

- *Private industries:* This group often generates a significant portion of the emissions.
- *Public sector:* This group is often tasked with developing, implementing, and monitoring existing and future air policy regulations; it might generate a portion of the emissions as well (particularly through utilities, generation of electricity, and use of governmental vehicles).
- *Nongovernmental Organizations* (NGOs, often called "nonprofits" in the United States): These organizations follow the policy debate and attempt to shape future policy to either tighten or loosen future air policy regulations (based on their social values and political affiliations).
- *Citizens:* This group often participates in generating emissions (most directly through mobile sources); it also might be concerned about the impact of air quality on human health and the environment. Some members are concerned with effects on other plants and animals and on ecosystems. It is important to remember that citizens themselves can be quite diverse in their concerns. For example, lower-income citizens might value an increase in local jobs over higher levels of air quality, while citizens with stable jobs might prefer better air quality over an increase in jobs.

Issues of social and economic equity, as well as issues of transboundary movement of air pollution, might be relevant for all of these stakeholder groups. Therefore, analysts and administrators need to think not only of the groups that are producing the emissions, but the groups that are "receiving" the pollution (that is, bearing the brunt of the emissions). Chapter 9 focuses in more detail on these environmental equity issues.

Transboundary Pollution

One characteristic of air pollution that makes policy development and monitoring difficult is the transboundary nature of the emissions. Chapter 3 discussed transboundary concerns when suggesting that governmental boundaries should match those of a common pool resource (CPR); yet, matching governance boundaries to effects can be more difficult for air than for water. For example, it is not uncommon to see industries in the midwestern United States generate significant levels of air pollutants. Because air is not constrained by state or local boundaries, this air pollution then drifts up to the northeastern portion of the United States and even into Canada, where citizens and companies have to deal with the negative impacts of air pollution that originated elsewhere. U.S. environmental regulations have attempted to address this issue by placing limits on emissions and using other controls (such as taxes, cap-and-trade mechanisms, etc.), but it is essential that analysts and administrators recognize that air pollution often does not stay in one place. Political and economic conflicts across states and metro areas can become significant problems for air pollution control.

Even though the laws and examples presented here focus largely on air pollution policy within the United States, several studies have explored the transboundary nature of air pollution within an international context— that is, addressing the question of how to form air quality policies when air pollution drifts between nations (Bruvoll and Foehn, 2006; Fraser et al., 2006; Kaldellis Chalratzis, and Spyropoulos, 2007; Kim, 2007; Liverman et al., 1999; Michaelowa, 2004; Park et al., 2004; Reuther, 2000; Sagar, 2000; Totlandsdal et al., 2007; Tuinstra, 2007; Tuinstra, Hordijk, and Kroeze, 2006). While these studies are largely international (and in fact cross-national), it is still possible to study their recommendations and apply many of them to negotiations about air pollution policy across U.S. states, regions, or metropolitan areas. The fact that negotiations and communications are required among different governmental structures makes many of the tensions and challenges of cross-national air policy negotiations similar to those experienced at the local or regional level in the United States.

Siddiqui and Quah (2004) explored the issue of transboundary air pollution that results from Indonesian forest fires. They argue that both the polluters and those who suffer from the haze generated by the fires are active stakeholder groups in the policy debate. The authors developed a regional model that takes into account the states that are responsible for generating the air pollution and the states affected by the air pollution. In their example, Siddiqui and Quah explicitly model the polluting industry and the role of regional governments, as well as the impacts of pollution on citizens in the area. They conclude that developing effective policy solutions requires the satisfaction of economic needs for all key stakeholder groups. In Case 6.1, you can see how the concepts of stakeholder groups, transboundary pollution, and equity all come into play in this case of air quality policymaking.

As this case outlines, it is necessary to include all stakeholder groups in the policy process. Many past studies have emphasized the importance of including stakeholder groups in decision making (for example, Beierle, 2002; Burger, 2004; Maynard et al., 2003; Sanderson et al., 2006), and this is particularly relevant for a transboundary issue like air pollution. Chapter 5 discussed how ecosystem management is one approach that encourages stakeholder collaboration on transboundary issues.

Transboundary air pollution issues have been addressed within the United States partly through the work of the Ozone Transport Assessment Group (OTAG) (Farrell and Keating, 2002). One goal of the OTAG effort is to reduce the flow of ozone and

■———— **Case 6.1** ————■

Policy Alternatives for Transboundary Air Pollution

Transboundary air pollution, popularly known as the "haze," is a recent but significant environmental crisis in Southeast Asia, and is primarily the result of Indonesian forest fires. . . . The fundamental motivation behind the practice of clearing forestland with fire by the polluters is economic in nature. . . . And the major victims of the forest fires and haze are likely to play a vital role in the solution of the problem, at least by motivating the polluters, even if they cannot force them not to pollute. Thus, the polluters and victims can be regarded as the "stakeholders" who would take interest and participate actively in the policy regime.

The region experienced its first case of transboundary pollution from the East Kalimantan forest fires in 1982–83. Since then, the recurrence of forest fires and haze has become an annual event, especially in the 1990s when the region experienced a few severe episodes of haze (1991, 1994, and 1997). Forest fires and haze have inflicted enormous environmental and economic damage on Indonesia, Malaysia, Singapore, Brunei Darussalam, Thailand, and the Philippines. . . .

Considering the severity and probable frequency of haze, the regional community has recognized the urgent need for a solution. In 1995 the adoption of the ASEAN Cooperation Plan on Transboundary Pollution marked the severity of the problem. But the formation of the Haze Technical Task Force, three months after the Cooperation Plan targeted the transboundary air pollution as a specific problem for the first time, could not prevent the haze episode of 1997. ASEAN governments in December 1997 dealt with the issue urgently and adopted the Regional Haze Action Plan or RHAP (ASEAN Secretariat, 1997). However, the effectiveness of the initiatives has often come under criticism for their lack of operational directives as problems persisted and a detailed implementation plan for the RHAP therefore became a necessity. In order to control the fires, fire monitoring and local law enforcement activities would require frequent reviews, and the funding of such activities would be critical to achieving a [positive] result.

Environmental policies have initially focused on the direct regulation of polluting activities of industries by using "command and control" strategies, such as imposing specific environmental quality standards and mandatory adoption of specific clean technology. These policy instruments have attracted criticism on the grounds of cost effectiveness and efficiency. Additionally, the implementation of these policy instruments has often been followed by inadequate monitoring, with incomplete and imperfect information and costly enforcement through civil or criminal trials, given the limited government budget (Callan and Thomas, 1996; Goodstein, 1999).

In order to address these problems, incentive-based strategies such as pollution taxes, tradable permits, etc. have been developed (Dietz and Vollebergh, 1999; Russel and Powell, 1999). This has allowed industries greater flexibility in decision making with respect to the development and choice of clean technology and pollution reduction while making pollution expensive, thereby making the monitoring and enforcement more efficient and cost effective. However, incentive-based strategies are not immune to monitoring and enforcement problems. In fact, the current environmental policy literature has not [as of 2004] adequately explored the issues of monitoring and enforcement. Furthermore, in practice, monitoring and enforcement are subject to

(continued)

Case 6.1 *(continued)*

bureaucratic discretion and political influence. Especially in developing countries, given weak governmental structures, the underpaid and inadequately trained inspectors often drag the system into corruption and inefficient enforcement. In order to address these issues, along with issues relating to efficiency and cost effectiveness, the stakeholder approach has been proposed here.

The stakeholder approach is an innovative class of the incentive-based mechanism, where the focus is on the stakeholders at various stages of the policy exercise and the institutions in question. In itself, the stakeholder approach is a mechanism for developing people-specific and institution-specific policy instruments and mechanisms. . . . The role of stakeholders is crucial in the policy regime as policy implementation relies heavily on cooperation from them. Further, funding and fund transfer among the stakeholders is crucial in fire monitoring and prevention activities. . . . These funds and incentives must be allocated efficiently among the stakeholders, so that each of them has optimum motivation to cooperate.

Source: Siddiqui and Quah, 2004. Used with permission.

other air pollutants between states. This two-year process was spearheaded by top management officials at thirty-seven state environmental agencies.[1] Farrell and Keating (2002) drew several lessons from their detailed analysis of the way the OTAG addressed the issue of transboundary air pollution. Since these lessons are relevant for analysts and administrators dealing with local or regional issues of transboundary air pollution, they are restated in Table 6.2. Lessons such as these are particularly salient for administrators who might have to facilitate negotiations about air pollution policies across stakeholder groups in different states or different metropolitan regions.

POLICY TOOLS IN THE AIR CONTEXT

Since the 1970s, environmental policy in the United States has shifted from a command-and-control approach to more of a market-based, incentive-based approach (Vig and Kraft, 2005). This trend has been particularly prevalent in the area of air quality regulations. One of the drivers of the shift in environmental policy tools for air pollution has been the cost-effectiveness of market-based incentive programs for lowering air emissions. The command-and-control approach was originally designed to target low levels of emissions with little regard for compliance costs, as well as little awareness of differences across industries, location, and types of pollutants. Market-based approaches are utilized because they can take compliance costs into account, and they allow for different emissions levels across different industries, locations, and pollutants. In fact, several policy and economics scholars have used economic analyses of command-and-control regulations and market-based policy tools, such as emissions trading or taxes, to demonstrate that command-and-control regulations might be less economically efficient than other policy tools for air pollution control.

Table 6.2

Transboundary Air Pollution Lessons for Administrators

There are limits to consensus	Farrell and Keating (2002) found that states could not be forced into agreeing to a policy that would go against their interests; therefore, assessments should focus on information gathering, communication, and the development of professional relationships across states.
Enhance communication and negotiation	Farrell and Keating (2002) concluded that the OTAG process led to an important opening of communication and negotiation channels on technical and political issues. Administrators should adopt a collaborative process that encourages stakeholders to begin communicating and negotiating about how to deal with the transboundary air pollution.
Seek stakeholder perceptions	Farrell and Keating (2002) found that it is important for all participants to have the opportunity to discuss their perceptions of the air pollution problem at the beginning of the process because this facilitates future communication processes.
Adopt an adaptable process	Farrell and Keating (2002) concluded that the leaders of the policymaking process should try to ensure that the process is adaptable because new (and better) solutions might come up in the middle of the policymaking process. New solutions that are promising and proposed in the middle of the process should not be ignored simply because they were brought up late.
Credible knowledge is important	Farrell and Keating (2002) argued that the facilitators of the communication and negotiation process must be interested in focusing the stakeholders on credible knowledge and letting the process play out by employing credible knowledge. This process is better than beginning the negotiation with a preconceived notion of what the final air pollution policy agreement should be.
Leaving a legacy is important	Farrell and Keating (2002) found that it is important for stakeholders to leave a legacy as a result of the negotiating process. In other words, if the results (both knowledge results and policy results) are not documented in some way, then they may not become fully institutionalized and, therefore, might not be as useful for future generations as they could be.
Transcend crisis management	Farrell and Keating (2002) concluded that it is important that the stakeholders are able to transcend crisis management and attempt to assess the air pollution problem before it reaches a state of crisis. If a crisis level has already been reached, then the negotiation process should be managed so the crisis does not take over and hinder future negotiations.

Source: Adapted from Farrell and Keating, 2002.

Requate (2005) provides an overview of the various incentives that environmental policy tools can provide for reducing emissions of pollutants. In this case, the focus is on advanced pollution-abatement technology. The author concludes from an extensive literature review that, when competitive conditions exist, market-based environmental policy tools are more economically efficient and effective than command-and-control regulations. Requate also indicates that taxing pollution might be an environmental policy tool that can provide an even stronger long-term incentive than tradable permits.

However, Soleille (2006) reaches a different conclusion than does Requate (2005) when comparing emissions trading regulations with command-and-control regulations in the European Union. Soleille argues that determining which environmental policy tool is the most efficient and effective depends largely on the context of the situation. He says that many scholars assume emissions trading programs are always the best policy tool because they might achieve the same level of emissions as a command-and-control program—but with a higher level of economic efficiency. Soleille's criticism of these assertions is that they are often based on theory and do not sufficiently take real-world conditions into account.

One particular assumption upon which he focuses is that of a perfect market for emissions trading. Soleille argues that the market for these allowances is often imperfect (for example, few participants may cause market power)—and that many scholars fail to incorporate full transaction and monitoring costs into their analysis. Yet the author does not believe that command-and-control regulation are always the best option either. Like his criticism of market-based regulations, he asserts that analysts who fully support command-and-control regulations neglect to include many real-world difficulties into their analysis. For example, he argues that some analysts who support command-and-control policies fail to acknowledge that not many countries are politically able to impose stringent environmental limits on pollution.

COMMAND-AND-CONTROL REGULATIONS

Some of the advantages of command-and-control regulations include clearly defined pollution targets/limits, as well as a reduction in overall emissions levels (from no regulation at all). However, this policy tool is not always the most desirable option for reducing air pollution. In particular, there are four somewhat significant disadvantages of employing a command-and-control regulation approach. First, this type of policy tool typically mandates the use of a specific technology. As a result, it fails to encourage technological innovation in the way that an emissions trading program or a taxing system might. Second, command-and-control regulations can be costly and time-consuming to implement, monitor, and enforce. While some of these costs (for example, implementation) might fall on the firms, other costs (monitoring and enforcement) typically fall on the government agency that is regulating the firm. Third, a command-and-control regulation is inherently inflexible for firms and does not provide an economic incentive for firms to find the most cost-effective method for reducing emissions. Finally, the costs of compliance with a command-and-control regulation can be quite high for firms, so they often resist this approach. In the next sections, we introduce additional policy tools for controlling air pollution.

EMISSIONS PERMIT TRADING SYSTEMS

Farrell and Lave (2004) outline two distinct types of emission trading regulatory systems. The first type is an emissions reduction credit program that allows a firm to trade emissions credits and, therefore, function above or below the baseline of pollutants that it emitted under the previous regulation (usually a command-and-control regulation). The second type of emission trading system is a cap-and-trade regulatory system. This type of regulation begins with a limit on total emissions in an area. Then, firms are allowed to trade emissions allowances among themselves. Typically, the emissions allocation given to a firm is lower than its historical emissions levels. Farrell and Lave offer four options for firms under these systems: (1) reduce emissions to match the allocation, (2) reduce emissions and sell extra allowances to other firms, (3) continue to have higher emissions and purchase allowances from other firms, or (4) reduce emissions and hold on to the allowances for use in future years.

Cap-and-Trade Systems

There are several ways to implement a tradable emissions allowance program, but one of the most common approaches is a cap-and-trade program. Given that it is the most common program it will be the primary focus of this section. Most of the advantages and disadvantages, however, are applicable to all tradable emissions allowance programs. One advantage of a cap-and-trade program is that it generally results in an overall reduction of emissions that is greater than a command-and-control regulation because the program is more flexible for firms that need to reduce emissions. Second, this market-based program allows firms to determine the most cost-effective balance between emitting pollutants and abating pollutants based on the monetary costs of each. Third, the flexibility of this type of system encourages firms to think about adopting (or creating) new technologies that might help with pollution abatement. This enhancement of technological innovation is something that generally does not thrive within a command-and-control regulation program. Fourth, if banking of allowances is permitted, then firms have even more flexibility in the way they control any future emissions. Fifth, this type of policy provides an incentive for some firms to drop their emissions below the standards that would be set with a command-and-control regulation (and to do this in a cost-effective way). Sixth, a cap-and-trade program allows regulators to set a cap on the total level of emissions that they are willing to accept in a given spatial and temporal range.

Burtraw and colleagues (2005) give an extensive overview of market-based incentives for SO_2 and NOx in their review article. They conclude that cap-and-trade programs for both NOx and SO_2 have contributed to a significant savings over the costs of command-and-control approaches. They point out that, however, a cap-and-trade approach is probably not the optimal policy tool for all air pollutants. When pollutants have local negative effects, it might not make sense from an environmental or a political perspective to allow for a cap-and-trade approach. However, for cases where the emissions are dispersed over a larger area, a cap-and-trade program can work quite efficiently (Burtraw et al., 2005).

In some cases, the adoption of a cap-and-trade program represents a significant policy shift for states. Farrell and colleagues (1999) outlined a U.S. NOx Budget program that was adopted by states in the Northeast in the late 1990s and early 2000s. The NOx Budget program was designed to be a cap-and-trade program for NOx that set specific limits on the total level of emissions that could be released into the participating states within a specific time period. These NOx pollution allowances could then be traded among polluters, allowing a firm with lower pollution-control costs to sell its permits to a firm with higher pollution-control costs. The major goal of the program was to reduce ground-level ozone concentrations, specifically during hot summer months when ozone concentrations are higher. Before the introduction of this program, NOx emission levels were governed in this area through command-and-control regulations. Thus, the introduction of the NOx Budget program represented a policy shift for states in the Eastern U.S. Farrell and colleagues argued that, while this new program might reduce emissions, it would not solve regulatory uncertainties (such as regulators' perceptions that a market-based approach might not be as certain in reducing emissions as a command-and-control approach).

Several environmental policy scholars have compared the effectiveness of cap-and-trade programs with command-and-control regulations. For example, Johnson and Pekelney (1996) conducted an economic comparison of policy alternatives for an emissions trading program in Los Angeles. Their economic models demonstrated that, when compared with command-and-control regulations, the emissions trading program yielded lower costs, fewer employment impacts, and comparable air quality results. Similarly, Conrad and Kohn (1996) discuss how early emissions trading programs under the Acid Rain Program (in the early 1990s) led to emissions permit prices for SO_2 that were lower than expected. After an economic analysis of emissions trading data, they argued that the prices of the allowances were low because of the large quantity of available allowances and the stringency of air quality standards, rather than because of regulatory uncertainty or transaction costs associated with trading. They concluded that since the price and the trading volume of the permits were below the rates expected, they could be a more cost-effective policy tool than a traditional command-and-control approach.

Weaknesses of Cap-and-Trade

As with command-and-control regulations, however, cap-and-trade programs also have some disadvantages. Here we discuss eight of the most significant disadvantages of adopting this policy tool for air pollution control.

First, cap-and-trade programs can lead to the creation of environmental hot spots. These are areas that have unacceptably high concentrations of pollutants—either in a given spatial area or a given time frame. For example, as mentioned in Chapter 3, Region A may end up having large concentrations of emissions of SOx, while Region B might have very small concentrations (and Region B sold their allowances to firms in Region A). This policy tool can also create discrepancies in pollutant concentrations across time. For instance, if allowances are traded to a firm that produces most of its NOx emissions in the summer (when ground-level ozone is often at peak levels because of the intense sunlight), then that area might have extremely high levels of ozone and NOx in the summer and very low levels the rest of the year.

The second disadvantage is related to the spatial accumulation of pollution in one location—a prime cause of equity problems. Residents in one area of a city might be exposed to higher levels of pollutants than residents in other areas of the state or city. If this situation exists, analysts and administrators need to think about any equity issues associated with this disparity in exposure to air pollutants. For more detail on equity issues, we discuss environmental justice issues explicitly in Chapter 9.

Third, a cap-and-trade program might not work well for some pollutants, particularly those that are extremely toxic. The potential for environmental hot spots (as a result of trading permits) makes this policy tool especially risky for highly toxic substances.

Fourth, the transaction costs of trading allowances are not trivial for firms. This is especially true when the cap-and-trade program is first implemented. Analysts and administrators should consider the transaction costs as part of their calculation when they are deciding if a cap-and-trade program would be more effective than a command-and-control regulation program.

Fifth, it is not uncommon for some firms to be granted an exemption or waiver from participating in the program. If the emissions from these firms are significant, this can decrease the overall environmental effectiveness of the program. Exemptions can also create political tension between firms that do receive exemptions and those that do not.

Sixth, a cap-and-trade program can cause unintended consequences by encouraging firms to shift to energy sources that are unregulated or that have more lenient regulations. Before implementing a cap-and-trade program, administrators should think about what sorts of shifts would be most likely and whether they are acceptable for the environmental quality of the region.

Seventh, a cap-and-trade program must have a minimum number of participants to ensure that the trading market is not distorted. Therefore, this program might not be effective in small cities with only one or two firms that emit air pollutants.

Finally, some environmental groups resist cap-and-trade programs because they believe that it is immoral to give firms a "license to pollute." Even though political opposition is possible with this policy tool, the overall political tensions are usually lower for a cap-and-trade program than they are for a taxation program.

Case 6.2 provides an overview for administrators of some of the lessons associated with implementing a tradable emissions program—whether cap-and-trade or otherwise.

Soleille (2006) provides a series of suggestions on how best to design an emissions trading program, when to adopt one, and how to evaluate it. He argues that the context is quite important when trying to choose between a command-and-control policy or an emissions trading policy. According to Soleille, some of the most important points for administrators that might be part of the implementation of an emissions trading program include the following:

- keeping transaction costs low,
- maintaining an active market to reduce the volatility of prices for allowances,
- measuring and monitoring emissions regularly and reliably, and
- allowing the banking of emissions allowances for future use.

TAXATION

So far, we have presented some details about emissions trading programs as a policy tool for air pollution control. Now we discuss another air pollution policy: taxation. Especially in Europe, taxes have been used to reduce air emissions from mobile sources

■――――― **Case 6.2** ―――――■

Lessons for Implementation of a Tradable Permits Program

The use of tradeable permits as an instrument in air quality and environmental policy has gained increasing attention in the environmental economics literature in recent years (Atkinson, 1994; Foster and Hahn, 1995; Hahn and Hester, 1989; Tietenberg, 1992). . . .

An allowance trading program requires a lot of administrative effort in the initial set-up, but once it is designed and implemented, the regulatory agency can step back into a rather passive role in the form of a market "watchdog" and data collection point, because market forces trigger the necessary adjustments to dynamic influences like changing costs, economic growth patterns, and inflationary pressures. . . .

. . . We identify a set of politico-economic influences, which we can categorize into (i) distributional economic interests, (ii) general moral reservations, (iii) concerns about environmental integrity and (iv) concerns about economic fairness. . . .

Distributional economic interests are reflected in the initial allocation of permits, namely in the choice of grandfathering and several special reserves (e.g., bonus allowances for polluters in high growth states). Considering the size and the diversity of these funds we conclude that tradable permits have an extraordinary flexibility to respond to distributional economic interests. . . .

Moral reservations against tradeable permits were expressed in a public controversy on "selling the right to pollute" at the time these programs were adopted. These reservations have been sufficiently addressed in a target instrument tradeoff, i.e., in a political agreement of ambitious environmental targets in combination with a market-based instrument. . . .

Concerns about environmental integrity are reflected in both programs by stipulation of advanced monitoring devices, tough penalties for non-compliance, and transparent reporting of emissions performance. To prevent damaging environmental effects on a local or regional scale, both programs are moreover backed up by a "safety net" of co-existing environmental regulations (air quality standards, NSR [New Source Review], etc.). . . .

Concerns about economic fairness (fair competition) have been voiced in lengthy political debates about the risk of "hoarding" of permits in the congressional hearings on SAT [Site Assessment Team] and (to a lesser extent) in the public debate preceding the adoption of RECLAIM [California's program for NOx and SO$_2$ reductions]. They are addressed in both programs by a set of special access provisions for newcomers (e.g., fixed prices reserves) and by designing the programs to assure a competitive market.

Subsuming these politico-economic influences to a broader concept of political acceptance, we are able to demonstrate the outstanding importance of this factor for the design of cap-and-trade programs. In fact, viewed through the lens of political acceptance, most similarities of these otherwise rather divergent programs can be attributed to this particular need.

In summary, provisions to assure political acceptance, functional interdependencies, and overlapping regulation (in descending degree of importance) emerge from our research as the most important features for the design of applied tradable permits. Further analysis of future cap-and-trade programs in the field of air pollution are, however, needed to validate this evidence.

Source: Schwarze and Zapfel, 2000. Used with permission.

(through a fuel tax). In particular, Sterner (2007) argues that taxes have been effective in constricting fuel demand—and, therefore, carbon emissions. He also addresses the increasing interest in adding transportation to carbon permit trading. Businesses in the transport sector seem supportive of this option because they expect that it could be less expensive than paying fuel taxes. Sterner notes that fuel taxes have a "long and reliable track record of reducing emissions in the countries that set them sufficiently high" (3194); thus, he believes that we should seriously consider this policy tool for reducing emissions. He concludes that "carbon emissions are essentially cut by more than half by introducing a long run policy of high taxes that raises the consumer price by a factor of around 3" (3201). For this reason, he strongly urges policymakers in Europe (where fuel taxes are much more common than in the United States) not to lower fuel taxes for either gasoline or diesel.

A *Pigouvian tax* is a tax that is levied to counter an economic negative externality that causes pollution in the environment.

Carbon taxes are another type of taxation that can reduce emissions from stationary sources. Bruvoll and Larsen (2004) explore whether or not carbon taxes are a useful policy tool for reducing air pollution in Norway. In 1991, Norway adopted a Pigouvian carbon tax for reducing air emissions. This carbon tax was among the highest in the world. The authors evaluated the effectiveness of the tax policy by analyzing changes in CO_2, methane, and NO_2 from the period 1990–1999. They found that, even though total emissions did increase during that time frame, there was a significant decrease in emissions per unit of GDP. In their study, they go on to break down the observed changes in these pollutants into eight potential driving forces, and then they examine the partial effects of the carbon taxes on the reduction in pollution. Their findings indicate that the estimated effect of the carbon taxes was a 2.3 percent reduction in total national CO_2 emissions. Thus, Bruvoll and Larsen concluded that the effectiveness of the carbon tax has been modest. They found that the carbon taxes caused an overall reduction in energy use, but at least a portion of this reduction was due to a change in the composition of energy use to less carbon-intensive energy sources. In addition, they found that the taxes had a somewhat negative impact on economic growth. They do point out that these results are somewhat surprising, since policymakers have often viewed carbon taxes as an effective and innovative tool for reducing emissions. Part of the problem with the taxes, they argue, is that a broad range of carbon-intensive industries gained an exemption from the tax because of concerns about competitiveness. They recommend that one solution would be a more broad-based and cost-efficient tax that is uniform across pollutants and sources. The results of this study provide some interesting points for analysts and administrators to consider when they think about adopting a carbon taxing system to reduce air emissions.

Scrimgeou, Oxley, and Fatai (2005) explored a similar policy tool used in New Zealand when that country decided to adopt a new carbon and energy tax because of the Kyoto Protocol. As the authors point out, a challenge for adopting an environmental policy tool like this is to try to maximize social welfare while also reducing air emissions and associated costs. New Zealand has had an extended debate about which environmental policy tool would be most effective and efficient in reducing greenhouse gas emissions. While many European countries have used taxation as a policy tool for reducing air emissions, New Zealand has not traditionally employed this tool. Scrimgeour and colleagues used a general equilibrium model to estimate the effectiveness of carbon, energy, and gasoline taxes. They found that the carbon tax would lead to an 18 percent reduction in carbon emissions—and that the energy tax would yield a reduction of about 16 percent for carbon emissions. However, the petroleum tax would lead to a reduction in carbon emissions of only about 0.9 percent. Thus, they concluded that the carbon tax yields the highest emissions reduction of the three types of taxes.

Political Considerations for Carbon and Energy Taxes

The economic efficiency of a policy tool is not the only consideration for an analyst or administrator. Political considerations are also important to take into account. Nakata and Lamont (2001) examined the use of carbon and energy taxes for the Japanese energy system. Instead of evaluating an existing tax program retrospectively, they used a partial equilibrium model to forecast changes in Japan's energy system through 2040. They found that both carbon and energy taxes would both be able to decrease the CO_2 emissions to target levels. Yet, even though they found that both the carbon tax and the energy tax would meet the environmental requirements, they concluded that carbon taxes would encourage a decrease in the use of coal and an accompanying increase in the use of gas. Since Japan imports almost all of its fossil fuel, the authors argue that limiting the variety of fuels used would make the country too sensitive to price variations in gasoline markets. Thus, from a political perspective, an energy tax might be more stable than a carbon tax.

Advantages of Carbon, Energy, or Fuel Taxes

There are several advantages of a carbon, energy, or fuel tax over a command-and-control approach or a cap-and-trade program. First, the taxes raise revenues for government agencies. If these taxes are used in an effective way, for example to ameliorate harms of the remaining pollutants, this can be a benefit for the government and for society. Second, the adoption of a tax provides a cost certainty for both the firms and the governmental agency because the rate is set and everyone knows what to expect. Third, as with the cap-and-trade program, a tax usually leads to an overall reduction of emissions beyond the reduction that would be accomplished with a command-and-control regulation. Fourth, like a cap-and-trade program, taxes are also market-based so they give firms the flexibility to determine the most cost-effective balance between emitting pollutants and abating pollutants based on the costs of each. Last, using taxes as a policy tool for controlling air pollution can also encourage firms to adopt new technology that might lower their emissions (and, therefore, lower their taxes).

Disadvantages of Environmental Taxes

There are, however, some disadvantages of environmental taxes. First, the presence of a tax might encourage firms to shift to an energy source that is unregulated or that has less strict regulations. This is not always a negative outcome, unless of course the new energy source is not more desirable (from an environmental perspective) than the source that is being taxed. One possible alternative to this situation would be to tax a suite of energy options together to reduce the likelihood that firms would simply shift to an unregulated (or less regulated) source. Second, it is often difficult for regulators to set an optimal tax level for a given total emissions level. Typically, it takes some time for regulators to determine what tax level will achieve a particular emissions target (although economic models can give them a solid first estimate). Case 6.2 and our recommendation of ecosystem- and adaptive-management approaches address this point. Third, if some firms are given tax exemptions or waivers, the system may not be optimal from an economic or environmental perspective. Fourth, there are potential equity issues with taxes (for example, in the case of a fuel tax, it is easier for higher-income citizens to pay more for fuel than it is for lower-income citizens). Fifth, the introduction of environmental taxes often faces political resistance from firms. They see the tax as an additional cost that they did not have before, and they often resist this policy tool more than they might resist a cap-and-trade program. Sixth, Scrimgeour and colleagues (2005) conclude that, while an energy tax and a carbon tax could be effective instruments for reducing carbon emissions, they could also have a negative impact on capital stocks. They encourage analysts and administrators to be cautious when making decisions about which policy tool is best.

Taxing and Then Refunding

Some policymakers and scholars have advocated the use of an emissions tax that can be refunded. Johnson (2007) has argued for the adoption of a refunded emissions tax and outlined some of the problems associated with adopting a cap-and-trade program. He explains that while a typical cap-and-trade approach will often reduce regulatory costs, sometimes it is not feasible to set the cap at a desirable level. Also, emissions taxes can "provide cost certainty, but their comparatively high cost makes it infeasible to set tax rates at levels commensurate with sustainability goals" (3115). The Tucson, Arizona, water-pricing example in Chapter 3 presents a similar problem for pricing in general. The solution that Johnson proposes is the implementation of an emissions tax that would allow the tax revenue to be refunded so the emissions reduction is actually profitable. (Exhibit 3.7 presents a worldwide refunding scheme advanced by Hans Gersbach, 2008). Johnson concludes that policymakers should consider refunded emission taxes as a viable policy alternative to the cons of both cap-and-trade systems and taxation.

Sterner and Isaksson (2006) also support a refunded emissions tax. They describe how polluting firms often resist the adoption of environmental taxes as a policy tool because they perceive future costs for both the pollution abatement *and* the tax. In the case that the authors propose, polluters would pay a fee for polluting and then the revenues from these payments would be refunded to the same groups of polluters based on their actual output of emissions. The researchers report that this policy tool was effective when it was applied to emissions reductions of NOx in Sweden. They also argue that it is possible for the emissions payment to be set at a higher monetary value than a tax because the money is refunded to firms. Other benefits of this type of regulation include the fact that each firm can choose its individual level of investment in pollution abatement, as well as the timing of that investment (Sterner and Isaksson, 2006).

Disadvantages of Tax-and-Refund

Johnson (2007), as well as Sterner and Isaksson (2006), point out some limitations of a refunded tax program, including the difficulties associated with setting the optimal payment amount and choosing a common denominator across firms for determining how much of the refund each firm gets. For example, should a refund be determined based on the energy output of the firm or the amount of money spent on abatement? Johnson (2007) points out another potential problem with this policy tool—that tax refunding might neutralize the economic incentive for a reduction in energy use over time. Nonetheless, Sterner and Isaksson (2006) conclude that refunded emissions payments are a possible alternative when taxes are not feasible. Also, refunded emissions payments could be an alternative to tradable allowances when policymakers want a price-type mechanism without putting large abatement costs on polluters.

CONCLUSION AND CHECKLIST FOR ADMINISTRATORS

Now that we have provided an overview of the most common policy tools that are utilized for air pollution—command-and-control, cap-and-trade, taxes, and refundable taxes—we present a checklist that can help administrators focus on some of the key issues when trying to make choices between policy tools (see Figure 6.1). Even though this list is not comprehensive and cannot take into account all contextual issues for every policy problem, administrators and analysts should use it as a guide when they are making decisions about air pollution policies. Since each question listed here is addressed individually, we encourage administrators and analysts to use this as a basic starting point for their choices among urban air policy tools; final decisions must also include understanding of a specific city's context.

NOTE

1. For a full overview of the process that led to the creation of the OTAG, as well as an assessment of its results, see Farrell and Keating, 2002.

REFERENCES

Ang-Olson, J.; Fischer, M.; and Dulla, R. 2000. Land use as an air quality control measure—Review of current practice and examination of policy options. *Energy, Air Quality, and Fuels 2000*, 1738, 33–38.

Association of Southeast Asian Nations (ASEAN). 1997. Regional haze action plan. http://www.aseansec.org/9059.htm.

Atkinson, S.E. 1994. Tradable discharge permits: Restrictions on least-cost solutions. In *Economic Instruments for Air Pollution Control*, ed. G. Klaassen and F.R. Forsund, 3–21. Boston, MA: Kluwer Academic Publishers.

Beierle, T.C. 2002. The quality of stakeholder-based decisions. *Risk Analysis*, 22, 4, 739–749.

Figure 6.1 **Checklist for Air Policy Tools**

A. How important is it for all polluting firms to adopt similar pollution abatement technologies?

B. Is it desirable to have a specific technology mandate?

YES ⇒ Then command-and-control regulations might be the preferred policy tool.

C. Is it important to include economic incentives for firms to reduce pollution?

YES ⇒ Then cap-and-trade, environmental taxes, or refunded environmental taxes might be preferred policy tools.

D. Does the regulatory system need to be highly flexible for firms?

YES ⇒ Then cap-and-trade might be preferred.

E. Is it politically important to allow firms some role in the decision-making process about how they reduce emissions?

F. Is it important to minimize compliance costs for firms?

YES ⇒ Then either a cap-and-trade system or refunded environmental tax might be the preferred policy tool.

G. How many firms will be affected by the adoption of the new policy?

H. Are there enough participants to ensure that there are not major distortions in an emissions trading market?

NO ⇒ Then a command-and-control regulation or an environmental tax (refunded or not) might be preferred over a cap-and-trade system.

I. Is there a high potential for temporal or spatial hot spots of pollution if firms are allowed to trade emissions allowances?

YES ⇒ Then command-and-control regulations might be preferred, especially if vulnerable populations reside in areas likely to be subject to hot spots.

J. Would lower-income individuals be more negatively impacted by a tax (especially a fuel tax)? Would certain areas of a community or region be more negatively impacted than others by potential environmental hot spots?

K. Is there a high potential for irresolvable equity issues?

YES ⇒ Then a command-and-control approach might be preferred.

L. Are there any highly toxic emissions that are part of the policy problem?

YES ⇒ Then a command-and-control regulation or environmental taxes (refunded or not) might be the preferred alternatives because they provide greater certainty of pollution-reduction levels.

M. Are governmental revenues needed to fund policy implementation?

YES ⇒ Then non-refunded environmental taxes might be the preferred policy.

N. Is it important to have cost certainty for individual firms that will be impacted by the emissions limitations?

YES ⇒ Then environmental taxes might be preferred over a command-and-control approach.

O. What are likely effects on water and land of the potential policies?

Bruvoll, A., and T. Foehn. 2006. Transboundary effects of environmental policy: Markets and emission leakages. *Ecological Economics*, 59, 4, 499–510.

Bruvoll, A., and B.M. Larsen. 2004. Greenhouse gas emissions in Norway: Do carbon taxes work? *Energy Policy*, 32, 4, 493–505.

Burger, J. 2004. Assessment methods for concerns about contaminated sites. *Journal of Toxicology and Environmental Health, Part A*, 67, 1, 31–42.

Burtraw, D.; Evans, D. A.; Krupnick, A.; Palmer, K.; and Toth, R. 2005. Economics of pollution trading for SO_2 and NOx. *Annual Review of Environment and Resources*, 30, 253–289.

Callan, S.J., and J.M. Thomas. 1996. *Environmental Economics and Management: Theory, Policy and Applications.* Chicago, IL: Irwin.

Conrad, K., and R.E. Kohn. 1996. The U.S. market for SO_2 permits—Policy implications of the low price and trading volume. *Energy Policy*, 24, 12, 1051–1059.

Dietz, F.J., and H.R.J. Vollebergh. 1999. Explaining instrument choice in environmental policies. In *Handbook of Environmental and Resource Economics*, ed. J.C.J.M. ven den Bergh, 339–351. Cheltenham, Glos.: Edward Elgar.

Farrell, A.; Carter, R.; and Raufer, R. 1999. The NOx Budget: Market-based control of tropospheric ozone in the northeastern United States. *Resource and Energy Economics*, 21, 2, 103–124.

Farrell, A.E., and T.J. Keating. 2002. Transboundary environmental assessment: Lessons from OTAG. *Environmental Science and Technology*, 36, 12, 2537–2544.

Farrell, A.E., and L.B. Lave. 2004. Emission trading and public health. *Annual Review of Public Health*, 25, 119–138.

Flugge, F., and S. Schilizzi. 2005. Greenhouse gas abatement policies and the value of carbon sinks: Do grazing and cropping systems have different destinies? *Ecological Economics*, 55, 4, 584–598.

Foster, V., and R.W. Hahn. 1995. Designing more efficient markets: Lessons from Los Angeles smog control. *Journal of Law and Economics*, 28, 19–48.

Fraser, D.A.; Gaydos, J.K.; Karlsen, E.; and Rylko, M.S. 2006. Collaborative science, policy development and program implementation in the transboundary Georgia Basin/Puget Sound ecosystem. *Environmental Monitoring and Assessment*, 113, 1–3, 49–69.

Gersbach, H. 2008. A new way to address climate change: A global refunding system. *The Economists' Voice*, 5, 4, 1–4. http://www.bepress.com/ev/vol5/iss4/art2 (accessed January 27, 2011).

Goodstein, E.S. 1999. *Economics and the Environment*, 2d ed. Englewood Cliffs, NJ: Prentice Hall.

Hahn, R.W., and G.L. Hester. 1989. Where did all the markets go? An analysis of EPA's emissions trading program. *Yale Journal on Regulation*, 6, 109–153.

Johnson, K.C. 2007. Refunded emission taxes: A resolution to the cap-versus-tax dilemma for greenhouse gas regulation. *Energy Policy*, 35, 5, 3115–3118.

Johnson, S.L., and D.M. Pekelney. 1996. Economic assessment of the regional clean air incentives market: A new emissions trading program for Los Angeles. *Land Economics*, 72, 3, 277–297.

Kaldellis, J.K.; Chalvatzis, K.J.; and Spyropoulos, G.C. 2007. Transboundary air pollution balance in the new integrated European environment. *Environmental Science and Policy*, 10, 725–733.

Kennett, S.A. 2002. National policies for biosphere greenhouse gas management: Issues and opportunities. *Environmental Management*, 30, 5, 595–608.

Kerr, S.; Liu, S.G.; Pfaff, A.S.P.; and Hughes, R.F. 2003. Carbon dynamics and land-use choices: Building a regional-scale multidisciplinary model. *Journal of Environmental Management*, 69, 1, 25–37.

Kim, I. 2007. Environmental cooperation of Northeast Asia: Transboundary air pollution. *International Relations of the Asia-Pacific*, 7, 3, 439–462.

Liverman, D.M.; Varady, R.G.; Chavez, O.; and Sanchez, R. 1999. Environmental issues along the United States–Mexico border: Drivers of change and responses of citizens and institutions. *Annual Review of Energy and the Environment*, 24, 607–643.

Maynard, R.; Krewski, D.; Burnett, R.T.; Samet, J.; Brook, J.R.; Granville, G.; and Craig, L. 2003. Health and air quality: Directions for policy-relevant research. *Journal of Toxicology and Environmental Health, Part A*, 66, 16–19, 1891–1903.

McNeil, B.I. 2006. Oceanic implications for climate change policy. *Environmental Science and Policy*, 9, 7–8, 595–606.

Michaelowa, A. 2004. Policy integration as a success factor for emissions trading. *Environmental Management*, 33, 6, 765–775.

Mitchell, G. 2005. Forecasting environmental equity: Air quality responses to road user charging in Leeds, UK. *Journal of Environmental Management*, 77, 3, 212–226.

Nakata, T., and A. Lamont. 2001. Analysis of the impacts of carbon taxes on energy systems in Japan. *Energy Policy*, 29, 2, 159–166.

Park, R.J.; Jacob, D.J.; Field, B.D.; Yantosca, R.M.; and Chin, M. 2004. Natural and transboundary pollution influences on sulfate-nitrate-ammonium aerosols in the United States: Implications for policy. *Journal of Geophysical Research—Atmospheres,* 109, D15.

Requate, T. 2005. Dynamic incentives by environmental policy instruments—A survey. *Ecological Economics*, 54, 2–3, 175–195.

Reuther, C.G. 2000. Winds of change: Reducing transboundary air pollutants. *Environmental Health Perspectives,* 108, 4, A170–A175.

Russel, C.S., and P.T. Powell. 1999. Practical considerations and comparison of instruments of environmental policy. In *Handbook of Environmental and Resource Economics,* ed. J.C.J.M. ven den Bergh, 307–328. Cheltenham, Glos.: Edward Elgar.

Sagar, A.D. 2000. Wealth, responsibility, and equity: Exploring an allocation framework for global GHG emissions. *Climatic Change*, 45, 3–4, 511–527.

Sanderson, E.G.; Fudge, N. Totlandsdal; A.I.; Brunekreef B.; and van Bree, L. 2006. Stakeholder needs for air pollution and health information. *Journal of Toxicology and Environmental Health, Part A: Current Issues,* 69, 19, 1819–1825.

Sartori, F.; Lal, R.; Ebinger, M.H.; and Parrish, D.J. 2006. Potential soil carbon sequestration and CO_2 offset by dedicated energy crops in the USA. *Critical Reviews in Plant Sciences*, 25, 5, 441–472.

Schwarze, R. and P. Zapfel. 2000. Sulfur allowance trading and the regional clean air incentives market: A comparative design analysis of two major cap-and-trade permit programs. *Environmental and Resource Economics,* 17, 3, 279–298.

Scrimgeour, F.; Oxley, L.; and Fatai, K. 2005. Reducing carbon emissions? The relative effectiveness of different types of environmental tax: The case of New Zealand. *Environmental Modelling and Software,* 20, 11, 1439–1448.

Siddiqui, A.I., and E. Quah. 2004. Modelling transboundary air pollution in Southeast Asia: Policy regime and the role of stakeholders. *Environment and Planning A,* 36, 8, 1411–1425.

Soleille, S. 2006. Greenhouse gas emission trading schemes: A new tool for the environmental regulator's kit. *Energy Policy*, 34, 13, 1473–1477.

Sperow, M.; Eve, M.; and Paustian, K. 2003. Potential soil C sequestration on U.S. agricultural soils. *Climatic Change,* 57, 3, 319–339.

Sterner, T. 2007. Fuel taxes: An important instrument for climate policy. *Energy Policy*, 35, 6, 3194–3202.

Sterner, T., and L.H. Isaksson. 2006. Refunded emission payments theory, distribution of costs, and Swedish experience of NOx abatement. *Ecological Economics*, 57, 1, 93–106.

Tietenberg, T.H. 1992. Relevant experience with tradable entitlements. In *Combating Global Warming: Study on a Global System of Tradable Carbon Emission Entitlements*, ed. United Nations Conference on Trade and Development, 37–54. New York: United Nations, September.

Totlandsdal, A.I.; Fudge, N.; Sanderson, E.G.; van Bree, L.; and Brunekreef, B. 2007. Strengthening the science-policy interface: Experiences from a European Thematic Network on Air Pollution and Health (AIRNET). *Environmental Science and Policy,* 10, 3, 260–266.

Tuinstra, W. 2007. Preparing for the European thematic strategy on air pollution: At the interface between science and policy. *Environmental Science and Policy*, 10, 5, 434–444.

Tuinstra, W.; Hordijk, L.; and Kroeze, C. 2006. Moving boundaries in transboundary air pollution: Co-production of science and policy under the Convention on Long-Range Transboundary Air Pollution. *Global Environmental Change: Human and Policy Dimensions*, 16, 4, 349–363.

U.S. Environmental Protection Agency (EPA). 2010. What are the six common pollutants? July. http://www.epa.gov/oaqps001/urbanair/ (accessed March 18, 2011).

Vig, N., and M. Kraft, eds. 2005. *Environmental Policy: New Directions for the Twenty-first Century,* 6th ed. Washington, DC: CQ Press.

Wilson, E.J.; Friedmann, S.J.; and Pollak, M.F. 2007. Research for deployment: Incorporating risk, regulation, and liability for carbon capture and sequestration. *Environmental Science and Technology*, 41, 17, 5945–5952.

7 | Water

> Over 70 percent of the Earth's surface is covered by water. . . .
> We should really call our planet 'Ocean' instead of 'Earth.'
>
> (University of Michigan, 2006)

As you already know, water, like air, is critical to the maintenance of human and much other life. Though there is variability, a healthy adult can live for several weeks—perhaps four to six weeks—without food (Lieberson, 2004), but only about one week without water (Packer, 2002). Some experts claim that the single most important contribution to the great increases in life expectancy in the modern era resulted from the management of clean drinking water and sewage. Whether or not this is true is debatable, but there is no doubt that water management has been a huge contributor to human health, particularly through the suppression of cholera and other waterborne diseases.

As illustrated in the model presented in Chapter 1, water is a central part of the Natural System and interacts with all other parts. Infrastructure for water and sewage distribution and management is an integral public utility system, and thus an important part of the Concretion System in most cities—and should be in all. Accidents or mismanagement in the realm of water—from the provision of drinking water, to stormwater management and the treatment of wastewater—can cause great human suffering. Potential problems include the destruction of plants and animals, the spread of diseases, flooding of built areas, and the distribution of poisons such as mercury. In many cities, the water Concretion System is managed by the city government or by other levels of government, making it part of the Governmental Subsystem. The water Concretion System includes not only the water distribution system and stormwater and wastewater management, but also ports and piers, for humans have long used water for transport. As illustrated in earlier chapters, water-use patterns can also be an important part of culture, making water part of the nongovernmental Social System as well.

For the urban policy manager or administrator, the most common concerns about water center on the provision of freshwater suitable for residential, commercial, and industrial use; the treatment of wastewater created by residents; and the management of stormwater. However, policy matters may also include the protection of saltwater and freshwater ecosystems, the monitoring of groundwater, and the allocation of water for agriculture and recreation. The placement of pollution in water can affect its usability, and urban stormwater can create pollution that, in turn, affects the usability of other resources. The urban environmental policy analyst may need to consider all of the following:

- Water quantity issues such as
  — too little water, resulting in the need for conservation ("demand management")
  — excessive water use, causing subsidence, increased salinity levels, and reduced sustainability
  — too much water due to sea-level rise or other flooding
- Water quality issues such as
  — pollution to water from other sources, including land and air
  — pollution due to stormwater runoff or other flooding
- Issues that combine quantity and quality concerns such as
  — water-energy trade-offs
  — water as a habitat for other animals, including fish and other aquatic creatures that may be food sources
  — water to support vegetation, also including food sources
  — water as a recreational element

Air can be analyzed as a pure public good susceptible to congestion, and some water may best be analyzed this way, as well. Typically, though, water presents itself as a common pool resource (CPR): It is provided by nature and is often rival in consumption (that is, subtractable), while exclusion can be difficult. In industrialized cities, the water distribution system may make water excludable, which can improve the ability to manage the resource. In some cases, water may appear to be a pure private good—as in bottled water, which is both rival and excludable—but it is important to remember that the water *source* is unlikely to be a pure private good.

INTERACTIONS

As discussed in Chapter 5, it is important to keep in mind the connections between all the environmental media: air, water, and land. Though environmental policy often may be crafted in a fashion that treats pollution in one medium as separable from pollution in another, in most cases the systems are tightly coupled. For example, we outline in Chapter 6 that CO_2 (carbon dioxide) in the air can be absorbed by the ocean. The ocean's water is a "carbon sink" from the perspective of the air, but the absorption of CO_2 is still a pollutant for the water: It affects the acidity of the water, directly changing its habitat characteristics (Williams, 2010) and also affecting its ability to dissolve and carry metals (Lenntech, 2009). Land pollution can directly affect the water table, as described in Case 7.1. Additionally, when land is polluted, flooding can spread the pollution widely across the land and increase concentrations of pollutants in water bodies. If water is scarce and this causes plants to die, then soil erosion may occur. When it comes to air, water and land we should always be on the lookout for interaction effects.

■——— **Case 7.1** ———■

Polluting the Land and Thereby the Water

Just Eight Hours to Keep Toxins at Bay (United Arab Emirates)

The Dubai-based firm EnviroFone in the United Arab Emirates collected nearly 65,000 outdated mobile phones in a campaign to prevent heavy metal residues from polluting the country's water tables. When cell phones are discarded in landfills and rubbish tips, their batteries leach beryllium, cadmium, lithium, mercury, and other toxins into the soil, and it's been estimated that one battery can contaminate up to 600,000 liters of drinking water. In the EnviroFone warehouse in Al Quoz, the old phones are stripped of their batteries before being shipped to a recycling plant in Singapore. It takes just eight hours to melt down a unit and recycle the plastics, silver, and other reusable materials.

Source: Landais, 2007.

Another important set of interactions is caused by relationships between energy and water. Water may produce energy directly, such as via hydroelectric dams. This can affect the use of water as a habitat for fish (such as salmon) and may broadly affect the former riverine (riparian) habitat. Water is also used in thermoelectric power plants (Young, 2009), as presented in Case 7.2. Therefore, drought can affect energy production. Energy may be used to create potable water, as in desalination plants, or to move water, as in pumping or irrigation, but the use of energy generally creates pollution (often air pollution). Another interaction between energy and water is explained in Case 7.3, which calls attention to a sometimes-unforeseen problem of desalination. The California Energy Commission points out that "the State Water Project, which moves large quantities of water great distances and over steep terrain, is the largest single user of electrical energy in the State" (California Energy Commission, 2010). For the urban administrator, more salient water-energy ties may revolve around heating water for residential and commercial use. Regardless of the geographical context, saving water—particularly hot water—saves energy, while also reducing the impact on sewer systems.

A growing awareness of energy-water linkages is indicated by (1) the introduction of U.S. federal legislation providing for analysis of potential problems (for example, the Energy and Water Integration Act of 2009); (2) an increase in research conducted at major colleges and universities such as Arizona State University (ASU News, 2009); (3) an entire issue of the *Journal of Contemporary Water Research and Education* devoted to the "energy-water nexus" (Sehlke, 2009); and (4) various research presentations at International Energy Association meetings (Young, 2009). "'Water and energy are inextricably linked,' says [David A.] Sampson, a . . . research scientist specializing in simulation and modeling. 'Energy is required to transport and purify water, and water is used in energy production'" (ASU News, 2009). Thus, the water interactions we should consider go beyond land and air to a *sine qua non* for desirable standards of living: energy.

■——— **Case 7.2** ———■

Water and Energy

Water Woes Loom as Thirsty Generators Face Climate Change (United States)

U.S. power plants are facing water shortages as climate changes intensify droughts and heatwaves in already arid regions of the country. At the same time that the demand for electricity to keep air conditioners running is growing, shortages of water to cool generators are threatening shutdowns. Nuclear power plants require even more water than conventional power stations to keep from overheating, the U.S. Department of Energy said in a report to Congress last year. This summer's [2007] record-breaking heatwaves in the western and southern states [led to] the partial shutdown of several reactors, and Illinois, Michigan, and Minnesota have scaled back their nuclear operations due to drought in the past two years, according to the Union of Concerned Scientists. Nuclear and conventional energy aren't alone in their heavy water requirements; concentrated solar technology and geothermal technology also use significant amounts of water. One practical solution is using recycled wastewater to cool power generators, an idea already being tried by some plants in Pennsylvania that are recycling mine water.

Source: Ling, 2007.

■——— **Case 7.3** ———■

Problems with Desalination

Making Water Potable Aggravates Global Warming (Switzerland)

"In Geneva, Switzerland, the World Wildlife Fund (WWF) released a report warning that the growing popularity of seawater desalination plants had the potential to aggravate global warming. Desalination is a popular solution to water shortages in Spain, Australia, and other arid countries and is becoming more common in the United Kingdom, the United States, China, and India; it supplies 60 percent of the potable water in the Persian (Arabian) Gulf. Unfortunately, the desalination process emits climate-damaging greenhouse gases and facilities dump briny residues back into the sea, harming nearby marine organisms, said Director Jamie Pittock of the WWF's World Freshwater Program" (El Universal, 2007).

"In many parts of the world, alternatives can provide the same freshwater benefits of ocean desalination at far lower economic and environmental costs. These alternatives include treating low-quality local water sources, encouraging regional water transfers, improving conservation and efficiency, accelerating wastewater recycling and reuse, and implementing smart land-use planning" (Cooley, Gleick and Wolff, 2006, 1).

KEY ECOLOGICAL ISSUES

For urban environmental policy administrators and analysts, the key ecological issues related to water are the many services water provides and the impact of humans—especially concentrated human populations—on those services. When considering ecological issues, the water sources with which humans interact can be divided into certain types: aquifers, wetlands, streams, rivers, lakes, estuaries, coastlines, and oceans. All of these are ecologically important, can affect urban areas, and are influenced by human behavior.

However, before discussing other ecological issues, it should be stressed that *all* water types—fresh, brackish, or salt; aquifer, estuary, or ocean—provide important resources and habitat for amazingly complex webs of plants, animals, and other organisms that interact throughout our biosphere:

> Thus, topsoil containing nutrients from an Oklahoma wheat field may be washed by spring rains into a nearby stream, which flows into larger rivers that reach the ocean. Phosphorus originating in deep marine sediments may eventually be transferred to terrestrial ecosystems in bird droppings from seabirds that feed on fish, which in turn, are nourished by crustaceans that eat algae, which absorb phosphorus from the ocean. Because of this, all ecosystems on Earth are linked and ecosystem disruption can have far-reaching effects. (Chiras and Reganold, 2005, 49)

The discussion here provides a broad-brush impression of human-water ecological interactions that are particularly relevant to urban environmental policy. But humans probably couldn't live on a planet denuded of wildlife even if we wanted to; in the back of your mind, then, you should always consider the breadth and depth of ecosystem links—and the importance of these ecosystems to urban residents many miles away.

WETLANDS

According to the U.S. Environmental Protection Agency (U.S. EPA), twenty-two states in the United States have lost more than half their original wetlands. Though considered by some to be wasteland that should be drained or used for "productive" purposes such as farming or building, wetlands are, in fact, of significant value to humans (in addition to their other ecosystem values), as work by leading ecologists bears out. Wetlands provide flood and stormwater control, water storage and support for groundwater aquifers, and filtration of pollution (Chiras and Reganold, 2005, 195). Some people also find them beautiful. The fact that wetlands can actually reduce pollution has led to interest in their intentional use—or artificial construction—for pollution control. However, the EPA warns that, without care, such intentional use can overwhelm the wetland and cause harm to wildlife (EPA, 2009b); the same potential risks exist for unintentional use.

Under Section 404 of the Clean Water Act, the EPA regulates wetlands. Some years ago, the EPA created a goal of "no net loss" of wetlands in the United States. No *net* loss allows for the loss of some wetlands as long as this is at least balanced by wetland restoration. "In 2009, [the] EPA, in partnership with the U.S. Army Corps of Engineers, states, and tribes achieved a 'no net loss' of wetlands under the CWA [Clean Water Act] Section 404 regulatory program" (EPA, 2009a, 65). Still, the loss of wetlands continues worldwide.

Streams, Rivers, and Lakes

"Streams are rather open ecosystems," note Chiras and Reganold (2005, 203). Thus, many things enter streams and rivers from the air and groundwater, and various types of debris "are all washed into streams during the spring runoff" (203). The openness of streams, as well as the fact that their flow carries much of what ends up in them to other areas, increases the potential for ecological harm. Runoff not only carries natural debris but also can transport various toxins, including heavy metal pollutants, to other locations.

> Between the end of the past century and now, the rivers Rhine and Meuse and their sediments have become increasingly contaminated with various pollutants (heavy metals, PAC's). As a result considerable amounts of heavy metals have accumulated in the soils of the embanked floodplains. (Faculty of Science, Radboud University Nijmegen)

In addition, many streams ultimately carry whatever ends up in them to lakes, while others carry organics and pollutants to the ocean. Streams may also flood, carrying their own contents—as well as anything that lies in their paths—into human habitations.

Surface and groundwater are the most directly useful water sources for human consumption, but both sources "are often polluted with toxic chemicals, pesticides, human waste, and many other contaminants" (Chiras and Reganold, 2005, 225). Increasingly, streams may even be contaminated with pharmaceuticals—with effects as yet unknown, but with some worrisome early findings: "In one instance, male fish beneath the outflow of a wastewater treatment plant emptying into Boulder Creek, Colorado, underwent a sex change into female fish. The same thing could be observed experimentally by exposing male fish contained in tanks to water from the plant outflow" (Hill, 2010, 83). The fact that rivers and lakes are often used for transport can cause other pollution problems, including pollution by boat fuels, damage to shorelines from boat wakes, and—perhaps the most difficult to manage—the introduction of non-native species (like the quagga mussels discussed in Chapter 1).

Estuaries, Coastlines, and Oceans

The relationship among humans, urban areas, and the oceans is powerful. In the United States, coastal regions comprise only 17 percent of the land area, but 53 percent of Americans live in those areas (Chiras and Reganold, 2005). "Worldwide, two thirds of the largest cities (population greater than 2.5 million) are located near estuaries" (Chiras and Reganold, 2005, 207). Elements of the ocean-land-human interaction can provide significant human protection. For example, estuaries, like wetlands, provide flood and erosion control and act as natural pollution-filtering systems. "According to one study,

---

■———— **Case 7.4** ————■

Human Causes of Damage to Coral Reefs

Reefs are not well adapted to survive exposure to long-term stress. Some examples include agricultural and industrial runoff, increased sedimentation from land clearing, human sewage and toxic discharges. Many land-based activities have important implications for reefs. Agricultural activities can introduce herbicides, pesticides, fertilizers and runoff from animal feed lots. Sewage discharges can introduce nitrogen and phosphate compounds along with pathogens and mixtures of toxics. Uncontrolled land clearing can result in erosion, with the resultant increase in sediment loads to surface waters. Roadways, parking lots and buildings consist of impervious surfaces. These surfaces increase runoff rates and carry with those waters mixtures of dissolved substances to surface waters. The surface waters in any watershed eventually discharge into coastal or near-coastal waters. These waters can then impact coral communities associated with these discharge points. Thus, activities occurring in distant locations have impacts to reefs which are far away from these activities.

There have been increasing efforts to establish better management and conservation measures to protect the diversity of these biologically rich areas. Management practices have historically focused on the coral reef proper and not considered associated communities, such as seagrasses, mangroves, mudflats or defined watersheds (which transport complex mixtures in their waters), in a meaningful manner. This attempted to manage the reef in isolation, like an island.

Current management efforts recognize the importance of including reefs as part of a larger system.

Source: EPA, 2011a.

---

an area of only 5.6 hectares (14 acres) of estuary has the same pollution-reducing effect as a $1 million waste treatment plant!" (Chiras and Reganold, 2005, 206). In addition, Chiras and Reganold note that estuaries provide important habitat for marine fish harvests, with 60 percent of harvested marine fish using the estuary for part of their life cycles (206). Yet, human impacts on estuaries often lead to serious degradation. For example, upstream dams reduce the flow of freshwater into estuaries, allowing saltwater intrusion. Naturally, streams also carry silt into estuaries, and this silt protects the estuary from excess erosion, but the reduced flow caused by dams reduces silt, too.

Coastal regions are often aesthetically beautiful and provide critical resources for humans such as food, oil, and transportation, but they also present hazards to humans caused by storms and rising sea levels. Barrier islands, estuaries, coral reefs, and natural shores all provide some protection against storm damage. Yet, human activities can erode natural shores, and human action is causing significant damage to coral reefs, as indicated in Case 7.4. Excess petroleum withdrawals can cause subsidence as well (Chiras and Reganold, 2005), and spills from the operation of transportation vessels or from oil extraction or transportation can produce serious impacts, as the sinking of the *Deepwater Horizon* oil drilling rig in 2010 graphically reminded us.

POINT SOURCE AND NONPOINT SOURCE WATER POLLUTION

Whether affecting surface waters, wetlands, or aquifers, water pollution can be divided into two main types: point source and nonpoint source. Point source water pollution comes from specific sources, such as a wastewater treatment plant (as described in the Boulder Creek example), or boats that emit oil and non-native species into waters, or the *Deepwater Horizon* oil spill. Much water pollution, however, comes from nonpoint sources. As mentioned earlier, when water runs over the land, it picks up pollutants and debris and carries them to its eventual destination. Even rainwater picks up air pollutants as it falls from the sky. These types of pollution are nonpoint source pollution.

In general, it is easier to develop policy for point source pollution because the sources can be identified; therefore, policy tools can be applied to change the behavior of individual entities. Stressing—again—the importance of a holistic approach to urban environmental policy, nonpoint source water pollution is often better managed by focusing on land and air pollution, for it is water's interaction with pollution of these media that causes nonpoint source pollution.

Whether pollutants come from point sources or nonpoint sources, there is a Total Maximum Daily Load (TMDL) that water bodies can receive before they become impaired. Among other agencies, the EPA works to develop TMDLs that identify "the total pollutant loading that a waterbody can receive and still meet water quality standards" (EPA, 2007, 1).

KEY SOCIAL ISSUES AND POLICY TOOLS IN THE WATER CONTEXT

With so many policy issues relating to water and society, it would be impossible for us to cover them all here. Therefore, we will focus on four broad areas of key importance to urban environmental policy analysis:

- household water use, with a particular focus on conservation (that is, demand management)
- water and production, including food production
- water runoff and other flooding issues
- recreational use of water

HOUSEHOLD WATER USE

Households use water to drink, to cook, for hygiene, for landscaping, for cooling (for example, through evaporative coolers, also known as "swamp coolers"), and for decoration or recreation (for example, fountains and swimming pools). The primary concerns of household water management include (1) ensuring sufficient clean water into the home, and (2) managing the dirty water that leaves the home. Many urbanized areas also consider the impact of stormwater created by concretions.

Though providing sufficient clean water for every household and properly managing wastewater can be challenging in certain parts of the world, in industrialized cities the main concern is the *amount* of water available for use (a serious concern for

---

■———— **Case 7.5** ————■

Supply Compared to Demand

Though Water Is Drying Up, a Chinese Metropolis Booms (China)

Above the ground, the capital of China's Hebei Province, Shijiazhuang, is flourishing, with a booming economy and a population to match. Below the ground, the picture is exactly the opposite: the overstressed water table is sinking fast. Hydrologists warn that aquifers below the North China Plain may be drained within 30 years. Studies show that five-sixths of the wetlands have dried up and that most streams and creeks have disappeared. Shijiazhuang's priority is to grow as quickly as possible, however, and planning for future water shortages is definitely in second place.

Source: Yardley, 2007.

---

developing cities as well). In most cities in Organisation for Economic Co-operation and Development (OECD) nations, water is clean enough to drink and is provided consistently; even so, there have been cases of major cities, such as Atlanta, Georgia, and Sydney, Australia, coming dangerously close to running out of potable water supplies. The delivery of potable water to households and the removal of wastewater are primarily well-understood engineering issues; however, as we have seen worldwide, successfully implementing engineering solutions requires the existence of effective governmental structures. This section focuses on household water conservation, which is often referred to as "demand management."

Too Little Water

Throughout the world, an increasing problem is insufficient water to meet demand—either presently or in the foreseeable future. Many people expect that a concern with sufficient water levels must be confined to the arid parts of the world, but this is not the case. First, the primary issue is the amount of water available in comparison to the demand for it. Worldwide population growth and the concentration of population in specific areas places ever-increasing pressure on freshwater supplies, as illustrated in Case 7.5. Second, even in areas where rainwater is plentiful, droughts can and do occur, and many climate scientists believe that global climate change may increase the rate of drought (Rogers, 2008). There is also very strong evidence that climate change will alter the timing of rain and snow, which will affect water systems fed by snow melt, including those in Los Angeles and San Francisco, California. Third, even where freshwater is plentiful, it is frequently polluted. For all of these reasons, it appears that water conservation will increasingly be an important urban environmental policy issue.

In the United States, there is considerable room for improvement in conservation measures. Although certain areas are becoming more efficient at managing water supplies, in general, residents in the United States "use more than three times as much water per person per day as average European countries, [many of] which themselves use much more than developing countries" (Graves, 1993, as quoted by Campbell, Johnson, and Larson 2004, 638).

Conservation/Demand-Management Policy Tools. The range of household conservation policy tools is broad. Both the feasibility of different water-saving options and their political acceptability can vary by society. Methods include education (suasion), pricing, regulation, plumbing replacement, and changes to allow for the use of "graywater" (water that has been used before but can be repurposed without purification). Other conservation methods include strict limits on water use, including the hours during which water is available or can be used for specific purposes (such as irrigating yards or washing cars).

Research in Phoenix, Arizona, a rapidly growing city in the U.S. Southwest, indicates that regulation and pricing are likely to be especially effective methods for conserving water (Campbell, Johnson, and Larson, 2004). This is because pricing and regulatory methods are typically more certain than other conservation methods and can be spread widely across large populations. In some cases, public administrators are skeptical about the efficacy of pricing. One reason for this may be the significant evidence that the price-elasticity of demand for water is inelastic, meaning that increasing the price of water by 1 percent results in less than a 1-percent decrease in the amount of water consumed. However, because even small price increases can be spread across an entire city, the amount of water savings can be significant (Campbell, Johnson, and Larson, 2004).

In order to price water effectively, its use must be metered. In America's largest city, New York (NYC), residential water use was not metered until 1985. When metering started, many members of NYC's water division were skeptical of the use of residential metering—and they were later astounded to discover that it led to great savings. For one thing, since people had to pay for water, it induced them to repair leaks, which in many cases they were not aware of before the meters were put in place (H. Tschudi, personal communication). In fact, leak detection and repair—whether in a home, a firm, a farm, or in the distribution infrastructure itself—can be an effective means of conserving water.

Multifamily buildings such as apartments can create a logistical difficulty for metering. A single water meter may record usage for an entire multifamily or multi-housing complex, and the price of water is often included in rent. If conservation is of importance, this is a bad policy: those who do not pay for their water will generally overconsume it. In fact, economists would predict that, at a *price* of zero, people will use water until the last unit of water they use is worth nothing to them—even though the *cost* of water is almost never zero. Cultural attitudes, including conservation attitudes, may prevent this extent of overuse, but overuse is still likely and common. Therefore, metering each unit in a housing complex, sometimes called submetering (EPA, 2010), can increase water-use efficiency. The term submetering can also refer to providing households with separate meters for indoor and outdoor use. In the United States, about 30 percent of all household water is devoted to outdoor use (EPA, 2008).

Designing appropriate water pricing regimes—or appropriate pricing structures for any public utility—can be quite complicated, and incorrect pricing can actually lead to water waste (Campbell, Johnson, and Larson, 2004). Therefore, before proposing specific water-conservation pricing structures, you should seek expert advice. Sources include the following:

- the extensive literature on public utility pricing, including *Fairness or Efficiency: An Introduction to Public Utility Pricing* (Zajac, 1978);
- appropriate conference proceedings such as those from conferences sponsored by the American Water Resources Association, the American Water Works Association, and the Association of Metropolitan Water Agencies;
- local public utilities' pricing divisions; and
- university faculty members.

In spite of some complexity, it is certain that water pricing can be an effective method for water conservation, as was illustrated in Exhibit 3.8. Case 7.6 suggests a different type of pricing scheme.

Regulatory methods can include a multitude of options, including rules about when water can be used for lawns ("lawns" are often referred to as "turf" in the demand-management literature), whether lawns are allowed at all (or only native plants or the water-saving landscaping method known as "xeriscaping" can be used), what limits are placed on yard sizes, and so on. In other countries, lawns may not be the issue, but other outside water use can be equivalent. For example, the Turkish government sought conservation through a reduction of residents' washing rugs in the street. (*Today's Zaman*, June 2008).

One effective means for reducing water consumption can be regulation of plumbing fixture types.[1] Low-flow showerheads, toilets, urinals, and faucets can reduce water

---

■——— **Case 7.6** ———■

A Pegged Scarcity-Pricing System

Water Bill Rises and Falls with Dam Level (Australia)

Domestic water rates may soon be pegged to weather conditions in the Australian state of New South Wales. The Independent Pricing and Regulatory Tribunal (IPART) is studying the adoption of "scarcity pricing," which would raise the price of water when rainfall and water levels in reservoirs both drop. Professor Quentin Grafton of the Crawford School of Economics and Government at the Australian National University said that prices could rise or fall by 50 to 80 percent, but emphasized that state residents would only pay more while droughts lasted. The goal of the scarcity pricing would be to discourage the use of water for landscaping, car washing, swimming pools, and other outdoor consumption.

Source: Masters, 2007.

issues w/ concretion system (handwritten margin note)

■————— **Case 7.7** —————■

An Unintended Consequence of Conservation Measures

Low-Water-Use Toilets Might Be Too Effective (Arizona)

A program to install low-flow toilets in older neighborhoods in Arizona's Pima County is on hold because—paradoxically—they may save too much water. The Regional Wastewater Reclamation Department agreed in 2006 to pay the Water Conservation Alliance, a University of Arizona group, $525,000 to manage the project, but after 450 of the planned 1,000 toilets were installed, the county decided to restrict where such toilets should go. A consultant found that some older sewer lines had slopes below minimum county standards, so that solid materials could settle and cause smells, clogs, and pipeline corrosion. In addition, because of efficient household water conservation, there isn't enough liquid in some lines to flush solids out of the system. Director Val Little of the Water Conservation Alliance contends that the studies aren't completely accurate.

Source: Davis, 2008.

---

consumption—though usually less than engineering estimates suggest. It appears that the estimate discrepancy occurs because some people overcompensate for low-flow fixtures. For example, some people may take longer showers when they know they have a low-flow showerhead than when they know they have a high-output showerhead, and this reduces water savings. However, if people do not realize that they have water-saving devices, the compensation effect is ameliorated and savings are much higher. Thus, installing low-flow fixtures in multihousing units with high turnover may be effective, and regulation that prevents sales of high-flow fixtures may be effective. But, ironically, providing low-flow fixtures directly to households can backfire and actually cause *increased* water use (Campbell, Johnson, and Larson, 2004). Chapter 2 encourages you to consider unintended consequences when making policy decisions. The increased use of water after provision of low-flow fixtures was an unintended consequence of a water conservation policy. Case 7.7 demonstrates another unintended consequence and reinforces the idea that analysts must be familiar with their own city's Concretion System.

One regulatory change that seems to hold out the potential for high water savings in some areas is increased use of graywater (that is, treated wastewater effluent or lightly used household water) or rainwater. In many arid regions, more than half of household water use occurs outside the house (for example, irrigating yards or filling pools) rather than inside. As indicated in Case 7.8, "graywater" is water that is no longer potable, but is also not polluted in ways that will certainly cause illness (the latter being known as "blackwater"). Incentives can be used to increase the use of graywater, but many codes prohibit the use of graywater for irrigation, even though use can be properly managed so as to limit the potential for harm. Currently, the regulation of graywater varies considerably by jurisdiction. Case 7.9 provides some

---

■——— Case 7.8 ———■

Graywater, Blackwater, and Household Water Conservation

As its name connotes, graywater is of lesser quality than potable water, but of higher quality than blackwater. Blackwater is water flushed from toilets. Also, water from the kitchen sink, garbage disposal and dishwasher usually is considered blackwater because of high concentrations of organic waste. Graywater derives from other residential water uses. Water from the bath, shower, washing machine [unless diapers or other sources of fecal matter are being washed (Barker and English, 2000–2010)], and bathroom sink are the sources of graywater.

Not a water for all uses, graywater is most suitably used for subsurface irrigation of nonedible landscape plants. Graywater could supply most, if not all the irrigation needs of a domestic dwelling landscaped with vegetation of a semiarid region. Along with its application to outside irrigation, graywater can be used in some situations for toilet flushing. . . .

Graywater recycling systems are commercially available.

Source: Gelt, n.d. Used with permission.

■——— Case 7.9 ———■

Some Arizona Guidelines for Household Graywater Use

Follow these best management practices to comply with Arizona's rules for graywater use

- First and foremost, avoid human contact with graywater, or soil irrigated with gray water.
- You may use gray water for household gardening, composting, and lawn and landscape irrigation, but use it in a way that it does not run off your own property.
- Do not surface irrigate any plants that produce food, except for citrus and nut trees.
- Use only flood or drip irrigation to water lawns and landscaping. Spraying gray water is prohibited.
- When determining the location for your gray water irrigation, remember that it cannot be in a wash or drainage carrying runoff.
- Gray water may only be used in locations where groundwater is at least five feet below the surface.

Source: Arizona Department of Environmental Quality, n.d. Used with permission.

---

regulations for household graywater use in Arizona. There are other nonhousehold uses of graywater, as well. For example, some golf courses use graywater for watering grass (City of San Luis Obispo, 2010; GCSAA, 2011). To increase the use of graywater as a conservation measure, cities may need to change regulations and also provide education and best-practice ideas to residents. One potential problem not

---

■――――― **Case 7.10** ―――――■

Rainwater Harvesting

The image of falling rain may be pure and refreshing, but harvested rain is not without water quality concerns. Rain in certain urban areas may contain various impurities absorbed from the atmosphere, including arsenic and lead.

Certain desert conditions also can cause rainwater quality concerns. Desert rain is infrequent and, therefore, bird droppings, dust and other impurities accumulate between rain events. They then occur in high concentrations in runoff when it does rain. As a result, the quality of harvested rainfall needs frequent monitoring if it is used for potable uses.

Various methods are used to purify rainwater. First-flush devices ensure a certain degree of water quality in harvested rainwater. The first five gallons of runoff from a gutter, roof or other surface is likely to contain various impurities such as bird droppings and dust. A first-flush device prevents this initial flow from draining into the storage tank.

Many first-flush devices are simply and cleverly designed. Such devices include tipping buckets that dump when water reaches a certain level. Also there are containers with a ball that floats with the rising water to close off an opening after an inflow of five gallons. Water then is diverted to another pipe leading to the cistern. This use of simple technology is an attractive feature of rainwater harvesting. (Water harvesting systems are not readily available on the market.)

Source: Gelt, n.d. Used with permission.

---

mentioned in the cases is that prolonged use of graywater can cause the buildup of salts in the soil (Barker and English, 2010).

Rainwater harvesting is another possible means of reducing household water use for irrigation, but as described in Case 7.10, its use also can benefit from governmental activity to provide education and best-practice guidelines. As for graywater, incentives can be used to increase the use of rainwater—and it might be possible for city governments either to develop and provide, or contract with another organization for the development and provision of, water harvesting systems.

Some nonpricing methods of water conservation may be more effective on a house-by-house basis than price-based methods, but these can be more difficult to deliver to each house. For example, Phoenix, Arizona, tried two programs: "Metrotech/ Neighbors Helping Neighbors" and "Seniors Helping Seniors." Neighbors Helping Neighbors involved teenagers from a technical high school helping neighbors to perform home audits for leaks and then repair and replace plumbing fixtures. Seniors Helping Seniors, a similar program, focused specifically on senior citizens. These programs were very effective on a per-household level—more effective per-household than some elements of conservation water pricing, for example. But because they could be delivered to only a relatively small number of households, the programs were less effective for the city overall (Campbell, Johnson, and Larson, 2004). However, another benefit of such programs is that they may develop long-range community and conservation attitudes.

It should be noted that water pricing for conservation may have a disproportionate impact on lower income groups. Thomas M. Babcock, formerly Water Conservation Coordinator for the City of Phoenix Water Services Department, believed that pricing hit poorer residents harder than richer residents because poorer residents didn't have the resources to repair leaks and upgrade fixtures to newer, more conserving, models (T.M. Babcock, personal communication). A solution to this problem might be found in combining a program like Neighbors Helping Neighbors—specifically targeted to low-income households—with conservation pricing.

There is some evidence that educational efforts can be effective, but the method of delivery must be carefully considered. For example, according to A.J. "Jack" Pfister, former General Manager of SRP, one of the largest energy and water providers in Arizona, SRP found that bill inserts, though an easy and inexpensive addition to monthly mailings, were not effective tools in water conservation efforts. Surveys performed for SRP revealed that only about 15 percent of recipients looked at the inserts at all, and only about half of those looked at them closely (A.J. Pfister, personal communication).

Estimating Effectiveness of City Water Conservation Policies. The Arizona Department of Water Resources (ADWR) commissioned a study to figure out which urban water conservation policies held out the most promise for Arizona. In addition to analyzing implemented policies, the study team was commissioned to develop an assessment model and do-it-yourself guide so cities could perform their own analyses of conservation-policy effectiveness. This guide, called *The Cookbook: Doing Multivariate Analysis of Residential Single-Family Water Conservation Programs,* is, as of this writing, publicly available at the website of the Morrison Institute for Public Policy of the School of Public Affairs at Arizona State University (Campbell and Johnson, 1999). It provides step-by-step instructions on how to estimate policy effectiveness for your own city. As we outlined in Chapter 5, adaptive management requires constant monitoring and assessment of environmental policies.

WATER AND PRODUCTION

At least in the United States, many water conservation efforts focus on residential water consumption. It is important to remember that producers, whether agricultural or otherwise, make high use of water. According to the United States Geological Survey (USGS), in 2000 only 11 percent of all water used in the United States was "public supply."

> Public supply refers to water withdrawn by public and private water suppliers that furnish water to at least 25 people or have a minimum of 15 connections. Public-supply water may be delivered to users for domestic, commercial, industrial, or thermoelectric-power purposes. Some public-supply water may be delivered to other public suppliers or used in the processes of water and wastewater treatment. Public-supply water is used for such public services (public uses) as pools, parks, and public buildings; [some is] unaccounted for (losses) because of system leaks or such nonmetered services as firefighting or the flushing of water lines. (Hutson et al., 2004)

Though this definition of "public-supply water" includes some commercial, industrial, and thermoelectric uses, it is still the case that separately measured (that is, nonpublic-supply) agricultural and horticultural irrigation accounted for 34 percent of total U.S. use, separate industrial accounted for 5 percent, and separate thermoelectric accounted for 48 percent in 2000. Excluding nonpublic-supply thermoelectric use,[2] public supply was still only 21 percent of total use, leaving nonpublic-supply agricultural irrigation at 65 percent and nonpublic-supply industrial use at 9 percent of all other U.S. water use (Hutson et al. 2004). The purpose of these statistics is to point out that household water use in the United States is almost certainly a lower percentage of total use than is agricultural and horticultural irrigation, and it is on a par with industrial use (unfortunately, from these data, we cannot tell exactly how industrial and residential uses compare).

Keep in mind that the percentage of total water use in each category can vary significantly by country. In 1996 in the southern African nations of Namibia, Botswana, and South Africa, agricultural water use was 58 percent, 73 percent, and 48 percent, respectively (compared with the 34 percent reported for the United States). In Namibia, Botswana, and South Africa, water use for mining was 10 percent, 3 percent, and 11 percent, respectively (Malan, 2006). In contrast, mining in the United States represented only about 1 percent of the country's total water use in 2000 (Hutson et al., 2004). Unfortunately, as shown by Case 7.11, mining itself presents significant land-water environmental problems.

Agricultural production is important to any society's well-being, and for the United States in particular, it is an important export. So, the point of this discussion is not to suggest that we should eliminate agricultural irrigation. However, agricultural irrigation is often very inefficient, not only because high water-use application technologies are still used, but also because distribution systems may be leaky. Additionally, agricultural water pumping can be energy intensive, and some agricultural uses drain aquifers (USDA, 2009). Local preferences for agricultural products may also affect agricultural water use. According to the Global Change Program at the University of Michigan:

> Agriculture is responsible for 87% of the total water used globally. In Asia it accounts for 86% of total annual water withdrawal, compared with 49% in North and Central America and 38% in Europe. Rice growing, in particular, is a heavy consumer of water. . . . Compared with other crops, rice production is less efficient in the way it uses water. Wheat, for example, consumes [less]. (University of Michigan, 2006)

At the same time, "irrigation systems often perform poorly, wasting as much as 60 percent of the total water pumped before it reaches the intended crop" (University of Michigan, 2006). Further, there are cases in which agricultural water reuse and recycling can be effective (EPA, 2010). Agricultural water is often underpriced, which is one reason for its inefficient use.

For some cities, it may be that agricultural irrigation is not an important policy issue, but there are at least three reasons why many urban policy analysts may need to consider agricultural use. First, water that flows into the city (or under-

6

■———— **Case 7.11** ————■

Mining Can Be Very Polluting

Unclean Water: The Lead Generation Is Still Paying (Greece)

A 1989 medical study of children living near the ancient silver mines at Lavrio in Greece's Attika Prefecture—still the site of mining activities today—revealed that 90 percent had excessive lead levels in their blood and that many suffered from lead-related ailments of the nervous system and brain. According to Dr. Angelos Khatzakis, who participated in that study, the soil and groundwater are still heavily contaminated and nothing has ever been done to clean it up. A similarly polluted mining town in Khalkidiki Prefecture, Stratoni, contains lead, zinc, and cyanide residues in the sand on its beaches to a depth of 5–6 m, according to Tolis Papageorgiou of the Observatory of Mining Activities. Children play frequently on those beaches, but nothing has been done to clean them up. In addition, Stratoni's groundwater contains ten times the permissible limits of lead, arsenic, and cadmium.

Source: Shaler, 2007.

---

lies the city in the case of aquifers) may be shared by agricultural users outside the city. Therefore, the efficiency of agricultural irrigation systems can be of crucial importance to cities. Recall that, in Chapter 1, we mention that cities are not fixed in space and that it may be useful for them to make agreements with extra-city organizations that affect resource flows important to the city. Heikkila (2004) explains,

> Institutional boundaries that coincide with natural resources are likely to be associated with the implementation of more effective resource management programs. At the same time, where jurisdictions can control through coordination, they can also facilitate more effective resource management [even] where jurisdictions do not match resource boundaries. (97)

Second, active agricultural lands may still exist in rapidly growing cities. The sight of a worked field or grazing stock, for instance, is not unknown within the city limits of rapidly growing cities in the American West. Third, there is increasing interest in urban agriculture worldwide. Starting in 1993, a UN-sponsored survey in Dar es Salaam, Tanzania, found that urban agriculture at that time produced over 100,000 tons of crops each year, in addition to around "95,000 litres of milk, 6,000 trays of eggs and 11,000 kilos of poultry" each *day* (Sustainable Cities, 2010).

Efficiency in industrial use of water should also be considered. Though the United States has seen a decline in water used for nonpublic-supply industrial use (Hutson et al., 2004), it seems clear that there are still water savings to be had. The EPA provides general suggestions for industrial water conservation measures (EPA, 2010). A 2003 report by the Pacific Institute provides detailed calculations for potential water savings in urban areas in California. Over all commercial, institutional, and industrial uses, they estimate that about 39 percent of water use in 2000 could be saved through conservation efforts (Gleick et al., 2003).

HOUSEHOLDS, PRODUCERS, AND DEMAND MANAGEMENT

Often, urban water conservation policies focus on household water consumption. But, as we said in the first chapter, if you want to hunt ducks, go where the ducks are. There are conservation gains to be made in household water conservation, but there are at least as many available in agricultural and industrial uses of water. When considering demand management, consider all three sectors, not just one.

TOO MUCH WATER: RUNOFF AND OTHER FLOODING[3]

Water runoff can be a significant problem in urban areas for two primary reasons. First, impermeable surfaces of the Concretion System affect the flow of water so that it is more rapid, does not soak into the ground, and concentrates in different ways than without them. Second, stormwater runoff in particular can cause pollution at outfall locations. A secondary reason is that agricultural runoff can pollute water bodies (including aquifers) that interact with cities.

Water flows much more rapidly over a concrete or asphalt surface than over most natural earth-and-plant surfaces. Just imagine the flow of water down a paved street compared with the flow of the same amount of water through a forest, where grasses, weeds, roots, dead leaves, and other debris slow its flow. Also, water flowing on a paved street doesn't soak in, but water in the forest does. Many of the surfaces of the urban Concretion System are impervious to water—consider paved sidewalks, driveways, parking lots, streets, and even the roofs of buildings. Thus, rainfall on a city has different effects than the same amount of rainfall in natural areas. The city of Denver, Colorado, has a large park that includes a lake. When the park was created, it was on the outskirts of the city; now, however, it is surrounded by residential areas. The decreased permeability surrounding the park has changed the amount of rainwater that flows into the lake—now much more water flows in at a faster rate—and this has affected habitat and necessitated changes in water management.

Stormwater runoff also presents a pollution concern for many cities, as described in Case 7.12. Clearly, a link exists between the problems of impermeability of much of the urban form and stormwater runoff pollution. The impermeability causes swifter flow that can overcome sanitary sewers in combined systems, and the impermeable surfaces hold other pollutants that are then swept away by the swift flows and deposited wherever the stormwater outfall is located.

There are four primary methods for dealing with these problems. The first is to decouple the stormwater and sanitary sewer systems; this process can be very expensive—especially in large, old cities—because it usually requires an entire additional system that must be large enough to accept significant storm events. The second method is treating stormwater runoff before it is discharged. Usually these two actions must be accomplished by the city government, either directly or through

---

■———— **Case 7.12** ————■

Stormwater Runoff Generates Pollution

The management of stormwater, especially in urban areas, has often involved the creation of elaborate infrastructure to move water away from streets, homes and business. Although effective in reducing flooding, this approach has created a new set of environmental impacts: the effluent at the end of the pipe carries everything that was on the streets or in the drains to the nearest body of water, usually in an untreated state.

Combined systems, where storm drains feed into the sanitary sewer system, obviate this problem in [milder] weather. But, during heavy precipitation, pollution problems are multiplied as a torrent of stormwater mixes with raw sewage and overwhelms the waste treatment system's capacity, usually forcing the municipality to dump a mix of stormwater and raw sewage into receiving waters. Pollution from combined systems is a major concern in over 770 cities in the United States, according to the EPA. Some cities, including New York City and Seattle, have invested heavily in both "end of pipe" improvements to treat stormwater overflow and in "green" best management practices to reduce stormwater flow into the combined system.

Source: Cain, n.d. Used with permission.

■———— **Case 7.13** ————■

Technology May Help Manage Stormwater Runoff

Water Pollution Can Be Reduced with New Storm Water Analysis System (Virginia)

A research team led by Professor Tamim Younos at Virginia Tech University in Blacksburg, Montgomery County, Virginia, is developing a new software program to help water managers deal with stormwater pollution. The U.S. Environmental Protection Agency is funding the project because contaminants washed into rivers, lakes, and coastal waters by runoff cause up to 50 percent of the country's water pollution. The new computer program will allow planners and water engineers to choose the "Best Management Practices," or BMPs, for a specific site by entering data on soil types, slopes, accessibility for maintenance, and other factors; its use will reduce both human errors and the time needed to make decisions, said researcher Kevin Young.

Source: Virginia Tech, 2007.

---

contracting, because the stormwater system is a pure public good. The third method is to reduce the impermeability of urban surfaces, and the fourth is to capture, slow, or delay stormwater flowing from roofs and buildings within impervious areas. Options three and four can be part of best management practices (BMPs); Case 7.13 conveys that technology may help in the management of stormwater runoff.

Stormwater best management practices (BMPs) involving capturing, slowing, or delaying stormwater are sometimes called *Natural Drainage Systems* (NDS) or *Sustainable Urban Drainage Systems* (SUDS).

Reduction of Impermeability

Reduction of impermeable urban surfaces can be accomplished through uses of nontraditional materials or methods. Case 7.14 describes a large U.S. city, Chicago, using a new type of asphalt that is pervious (permeable) to water. Interest in the development of such hard but pervious surfaces is increasing, and some universities have research programs focusing on their development.

Green roofs present another use of nontraditional materials. Green roofs include sod and plantings, as shown in Figure 7.1. Such roofs change water flow rates, retain more water on the property, and filter pollutants from rainfall (EPA, 2010). According to the EPA, as of 2007, the city of Portland, Oregon, had "6 acres (24,300 m^2) of green roofs" (2010). They have been used for decades in Germany and the Netherlands (Levine, 2004). Green roofs do not have to be high-tech marvels; in the U.S. settlement period, some pioneers and homesteaders lived in sod houses that they built themselves.[4] Some benefits can be realized simply by putting potted plants on suitable roofs.

Similar to green roofs, properly designed landscaping along the sides of streets can absorb and filter stormwater before it reaches storm drains. The city of Seattle, Washington, has successfully used this method in its Street Edge Alternative program (Stoner, Kloss, and Calarusse, 2006). In some cases, curb cuts can allow stormwater

---

■——— **Case 7.14** ———■

New Technology Can Produce Hard but Pervious Surfaces

Streets with "Green" Asphalt (Illinois)

In recent years, the "greening" of Chicago in Cook County, Illinois, propelled by Mayor Richard Daley, has encompassed roof gardens to harvest rainwater and the creation of 200 acres of parks and green areas to absorb pollution. The latest step: coating streets with porous asphalt to reduce the absorption of the sun's heat. In a city the size of Chicago, this alone would be valuable, but the new asphalt serves another function: it allows rainwater to seep into the subsoil and drains instead of running off road surfaces. The drains will transport the stormwater to treatment facilities and then into Lake Michigan.

Source: Saulny, 2007.

Figure 7.1 **A Photograph of a Green Roof**

This photo shows a green roof in a sustainable community in the Netherlands. The photo was accessed via Wikimedia Commons under the GNU Free Documentation License. This is a freely licensed work, as explained in the Definition of Free Cultural Works. The file is EVA- Lanxmeer Green roof2 2009.jpg, produced July 14, 2009 by Lamiot; use of this photo in no way implies endorsement by Lamiot of this work or opinions expressed herein.

to flow from gutters back into landscaping, reducing the amount of water that enters storm drains.

Another nontraditional use of materials is exhibited in a parking lot near the French impressionist painter Claude Monet's house in Giverny, France. It combines harder surfaces for driving with grass plots for parking. One problem with traditional parking lots is that they are inhospitable to trees, since the impervious surfaces direct water away from trees' roots and can be very hot. The Giverny lot would seem to solve this problem, and in fact includes many lovely trees; to those used to hard-surfaced parking areas, it gives new meaning to the British term "car *park*."

Policies for Impermeability. For reduction of impermeability, cities can directly replace impermeable materials on city-owned properties. Regulations can require other organizations or individuals to make changes. Additionally, incentives can be used to encourage other organizations and individuals to improve the permeability of surfaces.

The Urban Heat Island Effect. The many impervious surfaces of cities cause problems for water management and create an urban heat island effect, in which cities can become appreciably hotter than surrounding rural areas:

> The term "heat island" describes built up areas that are hotter than nearby rural areas. The annual mean air temperature of a city with 1 million people or more can be 1.8–5.4°F (1–3°C) warmer than its surroundings. In the evening, the difference can be as high as 22°F (12°C). Heat islands can affect communities by increasing summertime peak energy demand, air conditioning costs, air pollution and greenhouse gas emissions, heat-related illness and mortality, and water quality. (EPA, 2011b)

This effect is caused by increased absorption of the sun's rays by the many hard surfaces of the city. The hard materials radiate the heat back into the city, especially at night. Green roofs (and parking lots such as that at Giverny) serve to reduce urban heat: "On hot summer days, the surface temperature of a green roof can be cooler than the air temperature, whereas the surface of a conventional rooftop can be up to 90°F (50°C) warmer" (EPA, 2010). The EPA's discussion of the urban heat island and green roofs reinforces the reality of the many environmental interactions within the urban environment.

Catchments. Another solution to the problems of impervious surfaces and stormwater runoff is to create catchments that are interspersed throughout the city. Catchments vary in type. For example, parks can be created with large areas lower than the nearby landscape, and stormwater can be directed to these areas. When there is no rain, the park has other uses; when there is rain, runoff will fill the area and pool there until it naturally soaks into the ground. The city of Fresno, California, has used this method for several decades, as has the city of Scottsdale, Arizona. Especially if there is a chance that children will play in these dual-use catchments, it is important to monitor to make sure that no excess buildup of pollutants occurs. Wet detention ponds (essentially artificial wetlands), which "can also serve as an aesthetic or recreational amenity as well as habitat for some wildlife," are another option (Assembly of Rouge Communities, n.d.). In addition, cities may require new commercial (or other) development to include small catchment basins to retain water on the property. These types of catchments are sometimes called "dry wells" and can be easy to produce. For example, some catchment value is attainable simply by creating an earthen ridge at the drip line of a tree on its downslope side. Cities can produce catchments on their own properties, and individuals and organizations can be required or incentivized to create catchments.

Rainwater harvesting, mentioned before, can be considered a type of distributed catchment. Since stormwater runoff incurs significant costs, it might be a good idea to require property owners to retain all rainfall on their own properties—and perhaps even receive fines for water that escapes their property. Monitoring of such runoff has become possible due to the extensive availability of aerial photography and Geographic Information Systems (GIS).

Other Flooding

In general, flooding of streams and rivers presents the same problems as stormwater runoff. Many urban surfaces are impervious, streams may be polluted, and even if they are not they will carry and disperse pollutants that are present where they flow.

Ocean flooding is in some ways different—and should be of significant interest to administrators and analysts in coastal cities. On average, five hurricanes per year strike the eastern coastal areas of the United States, two of which, on average, measure Category 3 or above (which makes them major hurricanes). From 1988 to 1996, more than sixty Category 3 or higher hurricanes struck the eastern U.S. coastline from the tip of Texas in the Gulf of Mexico clear north to Cape Cod in Massachusetts (Chiras and Reganold, 2005). Other parts of the world are also susceptible to ocean flooding problems, as shown by recent tsunamis in the Indian Ocean and Japan and by historical typhoons in Japan and East Asia. To manage these potential disasters, people should protect barrier islands, reefs, natural shores, and estuaries, and limit human habitation and business activity in these areas, such as through zoning. Because of their function, some buildings (such as docks, shipyards, ferry terminals, etc.) must be present even in risky coastal areas, but specific rules for building practices should be put into place in these locations. *At War with the Weather: Managing Large-Scale Risks in a New Era of Catastrophes* (Kunreuther et al., 2009) provides detailed information on ocean and hurricane risks and presents zoning practices, building practices, and insurance methods for distributing that risk.

Though it seems harsh, from a policy perspective, homeowners should not be compensated by the government for damage to their houses or other possessions that are in flood zones and do not need to be. Compensating people for such flood damage creates a "moral hazard," or a situation in which people do not fully consider the costs of their actions because some costs can be shifted onto society at large. The U.S. Federal Coastal Barrier Resources Act of 1982 (as amended) "restricts federal financial assistance" within defined coastal barrier areas (U.S. Department of Housing and Urban Development, 2008).

WATER FOR RECREATION

Not only do humans value water for consumption, production, transport, and habitat, they also value it for recreation. Humans enjoy looking at water, swimming and boating in it, and using it for recreational (or subsistence) collection of foods such as fish and waterfowl. In an earlier chapter (Chapter 4), we discussed the use of hedonic pricing methods for determining the social value of hard-to-value amenities or disamenities. Various analyses (including hedonic) indicate that people place a high value on recreational uses of water.

Unless or until congestion becomes a significant problem, many recreational uses of water do not present environmental problems. Again, *absent congestion*, looking at water, swimming in it, and using it as a food source (whether for sport or from need) does not harm the water source, though some types of boating may. Additionally, such uses benefit from higher environmental quality, and so nearby landowners, sports enthusiasts (for example, hunters and fishers), and environmentalists may often share an interest in environmental protection. The University of Maine and the Department of Environmental Protection at the Maine Bureau of Land and Water Quality performed research on the economic value of lakes. The results of their survey "clearly demonstrated that the economic loss in property value is linked with a decline in lake water quality" and that "people are willing to pay for lake protection" (State of Maine, 2005).

With 330 million people in the United States, and almost 7 billion people on Earth (as of this writing), and so much use and preference for living near water, much of the planet's water has become congested. This congestion presents a typical Tragedy of the Commons, and standard corrections must be tried. In particular, water use that damages the resource must be limited, whether through licensing, lotteries, or pricing (for example, via fees for entry). If users have higher conservation standards and, for example, follow the saying "Take only pictures and leave only footprints," then a given resource can accept more use than if uneducated users damage the resource unnecessarily. This indicates that education/suasion campaigns can also be an important policy.

Unfortunately, because of air pollution, land pollution, polluted runoff, and direct placement of pollutants in water, many water bodies are polluted, making them harmful for swimming and food use. Several riverine, lake, and ocean fish in the United States are sufficiently contaminated that pregnant women and young children are advised not to consume them, and some are too contaminated for anyone to eat. This situation is not unique to the United States. However, as Case 7.15 shows, remediation can improve matters.

Preventing water and other pollution is often simpler than remediating pollution that already exists. Remediation can be technically complex, and expert advice should be sought, including from the EPA (see, for example, the EPA's Ground Water and Ecosystems Restoration Research website, and other resources of the National Risk Management Research Laboratory).

Conclusion and Checklist for Administrators

As we stated in Chapter 5, to make policies that increase sustainability, we must consider economic well-being, environmental quality, and social equity. Water is no different from air in this regard. For economic well-being, we require water for direct human use; for industrial, commercial, and agricultural purposes; and for habitat. Additionally, we value it for recreation. Water is part of all that we do.

Urban environmental policy administrators should think about certain policies, such as conservation pricing regimes, that may affect the poor or other disadvantaged groups disproportionately and devise plans to reduce such harm. With water, as with air, we must consider transboundary concerns: water flows into the city from other governments and habitats, and any specific city's use of water will affect those outside the city as well.

■——— Case 7.15 ———■

Shellfish Are Contaminated, but Remediation Works

Shellfish View on Derwent River Revival (Australia)

The Derwent Estuary Programme in Tasmania, Australia, reported that eight years of pollution mitigation in the Derwent River near Hobart are beginning to pay off. Shellfish from the river still aren't safe to eat, but levels of lead and zinc have dropped by 40 to 60 percent. Stricter regulation of industrial discharges has helped reduce the contamination, although runoff still carries pollutants into the river during heavy rains.

Source: ABC News (Australia), 2007.

■——— Case 7.16 ———■

Some Consensus Solutions to a Freshwater Crisis

Educate to change consumption and lifestyle . . .
Recycle wastewater . . .
Improve irrigation and agricultural practices . . .
Appropriately price water . . .
Develop energy efficient desalination plants . . .
Improve water catchment and harvesting . . .
Look to community-based governance and partnerships . . .
Develop and enact better policies and regulations . . .
Holistically manage ecosystems . . .
Improve distribution infrastructure . . .
Shrink corporate water footprints . . .
Build international frameworks and institutional cooperation . . .
Address pollution . . .
Innovat[e] . . .
[Apply] Water projects in developing countries/transfer of technology . . .
Climate change Mitigation . . .
Population growth control . . .

Source: Circle of Blue, 2010. Used with permission.

Some people believe that we are entering a global freshwater crisis, and Globe-Scan, a Canadian global survey research and strategy company, and SustainAbility, a think tank focused on sustainable business, performed a survey of "more than 1,200 leading international experts in 80 countries," asking them to rank the nineteen best solutions to this problem (Circle of Blue, 2010). Case 7.16 lists some of the solutions suggested by the international experts, one being "Look to community-based governance and partnerships." This approach is not discussed specifically in this chapter, but it is mentioned in Chapter 5 and is the focus of Chapters 10 and 11. Working

Figure 7.2   **Checklist for Considering Water Policy Tools**

The Problem: Too Little Water/Too Much Demand

A.   Remember that water can be gained from many sectors: industry, commerce, agriculture, the distribution system, and residents.

B.   Do other jurisdictions share the water?
YES ⇒ Be sure to consider and communicate both with those upstream and downstream.
YES ⇒ Can you create a single jurisdiction that encompasses the entire water source?

C.   Is water appropriately priced?
Note: Frequently prices are too low in at least one sector and sometimes in all. Be sure to consider equity effects of water pricing.
NO ⇒ Raise water prices to discourage inappropriate levels of consumption.
NO ⇒ Consider creative conservation pricing that directly ties higher prices to higher social costs.

D.   Is rainfall appropriately retained?
Does the stormwater system waste water or cause pollution?
YES ⇒ Can it be fixed? If it cannot be fixed, retain more water.
Can more rainwater be retained?
YES ⇒ Consider greater retention on all city properties.
YES ⇒ Create incentives for water retention on all properties (residential as well as commercial; taxes for failure to retain are also possible).
YES ⇒ Regulate greater retention.

E.   Does old infrastructure use more water than necessary?
YES ⇒ Educate people about leaks and water-saving devices.
YES ⇒ Provide incentives for people to replace water-wasting devices with water-saving ones.
Note: This may be particularly useful in the multihousing complexes, where residents are less likely to overcompensate for water-saving hardware and where unit-level meters may not be available.

F.   Is metering widespread?
NO ⇒   Consider installing meters so that people understand their water use.

G.   Do local ordinances allow the use of graywater?
NO ⇒ Consider changing ordinances along with development of best practices and education campaigns.
YES ⇒ Do people use graywater as much as would be desirable?
IF NOT,
⇒   Provide more information and best practices for use.
⇒   Subsidize installation of appropriate graywater systems.

The Problem: Too Much Stormwater/Runoff/Pollution

A.   Is the stormwater system joined with the sanitary sewer?
YES ⇒ Consider decoupling these systems.
YES ⇒ Consider treating stormwater at outflow sites.
YES ⇒ Consider whether new technology can help with stormwater management.
YES ⇒ Consider whether diversion of gutter water into planted areas is possible.

(continued)

Figure 7.2 *(continued)*

B. Is a high proportion of the urban Concretion System impervious?
    YES ⇒ Consider increasing the use of pervious surfaces.
    ____ This can be done by the city using more pervious surfaces on all properties it
    controls.
    ____ Incentives can be offered for adding pervious surfaces to new and/or old
    development.
    ____ Regulation can require more pervious surfaces in new and/or old
    development.

C. Is water retained on properties?
    NO ⇒ Look above for ideas regarding greater retention of rainwater on properties.

D. Consider increasing the number and use of catchments.
    NO ⇒ Consider many small catchments, or dual-use catchments such as parks.
    Note: They must be monitored for excess pollution build-up, *especially* if children will
    play in catchment areas.
    ____ Consider wet retention basins.
    ____ Cities can place catchments on city properties, and can regulate placement or
    incentivize placement on other properties.

E. Is the problem potential ocean/hurricane flooding?
    YES ⇒ Educate and inform.
    YES ⇒ Reduce use of risky area.
    ____ Consider zoning regulation.
    YES ⇒ Require best practices for risky areas.
    ____ Consider incentives for improvement of buildings/functions already in risky
    areas.
    ____ Consider taxation for buildings in risky areas.
    YES ⇒ Consider spreading risk through appropriate insurance mechanisms, especially for
    functions that must continue in the risky zone.
    YES ⇒ Do not add moral hazard incentives by providing assistance for those who continue
    nonnecessary functions in risky zones.

The Problem: Overuse or Excess Pollution of Recreational Waters

A. Do other jurisdictions share the water?
    YES ⇒ Be sure to consider and communicate both with those upstream and downstream.
    YES ⇒ Can you create a single jurisdiction that encompasses the entire water source?

B. Do point sources contribute to excessive daily load?
    YES ⇒ Use regulation (including command-and-control, taxes, incentives, or fines)
    to reduce point-source pollution.

C. Do non–point-sources contribute to excessive daily load?
    YES ⇒ Consider if land- or air-focused policies can ameliorate the problem.

D. Is overuse due to excessive "hard" use (e.g., littering, inappropriate consumption, etc.)?
    YES ⇒ Educate.
    YES ⇒ Implement a fine.

E. Is overuse due to excess population demand for the good even with education and/or "light"/
    appropriate use?
    YES ⇒ Limit use.
    ____ Methods include first-come/first-served up until the limit, licenses, lotteries, fees
    for use that are set high enough to reduce use to sustainable limits, etc.
    ____ Be sure to consider equity issues in limiting use.

with members of your community is an overarching technique that will serve you well in a variety of policy endeavors. The U.S. Agency for International Development (USAID) supports the use of Integrated Water Resources Management, which, like the ecosystem- and adaptive-management techniques suggested in Chapter 5, combines participative methods and science with a concern for economic benefits at the watershed or water-basin levels (USAID, 2006).

This chapter covers ecosystem and social issues regarding water, suggests policies for the management of urban water, and lists expert proposals for water policies overall. We end with a checklist that can help administrators and analysts focus on important issues that arise when choosing between different water policy tools (see Figure 7.2 on pages 188–189). Remember, though, that this list should be only a starting point: it is not complete. At the very least, you should consider interactions with air and land. As we reiterate throughout this book, environmental context is always important for administrators and analysts to bear in mind.

RECOMMENDED WEBSITES

American Water Resource Association (AWRA). Community, Conversation, Connections. http://www.awra.org/. From the website: AWRA's mission is "To advance multidisciplinary water resources education, management, and research."

American Water Works Association (AWWA). The Authoritative Resource on Safe Water. http://www.awwa.org/. From the website: "AWWA's mission is to unite the water community to protect public health and to provide safe and sufficient water for all."

Association of Metropolitan Water Agencies (AMWA). http://www.amwa.net/. From the website: AMWA "is an organization of the largest publicly owned drinking water systems in the United States."

Natural Resources Conservation Service (NRCS). U.S. Department of Agriculture. http://www.nrcs.usda.gov/. From the website: "NRCS works with landowners through conservation planning and assistance to benefit the soil, water, air, plants, and animals for productive lands and healthy ecosystems."

UN Water. United Nations Department of Economic and Social Affairs. http://www.unwater.org/.

U.S. Environmental Protection Agency. Ground Water and Ecosystems Restoration Research. http://www.epa.gov/ada.

U.S. Environmental Protection Agency. 2011. How to Conserve Water and Use It Effectively. http://water.epa.gov/polwaste/nps/chap3.cfm.

NOTES

1. Device-regulation methods can also be effective for home-generated air pollution. Some cities regulate power yard tools, for example, banning gas-powered leaf blowers.

2. Thermoelectric water use is often separated because much of it is mostly nonconsumptive, "once-through" use that returns much of the water to the source. In 2000, 91 percent of nonpublic-supply thermoelectric use in the United States was once-through (Hutson et al., 2004). It should be noted, however, that though once-through cooling wastes little *water*, it creates heat pollution in the water source that can damage habitats and ecosystems.

3. Some of the material in this section was developed by Nick Cain, author of Chapter 10 of this book. These materials are used with permission.

4. In fact, Heather Campbell's great-grandfather lived in a sod house.

REFERENCES

ABC News (Australia). 2007. Shellfish View on Derwent River Revival. November 9. http://www. abc.net.au/news/stories/2007/11/09/2086636.htm. Summary obtained from L. Shaler, *Global Water News Watch* (College of Science, University of Arizona), November 9.

Arizona Department of Environmental Quality. n.d. Using Gray Water at Home: Arizona Department of Environmental Quality's Guide to Complying with the Type I General Permit. Publication No. C 10–04. http://www.azdeq.gov/environ/water/permits/download/graybro.pdf (accessed February 18, 2011).

Assembly of Rouge Communities. n.d. Maintaining Your Detention Basin: A Guidebook for Private Owners in Southeast Michigan. Assembly of Rouge Communities, Canton Township, Michigan. http://www.canton-mi.org/uploadedfiles/Maintaining%20your%20detention%20basin.pdf (accessed February 18, 2011).

ASU News. 2009. Research looks at water, energy impacts of climate change. *ASU News*, November 30. http://asunews.asu.edu/20091130_dcdcgrant (accessed February 10, 2011).

Babcock, T.M. Various years. Personal communication with author. Former Water Conservation Co-ordinator for the City of Phoenix Water Services Department.

Barker, A.V., and J.E. English. 2010. Recycling gray water for home gardens. Fact Sheets: Plant culture and maintenance. UMass Extension. http://www.umassgreeninfo.org/fact_sheets/plant_culture/gray_water_for_gardens.html (accessed February 21, 2011).

Cain, N. 2007. Sustainable stormwater approaches for the urban environment. Introduction to Environmental Planning (Columbia University), December. Available at http://www.nicholas-cain.com/images/CAIN_sustainable_stormwater.pdf.

California Energy Commission. 2010. Industrial/Agricultural/Water End-Use Energy Efficiency, CA.gov. http://www.energy.ca.gov/research/iaw/industry/water.html (accessed March 12, 2011).

Campbell, H.E., and R.M. Johnson. 1999. *The Cookbook: Doing Multivariate Analysis of Residential Single-Family Water Conservation Programs*. Phoenix, AZ: Arizona Board of Regents. http://morrisoninstitute.asu.edu/publications-reports/TheCookbook-MultiVarAnalysisOfResFamH2OC-onservProg/view.

Campbell, H.E., with R.M. Johnson and E.H. Larson. 2004. Prices, devices, people, or rules: The relative effectiveness of policy instruments on water conservation. *Review of Policy Research*, 21, 5, 637–662.

Chiras, D.D., and J.P. Reganold. 2005. *Natural Resource Conservation,* 9th ed. Upper Saddle River, NJ: Pearson/Prentice Hall.

Circle of Blue. 2010. Experts name the top 19 solutions to the global freshwater crisis. Circle of Blue: Reporting the Global Water Crisis, May 24. http://www.circleofblue.org/waternews/2010/world/experts-name-the-top-19-solutions-to-the-global-freshwater-crisis/ (accessed February 21, 2011).

City of San Luis Obispo. 2010. Utilities: Water reuse: What is recycled water? http://www.slocity.org/utilities/reuse/reusewhat.asp (accessed February 18, 2011).

Cooley, H., P.H. Gleick, and G. Wolff. 2006. Desalination, with a grain of salt: A California perspective. Report, June. Oakland, CA: Pacific Institute. http://pacinst.org/reports/desalination/index.htm (accessed March 12, 2011).

Davis, T. 2008. Low-water-use toilets might be too effective. *Arizona Daily Star*, February 11. Summary obtained from L. Shaler, *Global Water News Watch* (College of Science, University of Arizona), February 11.

El Universal. 2007. Potabilizar agua agrava el calentamiento global [Water Purification Aggravates Global Warming]. ElUniversal.com.mx, July 19. http://www.eluniversal.com.mx/cultura/53427.html.

Translation and summary by L. Shaler, *Global Water News Watch* (College of Science, University of Arizona), July 19.

Faculty of Science. n.d. Spatial variability in ecological risk assessment: Ecological risk assessment in heterogene polluted Dutch river floodplains. Department of Environmental Science, Radboud University Nijmegen, The Netherlands. http://www.ru.nl/environmentalscience/research/rivers/ecological_risk/ (accessed February 11, 2011).

Gelt, J. n.d. Home use of graywater, rainwater conserves water—and may save money. University of Arizona Water Resources Research Center, College of Agricultural and Life Sciences. http://ag.arizona.edu/azwater/arroyo/071rain.html (accessed February 18, 2011).

Gleick, P.H.; D. Haasz; C. Henges-Jeck; V. Srinivasan; G. Wolff; K.K. Cushing; A. Mann. 2003. Waste not, want not: The potential for urban water conservation in California. Report, November. Oakland, CA: The Pacific Institute.

Golf Course Superintendents Association of America (GCSAA). 2011. Using effluent water on golf courses. http://www.gcsaa.org/solutions/facts/effluent.aspx (accessed February 18, 2011).

Graves, W. 1993. Introduction. *National Geographic*, November (special edition), 1.

Heikkila, T. 2004. Institutional boundaries and common-pool resource management: A comparative analysis of water management programs in California. *Journal of Policy Analysis and Management*, 23, 1, 97–117.

Hill, M.K. 2010. *Understanding Environmental Pollution*, 3rd ed. New York: Cambridge University Press.

Hutson, S.S.; N.L. Barber; J.F. Kenny; K.S. Linsey; D.S. Lumia; M.A. Maupin. 2004. Estimated use of water in the United States in 2000. USGS Circular 1268, March. Reston, VA: U.S. Geological Survey, revised 2004, 2005. http://pubs.usgs.gov/circ/2004/circ1268/index.html (accessed February 18, 2011).

Kunreuther, H.C.; and E.O. Michel-Kerjan, with N.A. Doherty; M.F. Grace; R.W. Klein; and M.V. Pauly. 2009. *At War with the Weather: Managing Large-Scale Risks in a New Era of Catastrophes.* Cambridge, MA: MIT Press.

Landais, Emmanuelle. 2007. Just 8 hours to keep toxins at bay. Gulfnews.com, September 1. http://gulfnews.com/news/gulf/uae/general/just-8-hours-to-keep-toxins-at-bay-1.197629. Summary obtained from L. Shaler, *Global Water News Watch* (College of Science, University of Arizona), September 1.

Lenntech. 2009. FAQ air pollution: The question library on air-related issues. Delft, The Netherlands: Lenntech Water Treatment & Purification Holding B.V. http://www.lenntech.com/faq-air-pollution.htm (accessed February 11, 2011).

Levine, K. 2004. 'Green' roofs sprout up all over: Growing plants on buildings said to offer environmental benefits. *Morning Edition,* NPR, June 23. http://www.npr.org/templates/story/story.php?storyId=1970286 (accessed February 18, 2011).

Lieberson, A.D. 2004. How long can a person survive without food? *Scientific American,* November 8. http://www.scientificamerican.com/article.cfm?id=how-long-can-a-person-sur (accessed February 4, 2011).

Ling, K. 2007. Water woes loom as thirsty generators face climate change. *Greenwire*, October 4. http://www.earthportal.org/news/?p=536. Summary obtained from L. Shaler, *Global Water News Watch* (College of Science, University of Arizona), October 4.

Malan, A. 2006. Water accounts in South Africa. PowerPoint presentation to the User-Producer Conference: Water Accounting for Integrated Water Resource Management, May 22–24. Voorburg: The Netherlands.

Masters, C. 2007. Water bill rises and falls with dam level. *Daily Telegraph* (Australia), September 7. http://www.highbeam.com/doc/1G1-168413482.html. Summary obtained from L. Shaler, *Global Water News Watch* (College of Science, University of Arizona), September 7.

Packer, R.K. 2002. How long can the average person survive without water? *Scientific American*, December 9. http://www.scientificamerican.com/article.cfm?id=how-long-can-the-average (accessed February 4, 2011).

Pfister, A.J. 2001. Personal communication with author. Former General Manager, Salt River Project (Arizona). May 23.

Rogers, P. 2008. Facing the freshwater crisis. *Scientific American*, August. http://www.scientificamerican.com/article.cfm?id=facing-the-freshwater-crisis (accessed February 11, 2011).

Saulny, S. 2007. In miles of alleys, Chicago finds its next environmental frontier. *New York Times*, November 26. Summary obtained from L. Shaler, *Global Water News Watch* (College of Science, University of Arizona), November 30.

Sehlke, G. (ed.). 2009. The energy-water nexus. *Journal of Contemporary Water Research and Education,* 143 (December), 1–62. http://www.ucowr.org/updates/143/Full-143.pdf (accessed March 12, 2011).

Shaler, L. 2007. Mining can be very polluting: Unclean water: the lead generation is still paying. *Global Water Watch News* (College of Science, University of Arizona), January 22. Translation and summary by L. Shaler from original source, *Ta Nea,* January 22, no. 16 (Greece).

State of Maine. 2005. The economics of lakes—Dollars and $ense. Augusta: Department of Environmental Protection, Maine Bureau of Land and Water Quality. http://www.maine.gov/dep/blwq/doclake/research.htm (accessed February 19, 2011).

Stoner, N., C. Kloss, and C. Calarusse. 2006. Rooftops to rivers: Green strategies for controlling stormwater and combined sewer overflows. Report, Natural Resources Defense Council, June. http://www.nrdc.org/water/pollution/rooftops/rooftops.pdf (accessed July 12, 2011).

Sustainable Cities. 2010. Dar es Salaam: Feeding the sustainable city. Case, Danish Architecture Centre, Copenhagen, July 15. http://sustainablecities.dk/en/city-projects/cases/dar-es-salaam-feeding-the-sustainable-city (accessed February 11, 2011).

Today's Zaman. 2008. Istanbulites must consume less water, ISKI head says. *Today's Zaman* (Istanbul, Turkey), May 28. http://www.todayszaman.com/newsDetail_getNewsById.action?load=detay&link=143188. Summary obtained from L. Shaler, *Global Water News Watch* (College of Science, University of Arizona), June.

Tschudi, H.F. Various years. Personal communication with author. Herbert Tschudi was the Assistant Commissioner for Water and Wastewater at the New York City Department of Environmental Protection—and a wonderful father-in-law.

University of Michigan. 2006. Human appropriation of the world's fresh water supply. Lecture, Global Change Program, University of Michigan, Ann Arbor. January 4. http://www.global-change.umich.edu/globalchange2/current/lectures/freshwater_supply/freshwater.html (accessed February 18, 2011).

U.S. Agency for International Development (USAID). 2006. What is integrated water resource management? http://www.usaid.gov/our_work/environment/water/what_is_iwrm.html (accessed March 12, 2011).

U.S. Department of Agriculture (USDA). 2009. Reducing water use in Midsouth rice paddies. *Agricultural Research,* January. http://www.ars.usda.gov/is/AR/archive/jan09/rice0109.pdf (accessed March 12, 2011).

U.S. Department of Housing and Urban Development (HUD). 2008. Coastal barrier resources act of 1984 (as amended): Guidelines for compliance. PowerPoint presentation, February. Environmental Planning Division, Office of Environment and Energy. http://www.hud.gov/offices/cpd/environment/review/qa/hud_guidance_cbra_compliance.pdf (accessed February 19, 2011).

U.S. Environmental Protection Agency (EPA). 2007. Total maximum daily loads with stormwater sources: A summary of 17 TMDLs. Report, EPA 841-R-07–002, July. Watershed Branch, Office of Wetlands, Oceans and Watersheds. http://water.epa.gov/lawsregs/lawsguidance/cwa/tmdl/upload/17_TMDLs_Stormwater_Sources.pdf (accessed March 12, 2011).

———. 2008. Outdoor water use in the United States. WaterSense, brochure, August. http://www.epa.gov/WaterSense/docs/ws_outdoor508.pdf (accessed March 12, 2011).

———. 2009a. Subobjective: Wetlands. Strategic Plan and Guidance Report prepared by the Office of Water, National Water Program, 64–65. http://water.epa.gov/aboutow/goals_objectives/waterplan/upload/FY_2009_EOY_WT.pdf (accessed February 19, 2011).

————. 2009b. Wetlands and runoff. January 12. http://www.epa.gov/owow/wetlands/facts/fact25. html (accessed February 19, 2011).

————. 2010. Heat island effect: Green roofs. February 23. http://www.epa.gov/heatisld/mitigation/ greenroofs.htm (accessed February 18, 2011).

————. 2011a. Coral reef protection: What are coral reefs? April 6. http://water.epa.gov/type/oceb/ habitat/coral_index.cfm (accessed February 19, 2011).

————. 2011b. Heat island effect. March 29. http://www.epa.gov/heatisld/index.htm (accessed February 18, 2011).

Virginia Tech. 2007. Water pollution can be reduced with new storm water analysis system. *Science Daily,* August 28. http://www.sciencedaily.com/releases/2007/08/070828110703.htm. Summary obtained from L. Shaler, *Global Water News Watch* (College of Science, University of Arizona), August 30.

Williams, P.L. 2010. Ice-free Arctic Ocean may not be of much use in soaking up carbon dioxide, a component of global warming, according to new study. News release, Office of Public Affairs, University of Georgia, Athens, August. http://www.uga.edu/news/artman/publish/100802_Ice_free_ocean. shtml (accessed February 10, 2011).

Yardley, J. 2007. Though water is drying up, a Chinese metropolis booms. *New York Times,* September 27. http://www.nytimes.com/2007/09/27/world/asia/27iht-water.3.7660278.html. Summary obtained from L. Shaler, *Global Water News Watch* (College of Science, University of Arizona).

Young, K. 2009. Current status of interaction between water issues and energy efficiency and renewable energy. Presentation at the IEA REWP55 Workshop on Renewable Energy and Water, Paris, France, March 23. http://www.iea.org/work/2009/rewp_water/Young.pdf (accessed February 10, 2011).

Zajac, E.E. 1978. *Fairness or Efficiency: An Introduction to Public Utility Pricing.* Cambridge, MA: Ballinger.

8 Land

Land, like air and water, is a natural resource that is affected by almost any urban environmental decision-making process. When analysts or administrators make decisions about water management, air pollution, transportation, urban open space, waste disposal, or urban development, they are making decisions that will have some impact on land use. In this chapter, we focus on land-use change, urban sprawl, brownfields, and urban open space as some core ecological issues associated with land as an urban natural resource. We also outline some social issues—mainly focusing on environmental equity—that result from urban land-use decisions. We do not go into great detail about smart growth initiatives or highway planning. Although these are important topics, they are covered in other textbooks, especially those focused on transportation planning. Here, we focus on how land-use changes in the urban environment can have an impact on the natural environment (for example, through species and habitat changes) and the social environment (for example, by changing the availability of open space) and exploring how that can affect humans.

LAND USE IN THE URBAN ENVIRONMENT

Land use is a key urban environmental policy issue. In most cities, land is a scarce resource, and the way that it is used has a significant impact on all other parts of the urban environment (including air quality, water quality, transportation systems, and energy use, among others). When we focus on land issues in urban environmental policy discussions, we typically concentrate on the following key issues: land use and development, soil erosion, and interactions with other systems (such as the impact of land use on water quality and air quality). The important components of the land-based Natural System include soil (or the actual land itself), vegetation, animals, terrestrial habitat/ecosystems, and humans. The components of the land-based Concretion System that are significant from a policy perspective include service infrastructure (electrical, water, trash, transportation, energy, and sanitation), buildings (including industrial, commercial, and residential), and transportation vehicles (for example, cars, subway systems, buses, light rail systems and motorcycles). Some planning and policy scholars have argued that administrators do not focus enough on the consequences of urban land-use patterns for the social, economic, and political aspects of urban life (Cutsinger et al., 2005). Therefore, in this chapter we introduce not only ecological issues but also social and political issues associated with land-use changes. Before jumping into the discussion of these topics, we first provide a brief overview of some of the recent trends in urban land-use management.

TRENDS IN URBAN LAND USE

A comprehensive overview of how urban land use has evolved over the last century is summarized nicely in Nechyba and Walsh (2004). They discuss the trend of increasing suburbanization and highlight how different academic disciplines focus on various aspects of this trend. For example, while the urban economics field has focused largely on higher incomes and lower transportation costs (for example, when gas prices are lower, people are willing to commute farther) as the drivers for suburbanization, the public finance field has focused more on household desires to live in places that match individuals' preferences for amenities and local taxes.

Also, we see a significant increase in the percentage of urban development in the United States. White and colleagues (2009, 37) reference the 2003 Natural Resources Inventory data (collected by U.S. Department of Agriculture, Natural Resources Conservation Service) when they point out that the "area of developed land in the United States (U.S.) increased by more than 48% between 1982 and 2003." As they discuss in their study, this dramatic conversion of natural and agricultural land to urban areas can have significant negative effects on wildlife, habitat, recreation opportunities, nonpoint-source water pollution, and the availability of other natural resources (such as forests, clean water, and clean air). Nuissl and colleagues (2009) outline some of those negative impacts on the environment. They introduce a model that assesses how land-use change affects the environment in urban areas. Figure 8.1 provides an overview of how Nuissl and colleagues (2009) conceptualize these interactions between land-use change drivers, impacts, and policy responses. Using the DPSIR Framework (an acronym for Driving Forces–Pressures–State–Impacts–Responses), they argue that analysts and administrators must view land-use change as an ongoing feedback loop between the drivers of the change, the environmental impacts of the change, and the development of policy tools.

Other scholars (Leo and Anderson, 2006) have analyzed the way that urban growth is portrayed in the media; they concluded that it is generally described as a positive trend with the potential to cure many of the problems associated with cities. Yet, these same researchers caution decision makers to make land-use (and urban growth management) decisions based on a range of variables, including an analysis of the advantages of rapid growth and slow urban growth. They argue that rapid growth is not always better for urban areas than slow growth, especially given the potentially negative social and environmental costs of rapid urban growth. Leo and Anderson (2006, 173) conclude that the current literature in the area of urban growth typically assumes that more is better; however, they believe we need to have increasing amounts of research focused on a "nuanced understanding of the policy implications of different rates of urban growth."

Next, we briefly discuss key ecological issues for land-use change before introducing the most relevant social issues.

Figure 8.1 **Conceptualization of Land-Use Transition, Inspired by the DPSIR Framework**

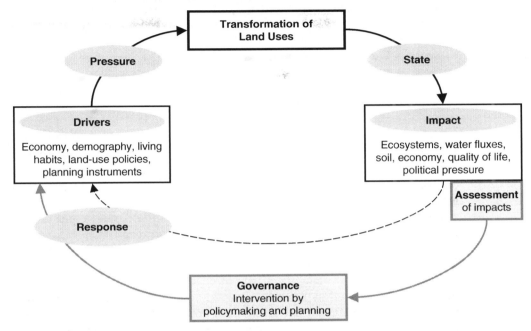

Source: From Nuissl et al., 2009. Used with permission.

KEY ECOLOGICAL ISSUES

LAND-USE CHANGE

The Ecological Society of America's (ESA) Committee on Land Use has identified five principles that address the potential ecological impacts of land-use change (Dale et al., 2000). We believe that these principles provide a comprehensive overview of the important policy dimensions that administrators should consider before making decisions about land use. The five principles are listed below. After introducing the list, we will briefly explain each principle and its relevance for administrators.

- Time
- Place
- Impacts on (and between) species
- Type of disturbances
- Size, shape, and characteristics of the landscape

According to the Committee on Land Use, the above five principles are land-use dimensions that should be considered by analysts and administrators who deal with the ecological impacts of land use. The "time" principle means that analysts should take into account the fact that ecological processes function at a variety of time scales (from short to long) and that human activities involving land changes can have an impact on the natural environment at all of these scales. In addition, managers need to keep in mind that it can take decades or centuries for ecosystems to adapt to—or recover from—the ecological impacts of human-imposed land-use changes.

Second, the committee's "place" principle suggests that managers should consider the local context of the location for proposed land-use changes. For example, there are only a few types of implementable land-use changes that allow ecological processes to "persist in a locale without continued management inputs (for example, irrigation of crops growing in a desert)" (Dale et al., 2000, 651).

In addition to considering time and place dimensions of land-use change, the committee also cautions analysts to consider the impacts of such changes on different types of species and the interactions between species. For instance, they point out that the disturbance of a keystone species[1] because of land-use changes can have a greater impact on the ecological processes within the ecosystem than if a non-keystone species is disrupted. Therefore, some important administrative questions for analysts might include the following: What are the keystone species for this ecosystem? What are the potential impacts of the land-use changes on the keystone species? And which species should be preserved or considered?

A fourth principle that the Committee on Land Use highlights is the "type of disturbance" (as well as the intensity and length of the disturbance) that will result from any proposed land-use changes. In particular, they argue that "land-use changes that alter natural disturbance regimes or initiate new disturbances are likely to cause changes in species' abundance and distribution, community composition, and ecosystem function" (Dale et al., 2000, 6).

The fifth and last ecological principle is related to the characteristics of the actual landscape. Since human activities can disrupt the land-cover patterns or fragment the existing landscape, it is important for analysts to consider the "size, shape, and other characteristics" of the landscape before they support major land-use changes.

In addition to outlining these five useful principles, the ESA (2000) also provides eight Ecological Guidelines for Land Use that we believe are particularly relevant for administrators dealing with land policy decisions. They include the following:

- "Examine the impacts of local decisions in a regional context."
- "Plan for long-term change and unexpected events."
- "Preserve rare landscape elements, critical habitats, and associated species."
- "Avoid land uses that deplete natural resources over a broad area."
- "Retain large contiguous or connected areas that contain critical habitats."
- "Minimize the introduction and spread of nonnative species."
- "Avoid or compensate for effects of development on ecological processes."
- "Implement land-use and management practices that are compatible with the natural potential of the area." (Dale et al., 2000, 8)

These five principles and eight guidelines form the basis for the important variables that administrators should analyze about the ecological impacts of land-use change.

Even though we highlight the ESA presentation of these dimensions, other scholars have outlined similar guidelines. For example, Naess (2001) introduces five principles for ecologically friendly urban development and land-use planning that have been discussed in the sustainable development literature. These include a focus on

- the reduction of energy use,
- minimizing the conversion of natural areas for food production,
- reducing the use of environmentally damaging construction materials,
- attempting to focus on closed resource loops that use more local natural resources, and
- reducing noise pollution and other types of pollution that can hinder the enjoyment of natural areas within cities.

These are all significant points for administrators and analysts to remember when they are incorporating the ecological impacts of land-use change into their decision-making process. When making policy decisions about land-use change, we encourage you to pay attention to the above principles just as you would pay attention to the checklist that we include at the end of this chapter.

Since we have already introduced some general principles for the ecological impacts of land-use change, we now turn to some specific land-use policy issues that have significant ecological impacts. In particular, urban sprawl is a case of land-use development that often involves uncontrolled and/or poorly planned, nondense urban growth. While we do not cover all examples of land-use change here, we do introduce some of the most common policy issues for land development and change.

URBAN SPRAWL

According to Carruthers (2002, 1960), urban sprawl consists of "spatially expansive, discontinuous, suburban-style development and is often characterised as the result of rapid, unplanned and/or uncoordinated growth." In addition, urban areas with high degrees of sprawl typically have "low-density, single-use, scattered, strip and leapfrog developments and [are] extensively criticized for being inefficient, inequitable and environmentally insensitive" (Carruthers, 2002).

So what are the drivers of urban sprawl? Several scholars have speculated about these drivers, and Brueckner (2000) has come up with three key variables that drive the increasing levels of urban sprawl in the United States: (1) increasing population levels, (2) increasing incomes, and (3) decreasing costs for commuting. He argues that these three factors contribute to urban sprawl because of market failures. So how does this happen? First, analysts and administrators often do not account for the benefits of open space because these benefits are difficult to quantify. Second, commuting rates and travel times tend to increase because people do not fully assess the negative social consequences associated with an increase in commuting. And, lastly, most metropolitan areas do not require developers to pay for the costs of infrastructure for new construction. This last point means that developers, as producers, do not take into account the full costs of their production decision and so, as with any negative externality case, they overproduce. As Brueckner (2000) suggests, these market failures typically can be addressed through tolls or fees for commuters and taxes on development.

Nechyba and Walsh (2004) have outlined the evolution of urban sprawl in the United States since the 1900s, while also providing an overview of the most common economic and public-finance models that are used to explain the drivers of urban sprawl. In Case 8.1, we provide an excerpt from their article explaining the concept of the monocentric city model that is often used by environmental and land economists to explain some of the drivers for urban sprawl. This case provides an overview of some key policy issues related to sprawl; it also defines the monocentric city model, which is sometimes used to explain how urban development is a result of the tension between commuting costs and land prices.

In addition to the monocentric city model, Wassmer (2008) introduces two other significant theories that attempt to explain the causes of urban sprawl: the "flight from blight" theory and the reliance of local governments on sales and land taxes. He notes that the "flight from blight" theory explains urban sprawl through the trend of urban decentralization that can be caused by increasing tax rates, increasing crime rates, and decreasing public school performance within cities, among other factors. Wassmer (2008) also explains how decentralization can be caused by local government reliance on sales and land taxes. When local governments rely heavily on these taxes, local decision makers have strong incentives to make land-use decisions based on how much revenue they can generate. For instance, the pattern of local retail development can be driven by decision makers' interest in generating revenue rather than their interest in land-use planning that yields positive outcomes for the environment and quality of life for residents. When decision makers gain profits from sales taxes, they might support zoning decisions that lead to low-density retail in previously undeveloped areas because they receive local revenue from this type of retail (in addition to receiving sales taxes from residents of adjacent communities). This type of decision making could lead to "outlet malls" with giant parking lots surrounded by empty land.

Addressing Urban-Sprawl Issues: Growth-Management Plans

A variety of land-use policy tools is available for dealing with urban sprawl, but one of the most common tools has been state growth-management plans. Carruthers (2002) explains how early state growth-management plans focused largely on the negative environmental effects of urban sprawl, while newer growth-management plans include an additional focus on how urban sprawl can have negative impacts on quality of life. He also points out that growth-management plans have been controversial because some scholars have argued that they do not increase urban density, and there is not much empirical evidence that these plans are very effective at reducing urban sprawl. Carruthers (2002) argues that the "details" of a growth-management plan are significant factors in whether or not it is successful at reducing urban sprawl. Growth-management programs that have high levels of consistency (across adjacent jurisdictions) and strict enforcement requirements are more effective at reducing urban sprawl than programs that do not have these qualities.

■———— **Case 8.1** ————■

The Case of the Monocentric City Model

Much of our understanding of this urban growth can be derived from the "monocentric city model" (Alonso, 1964; Mills, 1967; Muth, 1969), which explains urban spatial structure as arising from the trade-off between commuting costs and land rents. In equilibrium, this trade-off requires lower land rents at the urban edge to offset increased commute costs—with the declining rent gradients leading to declining density gradients as one moves out from a metropolitan area's central business district to the urban boundary. While the model captures the basic fact that downtown real estate is typically more expensive than equivalent land in the suburbs, it does not offer large insights into the development of the microstructure of the urban landscape. The urban economics literature that uses this model highlights the role of declining transportation costs—primarily cars on the consumer side and trucks on the producer side, combined with public infrastructure investment in roads—to explain the general decline in city density and expansion of city footprints, or urban sprawl, experienced over the last century. . . .

In this view, the advent of the automobile and accompanying lower transportation costs became the primary catalyst of sprawling cities through much of the twentieth century (Glaeser and Kahn, 2003). By 1910, the number of registered automobiles in the United States had passed the 500,000 mark, and in 1920, car registration reached eight million. In 1922, the first suburban, auto-oriented shopping center was constructed in Kansas City, Missouri (D.C. Williams, 2000), and by 1952, a majority of households in America owned at least one car (Glaeser and Kahn, 2003). The percentage of workers that drove to work stood at 64 percent in 1960 and rose to 78 percent by 1970 and 84 percent in 1980. It is difficult to imagine large increases in suburbanization without this rise of the automobile, even if other causes have contributed to the sprawling of cities in the presence of the automobile.

The monocentric city model also suggests that rising incomes have led to decreasing city densities to the extent that the income elasticity of demand for housing and land is sufficiently large relative to the income elasticity of commuting costs. . . .

Empirical evidence on the role of rising incomes in urban sprawl is provided by Margo (1992) and Brueckner (2000; 2001), with Margo's analysis suggesting that as much as half of the increase in suburbanization between 1950 and 1980 can be explained by rising incomes. Thus, the monocentric city model ultimately relies on the combined effect of increasing income and lower transportation costs to explain the phenomenon of suburbanization and sprawl.

While a variety of public policies have been suggested as potentially important contributors to urban sprawl within the monocentric city model, the empirical evidence suggests that these played at best a minor role—at least to the extent to which they did not contribute directly to enabling the rise of the automobile (such as through the construction of roads). Urban development may have been affected by the New Deal's creation of the Home Owners Loan Corporation and the Federal Housing Administration (FHA) (K. Jackson, 1981) and by increased post-World War II support for mortgage insurance programs through the FHA and the Veterans Administration (D.C. Williams, 2000). The federal deductibility of mortgage interest lowers the price of housing disproportionately

(continued)

Case 8.1 *(continued)*

for higher income families in higher tax brackets (Voith, 1999), potentially reinforcing the tendency of higher income households to suburbanize and commute. However, the U.S. General Accounting Office (1999) provides a skeptical review of the evidence of the extent to which such federal policies have created urban sprawl, at least as compared to the impact of lower transportation costs and higher incomes. At a more local level, the use of property taxes, as opposed to pure land taxes that do not tax improvements of land, provides incentives for low-density development in a monocentric city model (Brueckner and Kim, 2003). Again, it seems unlikely that local property taxation has played anything other than a supporting role in generating sprawl, especially in light of the fact that when interacted with minimum zoning rules, such taxes may in practice exhibit many of the features of land taxes (Fischel, 2001).

Source: Nechyba and Walsh, 2004. Used with permission.

Additionally, small local governments can increase the likelihood of urban sprawl because they lead to political fragmentation and are often driven by a preference for more separation from surrounding governmental units (Carruthers, 2002). Not surprisingly, the result of many small, local governments (each establishing its own land-use policies without paying attention to consistency in zoning regulations and development plans in adjacent areas) is often low-density development that encourages single-family homes. This pattern further encourages future urban sprawl. Carruthers (2002) illustrates how the creation of state growth-management programs in the 1960s and 1970s was designed partially to deal with this type of local fragmentation. The expectation was that individual local governments would act in their best interest, without regard for consistency in land-use policies across adjacent governments, unless the state supported a state-level growth plan.

Addressing Urban-Sprawl Issues: Urban Green Spaces

Another popular policy response to the negative impacts of urban sprawl has been local and state-level preservation of open, green spaces in urban environments. Many scholars have outlined the importance of green spaces in the urban environment (Baycan-Levent and Nijkamp, 2009; Chiesura, 2004). The positive aspects of green space are both ecological and social. From an ecological perspective, green spaces can serve as sinks for pollutants in the city. In addition, they can increase the biological diversity of the urban environment by providing habitat for a variety of plants and animals (Baycan-Levent and Nijkamp, 2009). Urban green spaces can moderate other negative human impacts on the urban ecosystem as well, namely by regulating air temperatures (which can be raised due to an urban heat-island effect) and catching runoff from streets (which is often due to impermeable surfaces like asphalt within the city).

Developing sustainable cities is not only about improving the ecological impacts of the urban environment but also improving the social aspects of urban life, such as life experiences and quality of life (Chiesura, 2004). From a social perspective, green spaces provide more opportunities for active lifestyles and, therefore, can have a positive impact on human health by increasing exercise, reducing stress, and lowering aggression levels (Baycan-Levent and Nijkamp, 2009). Chiesura (2004) found that relaxation is the most common reason why people visit urban green spaces or parks, followed closely by escaping the stress of the city and experiencing nature. Since social science research has demonstrated that many people view green spaces as a relaxing, quiet oasis in the middle of the often-stressful urban environment, Chiesura (2004) believes that the psychological and social benefits of green spaces should be incorporated into the overall analysis of a project when analysts or administrators are trying to place a value on a future green-space project. Green spaces in urban environments also provide positive health impacts. For example, Jackson (2003) addressed the public health component of open space and urban design by explaining how several public health issues—such as physical inactivity, cultural isolation, and social disparities—could be partly addressed by thoughtful urban design and an increased use of open space, public facilities, and parks.

From an economic perspective, green spaces can increase urban property values (Baycan-Levent and Nijkamp, 2009), though Backlund, Stewart, and McDonald (2004) completed a survey of 5,000 households in Illinois and found that the public supported certain types of open space over others. The most highly valued types of open space included "forest areas, stream corridors, wildlife habitat, and lakes/ponds." They note that a majority of U.S. states (46, in fact) have some sort of open-space preservation program. (Backlund, Stewart, and McDonald, 2004, 634)

Broussard and colleagues (2008) conducted a survey in Indiana to determine the differences in the ways that planners and the public value land-use changes and open space. The researchers concluded that, while planners view land-use changes from a perspective of the impacts on the whole community, the public is more likely to focus on the land-use changes that they value individually (rather than on community values related to open space and quality of life). Broussard and colleagues (2008) also concluded that, as people perceived lower quality of life for themselves, they were more willing to support measures that would control urban growth. This result is in line with previous studies that have demonstrated that respondents with a lower quality of life are more likely to think that natural resources are not sufficiently protected with existing policies.

One important question for analysts and administrators is "What level of government should be responsible for this development of open space?" Several scholars have shown that policy decisions about the preservation of open space, as well as the actual development of the space, will be increasingly handled at the local level (Fausold and Lilieholm, 1999). Fausold and Lilieholm (1999) provide a comprehensive overview of the way the literature has conceptualized the economic value of open space, and they highlight some of the challenges associated with the difficult task of measuring the economic value of open space. These challenges include estimating the value of multiple uses of open space (for example, recreation uses and wetland mitigation), dealing with issues of converting noneconomic values into monetary units such as dollars (or monetization, as discussed in Chapter 4), dealing with "double counting" of open-space values, and addressing the moral issue of trying to place a monetary value on something that many people say is priceless.

Fausold and Lilieholm (1999) further explain that open space serves as a key provider of multiple public goods such as wildlife, habitat, scenic views, and community activities. They discuss (as we do in Chapter 2) the fact that public goods are both nonexcludable and nonconsumptive. As we have stressed in this book, the market typically fails to provide these goods in an efficient way; therefore, the government is often involved in the provision of open spaces and the public goods that come along with them. If open spaces were provided only by the private sector, they would most likely be underprovided. Fausold and Lilieholm (1999) propose some interesting questions about green space decision making that can guide administrators who deal with this issue. These questions include the following:

- "What land should be preserved for open space and why?"
- "What level of public resources should be applied to the preservation effort?"
- "If we cannot protect all significant areas, then what are the priorities?"(Fausold and Lilieholm, 1999, 316)

There are several key issues that analysts and administrators should consider when trying to determine the economic value of open space for making policy decisions. First, according to Fausold and Lilieholm (1999), analysts must accept the fact that they will not be able to compute exact economic values for open space—and, therefore, they should not even try to make such calculations. The researchers believe that there will always be some nonuse values that will be undervalued if an administrator or analyst attempts to convert them to a monetary number. (As explained in Chapter 4, they are arguing for retaining some costs and benefits in their own units.) Second, they argue that administrators should recognize how the various methods available for calculating the economic values of open space differ significantly in their reliability and comprehensiveness. The solution to this issue is taking a multidisciplinary approach to calculating economic values, drawing from a variety of methods. Third, Fausold and Lilieholm (1999) argue that results of an economic analysis of open space can be misused if they are interpreted too narrowly. One solution to this challenge is to ensure that a wide range of values is included in the analysis and that economic-value results are discussed broadly before a decision is made about developing an open space. Fourth, the estimation of the economic value of open space can have unintended consequences. To help avoid these unintended consequences, administrators should think through the future implications of land-use decisions, and must also ensure that any economic valuation includes positive values and negative values, as well as the net value. The fifth challenge that Fausold and Lilieholm (1999) present is the fact that the economic value of open space can depend on whether or not it is protected. For example, protected space is an asset that will have increasing benefits over time, while nonprotected space has value because it can allow for future growth and development options. Finally, the researchers note that administrators and analysts must think carefully about how open-space values and their distribution might change over time. For example, some important questions for administrators to ask themselves include "Will different groups benefit from the open space as it changes?"

As previously mentioned, there is an explicit link between the concepts of urban sprawl and green space. Geoghegan (2002) points out that there are several policy tools that have been used to protect urban open spaces and therefore reduce urban sprawl. These include "cluster zoning; transferable development rights; proposed land taxes to fund purchases of remaining open spaces; and private organizations that buy land" (Geoghegan, 2002, 91).

So, which communities are most likely to use the preservation of open space as a way to combat the negative impacts of urban sprawl? Howell-Moroney (2004) studied suburban governments in the Philadelphia area and found that three characteristics of local governments make them more likely to protect open space: age, socioeconomic status, and degree of community growth. For example, younger governments with higher socioeconomic status and higher rates of development are more likely to support preserving open space. These findings represent only one study, and they might actually contradict some other studies on this topic; again, the context of your particular environmental community is important to consider when thinking about access issues and open-space availability. This introduction of demographic and social characteristics of communities brings us to our discussion of some of the key social issues associated with land-use changes.

KEY SOCIAL ISSUES

Even though there are many potential social issues associated with land-use change, one of the most important analysts and administrators is its impact on social equity. Therefore, we focus the majority of our discussion of social issues of land use on the topics of social and environmental equity. (Chapter 9 provides a broad overview of environmental equity considerations.)

EQUITY ISSUES AND LAND USE

> "*Brownfields* are real property, the expansion, redevelopment, or reuse of which may be complicated by the presence or potential presence of a hazardous substance, pollutant, or contaminant" (U.S. EPA, 2011).

Land-use development can be particularly laden with equity issues because most people do not want landfills, highways, smokestacks, or brownfields in their neighborhoods. Greenberg and colleagues (2000) explored how brownfield sites led to decreased property values in New Jersey. They also studied how those decreases were distributed across different neighborhoods based on geography. They found that about 10 percent of the neighborhoods they studied reported significant impacts of the brownfields on the neighborhood. They argue that brownfield remediation should be considered within the context of larger social and environmental equity issues, because the risks and benefits of these properties are not always distributed in a socially and environmentally equal way across different geographical areas.

In Case 8.2, Wiewel and Schaffer (2001) present a brief overview of some land-use issues associated with equity in the urban environment.

Social scientists have found that access to open space can vary significantly across different socioeconomic groups within an urban area (Barbosa et al., 2007). Barbosa and colleagues found that the groups having the highest access to green space include older citizens and those with the lowest income levels. Lindsey and colleagues (2001) also explored the distribution of access to urban greenways (that is, an urban trail system with open space) in Indianapolis across different socioeconomic groups. Their analysis indicated that the socioeconomic groups that had the most access to the greenways were underrepresented minorities, people with lower income levels or housing values, and people without vehicles. Like the Barbosa study, Lindsey and colleagues concluded that there is a significant degree of racial and social segregation in the populations that live near the greenways. Even though the residents that need access to the greenways are more likely to have access (that is, poorer residents and those without vehicles), distribution is not equitable according to all definitions of the word (because residents in all socioeconomic groups do not have equal access). However, as we discuss in Chapter 9, lower-income residents and minority residents are also more likely to be near environmental disamenities; perhaps relationships between these two sets of findings should be analyzed. It is also possible that Lindsey and colleagues' (2001) findings are in some way unique to Indianapolis.

HOW DOES ZONING IMPACT EQUITY ISSUES?

Cities can take a variety of policy approaches when addressing social equity issues related to land use. Several scholars have outlined how land-use policies (in general) and zoning (in particular) can often lead to situations in which lower-income or underrepresented minority groups can end up carrying the burden of more environmental hazards based on the location of these types of facilities (Agyeman and Evans, 2003; Bullard, 1995). Maantay (2001, 1033) explained how land-use zoning can play an important role in equity issues within the urban environment because "in its most basic form zoning separates land areas into broad categories of land use—for example, residential, commercial, and industrial—with the assumption that separation of land uses promotes the public health and welfare of the population." By using New York City as a case study, she concludes that industrial sites that are less healthy for the environment and human health are more likely to be located in poor and minority neighborhoods, largely because wealthier neighborhoods are zoned for other uses.

Some scholars have argued that zoning was originally used to keep minority residents separate from others residents (Pendall, 2000; Weiss, 1987). Even though most policymakers and residents would argue that this is no longer a goal of zoning, Pendall (2000) cautions that zoning might still lead to racially motivated decisions about land

---

■———— **Case 8.2** ————■

Equity and Land Use in the Urban Environment

For some, the main problem with the movement of people and jobs out of the central city is the resulting inequity. Residents left behind have less access to jobs; the loss of tax base leaves cities less able to provide needed services and quality education; and the disappearance of the middle class contributes to the loss of civic and social capital and positive role models for poor neighborhoods. Myron Orfield (1997) extends this analysis beyond the central city to the inner suburbs, noting that inner suburbs are often even worse off, since they usually do not even have a downtown commercial tax base.

... Furthermore, even in regions where supporters choose not to emphasize the equity benefits of their proposals (or are simply not cognizant of them), anti-sprawl campaigns may have important consequences for poverty. While some of these consequences may be negative (a region's urban growth boundary limits construction and raises housing prices, for example), 'smart growth' policies are also likely to increase the amount of transit in a region and direct jobs back to urban areas. ...

Source: Wiewel and Schaffer, 2001.

---

use. To further explore how current smart-growth initiatives might affect racial or ethnic equity in urban environments, Pendall (2000) studied data from the twenty-five largest metropolitan areas in the United States and found that low-density zoning leads to a reduction in the amount of available rental housing, and this, in turn, leads to fewer African American and Hispanic residents living in low-density areas.

In addition to the impacts of zoning policies, there are other ways that urban sprawl can disproportionately influence the lives of those in lower socioeconomic groups. For example, wealthier residents of an urban area have more resources and, therefore, a higher ability than poorer residents to move out of an unhealthy urban environment and into an area where there are fewer environmental and health concerns. Also, residents who do not own vehicles might be forced to live in central, urban areas that are unhealthy in order to have access to public transportation.

INSTITUTIONAL AND POLITICAL ISSUES

Despite our detailed discussions about the ecological and social aspects of land-use change, decision making about land use is often impacted by more than just consideration of ecological and social issues; some scholars have argued that the structure of local political institutions can have a significant impact on land-use change and urban growth. In particular, Lubell and colleagues (2009, 649) outline how "political institutions serve as the governance arena in which interest groups bargain over property rights." They discuss how property-rights models and interest-group models draw on different motivations to explain land-use change. While property-rights models argue that population growth and land availability drive land-use policy, interest-group models typically argue that land-use policy is propelled by local political bargaining between elected officials and various interest groups. Yet, Lubell and colleagues note that both of these models tend to ignore the fact that local political institutions play a large part in the development of local land-use policies. In response, they introduce a political-market framework that "conceptualizes institutional change as the result of a dynamic contracting process between the suppliers and demanders of change in a community" (2009, 650). Their model includes elements of both property-rights models and interest-group models to explain land-use change and urban-growth patterns, while also acknowledging the role of political institutions.

Lubell and colleagues (2009) concluded that mayors typically exhibit support for interests that are championed by the higher socioeconomic status groups in a local area. Therefore, in urban areas where mayors have more power over decision making, land-use change is more likely to be positive for environmental quality. Conversely, they found that city managers are more likely to make decisions based on the goals of economic development interests and the construction industry.

Now that we have looked at some social issues associated with land-use change, we turn to a discussion of the policy tools that are most commonly used to address this environmental issue.

POLICY TOOLS IN THE LAND CONTEXT

Some of the most common policy tools that have been used to reduce sprawl and efficiently manage urban land use include (1) zoning, (2) growth-management acts (including smart-growth efforts and urban containment), (3) taxation of land use, and (4) tradable development permits (TDP) (Frenkel, 2004). Scholars have argued that managers, administrators and analysts should focus on nonmonetary benefits for landowners (such as access to recreation and aesthetics) when considering policy incentives for land-use change (Koontz, 2001). Koontz found that nonmonetary benefits are significant motivators in landowner decision-making processes. Therefore, policy tools that focus only on the (private) financial incentives for land-use change might be less effective than programs that emphasize both financial and nonfinancial benefits of a land-use change. Later in this chapter, we discuss in more detail some of the pros and cons of these policy tools for land-use management.

ZONING AS A POLICY TOOL

Many scholars contend that traditional zoning is the most common policy tool for controlling land-use development in the United States (Diamond and Noonan, 1996; York and Munroe, 2010). Both zoning and growth boundaries are viewed by policymakers as regulatory (or command-and-control) tools for controlling urban sprawl—in contrast to taxes and tradable permits which are often classified as market-based tools (Nuissl and Schroeter-Schlaack, 2009). These policy tools use some type of land-use policy to restrict growth (in the case of growth boundaries) or to allow only specific types of development (in the case of zoning). Both of these mechanisms (zoning and growth boundaries) focus on regulating behavior rather than providing an economic incentive for alternative behaviors, which is the goal of market-based land-use policy tools such as taxes and tradable permits.

Zoning is one common policy tool that governments use to address (and reduce) landscape fragmentation. Landscape fragmentation in the United States is often caused by the conversion of agricultural or rural lands into developed, suburban (or urban) land (Munroe, Croissant, and York, 2005). This type of landscape fragmentation can have negative consequences on both the ecological systems of landscapes and the accompanying socioeconomic systems (Munroe, Croissant, and York, 2005). Yet, the political nature of zoning decisions might mean that zoning changes increase landscape fragmentation rather than decreasing it. This is particularly true in areas where zoning is not consistent across contiguous jurisdictions. For example, new residential development might be moved into more rural areas because of zoning restrictions in a nearby local area (Munroe, 2005). York and Munroe (2010, 471) argue that, in addition to restricting land development, zoning also has the ability to regulate the rate of urbanization in an area because of increasing "transaction costs and loss of use rights."

Using zoning as a policy tool can result in several beneficial outcomes for land-use planning. First, it can minimize habitat fragmentation when it is applied in a way that encourages contiguous land use that preserves habitat over larger areas (Munroe, Croissant, and York, 2005). Second, environmentally sensitive zoning regulations can effectively limit the amount of urban sprawl as rural and agricultural lands are considered for new development. On the other hand, as mentioned above, zoning regulations are often driven by political and social considerations, and it might be difficult for administrators to make decisions about zoning that are focused solely on improving environmental and public health.

GROWTH-MANAGEMENT PLANS AS A POLICY TOOL

Frenkel (2004) provides a comprehensive historical perspective of the evolution of "smart growth" policies for land-use management, focusing in particular on how cities utilized the concept of new urbanism as a growth-management tool in the 1980s and 1990s. This strategy included a focus on clustered, compact development and mixed use. Yet, some scholars have argued that growth-management strategies might not effectively prevent urban sprawl and this issue is hotly debated in the scholarly community (Bontje, 2001; Dieleman, Dijst, and Split 1999; Fulton, 1996; Kline, 2000; K. Williams, 2000).

Since the 1980s, growth-management plans have emerged in many U.S. metropolitan areas as a response to urban sprawl. These plans are often state-based and provide guidelines for local land uses. Therefore, relating back to the social component of our conceptual model in Figure 1.3, this state-based process for developing plans would be contained in the "other governmental systems" arrow that feeds into the city governmental system.

By 2001, eleven states (Arizona, Florida, Georgia, Maine, Maryland, New Jersey, Oregon, Rhode Island, Tennessee, Vermont, and Washington) had adopted statewide growth-management legislation (Carruthers, 2002). One of the goals of any growth-management plan is the coordination of development plans across local areas within a state to generate a regional approach for dealing with urban sprawl and population growth. If each local government functions on its own—and does not coordinate development plans with other local areas—this can lead to increased urban sprawl and decentralization of development. Carruthers (2002) outlines, however, that growth-management plans continue to be somewhat controversial as policy tools for reducing sprawl because of a general lack of empirical data that could demonstrate their effectiveness quantitatively.

Smart-growth theory is a more recent iteration of the concept of a growth-management plan, but smart growth typically includes a stronger focus on urban design issues than traditional growth-management plans (Hamin, Steere, and Sweetser 2006). Hamin and colleagues explain that the American Planning Association defines "smart growth" as including the following activities (paraphrased from two sources: American Planning Association, 2002; Hamin, 2006): (1) comprehensive planning that is focused on building communities with a strong sense of place, (2) preserving important cultural and natural resources, (3) ensuring that costs and benefits of development are distributed within the community equitably across different socioeconomic groups, (4) focusing on fiscally responsible decisions when expanding transportation, housing, and employment opportunities in the urban area, (5) including a long-term focus when thinking about sustainability of the region, and (6) encouraging healthy communities and residents.

TAXING LAND USE AS A POLICY TOOL

The overall policy goal of land-use taxes is to set the tax rate according to particular land-use classifications that reflect "the environmental value of the sites" (Nuissl and Schroeter-Schlaack, 2009, 273). Altes (2009) explains how taxation of land use can be one tool for governments to incorporate the market into their land-use development plans. Yet, he points out that many scholars disagree on whether taxation of land use is a simple solution for the negative environmental impacts of urban sprawl and increasing development. According to Altes (2009), the costs of converting agricultural land into newly developed land are not always fully incorporated into the market transaction associated with buying and selling the land. In other words, the conversion involves negative externalities. This phenomenon can lead to increased conversion of agricultural land (and other open, green space) into urban, developed land with the ultimate result being an increase in urban sprawl. The introduction of a development tax, however, can adjust the cost of agricultural land conversion by making the conversion more expensive for developers. As a result, this type of tax can lead to less conversion of agricultural land, leaving larger portions of land as green, agricultural space. Altes (2009) notes, however, that taxation is not an often-used policy tool for internalizing the value of agricultural land and open spaces.

TRADABLE DEVELOPMENT RIGHTS AS A POLICY TOOL

Tradable development rights are another type of market-based policy tool used to deal with the negative environmental and social impacts of urban sprawl. This tool requires that the governmental unit in charge of land development restrict the total amount of land available for future development. It does this by issuing a fixed number of permits for land development and then, as with tradable air pollution permits, developers can buy and sell these permits among themselves (Nuissl and Schroeter-Schlaack, 2009).

Tradable development rights are typically defined as a market-based policy tool based "on the notion that 'development rights' are one of many sets of rights associated with fee simple land ownership" (Kaplowitz, Machemer, and Pruetz, 2008, 379). Once an individual or an organization owns the land-based development rights, then they can choose to transfer them or sell them. In many ways, a tradable development permit (TDR) program is similar to the cap-and-trade programs that we describe in Chapter 6 when discussing air pollution, with the clear difference that the TDR program is focused on trading rights to land use while an air pollution cap-and-trade system is focused on trading rights to air use. In the case of a cap-and-trade air pollution program, the activity that is limited by the permits is the emission of air contaminants, while TDR programs restrict the development of ecologically sensitive or desirable land. The small-scale adoption of TDRs began in the 1970s and has grown over time (Kaplowitz, Machemer, and Pruetz, 2008).

CONCLUSION AND CHECKLIST FOR ADMINISTRATORS

Now that we have provided an overview of the most common policy tools that are utilized for land-use planning, we present a checklist that can help administrators focus on some of the most important issues when trying to make choices between land policy tools (see Figure 8.2). As we mentioned in the other media chapters, this

---

Figure 8.2 **Checklist for Land-Use Policy Tools**

____ A. From an environmental perspective, how important is it for administrators in one area to take into account the zoning decisions in adjacent areas?

____ B. Is it desirable to encourage coordination across adjacent local governments on zoning? If so, how could this be implemented?

____ C. Is it important to include economic incentives for environmentally friendly land-use change?
YES ⇒ Then land-use taxes or tradable development rights might be the preferred policy tool.
NO ⇒ Then zoning solutions or growth-management plans might be appropriate.

____ D. What are the keystone species for this ecosystem?

____ E. What are the potential impacts of the land-use changes on the keystone species and which species should be preserved or considered?

____ F. What land (or types of land) should be preserved for open space and why?

____ G. Are big contiguous areas required for habitat preservation?

____ H. What level of public resources should be applied to preserving open space?

____ I. If all ecologically important areas cannot be protected, which are most important from an environmental and social perspective?

____ J. Are there potential equity issues of the land-use change?
YES ⇒ If so, how can they be mitigated?

____ K. Would a different policy tool result in fewer social inequities? If so, is that tool a feasible alternative politically, economically, and administratively?

____ L. Are policy decisions regarding land use likely to affect air or water?

---

list is not comprehensive. This checklist should be used to guide administrators and analysts as they consider many aspects of policy problems related to land-use change, but we encourage administrators and analysts to use this simply as a starting point for their choice between policy tools and to be sure to think about their own local and regional contexts. We list some common questions that might come up, but there are many others that are not listed here that might be important for any particular policy problem. Some of these can be found in the literature that we discussed earlier.

NOTE

1. The ESA (Dale et al., 2000) document defines a "keystone species" as one that has "greater effects on ecological processes than would be predicted from their abundance or biomass alone."

REFERENCES

Agyeman, J., and T. Evans. 2003. Toward just sustainability in urban communities: Building equity rights with sustainable solutions. *Annals of the American Academy of Political and Social Science*, 590, 35–53.

Alonso, W. 1964. *Location and Land Use*. Cambridge, MA: Harvard University Press.

Altes, W.K.K. 2009. Taxing land for urban containment: Reflections on a Dutch debate. *Land Use Policy*, 26, 2, 233–241.

American Planning Association. 2002. Policy guide on smart growth. Chicago, April 15. http://www.planning.org/policy/guides/pdf/smartgrowth.pdf.

Backlund, E.A.; Stewart, W.P.; and McDonald, C. 2004. Public evaluation of open space in Illinois: Citizen support for natural area acquisition. *Environmental Management*, 34, 5, 634–641.

Barbosa, O.; Tratalos, J.A.; Armsworth, P.R.; Davies, R.G.; Fuller, R.A.; Johnson, P.; and Gaston, K.J. 2007. Who benefits from access to green space? A case study from Sheffield, UK. *Landscape and Urban Planning*, 83, 2–3, 187–195.

Baycan-Levent, T., and P. Nijkamp. 2009. Planning and management of urban green spaces in Europe: Comparative analysis. *Journal of Urban Planning and Development*, 135, 1, 1–12.

Bontje, M. 2001. Dealing with deconcentration: Population deconcentration and planning response in polynucleated urban regions in Northwest Europe. *Urban Studies*, 38, 4, 769–785.

Broussard, S.R. et al. 2008. Attitudes toward policies to protect open space: A comparative study of government planning officials and the general public. *Landscape and Urban Planning*, 86, 1, 14–24.

Brueckner, J.K. 2000. Urban sprawl: Diagnosis and remedies. *International Regional Science Review*, 23, 2, 160–171.

———. 2001. Urban sprawl: Lessons from urban economics. In *Brookings-Wharton Papers on Urban Affairs*, ed. W.G. Gale and J.R. Pack, 65–89. Washington, DC: Brookings Institution Press.

Brueckner, J.K., and H.A. Kim. 2003. Urban sprawl and the property tax. *Tax and Public Finance*, 10, 1, 5–23.

Bullard, R. 1995. Residential segregation and urban quality of life. In *Environmental Justice: Issues, Policies, and Solutions*, ed. B. Bryant. Washington, DC: Island Press.

Burby, R., and P. May. 1997. *Making Governments Plan*. Baltimore, MD: Johns Hopkins University Press.

Carruthers, J.I. 2002. The impacts of state growth management programmes: A comparative analysis. *Urban Studies*, 39, 11, 1959–1982.

Chiesura, A. 2004. The role of urban parks for the sustainable city. *Landscape and Urban Planning*, 68, 1, 129–138.

Cutsinger, J. et al. 2005. Verifying the multi-dimensional nature of metropolitan land use: Advancing the understanding and measurement of sprawl. *Journal of Urban Affairs*, 27, 3, 235–259.

Dale, V.H. S.; Haeuber, R. A.; Hobbs, N.T.; Huntly, N.; Naiman, R.J.; Riebsame, W.E.; Turner, M.G.; and Valone, T.J. 2000. Ecological principles and guidelines for managing the use of land. *Ecological Applications*, 10, 3, 639–670.

Diamond, H.L., and P.F. Noonan, eds. 1996. *Land Use in America*. Washington, DC: Island Press.

Dieleman, F.M.; Dijst, M.J.; and Split, T.1999. Planning the compact city: The Randstad Holland experience. *European Planning Studies*, 7, 5, 605–621.

Ecological Society of America (ESA). 2000. Ecological Principles for Managing Land Use. The ESA's Committee on Land Use. Washington, DC. http://www.epa.gov/owow/watershed/wacademy/acad2000/pdf/landuseb.pdf.

Fausold, C.J., and R.J. Lilieholm. 1999. The economic value of open space: A review and synthesis. *Environmental Management*, 23, 3, 307–320.

Fischel, W. 2001. Homevoters, municipal corporate governance and the benefit view of the property tax. *National Tax Journal*, 54, 1, 157–173.

Frenkel, A. 2004. The potential effect of national growth-management policy on urban sprawl and the depletion of open spaces and farmland. *Land Use Policy*, 21, 4, 357–369.

Fulton, W. 1996. The new urbanism challenges conventional planning. *Land Lines,* 8, 5, (September).

Geoghegan, J. 2002. The value of open spaces in residential land use. *Land Use Policy*, 19, 1, 91–98.

Glaeser, E., and M. Kahn. 2003. Sprawl and urban growth. NBER Working Paper No. 9733, National Bureau of Economic Research, Cambridge, MA, May.

Greenberg, M. et al. 2000. Brownfields, toads, and the struggle for neighborhood redevelopment—A case study of the state of New Jersey. *Urban Affairs Review*, 35, 5, 717–733.

Hamin, E.M.; Steere, M.O.; and Sweetser, W. 2006. Implementing growth management: The Community Preservation Act. *Journal of Planning Education and Research*, 26, 1, 53–65.

Howell-Moroney, M. 2004. Community characteristics, open space preservation and regionalism: Is there a connection? *Journal of Urban Affairs*, 26, 1, 109–118.

Jackson, K. 1981. The spatial dimensions of social control: Race, ethnicity, and government housing policy in the United States, 1918–1968. In *Modern Industrial Cities: History, Policy, and Survival*, ed. B. Stave, 79–128. Beverly Hills, CA: Sage.

Jackson, L.E. 2003. The relationship of urban design to human health and condition. *Landscape and Urban Planning,* 64, 4, 191–200.

Kaplowitz, M.D.; Machemer, P.; and Pruetz, R. 2008. Planners' experiences in managing growth using transferable development rights (TDR) in the United States. *Land Use Policy*, 25, 3, 378–387.

Kline, J.D. 2000. Comparing states with and without growth-management analysis based on indicators with policy implications. *Land Use Policy*, 17, 4, 349–355.

Koontz, T.M. 2001. Money talks—But to whom? Financial versus nonmonetary motivations in land-use decisions. *Society and Natural Resources*, 14, 1, 51–65.

Leo, C., and K. Anderson. 2006. Being realistic about urban growth. *Journal of Urban Affairs,* 28, 2, 169–189.

Lindsey, G. et al. 2001. Access, equity, and urban greenways: An exploratory investigation. *Professional Geographer*, 53, 3, 332–346.

Lubell, M. et al. 2009. Local institutions and the politics of urban growth. *American Journal of Political Science*, 53, 3, 649–665.

Maantay, J. 2001. Zoning, equity, and public health. *American Journal of Public Health*, 91, 7, 1033–1041.

Margo, R. 1992. Explaining the postwar suburbanization of population in the United States: The role of income. *Journal of Urban Economics*, 31, 2, 301–310.

Mills, E.S. 1967. An aggregative model of resource allocation in a metropolitan area. *American Economic Review*, 57, 197–210.

Munroe, D.K.; Croissant, C.; and York, A.M. 2005. Land use policy and landscape fragmentation in an urbanizing region: Assessing the impact of zoning. *Applied Geography*, 25, 2, 121–141.

Muth, R. 1969. *Cities and Housing.* Chicago, IL: University of Chicago Press.

Naess, P. 2001. Urban planning and sustainable development. *European Planning Studies*, 9, 4, 503–524.

Nechyba, T.J., and R.P. Walsh. 2004. Urban sprawl. *Journal of Economic Perspectives*, 18, 4, 177–200.

Nuissl, H. et al. 2009. Environmental impact assessment of urban land use transitions—A context-sensitive approach. *Land Use Policy*, 26, 2, 414–424.

Nuissl, H., and C. Schroeter-Schlaack. 2009. On the economic approach to the containment of land consumption. *Environmental Science and Policy*, 12, 3, 270–280.

Orfield, M. 1997. *Metropolitics: A Regional Agenda for Community and Stability.* Washington, DC: Brookings Institution Press.

Pendall, R. 2000. Local land use regulation and the chain of exclusion. *Journal of the American Planning Association*, 66, 2, 125–142.

U.S. General Accounting Office. 1999. Community development: Extent of federal influence on "urban sprawl" is unclear. Report to Congress Requesters, RCED-99-87, April.

Voith, R. 1999. Does the federal tax treatment of housing affect the pattern of metropolitan development? *Federal Reserve Bank of Philadelphia Business Review*, March, 3–16.

Wassmer, R.W. 2008. Causes of urban sprawl in the United States: Auto reliance as compared to natural evolution, flight from blight, and local revenue reliance. *Journal of Policy Analysis and Management*, 27, 3, 536–555.

Weiss, M.A. 1987. *The Rise of the Community Builders.* New York: Columbia University Press.

White, E.M. et al. 2009. Past and projected rural land conversion in the US at state, regional, and national levels. *Landscape and Urban Planning*, 89, 1–2, 37–48.

Wiewel, W., and K. Schaffer. 2001. Learning to think as a region: Connecting suburban sprawl and city poverty. *European Planning Studies*, 9, 5, 593–611.

Williams, D.C. 2000. *Urban Sprawl: A Reference Handbook.* Santa Barbara, CA: ABC-CLIO.

Williams, K. 2000. Does intensifying cities make them more sustainable? In *Achieving Sustainable Urban Form,* ed. K. Williams, E. Burton, and M. Jenks, 30–45. London and New York: Spon Press.

York, A.M., and D.K. Munroe. 2010. Urban encroachment, forest regrowth and land-use institutions: Does zoning matter? *Land Use Policy*, 27, 2, 471–479.

9 Environmental Justice

Since the ultimate goal of policy analysis is to improve society, policy analysis must concern itself with justice. However, the way people define justice varies considerably, and so determining whether or not policies are *just* can be even more difficult than determining if they are *efficient*.

Within the field of urban environmental policy, though, there is a particular issue of justice that has arisen over the last few decades: the distribution of what are often called "environmental bads" or "disamenities." This subfield of policy is usually known as "Environmental Justice" analysis, or EJ. In the scholarly community, there is much debate over the extent of environmental *in*justice in the placement of disamenities, but much less debate as to what we would observe in a just system. It is widely accepted that disamenity placement—whether in land, air, or water—should not be affected by race or ethnicity. Even those who do not agree with this perspective should be attentive to the issue, for ignoring it can incite significant political problems, especially because of the growth of national and international environmental justice political movements, in addition to the EJ field of analysis (Liu, 2001).

Using the model presented in Chapter 1, EJ should especially be considered during the Agenda Setting, Policy Formulation, and Implementation stages of policymaking (as described later, President Bill Clinton put EJ on the federal agenda). Furthermore, findings of environmental injustice may decrease citizens' beliefs in the legitimacy of policy, and therefore analyses of environmental injustice can be part of Policy Evaluation and Problem Identification.

THE EJ DEBATE

"There are years of data showing a disproportionate, harmful impact in communities of color and in poor communities, said Ngozi Oleru, director of environmental health for Public Health—Seattle and King County" (Stiffler, 2005).

The EJ movement started in the United States in the early 1980s (Liu, 2001). As a field of research and policy analysis, EJ was influenced significantly by a clear and careful analysis issued in 1987 by a commission of the United Church of Christ (UCC). This study was called *Toxic Wastes and Race in the United States* and "found that minorities and the poor bear a disproportionate burden of these waste sites in their neighborhoods" (Liu, 2001, 2). According to the UCC study, "Race proved to be the most significant among variables tested in association with the location of commercial hazardous waste facilities" (United Church of Christ, 1987, xiii). This study and other factors led the executive director of the UCC Commission for Racial Justice, Dr. Benjamin Chavis (who later headed the National Association for the Advancement of Colored People, the NAACP) to claim a finding of environmental *racism*, which is "the deliberate targeting of people-of-color communities for hazardous waste facilities" (Norment, 1993, 78). Another term associated with these concerns is "environmental equity."

DOES ENVIRONMENTAL INJUSTICE EXIST?

Whether environmental injustice—let alone the more pointedly invidious concept of environmental racism—really exists or not remains a matter of contention among scholars. There is little doubt that, on average, racial and ethnic minorities in the United States disproportionately bear environmental burdens (see, for example, Brown, 1995). However, the *causes* of this outcome are hotly debated. One reason is that the initial study by the United Church of Christ focused on relationships at a point in time (thus the phrase "association with" in the quote from p. xiii).[1] It found *colocation* of minorities and "treatment, storage, and disposal facilities," or what are called TSDFs, and toxic waste sites throughout the United States (Liu, 2001), even controlling for a few other factors (United Church of Christ, 1987). However, it would be possible for disproportionate levels of minorities to live near environmental bads without disproportionate *placement* of disamenities in people-of-color communities. In other words, we might observe environmental inequity without observing environmental racism.

How could this occur? As discussed in Chapter 4 on Benefit-Cost Analysis, economists believe—and there is evidence to support this belief—that housing prices reflect not only attributes of the house itself but also attributes of the neighborhood in which it is located. If an environmental disamenity affects a house's neighborhood, it follows that the price of that house should be lower than the price of a similar house that is not near an environmental disamenity. In the United States, racial and ethnic minorities other than Asians/Pacific Islanders are, on average, poorer than dominant-culture whites. For example, the U.S. Census reports 2008 median incomes for Asian/Pacific-Islander families to be $73,578, for white-alone families to be $65,000, for Hispanic families to be $40,466, for black-alone families to be $39,879 (U.S. Census, 2008, 456), and for families with American Indian/Alaskan Native householders to be $37,815 (U.S. Census Bureau, 2007). Because housing prices will be lower in neighborhoods with disamenities, the free market should lead to more lower-income people living near those disamenities. Therefore, assuming that racial and ethnic minorities care about environmental disamenities at the same level as do majority whites, proportionately more minority people (other than Asian/Pacific Islanders) should live near them.

Economists tend to believe that the workings of the free market lead to increased social efficiency and, therefore, such movement of poorer families into areas of proportionately higher disamenities should not be interfered with—as long as families who move to disamenities are fully informed as to their natures and the risks involved. In fact, at a meeting of the Association for Public Policy Analysis and Management (APPAM), professor Douglas Noonan pointed out that it would be paternalistic for us to try to prevent people from making the risk-housing trade-offs that they desire. Individuals should be able to exercise their own preferences given their tastes and budget constraints: "When an economist sees a landfill surrounded by poorer residents, he is as likely to see households shrewdly saving on rent as to see households suffering environmental injustice" (Noonan, 2008, 8, electronic version). One caution regarding such a free-market perspective is that, as mentioned in Chapter 3, there is significant evidence that people are not good at assessing changes in small levels of (statistical) risk.

Is Race/Ethnicity a More Accurate Predictor Than Class in the EJ Dilemma?

A significant empirical problem with the free-market perspectives on the EJ debate is the significant evidence that race and ethnicity, rather than lower income levels, are more important predictors of location near environmental bads. In fact, the initial United Church of Christ study found the following:

> The analysis also revealed that mean household income and the mean value of owner-occupied homes were not as significant as the mean minority percentage of the population in differentiating residential ZIP codes with lesser numbers of hazardous waste facilities versus those with greater numbers and the largest landfills. After controlling for regional differences and urbanization, the mean value of owner-occupied homes in a community was a significant discriminator, but less so than the minority percentage of the population. (UCC, 1987, 13)

Since then, these results have been supported with the use of more sophisticated investigatory methods. In a 1992 article, Mohai and Bryant reviewed fifteen EJ studies; in five of the eight that analyzed both race and class, race was a more powerful predictor. Shortly thereafter, Phil Brown (1995) extended this analysis via a systematic review of toxic hazards and actual health outcomes of multiple studies conducted from 1972 to 1994. He assembled the findings into four categories: (1) proximity to known hazards; (2) regulation, amelioration, and cleanup; (3) health effects; and (4) proximity to prospective hazards. Brown concluded, "The overwhelming bulk of evidence supports the 'environmental justice' belief that environmental hazards are inequitably distributed by class, and especially race" (1995, 15). In Evan Ringquist's 2005 meta-analysis of forty-nine EJ studies, he further found "that while there is ubiquitous evidence of environmental inequities based upon race, existing research does not support the contention that similar inequities exist with respect to economic class" (223). Though there is some research that does not find evidence of race effects in colocation with environmental bads, the overarching finding is that race, rather than class, is a more important predictor of such colocation. This undermines the idea that observed racial injustice (like that found in the UCC report) is due to rational, income-based decisions that just happen to be correlated with race and ethnicity.

Another reason to be skeptical of the free-market explanation for the disproportionate colocation of minorities and environmental disamenities is the finding that, statistically, minorities actually fear risk *more* than whites. "Numerous studies show that risk perceptions are skewed across gender and race: Women worry more than men, and minorities more than whites, about myriad dangers . . . [including] environmental pollution" (Kahan et al., 2005, 1). If minorities fear risk more than whites, that would add support to the theory that colocation with environmental disamenities is disproportionately related to income levels rather than to race and ethnicity. Assuming that the informed poor are making risk-pollution tradeoffs in housing, it follows that economically disadvantaged whites would be more affected by colocation issues than economically disadvantaged people of color. As already reviewed, however, this is not the general finding.

EVIDENCE OF INITIAL PLACEMENT IN DISPROPORTIONATELY MINORITY COMMUNITIES

Some studies have examined the nature of communities *before* the placement of environmental disamenities. These studies go beyond current colocation and allow us more nearly to infer causation. Pastor, Sadd, and Hipp (2001), for example, analyzed "the disproportionate siting and minority move-in hypothesis in Los Angeles County . . . over three decades with firm-level[2] information on the initial siting dates for toxic storage and disposal facilities" (1). They found that "disproportionate siting matters more than disproportionate minority move-in" (Pastor, Sadd, and Hipp, 2001, 1). Indeed, their results tend to suggest either no effect, or else a move-*out* effect (in which minorities move out of areas near TSDFs) (15). Similarly, Campbell, Peck, and Tschudi (2010) used three decades of U.S. Census data, combined with information about when Toxics Release Inventory Facilities (TRIFs) were located in Arizona's Maricopa County, to assess the effect of race on location. They found that—even after controlling for many other economic and political factors that could affect TRI firm location decisions—the strongest social predictor was Asian race, and poverty was relatively unimportant. Given that Asians are, on average, the richest racial group in the United States, this finding may be particularly indicative of racial factors—rather than income factors—as determinative.

The Toxics Release Inventory (TRI) Program of the EPA "compiles the TRI data on toxic chemical releases and waste management activities reported annually by certain industries as well as federal facilities and makes it available through data files and database tools" (U.S. EPA, 2011).

OVERALL, THERE IS EVIDENCE THAT RACE AFFECTS DISAMENITY PLACEMENT

Taken together, these studies indicate that environmental injustice is a part of American society and that it is due more to race and ethnicity than to social class and income.

To date, it seems that most minority-focused EJ research (at least the research published in English) has been conducted in the United States. Recently, however, there has been a motion to study EJ in England and in Central and Eastern Europe, and some initial research indicates that race- and ethnicity-based environmental injustice exists there also (ESRC Global Environmental Change Programme, 2001, Section 2). For example, in a case study of the Roma (or gypsies, also called Romany) in eastern Slovakia, it was found that "the municipality in Rudnany regularly collected waste from the non-Roma part of the village and illegally deposited it near the Roma shantytown in Patoracke" (Harper, Steger, and Filcák, 2009, 258–259). This finding—along with knowledge of worldwide discrimination against minority groups, even to the extent of genocide in some cases—suggests that American EJ findings may carry over to the rest of the world.

The findings regarding the Roma also point out that, especially in other countries, the groups that are discriminated against are likely to vary beyond the U.S. Census categories of Black, Hispanic, Asian/Pacific Islander, and American Indian. As just one example, it seems there is discrimination against Muslims in France and Germany: "Half of respondents [in a recent poll] said they believe France has too many immigrants, and just under half feel that Muslims have too many rights" (Keaten, 2011, 1). In a *Le Monde* poll, 42 percent of French people and 40 percent of Germans "considered the presence of a Muslim community in their country 'a threat' to their national identity" (news24, 2011). According to a report in the *Los Angeles Times*, a "public" park in Lebanon has been closed to most of the public, and some interviewees believe that whether people are allowed in or not has to do with their religious sects (Daragahi, 2011).

Though most of the EJ research to date has focused on the United States, urban environmental policy analysts in other countries should realize that environmental injustice may well be an issue for them, with disproportionate colocation of environmental bads among under-represented groups in their societies. Even in the United States, there may be yet-undetected environmental injustices against minority groups that are more difficult to track because they are not included in the U.S. Census.

European EJ studies tend to focus on social class and poverty rather than race or ethnicity. For example, Haines and colleagues (1998) suggest that chronic exposure to aircraft noise leads to poorer academic performance, particularly among children of lower socioeconomic status. However, they omit exploration of adverse noise impact on children by race or ethnicity. The European perspective also considers cross-country EJ, with concern about processes by which "the poorest people in the poorest countries" (ESRC Global Environmental Change Programme, 2001, Introduction) disproportionately bear costs created in wealthier countries.

DOES ENVIRONMENTAL INJUSTICE MATTER?

Another question is whether environmental injustice matters or not. The world is full of problems: Is this one that warrants attention? In the meta-analysis referenced

---

Figure 9.1   **Part of Executive Order 12898, Issued by President William J. Clinton**

Section 1–1 Implementation

1–101. Agency Responsibilities. To the greatest extent practicable and permitted by law, and consistent with the principles set forth in the report on the National Performance Review, each Federal agency shall make achieving environmental justice part of its mission by identifying and addressing, as appropriate, disproportionately high and adverse human health or environmental effects of its programs, policies, and activities on minority populations and low-income populations in the United States and its territories and possessions, the District of Columbia, the Commonwealth of Puerto Rico, and the Commonwealth of the Mariana Islands.

Source: The White House, 1994.

---

earlier, Ringquist (2005) indicates, "By most yardsticks, the magnitudes of class- and race-based environmental inequities [in the United States] are quite modest" (241). And so, he argues that "remedying inequities probably should not be the primary goal when reinventing environmental regulation" (241). Others disagree. The December 2002 issue of *PA Times*, the monthly newsletter of the American Society for Public Administration (ASPA), included a special section on environmental justice. One author argued that environmental justice is a core value for public administration as a field, as well as for Americans more broadly (Ortiz, 2002, 3). Certainly, Americans' self-concept includes a concern with "justice for all,"[3] and part of the ASPA Code of Ethics commits members to "oppose all forms of discrimination" (ASPA, 2006; Strong, 2002, 7).

Twenty years after its initial study, finding an even greater concentration of "people of color . . . and hazardous waste facilities than previously shown," the United Church of Christ firmly contends that environmental justice is an important issue (Bullard, et al., 2007, viii). Additionally, in some cases a concern with EJ is required by law. For example, in February 1994, U.S. president Bill Clinton signed Executive Order 12898, requiring "federal agencies to develop environmental justice strategies" (see Figure 9.1). Further evidence of the push for environmental equity comes from Europe, where "a strong environmental rights agenda based in law is building up" (ESRC Global Environmental Change Programme, 2001, Introduction). Thus, even if the social costs of environmental injustice are modest, a combination of ethics, ideals, and law may require attention be directed toward its reversal.

POLITICS AND EJ

There are other reasons to be concerned with EJ, and those stem from its political and logistical ramifications. While ethics and law may not *require* a jurisdiction's attention to environmental justice, it is politically prudent to be concerned with the issue nonetheless: Environmental justice advocates can cause significant problems for administrators and the policies they wish to implement. The U.S. Fish and Wildlife Service reports the following: For decades, numerous protests have been launched against "locally unwanted land uses" (also known as LULUs), but in the 1980s the "environmental justice movement became a national . . . movement that galvanized communities across [the] country" (U.S. Fish and Wildlife Service, 2010). Then, in 1991, "representatives from hundreds of communities across the country came together in Washington, D.C., to focus national attention on what they perceived as a national problem" (U.S. Fish and Wildlife Service, 2010). As of 2008, no new oil refineries had been built in the United States since 1976 (Schoen, 2004; AP, 2008). Though environmental justice concerns are by no means the only reason for this outcome, "Not In My Backyard" (NIMBY) and environmental justice protests have made building a new refinery more difficult (Pitzl, 2003; AP, 2008). Unfortunately, such protests against the building of new facilities may actually harm environmental progress; usually, newer facilities are much more environmentally friendly in every way—using less energy and water in addition to polluting less—than old facilities.

Though the EJ movement may be more advanced in the United States, EJ concerns are of political importance in other countries, as well. For example, in China, a country that discourages protesting (including through imprisonment), credible reports indicate that there were significant protests against relocation caused by the development of the country's massive hydropower plant, Three Gorges Dam (MacLeod and MacLeod, 2001).

Terms associated with environmental and infrastructure-location protest include "LULU"—Locally Unwanted Land Use; "NIMBY"—Not In My Back Yard; and "NOPE"—Not On Planet Earth.

What Should Analysts Do About EJ?

First, consider that EJ issues can affect any medium—land, air, or water—and can also be caused by other factors that are not clearly part of any of these media. For example, at high-enough levels, noise—whether from a new freeway, a change in airport landing procedures, or a green technology such as windmills—can be a harmful pollutant (see Case 9.1), and research findings now include the placement of noise as a form of environmental injustice (see, for example, Sobotta, Campbell, and Owens, 2007). Both the EPA and the World Health Organization have defined limits for healthy levels of noise (Sobotta, Campbell, and Owens, 2007).

Second, even if there is no evidence that something causes harm, the perception of potential harm coupled with distrust and/or perceived lack of control in vulnerable communities may be sufficient to prompt EJ-based protests and political anger. For instance, there is no significant evidence that high-voltage power lines present human health risks. More than one learned society has gotten as close as scientists ever do to stating that living near such power lines presents no risk (Zeman, 2009). Nonetheless, many people still believe that they cause cancer.[4] (Googling "high tension power lines" in 2011 brings up many claims that high-tension power lines harm human health.) Citizens do not always believe or trust governments or scientists. For a

---

■——— **Case 9.1** ———■

Noise Can Be a Harmful Pollutant

There is a growing body of evidence that various sorts of environmental pollution cause physical, emotional, psychological, and socioeconomic harm. But many people do not realize that it is not simply a matter of usage or of hyperbole to refer to "noise pollution:" significant evidence indicates that it causes physical and other harm to those overexposed. Research indicates aviation noise can cause a variety of harms, including (but not limited to) communication interference, sleep disturbance, elevated levels of blood pressure and cholesterol, immune system deficiency, lower birth weight and higher frequency of premature birth, and hearing damage including to unborn babies (Holland, 1997). Of particular relevance to minority children, some of these problems may themselves lead to reduced scholastic performance and test scores (ibid. and see Haines et al., 1998). In the economic realm it seems clear that aviation noise can cause significant property devaluation (Booz et al., 1994; Espey and Lopez, 2000; McMillen, 2004; Tomkins et al., 1998).

Source: Sobotta, Campbell, and Owens, 2007. Used with permission.

---

variety of reasons, minority communities in particular may distrust governmental and scientific representatives.[5] If minority citizens believe that a proposed high-voltage line in their neighborhood will cause cancer, they may engage in EJ protest. Many such protests have been organized in the United States against tower-based (rather than buried) high-voltage power lines.

Third, for political purposes, colocation (often measured as correlation in space) is more important than causation. Politically, it often does not matter *why* a minority community is disproportionately impacted by environmental bads, only that it is—and certain ethical perspectives accord with this view. Therefore, consider the following:

1. Part of prudent urban environmental policy analysis is checking to see if a proposed policy will have a negative impact on any minority community. One important way to check this is to engage community members early in the planning process.

If there is reason to expect EJ concerns:

2. Check to see if noticeable or perceived environmental injustice already exists—or is perceived to exist—in your city or urban region.
3. Check to see if the negative effects of the new policy are *disproportionately* placed on minorities or if they *proportionately* impinge on minority and majority communities (proportionate impact would occur if the same percent of majorities and minorities are negatively affected by the policy as their base percents in the community).

4. Check to see if a minority area that will be affected by the new policy is one in which minorities are already disproportionately affected by environmental bads and strive against placement of additional environmental disamenities in such areas. Note, however, that simply refraining from making a disadvantaged community worse off does not ameliorate existing problems (Pastor, Sadd, and Hipp 2001).

The EPA has a website that provides guidelines for conducting EJ analyses (U.S. EPA, 2010; see Recommended Websites at the end of this chapter), and these guidelines may help. In general, Geographic Information Systems (GIS) are used to analyze whether disproportionate colocation of minorities (or other disadvantaged groups) and disamenities exist. Figure 9.2 gives an example of a typical EJ mapping. In this figure, Hispanic ethnicity is mapped with Toxics Release Inventory Facilities (TRIFs). Many cities today have GIS groups (often in planning offices or departments), and one of these may be able to help you with the mapping project. The EPA also makes available the EnviroMapper product, which allows simple mapping of environmental information (U.S. EPA; see Recommended Websites). As illustrated by Figure 9.2, a problem with simple mapping is that there can be legitimate debate as to whether any observed colocation is "significant." In the map shown, there seems to be high correlation between Hispanic ethnicity and TRIF location in some areas (near the center), but not around the periphery. Therefore, in any EJ-centered evaluation, it is best to include some type of simple statistical analysis, such as a correlation analysis, along with the mapping.

Another factor to consider in EJ analysis is that, for some types of environmental disamenities, simple proximity may not be the best indicator. For example, within a certain distance from an airport, aircraft noise may affect some areas much more than others due to prevailing take-off and landing patterns. Additionally, facilities that emit air-carried pollution will affect downwind neighbors much more than upwind ones.

In the event that, for some technical or cost-related reason, a minority community simply is the best location for negative effects of a proposed policy, then (1) expect political difficulties, and (2) consider some type of compensation. In fact, even if a policy has positive net benefits, social welfare is not improved by that policy alone if there is no compensation for its negative effects (refer to Chapter 4). Though the Kaldor-Hicks principle justifies moving forward under the assumption that, *on average,* choosing many policies with net benefits will result in gains to all, this assumption is not tenable when costs will be imposed on a community that is already worse off than the average. Furthermore, such imposition of costs on a disadvantaged community would be viewed as unjust under many philosophies.

Compensation can include (1) money payment, (2) removal or amelioration of something else undesirable in the community, (3) amelioration of some of the harms of the policy under consideration (for example, sound walls to decrease freeway noise), or (4) provision of an offsetting benefit. The latter may be especially interesting, since some research finds racial disparities such that minority communities may have fewer amenities (see, for example, Moore et al., 2008) *as well as* more harms. Keep in mind, though, that some forms of compensation come with "strings," which members of

Figure 9.2 **Toxics Release Inventory Facilities (TRIFs) and Density of Hispanic-Ethnicity Residents, Central Portion of Maricopa County, Arizona, 2000**

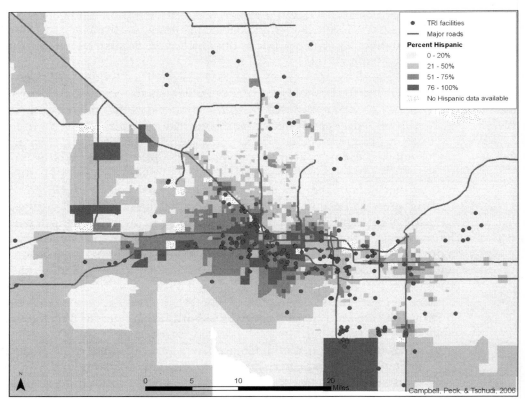

Source: GIS mapping produced by Michael K. Tschudi. Data from U.S. Census 2000 and EPA Toxics Release Inventory, http://www.epa.gov/tri/.

the affected groups may reject. In past exchanges for amelioration of future impact, residents have been required to relinquish compensation for past harm/injury in order to qualify for future protections. For example, aircraft-noise-impacted residents may be required to waive their right to seek damages from prior environmental impact if they wish to receive residential soundproofing (Sobotta, personal communication). Noonan (2008) argues in favor of creativity in considering compensations: "They might be environmental (ample greenery in exchange for high volatile organic compound emissions) or nonenvironmental (more jobs in exchange for industrial sitings), private (lower rent for more disamenities) or public (funding for public schools in exchange for a permit to operate a landfill)" (Noonan, 2008, 21, electronic version). Coming up with politically viable compensations can be especially difficult when predilections to cut taxes and reduce services are uppermost—all the more reason to communicate with citizens and use creativity in decision making.

Once such a breadth of options is considered, it is obvious that each community will have different preferences in the event that compensation is offered. Rather than trying to decide what compensation is best, analysts would do well to seek democratic input from those who will be affected. Citizen participation is in accord with Executive Order 12898 (see Figure 9.1), and Noonan (2008) argues that democratic input is especially important if the choice of compensation will be contentious. Irvin and Stansbury (2004) find that, under the right conditions, citizen participation can be effective and produce great gains in effective governance in general. Particularly relevant to many minority communities, they find that "winning the hearts of the citizens by meeting with them regularly and ultimately gaining their trust and friendship may be the only way for environmental regulators to promote new policies in communities where antigovernment sentiment runs high" (2004, 58).

In fact, given the many political problems with placement of new infrastructure and other projects, seeking citizen participation on a regular basis is good policy. Therefore, an important suggestion for dealing with EJ concerns—some type of democratic citizen participation—turns out to be a good procedure for urban environmental policy in general. In Chapter 10, we discuss standard methods of seeking citizen input.

However, it is important to keep in mind that many urban environmental policies are highly technical in nature. Uninformed citizen participation is not necessarily useful—either to citizens, the production of better policy, or the defusing of political anger—and in fact can be harmful (see, for example, Irvin and Stansbury, 2004). For example, increased participation might also lead to more NIMBY opposition by high-status groups, which could simply reinforce existing environmental inequities and further discourage low-status groups from participating. Participation is important; however, it must be conducted with the understanding that (1) technical/expertise constraints on some minority groups are likely, (2) political power/legitimacy constraints are also quite probable, and (3) divergent views of risk will often exist between residents and decision makers (see, for example, Cvetkovich and Earle, 1992, and Schively, 2007). For all these reasons, citizen participation should be structured to *engage and educate* citizens *before* gathering their opinions, and Chapter 11 focuses on creative methods for such educative processes.

CONCLUSION

Issues of environmental justice are woven through many urban policies. Land, air, and water can be affected by EJ issues, as can factors that you may not initially consider, such as noise, light, and electromagnetic spectra. Environmental injustice can affect ethics, efficiency, and politics. Though research and advocacy have tended to focus on environmental "bads," some research is also beginning to consider the placement of "goods," along with the amelioration of disamenities (Eckerd, 2010). In the United States, the latter is already part of federal policy on brownfields remediation (Public Law, 107–118). If only for political protection, every urban environmental policy analysis should include an EJ component that addresses the following questions: Are harms disproportionately affecting minority communities? Are positive outcomes disproportionately affecting majority communities? Depending on the circumstances, either outcome may be unjust, inefficient, and/or politically dangerous. If there is environmental injustice in a policy and no better policy is available, then analysts should consider careful and appropriate citizen engagement, along with compensation for disproportionate receipt of harms.

This chapter began by stating that, if policy analysis is to be a tool of social improvement, then a key element in any analysis must be the concept of *justice.* While there are clear definitions of *efficiency,* what is *just* or *unjust* at a particular point in time, in a particular society, and in relation to a particular policy is much more difficult to determine. Because of this, one of the best ways to achieve policy justice in general—not just environmental justice—is through appropriate citizen engagement. The next two chapters of the text discuss methods of appropriate citizen engagement.

RECOMMENDED WEBSITES

U.S. Environmental Protection Agency. 2011. Toxics release inventory (TRI) program. January. http://.epa.gov/tri/. From the website: "The goal of the Toxics Release Inventory (TRI) program is to provide communities with information about toxic chemical releases and waste management activities and to support informed decision making at all levels by industry, government, nongovernmental organizations, and the public."

U.S. Environmental Protection Agency. 2010. *Guidelines for Conducting Environmental Justice Analyses: Section 2.* October. http://www.epa.gov/region2/ej/guidelines.htm. From the website: "The *Guidelines for Conducting Environmental Justice Analyses* provide guidance and procedures, and identify sources of data for conducting EJ analyses to evaluate if a community is an EJ community."

U.S. Environmental Protection Agency. 2010. EJView. November. http://epamap14.epa.gov/ejmap/entry.html. From the website: "EJView, formerly known as the Environmental Justice Geographic Assessment Tool, is a mapping tool that allows users to create maps and generate detailed reports based on the geographic areas and data sets they choose."

U.S. Environmental Protection Agency. EnviroMapper for Envirofacts. http://www.epa.gov/emefdata/em4ef.home. From the website: "This Website provides access to several EPA databases to provide you with information about environmental activities that may affect air, water, and land anywhere in the United States."

NOTES

1. Statistical methods have advanced since the initial UCC report was published. Even so, the study used discriminant analysis, which allowed for some controlling of multiple variables, as well as difference of means tests and matched-pairs tests (see United Church of Christ, 1987, 41, Table B-1).

2. A methodological issue in EJ research is the unit of analysis. Here Pastor, Sadd, and Hipp (2001) are stressing that they model the decision process of the firm and that they have firm-specific data on firm siting.

3. The Pledge of Allegiance states that the republic of the United States is dedicated to "liberty and justice for all."

4. A 1979 study "associated increased risk of childhood leukemia with residential proximity to power lines," but evidence since indicates otherwise (Zeman, 2009).

5. One of the most horrific blots on American science and government was the Tuskegee syphilis experiments, in which 400 poor black men—and those they infected—were allowed to suffer with syphilis over many decades in the name of scientific knowledge (Chadwick, 2002). One ramification of this has been distrust within the African American community of both governmental representatives and scientists.

REFERENCES

American Society for Public Administration (ASPA). 2006. ASPA's Code of Ethics. http://www.aspanet. org/scriptcontent/index_codeofethics.cfm (accessed January 14, 2011).

Associated Press (AP). 2008. South Dakota voters approve what could be first new U.S. oil refinery in decades. Fox News.com, June 4. http://www.foxnews.com/story/0,2933,363121,00.html (accessed January 20, 2011).

Booz-Allen & Hamilton. 1994. The Effect of Airport Noise on Housing Values: A Summary Report. Prepared for the Office of Environment and Energy, Federal Aviation Administration, Washington, DC, September 15. http://www2.oaklandairport.com/pdf/effects_aircraft_noise_home_values.pdf .

Brown, P. 1995. Race, class, and environmental health: A review and systematization of the literature. *Environmental Research,* 69, 1, 15–30.

Bullard, R.D., P. Mohai, R. Saha, and B. Wright. 2007. *Toxic Wastes and Race at Twenty: 1987–2007.* United Church of Christ Justice and Witness Ministries.

Campbell, H.E., L.R. Peck, and M.K. Tschudi. 2010. Justice for all? A cross-time analysis of Toxics Release Inventory facility location. *Review of Policy Research,* 27, 1, 1–25.

Chadwick, Alex. 2002. Remembering Tuskegee: Syphilis study still provokes disbelief, sadness. National Public Radio, *Morning Edition,* July 25. http://www.npr.org/programs/morning/features/2002/jul/tuskegee/ (accessed March 13, 2011).

Cvetkovich, G., and T. Earle. 1992. Environmental hazards and the public. *Journal of Social Issues,* 48, 4, 1–20.

Daragahi, B. 2011. Beirut's lone public park isn't: Officials have barred the masses from the city's only green refuge, saying they don't know how to enjoy such places. *Los Angeles Times,* January 7, A1, A6.

Eckerd, A. 2010. From brownfields to greenfields: Assessing the environmental justice of cleaning up brownfields. Edward F. Hayes Graduate Research Forum. http://hdl.handle.net/1811/45584.

Espey, M., and H. Lopez. 2000. The impact of airport noise on residential property values. *Growth and Change,* 31, 408–419. As cited in Sobotta et al., 2007.

ESRC Global Environmental Change Programme. 2001. Environmental justice: Rights and means to a healthy environment for all. Special Briefing No. 7, November. http://www.foe.co.uk/resource/reports/environmental_justice.pdf (accessed January 20, 2011).

Haines, M.M. et al. 1998. Chronic aircraft noise exposure and child cognitive performance and stress. In *Proceedings of the Seventh International Conference on Noise as a Public Health Problem,* ed. N. Carter and R.F.S. Job, 1, 329–334. As cited in Sobotta et al., 2007.

Harper, K., T. Steger, and R. Filcák. 2009. Environmental justice and Roma communities in Central and Eastern Europe. *Environmental Policy and Governance,* 19, 4, 251–268.

Holland, W. 1997. Health effects of aircraft noise. Unpublished report. As cited in Sobotta et al., 2007.

Irvin, R.A., and J. Stansbury. 2004. Citizen participation in decision making: Is it worth the effort? *Public Administration Review,* 64, 1, 55–65. http://glennschool.osu.edu/faculty/brown/home/810/Class%20Materials/Irvin.pdf (accessed January 20, 2011).

Kahan, D.M. et al. 2005. Gender, race, and risk perception: The influence of cultural status anxiety. Available at SSRN: http://papers.ssrn.com/sol3/papers.cfm?abstract_id=723762.

Keaten, J. 2011. France: Marine Le Pen seeks to show softer side of National Front. *The Scotsman,* January 13. http://news.scotsman.com/news/France-Marine-Le-Pen-seeks.6688631.jp (accessed January 12, 2011).

Liu, F. 2001. *Environmental Justice Analysis: Theories, Methods, and Practice*. Boca Raton, FL: Lewis Publishers.

MacLeod, C., and L. MacLeod. 2001. China's dam busters protest controversial resettlement project. *The Independent*, July 19. http://www.independent.co.uk/news/world/asia/chinas-dam-busters-protest-controversial-resettlement-project-678191.html (accessed January 20, 2011).

McMillen, D.P. 2004. Airport expansions and property values: The case of Chicago O'Hare airport. *Journal of Urban Economics*, 55, 3, 627–640. As cited in Sobotta et al., 2007.

Mohai, P., and B. Bryant. 1992. Environmental racism: Reviewing the evidence. In *Race and the Incidence of Environmental Hazards,* ed. B. Bryant and P. Mohai, 163–176. Boulder, CO: Westview. As cited in Brown (1995).

Moore, L.V. .; A.V. Diez Roux; K.R. Evenson; A.P. McGinn; and S.J. Brines. 2008. Availability of recreational resources in minority and low socioeconomic status areas. *American Journal of Preventive Medicine,* 34, 1, 16–22. http://www.ncbi.nlm.nih.gov/pubmed/18083446 (accessed January 20, 2011).

news24. 2011. Muslims seen as a threat in France, Germany. news24, January 4. http://www.news24.com/World/News/Muslims-seen-as-threat-in-France-Germany-20110104 (accessed January 18, 2011).

Noonan, D.S. 2008. Evidence of environmental justice: A critical perspective on the practice of EJ research and lessons for policy design. *Social Science Quarterly*, 89, 5, 1154–1174. http://www.prism.gatech.edu/~dn56/EJ.SSQ.pdf (accessed January 12, 2011).

Norment, L. 1993. Ben Chavis: A new director, a new direction at the NAACP. *Ebony*, 48, 9 (July), 76–80. http://books.google.com/books?id=_MsDAAAAMBAJ&pg=PA78&lpg=PA78 (accessed January 11).

Ortiz, J. 2002. Environmental justice is part of our core values. *PA Times*, 25, 12, 3.

Pastor, M., Jr., J. Sadd, and J. Hipp. 2001. Which came first? Toxic facilities, minority move-in, and environmental justice. *Journal of Urban Affairs*, 23, 1, 1–21. http://www2.ucsc.edu/cjtc/docs/a_Which_Came_First.pdf (accessed January 12, 2011).

Pitzl, M.J. 2003. Oil refinery at Mobile may not fly: Issues involve race, ozone. *Arizona Republic*, October 13, B1, B5.

Public Law 107–118 (H.R. 2869). 2002. Small Business Liability Relief and Brownfields Revitalization Act. http://epa.gov/brownfields/laws/sblrbra.htm.

Ringquist, E.J. 2005. Assessing evidence of environmental inequities: A meta-analysis. *Journal of Policy Analysis and Management,* 24, 2, 223–247.

Schively, C. 2007. Understanding the NIMBY and LULU phenomena. *Journal of Planning Literature,* 21, 255–266.

Schoen, J.W. 2004. U.S. refiners stretch to meet demand: Can existing plants continue to squeeze more output? Oil & Energy on MSNBC.com, November 22. http://www.msnbc.msn.com/id/6019739/ns/business-oil_and_energy/ (accessed January 20, 2011).

Sobotta, R.R. 2011. Personal communication with author. Robin Sobotta is Chair of the Embry-Riddle Aeronautical University Aviation Business Administration degree program.

Sobotta, R.R., H.E. Campbell, and B.J. Owens. 2007. Aviation noise and environmental justice: The barrio barrier. *Journal of Regional Science,* 47, 1, 125–154.

Stiffler, L. 2005. Toxic burden for poor, minorities and EPA looks set to ease remedy efforts. *Seattle Post-Intelligencer,* August 26.

Strong, D.E. 2002. Continuing challenge of environmental justice. *PA Times*, 25, 12, 6, 7.

Tomkins, J.N. et al. 1998. Noise versus access: The impact of an airport in an urban property market. *Urban Studies*, 35, 2, 243–258. As cited in Sobotta et al., 2007.

United Church of Christ (UCC). 1987. Toxic wastes and race in the United States: A national report on the racial and socio-economic characteristics of communities with hazardous waste sites. UCC Commission for Racial Justice. http://www.urbanhabitat.org/node/5346 (accessed January 20, 2011).

U.S. Census Bureau. 2007. American Indians by the numbers. Information Please. http://www.infoplease.com/spot/aihmcensus1.html (accessed January 14, 2011).

————. 2008. Table 696. Money income of families—Median income by race and Hispanic origin in current and constant (2008) dollars: 1990 to 2008. In *Statistical Abstract of the United States: 2011.* http://www.census.gov/compendia/statab/2011/tables/11s0696.pdf (accessed January 12, 2011).

U.S. Environmental Protection Agency. 2010. *Guidelines for Conducting Environmental Justice Analyses: Section 2.* October. http://www.epa.gov/region2/ej/guidelines.htm.

————. 2011. Toxics release inventory (TRI) program. http://www.epa.gov/tri/ (accessed January 12, 2011).

U.S. Fish and Wildlife Service. 2010. Environmental justice legacy. Office of External Affairs, December 22. http://www.fws.gov/dpps/envirojustice.html (accessed January 20, 2011).

The White House. 1994. Executive Order 12898. 59 F.R. 7629, February 16. http://www.archives.gov/federal-register/executive-orders/pdf/12898.pdf (accessed March 14, 2011).

Zeman, G. 2009. Health risks associated with living near high-voltage power lines. Health Physics Society, HPS Publications, December 19. http://www.hps.org/hpspublications/articles/powerlines.html (accessed January 20, 2011).

Part IV

Communicating About
Environmental Policy

10 Learning from Citizens: Public Participation in Environmental Policy

Nicholas L. Cain

Across the world, public participation in government policy has never been more common. As the use of participation has grown to include a broad range of policy areas and national contexts, innovative approaches and tools have multiplied—and so have the challenges and issues that practitioners confront. As public participation has grown more prevalent, it has also undergone a shift in emphasis. Conceived initially as a check on the excesses of bureaucracy, participation increasingly is being used to defuse controversy and build consensus, plan and implement policy, and engage the community in collaborative projects.

Many facets of democracy involve public participation in some form. For our purposes, however, public participation is defined as involvement in formal "administrative decision making" outside of the activities of electoral politics (Beirele and Cayford, 2002, 6). In United States law, public participation rests on a three-part foundation of information transparency, participation in the rule-making process, and judicial review. This three-pronged approach has been echoed in the practices of other nations and also used as the foundation for major international agreements such as the Aarhus Convention [a treaty of the United Nations Economic Commission for Europe (UNECE), adopted in Aarhus, Denmark, in 1998, to facilitate communication on environmental matters; for more information, see "Europe, Asia, and the Developing World" later in this chapter] (Toth, 2010).

As participation has become more common around the world, and as the range of agencies that seek public input has expanded, the methods for soliciting public input have also grown in number and complexity. Traditional forms, such as listening to spoken comments at a public hearing, are being joined by innovative practices such as distributed decision making and the use of computer-aided visualization and mapping systems.

Looking at the model framework set out in Chapter 1 of this book, public participation can be found in almost every area of the Social System (Figure 1.3). Although our focus here will be on the role of public participation in the Policy Process layer of the model, participation activities frequently involve a range of actors from the Nongovernmental Subsystem as well as from different levels of government. In the

United States, participation has long been a part of local government, especially around land-use decisions and changes to the urban form. It is also a longstanding feature of the work of federal environmental regulatory agencies, going back to the 1969 passage of the National Environmental Policy Act (NEPA). More recently, per a 2011 Executive Order, participation has become a requirement for all U.S. federal agencies (The White House, Executive Order 13563, 2(a)).

For practitioners, the basic requirement of participation is often obvious—a local, state, or federal law requires a government agency or department to hold a hearing, announce a change in zoning, or form an advisory committee on a given issue. However, within these broad confines, managers and staff often have substantial discretion in how they will perform outreach, gather and analyze comments, and present the data. And of course, there may be cases in which citizen participation is not mandated but is still a good idea.

This chapter will discuss recent trends, briefly examine some cautions, and then detail successful approaches for ensuring that public participation meets the needs of policymakers and improves urban environmental public policy.

RECENT TRENDS IN PUBLIC PARTICIPATION

THE UNITED STATES

Executive Order 13563, signed by President Barack Obama in January 2011, makes substantial public participation the new standard for all major policy activities of U.S. federal agencies. As set forth in Figure 10.1, the order makes explicit and extensive references to Internet-based approaches for comment gathering and for information sharing. Each federal agency is required to afford the public a "meaningful opportunity to comment through the Internet on any proposed regulation." In the same fashion, information on both proposed and final regulation, "including relevant scientific and technical findings" is required to be posted on Regulations.gov (The White House, E.O. 13563).

Along with these changes, the new executive order greatly expands the scope of participation, requiring "public comment on all pertinent parts of the rulemaking docket" (The White House, E.O. 13563, 2(a)). Although this order "reaffirms many core principles" reflected in prior executive orders, it also sets a new standard—especially regarding the requirements for information transparency and the broad scope of agencies now required to participate (Coglianese, 2011).

This 2011 executive order is just the culmination of a decades-long trend that has seen public participation spring from executive, legislative, and court efforts to exercise oversight on the activities of post–New Deal federal agencies (Beirele and Cayford, 2002, 2). The first major legislative reaction took the form of the Administrative Policy Act (APA) of 1946, which requires that agencies provide notice of impending rules and information about them (*transparency*), an opportunity for *participation* in rule making, and *judicial review* of agency proceedings. These three elements have formed the basis of most participation efforts in the United States, in Europe, and elsewhere ever since (Beirele and Cayford, 2002, 3).

Figure 10.1 **Excerpt from Executive Order 13563 on Improving Regulation and Regulatory Review**

Executive Order 13563 of January 18, 2011 Improving Regulation and Regulatory Review

By the authority vested in me as President by the Constitution and the laws of the United States of America, and in order to improve regulation and regulatory review, it is hereby ordered as follows:

. . .

Sec. 2. Public Participation.

(a) Regulations shall be adopted through a process that involves public participation. To that end, regulations shall be based, to the extent feasible and consistent with law, on the open exchange of information and perspectives among State, local, and tribal officials, experts in relevant disciplines, affected stakeholders in the private sector, and the public as a whole.

(b) To promote that open exchange, each agency, consistent with Executive Order 12866 and other applicable legal requirements, shall endeavor to provide the public with an opportunity to participate in the regulatory process. To the extent feasible and permitted by law, each agency shall afford the public a meaningful opportunity to comment through the Internet on any proposed regulation, with a comment period that should generally be at least 60 days. To the extent feasible and permitted by law, each agency shall also provide, for both proposed and final rules, timely online access to the rulemaking docket on regulations.gov, including relevant scientific and technical findings, in an open format that can be easily searched and downloaded. For proposed rules, such access shall include, to the extent feasible and permitted by law, an opportunity for public comment on all pertinent parts of the rulemaking docket, including relevant scientific and technical findings.

(c) Before issuing a notice of proposed rulemaking, each agency, where feasible and appropriate, shall seek the views of those who are likely to be affected, including those who are likely to benefit from and those who are potentially subject to such rulemaking.

Source: The White House, 2011.

Although the 1946 APA set out broad principles, it wasn't until a series of subsequent legislative efforts and court rulings that participation became more common in the United States. In the area of environmental policy, the 1969 National Environmental Policy Act (NEPA)—and related state policy acts—established participation as an "important component of environmental planning and decision making" at all levels of government (McKinney and Harmon, 2002, 149). By the late 1970s, over 225 laws required participation in environmental policymaking at different contexts (Berry et al., 1984, 8). As Figure 10.2 shows, the prevalence of the term "public participation" in various kinds of documents held steady through the 1950s and 1960s at a relatively low level before increasing rapidly in the 1970s, and then again in the 1990s. According to a review of search results, the spike occurring in 1998 was triggered by the passage of the Aarhus Convention.

In U.S. courts, the right of the public and nongovernmental organizations to have standing in federal rule making was "reasonably well established" by the time of a 1970 federal appeals court decision dealing with welfare policy. Since that ruling, which in turn drew on a series of earlier rulings by the Supreme Court, federal agencies have increasingly included public participation in rule making (Cramton, 1972, 538).

The growth in public participation in the United States in the 1960s and 1970s, according to Jeffrey M. Berry and his colleagues at Tufts, was part of a broader shift in the United States toward a "new public administration" that moved agencies from a primarily managerial approach toward a more pluralist practice. This was due in part (1) to recognition that agencies were inherently undemocratic, and

Figure 10.2 **Google Timeline for "Public Participation," 1950–2011**

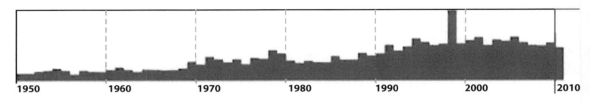

Source: Google News Archive Search, 2011.
Note: This Google Timeline graph shows the frequency of the occurrence of the phrase "public participation" in various publications and other documents over the past sixty years in a unitless graphical fashion. According to a review of search results, the spike in 1998 corresponds with the passage of the UN/ECE Convention on Public Access to Information, Public Participation in Decision Making and Access to Justice in Environmental Matters (the Aarhus Convention).

(2) to a "de facto acknowledgment" that agencies were sometimes overly influenced by private entities such as firms and associations (Berry et al., 1984).

According to the legal thinking of the APA and later laws, increased public participation will help agencies make "wiser and more informed decisions" while countering the undemocratic nature of rule making. But even early advocates saw participation as a potential fad that, if not used judiciously, could undermine effectiveness and make policy subject to the capricious whims of the public (Cramton, 1972, 530). The tension created by public involvement—acute in the environmental realm—is how to reconcile "the need for expertise" in dealing with complex, technical programs, with the "transparency and participation" that democratic governance requires (Beirele and Cayford, 2002, 3).

To help meet this challenge, public participation in the United States has evolved significantly over the last five decades. What was once seen as citizen oversight of rule making is now being viewed as a kind of "collaborative problem solving" that can help solve tough policy challenges (McKinney and Harmon, 2002, 149). As the extent of participation in the United States has become more common, the scope of participation has also grown. Today, at both the federal and state levels, participation is usually required at all major stages in the policy process: agenda setting, intermediate development, and implementation.

Europe, Asia, and the Developing World

Until recently, most of Europe lagged decades behind the United States in the use of public participation. It wasn't until the adoption of the "Convention on Access to Information, Public Participation in Decision Making and Access to Justice," in Aarhus, Denmark, in 1998 (which entered into force three years later) that a "shift in thinking" regarding the importance of public participation in Western Europe was solidified (Dette, 2004, 20). The Aarhus Convention, as it came to be called, was described as a "giant step forward" in the area of participation by then–United Nations Secretary-General Kofi Annan.

The convention grew out of the process of European integration and from the evolution of global international agreements such as the United Nations' Agenda 21 (Bell,

Stewart, and Nagy, 2002, 36). It is built around the three main pillars of participation discussed above: access to the process, to information and to judicial oversight. Much like the laws in the United States, the Aarhus Convention requires member states to provide access to information about a policy, public access to the rule-making process, and oversight of the process by the courts (Toth, 2010, 295).

Prior to the passage of the convention, major European nations such as Germany and France favored a decidedly technocratic approach to regulatory policy that was only minimally open—although other nations, such as Finland, the Netherlands, Norway, and Sweden offered access to information and public participation, especially in environmental policy (Bell, Stewart, and Nagy, 2002, 36). Denmark, which played host to the signing of the convention, has pioneered innovative participation tools such as the consensus conference and the scenario workshop, both of which we cover in greater detail in the next section (Einsiedel, Jelsøe, and Breck, 2001)

Analyzing the situation in Asia, authors led by Shui-Tan Tang at the University of Southern California trace the use of Environmental Impact Assessments (EIAs) in China and Taiwan to their introduction in the United States in 1969 as part of NEPA. Since then, the authors note, citizen participation in EIAs has become a standard practice in more than one hundred nations around the world (Tang, Tang, and Lo, 2005, 2). Established by China's 1979 Environmental Protection Law and finalized a decade later, the EIA system in China is now quite extensive. However, as Tang and his colleagues discuss, local-federal competition, bureaucratic corruption, limited governmental transparency, and limited participation diminish the practical effectiveness of much of China's legal participation requirements. With that said, improving environmental performance is at least a stated goal of the regime (Toth, 2010, 329).

Public participation is now also growing in the developing world. Driven by international treaties, environmental and health NGOs, and local governmental innovation, the use of public participation has grown rapidly in nations such as India, Indonesia, South Africa, and Argentina. John C. Dernbach observes that public participation has become an international standard with the adoption by United Nations member states of Agenda 21 and the Rio Declaration—each of which has substantial requirements for public participation for participating nations and NGOs (Dernbach, 2002, 56). "Painting the Landscape," a 2010 report on public participation by the International Association for Public Participation, tracks the extent to which this set of approaches has spread to all corners of the world. The report finds that developing nations in regions including Africa, Asia, and Latin America are adapting public participation techniques (Offenbacker et al., 2010).

SUMMARY

From the Administrative Policy Act of 1946 to 2011's Executive Order 13563, public participation has become a common feature of a wide range of policy at all levels of American government. As participation has grown in the United States, it has also become far more common in Europe, Asia, and, most recently, the developing world. This growth and evolution has brought out a range of challenges and also sparked refinement and innovation in the techniques used to learn from citizens. After a brief look at benefits, limits, and cautions, it is to these techniques we will next turn.

Benefits, Limits, and Cautions: Is It Worth the Effort?

Despite the widespread acceptance of public participation and its use in almost every area of public policy, questions remain: Is it worth all the effort? Does public participation improve public policy? Although a definitive answer is hard to muster, a range of evidence indicates that public participation is indeed effective. Scholars Thomas C. Beierle and Jerry Cayford make a strong case, based on an analysis of over 230 case studies, that participation by the public "frequently produces decisions that are responsive to public values and substantively robust" while also helping to reduce conflict, improve public trust, and educate the public about the issues at hand. These benefits, the authors argue, are mostly likely to be found when "agencies are responsive, participants are motivated, the quality of deliberation is high" and those who participate have some influence; processes that lack these characteristics may not lead to successful outcomes (Beirele and Cayford, 2002, 74).

Other challenges confront administrators as well. Setting up an effective event and then incorporating feedback into decision making can be "time consuming" and expensive for government agencies (Irvin and Stansbury, 2004, 58). To ensure that organizing and incorporating feedback doesn't overwhelm administrators, it is important to carefully consider how to best structure a participatory process. Unstructured participation and "qualitative methods," such as transcribing public comments made at a hearing, can provide rich narrative detail—or become an incoherent jumble where useful ideas are difficult to find (Halvorsen, 2001, 180).

Another issue that practitioners confront is that the public can be very complacent and difficult to motivate. Thus, ensuring that events are representative of the views of the larger community may be difficult. Those citizens that do show up for public events or comment periods may represent strong partisan or economic interests (Irvin and Stansbury, 2004, 58).

The most troubling potential problem is that public participation may create decisions that are counterproductive or even harmful. Although participation can help "break political gridlock," these same approaches can also "ratify selfish decisions that favor the most powerful or persuasive members" of the community (Irvin and Stansbury, 2004, 60; issues specific to environmental justice are raised in Chapter 9). In short, without proper care, public participation can be inefficient or even counterproductive to the goal of good policy. It can also lead to a loss of control that makes a poor decision, now ratified by participation, all the more difficult to undo. With these cautions in mind, let us now turn to discuss specific approaches to public participation and examine how they can be most effectively implemented.

Tools for Public Participation

In this section, we consider issues and opportunities in eight groups of approaches to collecting information from the public: (1) public events; (2) workshops and juries; (3) charrettes and visualization; (4) citizen advisory committees; (5) opinion surveys, polls, and written comments; (6) crowdsourcing; (7) GIS, the World Wide Web, and social media; and (8) community-based research.

PUBLIC MEETINGS AND BEST PRACTICES

Public meetings are the bread and butter of public participation, but in our current climate, they hold out the possibility of conflict. Are public meetings worthwhile? How can they be conducted in a way that helps ensure dialogue will be respectful and the outputs useful to the policy question at hand? Although criticisms of public meetings are many, there is ample evidence that—with proper structuring—they can generate a useful level of detail and bring forward a representative sampling of opinion.

From their survey of the literature, Chess and Purcell (1999) make the case that public meetings are, in large measure, a robust way to gather representative public views, even though attendance may not be strictly representative of the larger demographics. They argue for participation practices that promote "fairness" and "competence, using the best available information," which they believe will lead to the best outcomes (Chess and Purcell, 1999, 2686).

However, the evidence is not all positive: From the perspective of the administrator, public meetings are potentially problematic because they can serve as a "focal point" for opposition to a proposal (Chess and Purcell, 1999, 2687). From the perspective of public-interest groups or citizens, public meetings can also disappoint, with proceedings conducted in a perfunctory way that meets the letter of the law, but doesn't give much weight to the comments made (McComas, 2001, 38). A wide range of researchers have criticized public hearings as being demographically unrepresentative and lacking in "two-way dialogue, information sharing, and deliberation" (Halvorsen, 2001, 179).

Despite this criticism, public meetings are often required for a wide range of urban environmental issues. Research and experience have generated some techniques that are widely considered best practices. Chess and Purcell recommend:

- holding meetings in concert with other kinds of participation,
- providing technical assistance to the public as needed,
- conducting "vigorous outreach" to the public,
- encouraging the participation of underrepresented communities,
- discussing social issues where appropriate, and
- having enough staff on hand to field questions properly (Chess and Purcell, 1999, 2688).

Using a 1999 dataset drawn from thirty-five phone-based interviews with New York State health and environment officials, Katherine A. McComas put together the following list of best practices for public meetings, which is provided in a shortened version in Figure 10.3 for easy reference.

Before the meeting, know your audience and communicate effectively. This includes anticipating the audience's concerns and planning accordingly. It also means ensuring that effective public notice goes out and that the meeting is scheduled appropriately (McComas, 2001, 46). A significant portion of respondents to the survey that McComas conducted also emphasized the importance of outlining a clear purpose for

---

Figure 10.3   **What Makes a Successful Public Meeting? Officials' Rules of Thumb**

Before the Meeting
- Know the audience and anticipate their needs and concerns.
- Make sure that the meeting is well publicized and timed appropriately to ensure good turnout.
- Agree upon a clearly stated purpose for the meeting.
- Plan the presentations carefully (e.g., limit the length and complexity of technical presentations, and rehearse the presentations in front of colleagues to ensure they are smooth and cogent).
- Select the right location, building, and room for the meeting (ideally an easily found location that can accommodate the expected group with some extra capacity).
- Use a format that is appropriate to the meeting's topic and purpose.
- Schedule the appropriate equipment, staff, and agencies.
- Prepare clear, concise handouts (e.g., fact sheets and agendas) and multimedia.

At the Meeting
- Encourage dialogue and one-on-one interaction between officials and the public before, during, and after the meeting (e.g., arrive early and leave late).
- Employ a strong and experienced facilitator to run the meeting, and set and uphold "ground rules" of civility.
- Be open, honest, and candid with the audience.
- Be flexible enough to allow for a quick change in formats (e.g., if a larger-than-anticipated audience arrives).

After the Meeting
- Thank participants as they leave and ensure they have left their contact information and taken any follow-up materials.
- Demonstrate to the audience how comments were incorporated into the outcome (e.g., by providing thorough summaries that are available to the general public).
- Promote continued dialogue with citizens (e.g., via phone calls, electronic communications, site visits, or additional meetings).
- Track any media coverage related to the event and share it with stakeholders.

Feelings That Suggest the Meeting Was Successful
- Believing that the audience considered the meeting worth their time in attending.
- Perceiving that officials connected with the audience (e.g., officials left with a better understanding of the audience's expectations, as did the audience of the agency's).

Source: Adapted from McComas, 2001.

---

the meeting and communicating this purpose in preliminary materials, as well as in the agenda and meeting materials.

There was strong agreement that *at the meeting*, ensuring true dialogue—being able to take criticism, respond to questions, and engage in deliberation—was critical to success. Also key, according to respondents, was putting a "strong facilitator" or moderator in place to keep the meeting on track (McComas, 2001, 47). In addition, administrators highlighted the importance of being "open, honest and candid" during the meeting, as well as being flexible enough to allow adaptation to changing conditions and audience needs (McComas, 2001, 48).

Following up *after the meeting* is also critical. The key, according to respondents, is making clear to those who attended how the feedback and comments gathered at the event were incorporated into the final product (McComas, 2001, 48). To facilitate this, be sure to gather contact information and then keep the conversation going via emails or other outreach communications.

Improving Public Events: Bounded Rationality and Embodied Cognition

"Bounded rationality" is a political science concept that almost every practitioner understands viscerally: sometimes members of the public simply don't have the information or cognitive resources to participate in a productive fashion in policymaking. Originally developed by Nobel laureate Herbert Simon, more recent research in this tradition finds that humans make sense of the world using a set of decision rules that are "fast, frugal and computationally cheap" and are subject to a range of biases, such as a preference for familiar concepts or images (Gigerenzer and Selten, 2002, 35).

Drawing from this, one can assume that a significant portion of the audience at a public engagement event is always looking for cognitive shortcuts as well as for signs of patterns. At a practical level, this argues in favor of keeping presentation segments short and making clear connections to the topic at hand in between each segment. Reducing the cognitive burden on your audience is also a reason to make good use of visual aides. A digital projector, white boards, or even simple posters displaying key concepts and goals can help offload some of the mental work you are asking your audience to perform onto the room itself. Charts, maps, and visualizations (which are discussed further in the next section and in Chapter 11) can also greatly increase audience understanding of more detailed concepts and plans.

A set of theories dubbed "embodied cognition" also provides useful insight on conducting effective events. These psychological theories hold that it is almost impossible to divorce the mental processes of thinking from the physical setting where the thinking takes place. This emerging picture of decision making is in direct contrast to the model of the human mind as a computer-like "central processor unit" that takes input from the senses and returns a decision. Instead, embodied cognition is based on research that finds that even abstract reasoning is influenced by feedback from our body including our physical setting (Wilson, 2002, 625).

Research in this area has found that a range of "seemingly trivial sensations and actions—mimicking a smile, holding smooth or rough objects, nodding or giving a thumbs up—can influence social judgment, language comprehension, visual perception and even reasoning" (Carpenter, 2010, 1). Studies have found, for instance, that whether a person is sitting in a hard or plush seat is associated with how hard of a bargain they drive in a mock negotiation. In fact, even gesturing while you speak can help your audience remember what you are saying. Other research has shown that the temperature of a beverage held during an interview influenced the person's perception of the other (Carpenter, 2010, 4). Although draping a room in soft fabric and serving tea and sandwiches is not always practical, when preparing for a policy forum, practitioners should take care that the environment is as comfortable as possible. If the budget allows, providing beverages and snacks is also a good idea.

WORKSHOPS AND JURIES

We next turn our attention to workshops and related forms, which occupy a "middle ground" that lies between public meetings and more in-depth events such as advisory committees. Workshops are beneficial because they enable more in-depth discussion than a public meeting, but take less time than a full-blown advisory committee (Chess and Purcell, 1999, 2686). Although workshops have the potential to create richer data sets than a public meeting, a well-designed process should lead to a comprehensible set of outputs. Workshops can also impose a bigger burden on participants: multiple days of sometimes-difficult decision making can tax even a dedicated policy wonk. However, workshops can be beneficial in the sense that participants have more time to understand the issues and provide more detailed feedback.

Workshops are sometimes open to the public and sometimes require invitation or sign-up. Even open workshops, since they require substantially more time then attending a meeting, impose a higher barrier on participation. Citizen juries, consensus conferences, and other kinds of events are usually by prior arrangement. Although workshops differ from public meetings in their openness, length, and scope, practitioners face similar issues in regards to planning effective events: pre-event planning is a critical foundation, a clear agenda and strong presenters are key to a successful event, and thorough follow-up after the event is needed to ensure participants understand the impact of their contributions (Simon, 2003).

Scenario Workshops

A now-common variation on a public participation workshop is the *scenario workshop*. Like a standard workshop, this event usually involves a day or more of activity but is focused on crafting a "vision of the future" for a region, a community, or a neighborhood. The benefit of this kind of scenario planning is that it allows communities to develop a range of potential options and compare their benefits and costs. This approach improves understanding of "plausible futures" and gets stakeholders involved early in a planning process. Early involvement and education of stakeholders may lead to participants who are "more willing to make tradeoffs" in the planning process (McCullough, 2007, 2). Scenario workshops are discussed in greater detail in Chapter 11.

Consensus Conferences

Related to the scenario workshop is the *consensus conference*, which is based on work by the Danish Board of Technology. A consensus conference brings together a small group of roughly a dozen citizens to discuss in detail a more complex policy issue, usually related to science or technology. The panel hears testimony from experts whom they can cross-examine. After deliberation, the panel develops a policy statement, which is presented to policymakers and the public (Chopyak and Levesque, 2002, 161). The benefits of this approach for urban environmental policymakers are that more complex material can be presented and more sophisticated input garnered; one drawback is that a small group may not represent the full range of views in the community.

Citizen Juries

The *citizen jury* represents the American approach to the consensus conference. As in the consensus conference, the core idea is that "average citizens" can "understand complicated issues," deliberate on potential responses and make "well-reasoned decisions"—if they are properly educated and empowered. Like the consensus conference, the citizen jury brings together a group of citizens that practitioners hope will be representative of community views, and it proceeds along a quasi-judicial path (Beierle and Konisky, 1999, 34).

A citizen jury begins when a facilitator picks members from a "jury pool" that is designed to be representative of the demographics of the larger target population. A problem statement is presented to the citizen jury and a list of witnesses representing "different points of view" on the topic is created. After participants hear testimony and cross-examine witnesses, depending on the ground rules, the jury will either reach consensus or take a vote (Beierle and Konisky, 1999, 35).

Study Circles

Along with the citizen jury, Beierle and Konisky analyze a range of related approaches to public participation in their analysis of planning around the Great Lakes. One less-formal version of the small-group approach is the *study circle*, which typically includes eight to twelve people who meet consistently over several weeks or months to discuss policy issues. Instead of expert testimony, the organizers of the study circle provide background materials that encompass a range of perspectives. Sessions emphasize the "search for common ground through considering an issue from many points of view" (Beierle and Konisky, 1999, 36). The approach can bring useful feedback to policymakers at a low cost.

Strengths and Weaknesses of In-Person Group Approaches

Looking at this constellation of innovative approaches, Beierle and Konisky find that one major strength is that they "focus on deliberative processes" and thus emphasize communication and consensus building, which are sometimes missing from more traditional approaches (1999). These kinds of processes "are most useful for values-orientated activities such as visioning or priority-setting" and, if planned appropriately, can bring together stakeholders with a contentious history (Beierle and Konisky, 1999, 43). Along with these strengths, there are, of course, some weaknesses. Most of these approaches are limited to a small number of participants and thus run the risk of excluding important perspectives—especially from underrepresented groups such as recent immigrants, low-income residents, and those who may not be prone to engaging in intensive participatory events. They also require participants to make a significant and consistent commitment.

CHARRETTES AND VISUALIZATION

Charrettes are related to workshops and small-group events but are more oriented toward issues of design and collaborative planning. These intensive, community-based, participatory events usually last from four to seven days, during which a team of design professionals and stakeholders work collaboratively to create a detailed plan (Walters, 2007, 3398). Charrettes are often used for redevelopment planning, infrastructure planning, and land-use planning tasks, and they emphasize collaboration between architects, planners, administrators, and the public. They usually follow a similar four-step sequence (Girling, Kellett, and Johnstone, 2006, 113):

1. Information regarding project goals and issues is gathered.
2. "Alternative arrangements" and land-use plans are discussed.
3. Plans for the project are proposed, compared, and "evolved through iteration."
4. A preferred plan emerges and "is refined" until it wins approval from the group.

Walters (2007) argues that getting all points of view on a potential project out in the open is an essential first step for a successful charrette, and he puts forward five "guiding principles" to ensure a successful workshop:

1. Involve all stakeholders from the beginning "to foster a shared community vision."
2. Manage the outreach process effectively in terms of sending out well-crafted materials, which builds trust between participants.
3. Work across disciplines (architecture, planning, urban design) to maximize the effectiveness and productivity of the charrette.
4. Use short, iterative, "feedback loops" to stimulate public participation and test ideas.
5. Work in enough detail so that achievability of different visions can be accurately assessed (Walters, 2007, 3338).

You may notice the repeated point (for example, see Figure 10.3) that *planning* and *management* are key to successful public participation. This includes thinking through the design of your participation event, providing well-edited and -written materials and meeting external deadlines.

Although charrettes can make use of low-tech tools, such as plans presented on paper, they increasingly take advantage of computer-based visualization systems. Digital maps and photomontages are increasingly being used to engage the public in visioning; these tools can help a community "visualize, measure and compare competing alternatives" across various criteria (Girling, Kellett, and Johnstone, 2006, 109).

Urban planner Kheir Al-Kodmany puts forward the idea that visualization, if handled properly, can help overcome some of the traditional barriers to participation in land-use decisions, which include the often-inscrutable nature of maps and documents, and the long time-lag involved in generating new plans. His 1999 paper compares the use of an in-person artist against both a computer-based mapping system (also known as a Geographic Information System or GIS) and a digital photo-visualization approach (which displays photo-realistic renderings of a project). Based on his analysis, he finds each technique has an optimum role: the in-person artist for rendering quick sketches during the visioning process, the GIS maps for providing critical spatial information to the public, and the computer-based visualization approach for the more detailed development of various scenarios (Al-Kodmany, 1999). We examine these techniques in more detail later in this chapter.

THE CITIZEN ADVISORY COMMITTEE

At the other end of the spectrum from a public meeting is the citizen advisory committee: a longer-term, highly participatory approach that encourages more interaction among participants and policymakers (Chess and Purcell, 1999, 2689). The citizen advisory committee is probably one of the most common participation techniques in the United States, and almost every major American city makes use of the committees in some fashion. They are usually relatively inexpensive to organize, provide a useful level of detail (which can be tailored to different uses by the group), and don't impose a huge burden on participants or administrators. Cities often make use of standing advisory committees for resource planning and environmental issues, and many cities have integrated citizen advisory committees with ongoing sustainability planning efforts.

The city of San Antonio, Texas, is a perfect example. The city council established a Citizen's Environmental Advisory Committee (CEAC) in April of 2009 to support the city's "Mission Verde" sustainability plan. The eleven-member CEAC meets monthly and advises city staff and the city council (City of San Antonio, Texas, 2011). In some cities, the advisory group may be independent of any particular sustainability project. The Citizens Environmental Advisory Committee for the city of Minneapolis, for instance, is one such group. It is one of almost two dozen commissions and committees the city convenes across all major policy areas. The sixteen members of the CEAC are appointed for two-year terms to discuss environmental issues and projects "of concern to the City" (City of Minneapolis, Minnesota, 2011).

Citizen advisory committees are often convened by public utilities or public benefit organizations as well. Almost every major water utility in the United States makes use of the approach—from Colorado's Denver Water and New York City's massive Department of Environmental Protection to smaller agencies in Albuquerque and San Francisco (Albuquerque Bernalillo County Water Utility Authority, 2011; City of New York, NY, 2007; Denver Water, 2011; San Francisco Public Utilities Commission, 2011). The approach has also been used for broader regional partnerships, such as the Chesapeake Bay Program. In this case, the committee consists of over two dozen representatives from "agriculture, business, conservation, industry and civic groups," who, since 1984, have been advising the Bay Program on its efforts to improve water quality in the Chesapeake (Chesapeake Bay Program Office, 2008). In addition, the federal government utilizes advisory committees, with agencies such as the Environmental Protection Agency, the Department of Interior, and the Federal Highway Administration all making extensive use of advisory bodies.

OPINION SURVEYS, POLLS, AND WRITTEN COMMENTS

Opinion surveys are a powerful tool for assessing public sentiment, and they can be used in conjunction with public meetings, workshops, and other events, or as a stand-alone tool. Although web-based software has made conducting surveys much easier, electronic surveys present special challenges, which we look at in greater detail in Case 10.1. Whatever the method of opinion survey, a clear understanding of the basics of survey design and data interpretation is critical.

There are several types of survey designs, with the major divide being whether the data set will be cross-sectional—that is, sampling a representative cohort of individuals—or longitudinal—that is, sampling cases over time—or include both as panel data. The most fundamental consideration when conducting a poll or survey is ensuring that the sample is representative of the larger population to which you wish to generalize. A representative sample "has every major attribute of the larger population present in about the same proportions" (Folz, 1996, 43). Problems with this aspect of sampling, often called sample bias, are endemic to opinion research and can be difficult to correct.

An estimate of an attribute of a population is often called a statistic. "The difference between a sample statistic and the actual population parameter is known as *sampling error*" (Folz, 1996, 44). All sample statistics have this kind of error, which can be expressed as a range above and below the estimate that is expected to contain the true value. Another related measure of the accuracy of the sample is the "level of confidence," which measures how sure we are that a sample's estimates will fall within this specified range. In public policy, we often accept a confidence level of 95 percent; this translates into an understanding that "there is a 5 percent chance that the actual population parameter falls outside the estimated range," but this is usually considered accurate enough for our purpose of gauging public sentiment (Folz, 1996, 45).

The best surveys make use of random selection, which is a process for choosing cases whereby any member of a population has an equal chance of being selected for the sample. We strive for random selection, because this "eliminates any conscious or unconscious bias" in terms of which cases are chosen (Folz, 1996, 54). This kind of bias can be a particular problem with online polls or any method that produces statistics from a nonrandom or otherwise skewed sample set. Remember the old saying in computer programming: garbage in, garbage out.

There are five common ways of conducting a survey: in person, by mail, by telephone, by electronic mail, or via the web. According to Jason T. Siegel, a professor at Claremont's School of Behavioral and Organizational Sciences, there are three major practical factors to consider: "coverage," "content," and "cost" (personal communication, November 2, 2009). *Coverage* means ensuring you have enough cases so that, even with nonresponders, you have a large enough sample to ensure statistical validity. *Content* is ensuring that questions are cogent, complete, use neutral language, and avoid common pitfalls. *Cost* involves considering the practical realities of adding one more question—both to the bottom line and to the cognitive resources of your respondents. Poorly written, overly complex, or excessively detailed surveys can drive down the response rate and undermine the quality of the data (personal communication, November 2, 2009).

Since we've already discussed some of the key issues of coverage, let's move to the topic of content. When writing survey questions for any medium, Dr. Siegel offers these guidelines (based in part on Dillman, 2007):

- Write in a simple, clear style that avoids jargon (for environmental matters, this may mean that scientific or technical terms must be explained so that respondents can understand the issue with little prior knowledge; an example of this is given in the text from the anti-idling brochure shown in Chapter 3).
- Use as few as words as possible to ask the question, but write in clear, complete sentences.
- Avoid vague qualifiers when more precise information can be obtained (for example, ask for level of support instead of merely a yes/no answer), but also avoid excessive specificity.
- Use equal numbers of positive and negative categories for scalar questions: if you give someone the choice of "support" and "strongly support," you must also give them "oppose" and "strongly oppose" as well as a midpoint of neutral (which in this case creates a five-point Likert scale).
- To reduce bias, provide an "undecided" category (along with the "neutral" option) on Likert-scale questions.
- Eliminate questions in the "check-all-that-apply" format, as they are subject to question-order bias (where early choices are more favored simply due to physical location).
- Develop response categories that are mutually exclusive.
- Avoid double-barreled questions (asking two things at once) and avoid double negatives (making a respondent say "yes" to say "no").
- Carefully check and recheck the technical accuracy of your questions.

Another related suggestion is to have a small group of colleagues read over your questions and tell you how they interpret them. What seems perfectly clear to you may be interpreted differently by someone else. Many surveys are moving from phone-based methods to web-based tools to reach respondents. Although these approaches can be useful, they are also subject to some particular biases that are worth further scrutiny. Online surveys are discussed in greater detail in Case 10.1.

Contingent Valuation Method and the Microeconomic Lens

Contingent valuation, grounded in microeconomics, is a survey-based approach that can help administrators assign a value (or shadow price) to a "nonmarket" good such as reducing congestion with a public transit project. Despite various problems and controversies about the proper use of this technique, contingent valuation is now quite common. It works by assessing, via a survey, a respondent's willingness to pay for either the services provided by a public good (such as the recreation value of a forest) or for access to the resource.

As Boardman and his coauthors discuss, economists prefer using observations of market behavior to assign values to goods. However, for some kind of public goods, market-based proxies may not exist. Examples include reducing air pollution, protecting a pristine forest, or reducing a driver's wait-time in traffic. In these circumstances, a survey-based approach to valuation may be used (Boardman et al., 2005, 369). Although there are a variety of specific techniques, the basic most common approach

■———— **Case 10.1** ————■

How to Use Online Surveys Accurately

Online surveys are cheap, easy to create, and increasingly common. But are they accurate? The good news is that a range of efforts to test online surveys has shown that they garner similar answers to more traditional approaches. There are also potential advantages: Internet-based approaches are easier to complete and hence garner a higher response rate; they reduce bias created by the interviewer and improve reliability, and they are less expensive to carry out (Hutson and Rothery, 2010, 134). All the cautions regarding paper and pencil surveys still apply—and two important cautions must be added: (1) online surveys should not be confused with online polls, and (2) although access to the Internet has increased, the digital divide still persists.

Despite similarities, the online poll, often published on a media outlet's website, can't substitute for a survey. Because online polls are not based on a random sample, they represent only a snapshot of those who decide to respond. Since this group can be easily influenced by partisan appeals, the results of an online poll are easy to manipulate. Even surveys that are emailed or sent out electronically can be subject to deception, as it is harder to verify the identity of the respondent (Paul, 2005). However, when the administrator is doing the outreach, they can ensure that the initial list is drawn randomly or represents the desired target group.

Another issue to consider with Internet-based surveys is accessibility: Although the digital divide has diminished (with almost 75 percent of Americans having home access to the Internet), it still exists: according to a 2010 survey by the Pew Internet and American Life Project, while 95 percent of households making more than $75,000 a year have access to the Internet at home, only 70 percent of people living in households that make less have access (Jansen, 2010).

Just as in standard surveys, context effects—the influence of nearby questions—can influence the results of Internet-based surveys as well. This means that earlier responses to questions can color the way a respondent may answer later questions (although with certain kinds of intelligent survey software, the order of questions can be varied automatically to minimize context effects (Smyth et al., 2007, 3).

Suggested best practices for online survey design (Granello and Wheaton, 2004) include:

- If consent and contact information is required, place it on a separate screen before the survey begins.
- Ensure that the survey's design is simple and clear, has a consistent typographical style and contains pages that are easy to both read and navigate.
- Determine what data format your analysis software will require and ensure that your survey software can output the needed format.
- Test your survey by putting data into each and every field in the survey—you want to test likely variables and find any errors.
- Launch the survey at an appropriate time to reach your intended audience (for instance, not during a holiday or during a time when you know respondents are likely to be busy).
- Download and back up your data frequently and ensure that only authorized users will be able to access the data by using a strong password to protect the survey.

to contingent valuation uses a survey to estimate a population's willingness to pay for the good in question (Boardman et al., 2006, 370).

One serious concern with the use of contingent valuation is whether those who respond can really estimate the value of something that is intangible or difficult to monetize (Boardman et al., 2006, 379). The issues here include both the problems of using a survey to value any good (such as issues of wording and question-order discussed above) and the more specific set of challenges surrounding the difficulty people may face in valuing the attributes "of new and unfamiliar products in market contexts" (Boardman et al., 2006, 380). In other words, because a good is not priced in the market, imagining that good's price is sometimes difficult to do. The framing of the "good" to be valued is also a key concern—it is critical that the explanation of the good, such as a reduction in traffic or pollution, is explained in neutral terms.

There is also the issue of "judgment bias"—that is, in the context of a contingent valuation survey—can the respondent accurately judge the value of a nonmarket good? (Boardman et al., 2006, 382). Prospect theory holds that most people are more averse to a loss than favorable to a gain. Along with this, people tend to "prefer a smaller certain gain over a larger probable gain, when the expected values of the two alternatives are the same" (Boardman et al., 2006, 384). All these biases can distort the valuations that people express during a willingness to pay (WTP) survey.

Along with these potential biases in judgment and valuation, there is also a well-known bias that people responding to surveys "tend to overstate" the value of the good being scrutinized. Research on this phenomenon has found that "'hypothetical WTP is consistently and significantly higher than the WTP that reflects real economic commitments." Ensuring that respondents understand the economic impacts of their choices can help counter this phenomenon and produce more accurate valuations (Boardman et al., 2006, 384).

CROWDSOURCING

Taking computer-assisted interactivity a step further than an online survey, "crowdsourcing" is a method of distributed decision making that makes use of the Internet to harness the collective intelligence of large groups of people. The concept, coined by Jeff Howe (2006) in an article published in *Wired* magazine, "is a mechanism for leveraging the collective intelligence of online users toward productive ends" (Brabham, 2009). The social web is familiar to many users through sites like Facebook and LinkedIn; these kinds of platforms are also seeing increasingly greater utilization for community planning and other types of communication between the public and various agencies, including local government departments.

Crowdsourcing, Brabham argues in a 2008 article, is more than just digitized participation: It is a model of interaction "capable of aggregating talent" and "leveraging ingenuity" in a fashion that can greatly reduce the resources required to solve public policy problems (Brabham, 2008, 250). Brabham makes the case that this distributed model of decision making "holds enormous promise" for policy makers, especially for urban planning projects, because it reduces traditional barriers to participation that often keep people from attending public events (Brabham, 2008, 252).

Although recent efforts in the United States and the UK have demonstrated some of the challenges of crowdsourcing (Wintour, 2010), Brabham argues that the distributed, diffuse nature of the technique overcomes many of the problems of face-to-face meetings. Among the obstacles sidestepped by crowdsourcing are the time and money involved in traveling to a meeting, and the potential challenges of gaining input from nonexperts, who may be afraid to speak up for fear of humiliation.

One major limitation of crowdsourcing—or of any computer-based participatory approach—is the so-called "digital divide," which is the gap between those who have computers and understand how to use them, and those who don't. Brabham notes that "members of low-income households," certain minority groups, rural populations, older citizens, and other subgroups may not have access to computers or the World Wide Web. Other potential issues are related to the design and usability of the interface. Yet another challenge involves standing: There is a fundamental tension between the practice of collective intelligence, which involves casting "as wide a net as possible," and the legal and administrative limits of participation (Brabham, 2009, 256).

GIS, THE WORLD WIDE WEB, AND SOCIAL MEDIA

Using the World Wide Web to share and comment on GIS visualizations is a powerful combination. As a group of authors based out of the University of Leeds argues, this combination holds out the promise for improving public participation in a wide range of land-use planning and infrastructure-siting issues. Some of the innovative, web-based systems being developed by cities such as East St. Louis mate a relatively intuitive and user-friendly "graphical user interface" (or GUI) with a powerful server-based mapping program. This combination can open up GIS technology to a nonexpert audience and thereby better clarify the choices that planners face (Carver et al., 2000).

Web 2.0 and Social Media Technology

A broad range of analysts sees social media technology as being fundamentally transformative for government. What began as e-government—placing government information online—has moved toward making use of more interactive technology. These interactive "Web 2.0" approaches, as they are often called, are being used "to transform service delivery, make smarter policies, flatten silos and, most importantly, reinvigorate democracy" (Klein, 2008, 1).

Of course, Web 2.0 interaction is part of a now decades-long trend to place public information online. And, as writer Anthony D. Williams argues in an interview with journalist Paula Klein, although early proponents of e-government had high hopes that digital technology would "usher in sweeping changes in the way governments are organized"—this halcyon future has not yet arrived; and so we should take claims for the benefits of new Web 2.0 technology with at least a grain of salt (Klein, 2008, 1).

Cautions noted, some observers argue that it is only now, with the World Wide Web becoming ubiquitous, that we can begin to make proper civic use of these technologies. As Williams discusses, the more interactive nature of Web 2.0 technology opens up new avenues "for collaboration between any combination of public agencies, the private sector, community groups and citizens." The result, what he calls "government webs" or "G-webs," could significantly increase and improve public participation. Williams makes the case that government webs will integrate disparate agencies by allowing the synthesis of services and information, while also providing a greater opportunity for engagement by a wide range of stakeholders (Klein, 2008, 3).

Despite the huge potential of these tools, most government agencies are not using social media effectively. As researcher and journalist Mark Drapeau discusses, current efforts are, by and large, organized around existing agencies instead of around topics or issues, and are often deployed in a somewhat clumsy fashion. For instance, agencies all too often create social web pages that attract just a few "fans," offer little interactivity, and feature content that is written by and about the agency at hand (Drapeau, 2011, 1). There are exceptions to this lackluster deployment, however. One example that Dr. Drapeau discusses is the EPA's Facebook page called "Water Is Worth It" (see EPA, 2011, for the URL).

COMMUNITY-BASED RESEARCH

Community-based research (CBR) is the real world counterpart to crowdsourcing. A CBR project, also sometimes called community-based participatory research (CBPR), is a "collaborative partnership" between researchers and the community where work is conducted by or with those who are affected. This is a technique that was used heavily in South America and in developing nations, and is now also being used in the United States and other wealthy nations (Chopyak and Levesque, 2002, 159).

Community-based research practices may be of special use to urban environmental policy managers. Through "bucket brigades" that sample air, water, soil, or other impacted resources, often in inner-city environments, participants have begun to advance a model of "community environmental policing." These kinds of efforts have created major benefits by empowering and educating community members, creating new empirically based sources of information on pollution, and spotlighting gaps in existing monitoring systems—the sum of which helps to improve the accountability of regulators and companies (O'Rourke and Macey, 2003, 15). In Case 10.2, we look in greater depth at a community-based research effort in Oakland, California.

CONCLUSION

Since the passage of NEPA in 1969, public participation has become a key concern for environmental policymakers at every level of government. And with the 2011 Executive Order in the United States and the growth of innovative digital tools, participation now encompasses a wide array of policy contexts and techniques. Successful events can be challenging to design and carry out, but with attention to the issues discussed in this chapter, public participation can pay off for policymakers by reducing conflict, improving trust, educating the public, and improving the work of government.

■────── **Case 10.2** ──────■

The West Oakland Environmental Indicators Project as a Case of Community-Based Research

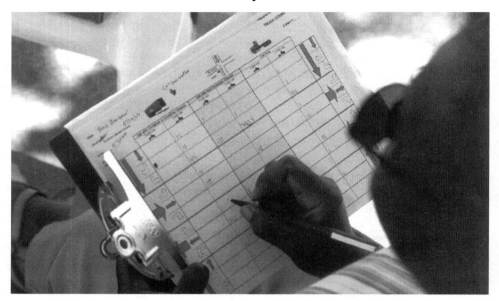

A resident of West Oakland, California, participates in a "truck count" survey of commercial vehicles in 2005 as part of the West Oakland Environmental Indicators Project (WOEIP). Using data from the survey, residents, working with the Pacific Institute, determined that trucks traveling to the Port of Oakland were frequently using city streets instead of the required truck route. After the publication of these findings, WOEIP worked with truckers, the port, and the city of Oakland to improve signage and successfully reduce illegal truck traffic. Photo by Nicholas L. Cain. Used with permission.

Community-based research (CBR) is a form of public participation where citizens design and conduct a research project on the behalf of a community or neighborhood. The West Oakland Environmental Indicators Project (WOEIP), begun in 1997 as a project of the Pacific Institute of Oakland, California, is one such effort.

Fundamental to CBR is ensuring that citizens shape the direction of the research. "The whole idea of WOEIP is changing who gets to ask the research question," said Meena Palaniappan, Director of the International Water and Communities Initiative at the Pacific Institute and then-director of WOEIP. More than just tasking residents to help with a research project, the goal is to put "the power of research at the disposal of people who were most at need" (personal communication, January 11, 2011).

The other dimension is moving communities away from anecdotal research to "hard data" that can influence the policy process. Ms. Palaniappan, an engineer by training, emphasizes that a quantitative project "allows residents to go to planning meetings with real data to back up their lived experience" (personal communication, January 11, 2011). These kinds of research projects may require assistance from a nongovernmental organization to help residents gain the technical and administrative capacity needed.

(continued)

Case 10.2 *(continued)*

Nevertheless, Palaniappan maintains, community-based research can often create a participatory process that is far more robust then the usual approach, which is too often "participation in name only" because the comments don't really change policy.

Two points were emphasized: administrators should "ensure that there are key inputs that can really affect the outcome," and they should also "detail the decision-making process and how community input will influence the eventual decision." New electronic approaches to visualization and interaction were seen as positives by Ms. Palaniappan: "The idea of using community mapping as a tool to effect planning is an exciting [one] that" decentralizes decision-making and also allows the community to be involved earlier in the process. "The earlier a community can be involved, the better" as this ensures community participation in the all-important "conceptualization phase of a project."

Source: Nicholas L. Cain was Meena Palaniappan's colleague and worked with her on the West Oakland Environmental Indicators Project as communications director for the Pacific Institute of Oakland, California. These cases were developed through an interview with Ms. Palaniappan on January 11, 2011, and are used with permission.

RECOMMENDED WEBSITES

International Association for Public Participation. 2011. http://www.iap2.org/. From the website: "IAP2 is an international association of members who seek to promote and improve the practice of public participation in relation to individuals, governments, institutions, and other entities that affect the public interest in nations throughout the world."

Lawson, B.R., E.P. Ryan, and R.B. Hutchison. 2002. *Reaching Out, Reaching In: A Guide to Creating Effective Public Participation for State Historic Preservation Programs,* web ed. National Park Service, Heritage Preservation Services. http://www.nps.gov/history/HPS/pad/plancompan/PublicPartic/RORIhome.html. This guide includes valuable tips for administrators.

National Institute of Environmental Health Sciences (NIEHS). 2010. Environmental Justice & Community-Based Participatory Research. National Institutes of Health. http://www.niehs.nih.gov/research/supported/programs/justice/. From the website: "This program has been instrumental in enhancing and strengthening community-university partnerships in the pursuit of addressing environmental health research and interventions. . . . As outlined in the NIEHS Strategic Plan, community participation is essential to the mission of the Institute."

Sector: Public. American Progress Through Technological Innovation. 2011. Microsoft Corporation. http://sectorpublic.com/. Features articles and updates on using social media technology in the public sector.

U.S. Department of Energy (DOE). 1998. *Effective Public Participation Under the National Environmental Policy Act (NEPA),* 2d ed. http://nepa.energy.gov/753.htm.

REFERENCES

Al-Kodmany, K. 1999. Using visualization techniques for enhancing public participation in planning and design: process, implementation, and evaluation. *Landscape and Urban Planning*, 45, 37–45.

Albuquerque Bernalillo County Water Utility Authority. 2011. Advisory committees. January 18. http://www.abcwua.org/content/view/262/464/ (accessed March 18, 2011).

Beirele, T., and J. Cayford. 2002. *Democracy in Practice: Public Participation in Environmental Decisions*. Washington, DC: Resources for the Future.

Beierle, T.C., and D.M. Konisky. 1999. Public participation in environmental planning in the Great Lakes region. Resources for the Future Discussion Paper 99–50, September.

Bell, R., J. Stewart, and M. Nagy. 2002. Fostering a culture of environmental compliance through greater public involvement. *Environment*, October, 34–44.

Berry, J. et al. 1984. Public involvement in administration: The structural determinants of effective citizen participation. *Nonprofit and Voluntary Sector Quarterly,* 13, 7, 1–18.

Boardman, A.E., Greenberg, D.H., Vining, A.R., and D.L. Weimer. 2005. *Cost-Benefit Analysis: Concepts and Practice*, 3d ed. Prentice Hall.

Brabham, D. 2008. Crowdsourcing as a model for problem solving: An introduction and cases. *The International Journal of Research into New Media Technologies*, 14, 1, 75–90.

———. 2009. Crowdsourcing the public participation process for planning projects. *Planning Theory*, 8, 3, 242–262.

Carpenter, S. 2010. Body of thought: How trivial sensations can influence reasoning, social judgment and perception. *Scientific American Mind*, December 23. http://www.scientificamerican.com/article.cfm?id=body-of-thought (accessed January 2011).

Carver, S. et al. 2000. Accessing geographical information systems over the World Wide Web: Improving public participation in environmental decision making. *Information Infrastructure and Policy*, 6, 157–170.

Chesapeake Bay Program Office. 2008. Citizens Advisory Committee. February 15. http://www.chesapeakebay.net/cac.htm.

Chess, C., and K. Purcell. 1999. Public participation and the environment: Do we know what works? *Environmental Science and Technology,* 33, 16, 2685–2692.

Chopyak, J., and P. Levesque. 2002. Public participation in science and technology decision making: Trends for the future. *Technology in Society*, 24, 155–166.

City of Minneapolis, Minnesota. 2011. Citizens environmental advisory committee (CEAC). http://www.ci.minneapolis.mn.us/boards-and-commissions/Citizens-Environmental-Advisory-Cmte.asp (accessed March 2, 2011).

City of New York, NY. 2007. Biosolids and pollution prevention citizens advisory committee (CAC-PP). http://www.nyc.gov/html/dep/html/wastewater/cac-pp.shtml (accessed March 2, 2011).

City of San Antonio, Texas. 2011. Citizen environmental advisory committee. Office of Environmental Policy. http://www.sanantonio.gov/oep/CEAC.asp?res=2560&ver=true (accessed March 2, 2011).

Coglianese, C. 2011. New executive order promotes public participation. Reg Blog, January 18. http://www.law.upenn.edu/blogs/regblog/2011/01/new-regulation-executive-order-promotes-public-participation.html.

Cramton, R.C. 1972. The why, where, and how of broadened public participation in the administrative process. *Georgetown Law Journal*, 60, 525–550.

Denver Water. 2011. Citizens advisory committee (CAC) members. Denver, CO. http://www.denverwater.org/AboutUs/CitizensAdvisoryCommitteeCAC/Members/.

Dernbach, J.C. 2002. Sustainable Development: Now More Than Ever. In *Stumbling Toward Sustainability*, ed. J.C. Dernbach. Environmental Law Institute: Washington, DC.

Dette, B. 2004. Access to justice in environmental matters: A fundamental democratic right. In *Europe and the Environment: Legal Essays in Honour of Ludwig Kramer*, ed. M. Onida, 1–20. Amsterdam, NL: Europa Law Publishing.

Dietz, T., and P.C. Stern, eds. 2008. *Public Participation in Environmental Assessment and Decision Making.* Panel on Public Participation in Environmental Assessment and Decision Making; Committee on the Human Dimensions of Global Change, Division of Behavioral and Social Sciences and Education. Washington, DC: The National Academies Press.

Dillman, D.A. 2007. *Mail and Internet Surveys: The Tailored Design Method,* 2d ed. Hoboken, NJ: Wiley.

Drapeau, M. 2011. Government social media: Five questions for 2011. *Fast Company,* January 21. http://www.fastcompany.com/article/government-social-media-five-questions-for-2011.

Eden, S. 1996. Public participation in environmental policy: Considering scientific, counter-scientific and non-scientific contributions. *Public Understanding of Science,* 5, 3 (July), 183–204.

Einsiedel, E.F, E. Jelsøe, and T. Breck. 2001. Publics at the technology table: The consensus conference in Denmark, Canada, and Australia. *Public Understanding of Science;* 10, 83.

Folz, D.H. 1996. *Survey Research for Public Administration.* Thousand Oaks, CA: Sage Publications.

Gigerenzer, G., and R. Selten, eds. 2002. *Bounded Rationality: The Adaptive Toolbox.* Cambridge, MA: MIT Press.

Girling, C., R. Kellett, and S. Johnstone. 2006. Informing design charrettes: Tools for participation in neighbourhood-scale planning. *The Integrated Assessment Journal,* 6, 4, 109–130.

Google News Archive Search. 2011. Search on "public participation." http://news.google.com/archivesearch (accessed February 11, 2011).

Granello, D.H., and J.E. Wheaton. 2004. Online data collection: Strategies for research. *Journal of Counseling and Development,* 82, 4, 387–394.

Halvorsen, K. 2001. Assessing public participation techniques for comfort, convenience, satisfaction, and deliberation. *Environmental Management,* 28, 2, 179–186.

Howe, J. 2006. The rise of crowdsourcing, *Wired Magazine,* 14, 6, 1–4.

Hutson, R.A., and M.A. Rothery. 2010. Survey studies. In *The Handbook of Social Work Research Methods,* 2d ed., ed. Bruce Thyer. Thousand Oaks, CA: Sage.

Irvin, R., and J. Stansbury. 2004. Citizen participation in decision making: Is it worth the effort? *Public Administration Review,* 64, 1, 55–65.

Jansen, J. 2010. Use of the Internet in higher-income households. Pew Internet and American Life Project, November 24. http://www.pewinternet.org/Reports/2010/Better-off-households.aspx.

Jones, B. 1999. Bounded rationality. *Annual Review of Political Science,* 2, 297–321.

Kahneman, D., and A. Tversky. 1979. Prospect theory: An analysis of decision under risk. *Econometrica,* 47, 2, 263–292.

Kingston, R., S. Carver, A. Evans, and I. Turton. 2000. Web-based public participation geographical information systems: An aid to local environmental decision-making. *Computers, Environment and Urban Systems,* 24, 109–125.

Klein, P. 2008. How Web 2.0 can reinvent government. *CIO Insight,* April 1. http://www.cioinsight.com/c/a/Expert-Voices/Web-20-Reinventing-Democracy/.

Lowndes, V., L. Pratchett, and G. Stoker. 2001. Trends in public participation: Part 1—Local government perspectives. *Public Administration,* 79, 1, 205–222.

———. 2001. Trends in public participation: Part 2—Citizens' perspectives. *Public Administration,* 79, 2, 445–455.

McComas, K. 2001. Theory and practice of public meetings. *Communication Theory,* 11, 1, 36-55.

McCullough, J. 2007. Overview of Scenario Planning. Scenario Planning Peer Workshop, Sponsored by the Federal Highway Administration, Burlington, VT, November 9.

McKinney, M., and W. Harmon. 2002. Public participation in environmental decision making: Is it working? *National Civic Review,* 91, 2, 149–170.

McManus, R. 2007. E-government meets Web 2.0: Goodbye portals, hello web services. Read Write Web, November 5. http://www.readwriteweb.com/archives/e-government_meets_web_20.php.

Obama, B. 2011. Toward a 21st-century regulatory system. *The Wall Street Journal,* January 18, 1–4.

Offenbacker, B., S. Springer, and Leah Sprain. 2010. Painting the landscape: A cross-cultural exploration of public-government and decision-making. International Association for Public Participation and the Charles F. Kettering Foundation.

O'Rourke, D., and G. Macey. 2003. Community environmental policing: Assessing new strategies of public participation in environmental regulation. *Journal of Policy Analysis and Management,* 22, 3, 383.

Palaniappan, M. 2011. Personal communication with author. Nicholas L. Cain is Meena Palaniappan's colleague and worked with her on the West Oakland Environmental Indicators Project as communications director for the Pacific Institute of Oakland, California. Information was taken from an interview with Ms. Palaniappan on January 11, 2011, and is used with permission.

Paul, B. 2005. Are online surveys as accurate as offline surveys? The Nielsen Company. http://lk.nielsen.com/pubs/2005_q1_ap_surveys.shtml.

San Francisco Public Utilities Commission. 2011. Citizens' advisory committee. http://www.sfwater.org/msc_main.cfm/MC_ID/18/MSC_ID/125.

Siegel, J.T. 2009. Personal communication with author. Dr. Siegel is a health psychologist at Claremont Graduate University's Health Psychology and Prevention Science Institute.

Simon, J. 2003. How to coordinate and host a successful workshop; or, how NOT to get lost in the details! In *Affiliate Chapter Handbook*, 3d ed., ed. R.A. James, 22–39. Registry of Interpreters for the Deaf and Affiliate Chapter Relations Committee. http://www.rid.org/UserFiles/File/pdfs/AC_Handbook.pdf.

Smyth, J.D., D.A, Dillman, and L.M. Christian. 2007. Internet Surveys: New Issues and Evidence, In *Handbook of Internet psychology*, Ed. A.N. Joinson. Oxford University Press: New York.

Tang, S.-Y., C.-P. Tang, and C.-H. Lo. 2005. Public participation and environmental impact assessment in mainland China and Taiwan: Political foundations of environmental management. *Journal of Development Studies*, 41, 1, 1–32.

Toth, B. 2010. Public participation and democracy in practice—Aarhus Convention principles as democratic institution building in the developing world. *Journal of Land Resources and Environmental Law*, 30, 2, 295.

U.S. Environmental Protection Agency (EPA). 2011. Water is worth it. Facebook page. http://www.facebook.com/EPAWaterIsWorthIt?

Walters, D.R. 2007. *Designing community: Charrettes, master plans and form-based codes.* Architectural Press: Oxford, UK.

Wilson, M. 2002. Six views of embodied cognition. *Psychonomic Bulletin & Review,* 9 (4), 625–636.

The White House. 2011. Executive Order 13563: Improving Regulation and Regulatory Review. January 18, 1–3.

Wintour, P. 2010. Coalition's first attempt at crowdsourcing fails to alter Whitehall line. *The Guardian* (London), August 3. http://www.guardian.co.uk/technology/2010/aug/02/coalition-crowdsourcing-results-unheeded-whitehall.

11 Creative, Democratic Methods for Teaching and Learning from Citizens

One of the ongoing challenges of serving as a policy analyst, planner, or public administrator is the need to explain complex phenomena to people who have little training in them and/or little time to devote to the explanation. This difficulty not only pertains to the goal of presenting information to "the person on the street," but also to the need to present the results of analyses to decision makers such as members of the city council. It can be a particularly difficult task for those engaged in the formation of environmental policy, where both the science and the structure of trade-offs can be complex.

Consider again the system model of the city that was presented in Chapter 1. Taken as a whole (as seen in Figure 1.5), the system model reminds us of the complexity of the trade-offs and interactions involved in urban environmental policy analysis. Next, focus on the Social System portion of the model, illustrated in Figure 1.3. As explained before, the Governmental Subsystem is part of the Social System. For both efficiency (that is, the improvement of overall social welfare) and for ideals of democratic governance, the nongovernmental part of the Social System and the Governmental Subsystem need to communicate with each other. The two parts are permeable to each other but generally communicate through elected and appointed officials—including policy analysts, planners, and public administrators—and via the policy process (Figure 1.4).

As explained in Chapter 10, to improve democratic governance, citizen input may be sought during the Problem Identification stage in order to understand what areas citizens think are in greatest need of policy response, and also to understand which dimensions of a particular policy issue are most important to citizens. To develop better policies, citizen input may be sought during the Policy Formulation and Policy Implementation stages. With an eye toward improving understanding of a policy's outcomes—by citizens or by analysts—citizen input may also be sought during the Policy Evaluation stage. Chapter 10 focuses on how analysts and administrators can gain useful information from the public.

However, citizens, often uneducated in the policy process and busy with their own lives, may feel that barriers prevent them from moving their opinions and preferences into the policy process. For complex topics, they may feel unprepared to participate.

On their side, government employees often feel it is difficult to engage citizen attention in a meaningful way. When standard public hearings are held, administrators are often frustrated by the presence of the same industry representatives and local crackpots who always show up, with only a sprinkling of open and engaged citizens.

On the other hand, when presenting to decision makers, analysts are often frustrated by the meager amounts of time and attention decision makers can give to even the most complex policy questions. Analysts must communicate with decision makers, especially during the Formulation and Legitimation stages. However, decision makers are busy and can give little time to any particular policy communication: "Time is the lawmakers' most precious commodity; lack of it is their most often-voiced complaint. . . . Little of this time is devoted to serious or sustained study of the legislation they are working on. . . . [In] 1965, representatives spent almost a full day every week on 'legislative research and reading'; by 1977, the time spent on reading was down to an average of eleven minutes per day" (Davidson, 1988, 98); there is no reason to think this amount of time has increased since. In the Arizona state legislature, for example, it is rare when a policy brief provided by the staff of the Joint Legislative Budget Committee is more than two pages long (D. Hunting, personal communication, 2008). When considering people for policy jobs in his division, the Deputy Director of the U.S. Environmental Protection Agency's (EPA) Office of Civil Enforcement requires a two-page policy memo on a complex environmental topic (R. Hill, personal communication, 2008).

This chapter focuses on ways to provide complex information to the public and to decision makers. Naturally, the two modalities of gaining information from the public and providing information to the public have some overlap, so some topics in Chapter 10 are also discussed here, and some techniques presented here can assist in gathering citizen opinions.

In their book *Policy Designs for Democracy*, Schneider and Ingram (1997) argue that currently democracy is troubled; people have little faith even in democratic governments. One part of the problem, they contend, is that policies are not designed with sufficient "public involvement in decision making" (204). Concerns with time-and-attention limits to policy communication have led to the development of creative methods of engaging and educating all citizens—including politicians and other decision makers. Several such methods are presented in this chapter. However, don't be constrained by them, because they are not comprehensive but rather illustrative. These methods should set your creativity flowing and help you think outside the standard PowerPoint-presentation box. You can use the methods presented as warranted, but also draw general principles from these examples—develop your own creative and democratic methods for communicating and learning about policy trade-offs and preferences. As indicated in Chapter 10, technology-assisted methods are constantly changing. And keep in mind that different methods can be used in combination: A mix-and-match approach is sometimes best.

USE EXCELLENT GRAPHICS

This section deals with the savvy use of graphical images for the purpose of better policy communication. For years, Edward R. Tufte has argued that many graphi-

---

■————— **Case 11.1** —————■

Graphical Excellence by Edward R. Tufte

Excellence in statistical graphics consists of complex ideas communicated with clarity, precision, and efficiency. Graphical displays should

- show the data
- induce the viewer to think about the substance rather than about methodology, graphic design, the technology of graphic production, or something else
- avoid distorting what the data have to say
- present many numbers in a small space
- make large data sets coherent
- encourage the eye to compare different pieces of data
- reveal the data at several levels of detail, from a broad overview to the fine structure
- serve a reasonably clear purpose: description, exploration, tabulation, or decoration [and]
- be closely integrated with the statistical and verbal descriptions of a data set. Graphics reveal data.

Source: Tufte, 1983, 13.

---

cal presentations of information are misleading and that it is imperative that visual explanation be improved (for example, see Tufte's 1983 work *The Visual Display of Quantitative Information,* widely considered a classic).

Case 11.1 presents some key points about communicating with graphics, stated in Tufte's (1983) own words, as is only right given his longstanding crusade for the better use of graphics.

Case 11.2 and the accompanying figures display two maps that present statistical information relevant to urban policymakers. Because of Tufte's point regarding the integration of the image with the verbal description ("Graphical displays should . . . be closely integrated with the statistical and verbal descriptions of a data set"), the verbal descriptions below each map in the originals are included. The two maps in Case 11.2 are both based on United States Geological Survey (USGS) data. Essentially, the images present the same information, though the second map is presented at a smaller scale (that is, it covers more area). Study the two maps and their captions carefully. Ignoring the scale difference, which map seems better for communication relevant to policy decisions?

We argue that, while the second map might be superior for some uses, the first map is likely to be more useful for policy communication.

1. The first map and its text are simpler, yet they explain the key points for policy. For example, some will find it interesting that there is a greater risk of sand boils in some areas than in others (as is explained in the descriptive text for the second map), but what really matters for policy is the risk of structural damage.

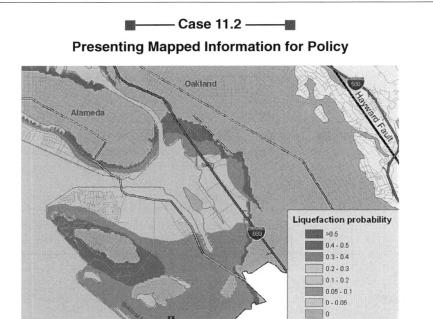

■——— **Case 11.2** ———■

Presenting Mapped Information for Policy

Liquefaction models show where earthquakes could cause the greatest structural damage.

(continued)

2. The use of color[1] is better on the first map because the gradation of danger is visually clear—from yellow through orange to orange-red and on to red represents an unambiguous progression of risk—especially in the U.S. context, where yellow signals caution and red indicates danger. In the second map, pink areas are less risky than red, which makes intuitive sense, but pink areas are more risky than orange, which is ambiguous.
3. Furthermore, on the second map, the most prominent orientation information is the latitude-longitude squares that overlie the map. This may be ideal for geographers, but for average citizens and council-members, the use in the first map of freeways as orientation devices is likely to be more effective.

Geographic Information Systems (GIS) are making the use of information-rich maps such as those featured in Case 11.2 much more easily and commonly available. However, the illustrations above point out that maps must be carefully designed to communicate what is needed for policy understanding (Desai, Greenbaum, and Kim, 2007, also make this point). Yet, Tufte (1983) reminds us that "graphical excellence

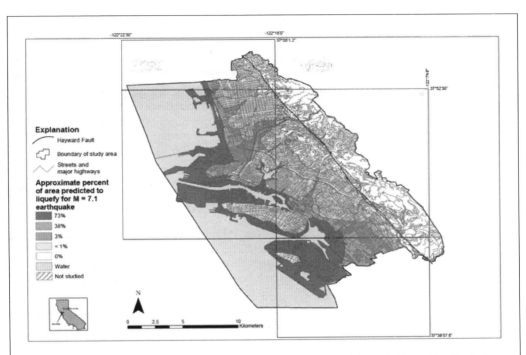

This map shows the liquefaction hazard in the communities of Alameda, Berkeley, Emeryville, Oakland, and Piedmont [California] for a magnitude 7.1 earthquake on the Hayward fault. The map predicts the approximate percentage of each designated area that will liquefy and show surface manifestations of liquefaction such as sand boils and ground cracking. Liquefaction is a phenomenon that is caused by earthquake shaking. Wet sand can become liquid-like when strongly shaken. The liquefied sand may flow and the ground may crack and move, causing damage to surface structures and underground utilities. The map depicts the hazard at a regional scale and should not be used for site-specific design and consideration. Subsurface conditions can vary abruptly and borings are required to address the hazard at a given location.

Sources: First map: ESRI, 2008, used with permission; second map: USGS, 2008.

requires telling the truth about the data." Graphics for policy should be as simple as possible without being deceptive.

Tufte (1983, 51) argues, "Graphical excellence is that which gives to the viewer the greatest number of ideas in the shortest time with the least ink in the smallest space." However, for policy communication, it is more important to give viewers the key information than it is to give them a great number of ideas. This point does accord with Tufte's closing words in *The Visual Display of Quantitative Information*: "What is to be sought in designs for the display of information is the clear portrayal of complexity . . . that is, the revelation of the complex" (1983, 191). The first map in Case 11.2 does this. In some cases, as described in the next section, reimagining graphics can perform this function.

Reimagine Graphical Concepts

One policy-decision concept that can be difficult to present is "risk"—that is, the combination of two key facts: (1) there are different possible outcomes to a given situation, and (2) these different outcomes have different probabilities of occurrence. In order to deal with this difficulty, Ronald Prinn, director of the Massachusetts Institute of Technology's Center for Global Change Science, and his group have reimagined pie charts as roulette wheels, or "wheels of global fortune" (Bourzac, 2008). Prinn's doctorate is in chemistry, and he has studied atmospheric chemistry since the late 1960s. Fairly early on in his career, he felt it was important to communicate his findings to policymakers, but he often had the experience of watching "policymakers' eyes glaze over" (Bourzac, 2008).

Case 11.3 and the accompanying figures show Prinn's wheels of global fortune, or the "Greenhouse Gamble" (The MIT Joint Program on the Science and Policy of Global Change, 2011). This re-envisioning brings home the ideas of probabilities and the riskiness of gambling on the future. Both pie charts indicate that the future is uncertain—our understanding of the complexities of atmospheric interactions is not good enough to give us certainty regarding future outcomes under different possible scenarios. But, they also indicate that the *structure* of uncertainty is different between a future in which we institute greenhouse-gas caps and one in which we don't. The risk tradeoffs are made clearer by the reimagining. To enhance policy communication, Prinn has versions of the wheels that actually spin (both online virtual wheels and physical versions). It appears that the actual spinning also creates a sense of tension and realism. The first time that the wheel was used in public, "the auditorium filled with former Presidential Science Advisors anxiously awaited a result" (The MIT Joint Program).

In considering the wheels of global fortune, look at the figures and notice the use of color. First, blues and greens are used for lesser temperature increases, while yellows through reds are used for greater increases. The size of each sliver of the roulette wheel indicates the probability of a certain outcome occurring by the year 2100. Across wheels, each color indicates the same number of degrees of temperature increase. So, on both wheels, green indicates an average temperature increase of 3–4 degrees Celsius (approximately 5–7 degrees Fahrenheit). Green is the highest predicted increase on the "with policy" wheel but nearly the lowest on the "no policy" wheel. The lack of orange, red-orange, and red slices on the "Cap" wheel also calls attention to the fact that the probability of temperature increases this great are minimal if we cap greenhouse-gas emissions as described. Had the group used different colors on the two wheels, comparing the two scenarios would be difficult rather than intuitive.

Consider Policy Games

Beyond just using graphics as described above, a newer method for both educating citizens and encouraging useful communication around complex policy issues is the policy game. (Yes, you read that right.) Scholars and practitioners alike have found that policy games can

■———— **Case 11.3** ————■

Pie Charts Re-envisioned as Roulette Wheels

Which Wheel Would You Rather Spin?

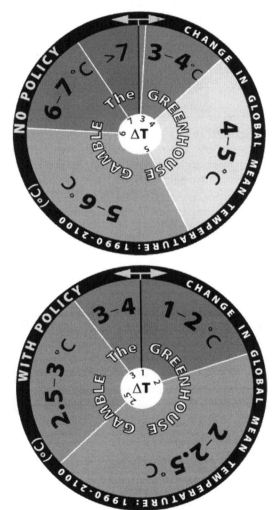

Betting how hot the planet will get if we do—or don't—cap greenhouse-gas emissions (Bourzac, 2008).

The first wheel presents the risk of temperature increase with no policy change, and the second the risk of temperature increase with policy change.

Source: Figures by the MIT Joint Program on the Science and Policy of Global Change. Used with permission.

be useful teaching tools that also reveal citizens' insights and opinions. Because of their interactivity, it is difficult to fully represent policy games in the static format of a bound book. However, here we give some examples (with web links that are current at the time of writing), and some images to suggest the potential attractiveness of policy games.

IN-PERSON GAMES FOR PRESENTING POLICY INFORMATION AND GAINING CITIZEN PREFERENCES

Stabilization Wedges is a game developed by Robert Socolow and Stephen Pacala of the Princeton Environmental Institute and Carbon Mitigation Initiative (Hotinski, 2009). It is a game that:

- helps people to understand the carbon and climate problem,
- helps people to understand what can be done about it with current technology (fifteen different current-technology possibilities are presented),
- breaks the problem into (relatively) manageable sizes (eight stabilization wedges of one billion tons each are required to stabilize carbon emissions),
- encourages understanding of trade-offs in choosing from current carbon mitigation technologies,
- creates an environment for discussing trade-offs and people's varying perceptions and preferences around those trade-offs—thus improving political discourse and encouraging desirable democratic processes—and
- encourages consensus building regarding preferable solutions.

The game is played in groups, and it involves significant education in carbon issues, climate change, current technologies, and trade-offs between them.

The materials designed by the Princeton team are publicly available, so teachers can use the Stabilization Wedges game in classes. Case 11.4 shows graphics that present the concept of the Stabilization Triangle, the concept of the Stabilization Wedges, and some excerpts from the Wedge Table worksheet. These examples, small parts of the available materials, show that games often incorporate high-quality graphics such as those discussed previously.

Note that the Stabilization Triangle is another case of re-envisioning a standard graphic so that it makes a complex concept more salient (like the "wheels of global fortune" used by the MIT group). We are sure that you have seen graphs with upward trendlines many times before. By considering the straight line of no change as the base of a triangle, we change how we think about what is needed to move from the growth position to the stability position.

Policy games do not need to stand alone, as the Princeton Stabilization Wedges game does. They can be part of broader citizen-engagement processes such as those discussed in Chapter 10. This is the case with a three-part citizen-engagement process that occurred in Maui County in the state of Hawaii. Focus Maui Nui, WalkStory, and PlanStory included games—and other data collection methods—as parts of overarching engagement plans. Case 11.5 presents information about the sociopolitical environment within which the larger, initial Focus Maui Nui process was developed.

■———— **Case 11.4** ————■

Excerpts of Materials from Princeton's
Stabilization Wedges Policy Game

The first image presents the concept of the Stabilization Triangle. This is a simple representation of a complex concept. By conceptualizing the trendline as a ramp up from a base that represents the current level of carbon emissions, what is needed to stabilize carbon emissions can be thought of as a triangle that needs to be filled with solutions.

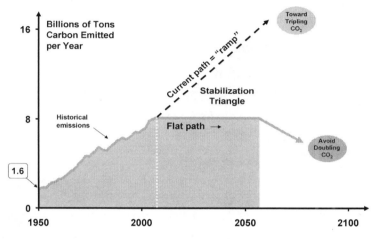

The second image then expands this idea via the Stabilization Wedges—8 wedges of 1 billion tons of carbon each that will fill in the triangle, thus leading to a path of stability, rather than the projected path, which leads to the doubling of the amount of carbon in the atmosphere in the next fifty years. (Here and in the next graphic, the right-most arrow points down from the interim goal to indicate that we may wish to have a longer-term goal, beyond the interim goal, of reducing emissions below their current levels.)

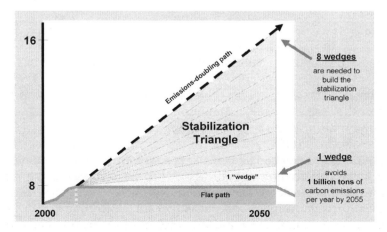

(continued)

Case 11.4 *(continued)*

The next excerpt shows portions of the alternatives matrix that players can use to remind themselves of the trade-offs represented by different solutions as they play the game with others. The trade-offs are presented more thoroughly in several pages of educational materials that precede the matrix. The Stabilization Wedges game matrix uses symbols to indicate which sector a proposed solution comes from, and uses easily understood dollar signs to indicate the relative expense of different options. The full sheet includes fifteen different options (note that the numbers in the sheet are not continuous because some options are omitted for brevity).

Wedge Table

STUDENT GAME MATERIALS

(f)= Electricity Production, =Heating and Direct Fuel Use, =Transportation, = Biostorage

Strategy	Sector	Description	1 wedge could come from...	Cost	Challenges
1. Efficiency – Transport		Increase automobile fuel efficiency (2 billion cars projected in 2050)	... doubling the efficiency of the all world's cars from 30 to 60 mpg	$	Car size & power
3. Efficiency - Buildings	(f)	Increase insulation, furnace and lighting efficiency	... using best available technology in all new and existing buildings	$	House size, consumer demand for appliances
7. CCS Synfuels		Capture and store CO$_2$ emitted during synfuels production from coal	... using CCS at 180 large synfuels plants	$$	Emissions still only break even with gasoline
9. Nuclear Electricity	(f)	Displace coal-burning electric plants with nuclear plants (2 x current capacity)	... ~3 times the effort France put into expanding nuclear power in the 1980's, sustained for 50 years	$$	Weapons proliferation, nuclear waste, local opposition
14. Forest Storage		Carbon stored in new forests	... halting deforestation in 50 years	$	Biodiversity, competing land use

Sources: First two graphs are from Princeton University, 2009; last image is from Hotinski, 2009. Used with permission.

Focus Maui Nui (as described in Case 11.5) occurred in 2003. It involved nearly 1,700 people engaged in information exchange over the course of ten weeks. Three years later, county planners sought to build on the results of Focus Maui Nui through the use of community-involvement "games"—games with a serious policy purpose, involving participatory tools and facilitated activities (Fern Tiger Associates, 2006, 5). To do this, they engaged Fern Tiger Associates (FTA),[2] the organization that had designed and developed Focus Maui Nui. Grounded in the values that evolved from Focus Maui Nui, the exercises in the WalkStory process were intended to guide planners in their ultimate mission: "WalkStory was designed . . . to inform participants and also to gather information, opinions, and ideas from participants through structured experiences at each station" (FTA, Appendix D, 3). During the WalkStory process, participants rotated between five different stations.

■———— **Case 11.5** ————■

**An Engagement Process for Achieving a Shared Vision:
Focus Maui Nui**

From May through August 2003, the people of Maui County [on the island of Maui, Hawaii]
engaged in a groundbreaking process to begin to define a vision for Maui County. . . .

Focus Maui Nui was the response to a community-wide concern, expressed frequently
at public meetings and gatherings in Maui County: that the islands lacked a [shared]
vision and sense of clear direction for the future. Frustrated with the often contentious
results of development and planning processes, residents repeatedly voiced a consensus
that the county needed a plan that would provide a vision for all communities and a
creative set of actions to tackle over the coming years. . . .

Advisory committee members determined that, while efforts to plan for the future of
Maui County had been attempted many times before, opportunities existed for a new process that would build on the findings of prior efforts and would address areas overlooked
in the past. And due to the historically low rates of voting and civic participation on the
islands, committee members also believed it was essential to reach beyond the typical
outreach efforts to truly engage residents, particularly those who rarely participated in
public dialogues, in ways more meaningful than a cursory survey or poll [or a one-day
workshop that generally attracts those already involved in the issue]. . . .

To ensure a representative group of residents would participate in the process, Focus
Maui Nui led a concerted outreach effort. More than 50 volunteers, including elected
state and local leaders, conducted a countywide door-to-door canvassing campaign,
disseminating information about the project. Fliers were inserted in 30,000 water bills,
and extensive news media coverage in print and broadcast outlets helped to position
the process in the public eye. . . .

A total of 167 participatory small group sessions were held countywide, involving at
least 1,639 participants (each of whom filled out a survey at the end of the session . . .).

Source: Focus Maui Nui, 2003, i–iii. Words in brackets inserted by Fern Tiger of Fern Tiger
Associates. Used with permission.

Case 11.6 briefly describes the five areas of focus and the facilitated activities of
WalkStory (FTA, Appendix D, 7), some of which resembled games and some of
which mirrored the activities of a focus group. Again, this stresses that successful
policy presentation methods can combine traditional methods with more creative
methods such as games.

The designers of the Maui processes (FTA) included educational information before each of the three elements (Focus Maui Nui, WalkStory, and PlanStory) of the
overarching process. Prior to participation in Focus Maui Nui, participants viewed
many panels around the presentation area that included short facts about demographic
projections and other data. Before starting the five WalkStory activities, participants
were asked to fill out a questionnaire and were encouraged to view educational exhibits (FTA, Appendix D, 7), including:

■——— **Case 11.6** ———■

The Five Topics and the Exercises, Discussions, and Games of WalkStory

1. Topic: Education and Needs of Young People
   - Facilitated discussion, incorporating large-scale maps featuring school locations in relation to nearby services, resources, and density of development, of key questions regarding potential locations for future schools.

2. Topic: Infrastructure, Particularly Housing
   - Game involving assigning participants to different fictitious households via cards that defined size of household and housing budget; a chart of community housing prices; a game board indicating different parts of a town (urban, residential, and suburban) that have different types of housing, density, and ownership (owned, rented); and "housing squares" that can be aggregated to produce different housing sizes. During the exercise, a facilitator sells and rents housing squares, each of which represents 300 square feet but sell for different prices in different parts of the town and reflect different densities and quantities of housing. This game focuses particularly on tradeoffs (more space and further from amenities versus less space and closer to amenities; affordability, etc.).

3. Topic: Protecting the Natural Environment
   - A list of possible changes in Maui is presented, and teams of two people (dyads) created out of the larger group choose which of those changes receive the go-ahead (via green dot stickers) and which of those changes do not (via red dot stickers). This leads to a larger group discussion of the extent to which participants agree or disagree with each other. Next, an explicit link is made with the need for resources to implement policy choices by considering whether they should come from subsidies, tax credits, etc., or penalties, taxes, etc.

4. Topic: Creating Economic Development
   - Two teams debate to compete "for public and County Council support and approval of a zoning permit to develop a piece of land in an urban area." Each team must support its assigned economic development project even though the individuals on the team may or may not like that particular project. Each team receives the identical list of facts with which to build an argument.

5. Topic: Preserving Local Culture and Traditions
   - An exercise in which the participants create an idealized map of "The Real Maui." Participants begin with a blank map and a set of index cards on which they write things that would be part of "a very special tourist map that doesn't focus on sights or tours . . . rather, your charge is to create a map that illustrates how Maui has preserved (and is preserving) its culture and how it takes care of its people." Participants indicate the locations of these places through the placement of sticky dots, which again allows for discussion as to where there is agreement and disagreement.

Source: Fern Tiger Associates, 2006. Used with permission.

■——— **Case 11.7** ———■

Focus Maui Nui PlanStory

At PlanStory, participants—working in groups of four and eight—focused on a large format (36" × 60") map of Maui Island, which depicted topography, protected lands, existing roads, and developed areas. Throughout the two-hour session, participants concentrated on the sequential development of the island, including decisions about areas to protect (and to remain totally restricted from development); siting 16,000 units of new housing (with decisions about density and settlement areas); and the need [for] and placement of roads and infrastructure (FTA, 8).

Source: Fern Tiger Associates, 2006. Used with permission.

- Nine historical photographic panels
- Four historical maps of Maui
- Four panels explaining the General Plan, including the process
- Blow up of the "instructions" for WalkStory and the names of the . . . stations
- Focus Maui [Nui] Vision and Goals

As is necessary with facilitated citizen-engagement games like Focus Maui Nui, WalkStory, and PlanStory, workshop facilitators were well prepared in the use of formal training materials. The brief descriptions in Case 11.6 do not fully describe the games that were played at the various stations, but more detailed information is available from online training documents. As part of the game atmosphere at WalkStory, participants were issued "passports" with a page for each station (FTA, Appendix D). Individuals had to complete the circuit in order to participate in the final WalkStory activity and become eligible for a raffled prize. The WalkStory examples, along with Focus Maui Nui PlanStory's activities, (described in Case 11.7) illustrate a variety of types of gamelike activities that can be used to facilitate and encourage educated policymaking.

All of the games discussed so far involve explicit interaction between participants. Actual interaction is desirable because it creates direct citizen communication around important policy issues, not only enhancing policy outcomes, but also nurturing community and democracy. When designed correctly, games, exercises, and workshops can increase understanding among citizens with different incentives, tastes, and constraints. However, even well-funded and well-designed in-person events are limited by the number of people who can participate. Focus Maui Nui itself involved just under 1,700 participants—more than 10 percent of the county's population—which is an impressively large number for in-person interaction. To get that many participants, Focus Mau Nui events were held in more than 160 different locations throughout the county. About 230 people participated in WalkStory (FTA, 2006, 13), and PlanStory engaged around 100 (15). With even the best in-person participation processes, representativeness can be an issue of concern. For example, only 9 percent of those involved in WalkStory were between 18 and 24 years of age, and men and those who described themselves as Asians were underrepresented in both WalkStory and PlanStory (FTA, 2006, 13, 15).

Games that don't involve in-person contact can still educate citizens about important policy issues, however, and using more than one type of game has the potential to engage different groups with different interests and time constraints. Computer games, as discussed in the next subsection, are sometimes used to educate citizens on important policy issues. Moreover, though game development itself is resource intensive, once a computer game is developed, it can reach far more people than an in-person game that must be facilitated by experts.

COMPUTER GAMES FOR POLICY EDUCATION

Computer games are increasingly used for serious purposes. Consider recent suggestions to use Wii and Kinect for Xbox 360 games to increase exercise, especially for children. This trend is sufficiently strong that there is a website devoted to what are known as "Social Impact Games" (http://www.socialimpactgames.com/). The subtitle at the Social Impact Games site is "Entertaining Games with Non-Entertainment Goals (a.k.a. Serious Games)." As the site says,

"Game" (i.e., video and computer) has become a language—i.e., a medium of expression—in which almost any idea can be, and is being, expressed. It is our intention to help document this growing phenomenon and list, so that: 1. People who want to locate Social Impact Games can find them, and 2. People who want to create Social Impact Games can see what others have done." (Social Impact Games, 2005)

Public Policy Games are one category of Social Impact Games, with the following description given: "Note: These are games designed to educate the public (or some element thereof) on some aspect of policy, to help them better understand and fulfill their role as citizens in a democracy" (Social Impact Games, 2006). Thus, these games do exactly what we discuss in this chapter. Lending respectability to the idea of policy games, the Woodrow Wilson International Center for Scholars has a serious games initiative, with an accompanying website (Serious Games Initiative at http://www.seriousgames.org/about2.html). It focuses specifically on "uses for games in exploring management and leadership challenges facing the public sector" (Serious Games Initiative, 2002). Since "97 percent of youngsters ages 12 to 17—99 percent of boys and 94 percent of girls—play some sort of video games according to a national survey . . . from the Pew Internet and American Life Project" (Bland, 2008, E1), video games seem likely to be an intuitive and comfortable method for younger citizens to process policy information.

Some of the earliest policy games were budget games, and there are already many computerized budget games in existence. The Woodrow Wilson Center, in concert with American Public Media, developed one for the U.S. Federal Budget (Science and Technology Innovation Program, 2011). Debuting in 2008 as "Budget Hero," the game was relaunched in 2011 as "Budget Hero 2.0." Case 11.8 discusses games for balancing New York City's budget, as well as a budget game developed by the French government.

The games mentioned in Case 11.8 do not relate *directly* to urban environmental policy—though clearly the budget will affect urban environmental policies and vice versa—but they do help illustrate the possibilities in serious games. Budget games also frequently have the advantage of clarifying trade-offs between goals. Note that these budget games can educate citizens about the difficulties inherent in the budgeting task, while also providing decision makers with insight into what citizens (who play the game) think are reasonable solutions.

Other games available on the Social Impact Games site are more directly relevant to urban environmental policy: One on city planning, called "Plan Your Future Park!" is available at http://www.gothamgazette.com/parksgame/; one on city services, called "Breakdown! Save the City from Kaput," is available at http://www.gothamgazette.com/breakdown/; and one on disaster management, called "Incident Commander," is available at http://www.ojp.usdoj.gov/nij/pubs-sum/217516.htm.

■———— **Case 11.8** ————■

Computerized Budget Games

In an effort to close [New York] city's $3.8 billion deficit, public officials have been playing the usual budget games—laying off workers, raising taxes, and threatening to close firehouses and zoos. Now, with our interactive NYC Budget Game, you can play, too. You spend the money. You make the cuts. You raise and lower the taxes.

(continued)

"Incident Commander" was developed by the U.S. National Institute of Justice (NIJ, the U.S. Department of Justice's Research and Development arm). "The game is intended to help incident commanders and other public safety personnel train and plan for how they might respond to a wide range of critical incidents. [It] will be distributed free of charge by NIJ to more than 30,000 city, county and state public safety agencies nationwide" (Social Impact Games, 2005). The wide distribution of "Incident Commander" stresses the point made earlier: for almost all purposes, it would be prohibitively expensive to perform a facilitated in-person game or other exercise engaging 30,000 people, but it is relatively inexpensive to distribute a computer game to 30,000 people.

The World Wide Web and the increasing rate of Internet connectivity make the distribution of games to the public economically feasible. Organizations that seek to improve policy can adopt this method easily. For example, the Decision Center for

Case 11.8 *(continued)*

The French government has taken a gaming approach to try to find a solution to the country's financial challenges. Budget Minister Jean-François Cope has launched an online Cyber-budget game that allows people to balance the books. The challenge is to ensure the €300 billion budget is spent wisely and that if tax cuts are made then services do not fall into deficit. There are a range of tests to face, including having to present the budget to a virtual parliament.

Sources: First image, *Gotham Gazette*, 2003 and 2009; second image, Social Impact Games, 2006. See also http://www.cyber-budget.fr/jeu/index.html.

a Desert City (DCDC) of the Global Institute of Sustainability at Arizona State University is a National Science Foundation–funded program studying decision making under uncertainty (http://dcdc.asu.edu/). Given its location in a large, rapidly growing city in the middle of a desert (the Phoenix metropolitan area's population was over 1.4 million in 2010, and average rainfall in the Phoenix area is less than eight inches per year), DCDC focuses on water use and creating better policymaking around this essential resource. DCDC has created the WaterSim program, which allows users to simulate different situations so they can better understand the impacts of climate and policy on water availability and groundwater depletion. At first, WaterSim was available only to those who could attend a presentation, which still meant it was useful for policy decision makers. However, to make it more broadly available to students, citizens, and even decision makers when they are not attending a DCDC presentation, WaterSim became available for free on the DCDC website. Anyone with Internet access can play WaterSim, choosing his or her own water scenarios (simulation available at http://watersim.asu.edu/).

In this context, it is interesting to note that the Princeton Stabilization Wedges game (discussed above), while not itself a computer game, is made widely available online. This means that the game is distributed much more broadly than is possible through the in-person sessions held by the Carbon Mitigation Initiative group alone. Thus, Stabilization Wedges is a midpoint on a spectrum that has interactive, single-player computer games at one end and facilitated, multi-player in-person games at the other. As you consider how to best distribute policy information, keep this game spectrum in mind.

USE CUTTING-EDGE TECHNOLOGY TO PRESENT DECISION-MAKING DATA CREATIVELY

While it has become almost a cliché to say that our society is in a period of rapid change in methods of gaining and presenting information, the claim is nonetheless true. Policy analysts need to keep in mind constantly evolving, cutting-edge methods of presenting policy information. Chapter 10 discusses crowd sourcing. The Alliance for Innovation (an international network comprised of progressive local governments) presents webinars on how local governments can use newer technologies such as Mobile Apps for Citizens (Alliance for Innovation, 2011). It is quite possible that other technologies such as YouTube, wikis, or Second Life might be helpful ways to disseminate and gain policy information.

YouTube, the amazingly popular online service that allows web users to post videos online (http://www.youtube.com/), has real potential for expanding public policy goals. In 2007 and 2008, the National Association of Schools of Public Affairs and Administration (NASPAA; http://www.naspaa.org/) held a YouTube video competition, the You-Tube Public Policy Challenge for MPA/MPP Students (http://www.naspaa.org/Media/index.asp). In some classes, students in master's of public affairs (MPA) and master's of public policy (MPP) programs have been asked to post policy videos on YouTube. Among others, policy video topics have included immigration reform, mental health care for soldiers, sex trafficking, adaptive reuse, and railway policy.

Wikis are websites that multiple people can edit (LeFever, 2007). "The collaborative encyclopedia Wikipedia is one of the best-known wikis" (Wikipedia, 2008). "Wikis are often used to create collaborative websites and to power community websites" (Wikipedia, 2008). Though we are not aware of such a use, because of the ability to collaborate, it seems a wiki could be used to create a collaborative element to policy games or other citizen-engagement exercises that are not performed in person. The Alliance for Innovation in Local Government, a unique partnership of the Innovation Group, the International City/County Management Association, and Arizona State University (Alliance for Innovation, 2008), has a wiki on the subject of urban sustainability (ICMA, 2008).

Second Life (http://secondlife.com/) is a free, online "virtual world" (2008a). It, too, has the potential to serve as a virtual location for collaboration and communication. Specifically, Second Life provides a system for "education and enterprise," which is designed for organizations to engage in "communication, collaboration and community engagement" (Second Life, 2008b). According to the Second Life Wiki website, some real-life government agencies are using Second Life for task simulations such as fighting virtual fires, analyzing traffic patterns, and virtually testing water samples (Second Life Wiki, 2008c). NASA has a virtual "island" that is "a member of the SciLands 'continent.' By putting a wide range of educational content in close virtual proximity, the goal is to foster conversations and ideas that might not have occurred had each been separate" (2008c). The State of Missouri uses Second Life as a job recruitment site. These examples of uses suggest that there might be a way to reach many citizens via a Second Life presence, either for education or for collaboration.

Given the speed at which things change on the web, odds are that by the time this book is in your hands, there will be other technologies that could be used for educating citizens, including decision makers, about important issues. Some, like wikis and Second Life, may be interactive, also allowing policy analysts to learn about citizen preferences. If used properly, these could enhance democratic governance and policymaking. Keep your mind open to new developments and how they might be used for policy communication.

APPLY SEVERAL CREATIVE METHODS TO LEGITIMATION: USE AN SVR

So far in this chapter, we have discussed a variety of creative, graphic, and interactive ways to provide citizens with policy information. We have also stressed that these ways can be used in combination: for example, high-quality graphics can be used on their own, as in the liquefaction maps presented in Case 11.2; as part of an interactive game like the Princeton Stabilization Wedges Game; or as part of an entire citizen-engagement process along the lines of Maui's WalkStory.

Beyond their uses as described above, any or all of the methods discussed in this chapter can be used as part of an educational process that leads to a specific policy legitimation event. This section presents the structured value referendum (SVR), a particular type of referendum designed to enhance *educated* citizen voting engagement, and therefore designed to make use of any or all of the creative methods of providing policy information discussed heretofore.

Though surveys, as discussed in Chapter 10, can be quite useful instruments for understanding public opinion, some policy analysts are somewhat suspicious of them (for example, see Boardman et al., 1996, especially Chapter 15). As discussed in Chapter 10 regarding contingent valuation method, there is significant evidence that what people state they will do during surveys and what they actually end up doing are not always the same. And so the problem becomes finding out what people *actually* will do. The psychological literature points out that there are two ways individuals can respond to a stimulus such as a survey. The first method is spontaneous and may result in influence by "momentarily salient, and potentially unrepresentative, features" (Fazio and Towles-Schwen, 1999, 98). In this situation, behavior may be less consistent with attitudes than in the second, deliberative type of response, which involves "significant cognitive work[,] . . . the scrutiny of available information and an analysis of positive and negative features, of costs and benefits" (99). Whether using a standard survey, contingent valuation method, or any other method of gaining citizens' opinions, for the greatest consistency between expression and action, participants must engage in the deliberative, cognitive work that Fazio and Towles-Schwen (1999) reference.

In addition, there are several other reasons that some policy analysts are suspicious of standard surveys: (1) standard surveys usually don't present trade-offs (making it harder to engage the deliberative analysis of costs and benefits), (2) they don't take into account strengths of preferences, and (3) responses can be sensitive to wording and ordering (see, for example, Fischhoff, Slovic, and Lichtenstein, 1980; Hogarth, 1982; Schuman and Scott, 1987). In fact, some surveys, called "push polls," actually exploit the known problems with surveys in order to obtain desired outcomes or even to influence voters' ideas. This presents perhaps the most significant problem with standard surveys within the context of policy analysis and good governance: standard surveys measure opinions at a certain point in time based on whatever knowledge and preferences people have at that point. In many cases, though, respondents' knowledge is sketchy, and they haven't thought much about the issue; therefore, their preferences aren't strong, and additional knowledge would change opinions and strengthen their preferences.

Direct democracy also suffers from many of these same problems. Standard referenda and initiatives usually do not present trade-offs, and potential voters often are not well educated on the topics—and lack incentives to become educated about them. At times, the information that is presented during the lead-up to a public vote is severely biased because most information is provided by groups of supporters or opponents, both of whom may spin the information so that it supports only their desired outcome.

So, what is a policy analyst or decision maker who wants an educated public opinion on a complex topic to do? Timothy L. McDaniels, a professor in the School of Community and Regional Planning at the University of British Columbia, is a developer of the structured value referendum (SVR) method of first educating citizens as to trade-offs involved in complex decisions, and then garnering their educated preferences via a carefully structured referendum (McDaniels, 1996; McDaniels and Thomas, 1999). The SVR has been used at least once: McDaniels worked with a regional governmental team that implemented this method to make an environmental policy decision in Victoria, British Columbia (McDaniels, 1996). During the early 1990s, the Capital Regional District needed to decide whether to begin treating their sewage, and the Board of Director's decided to use an SVR so that citizens could make an educated decision.

The SVR is designed to make use of knowledge that has been gained from the fields of risk communication and risk perception about how decisions are made and improved. For example, Fischoff and Cox (1986) explain that preference elicitation is more meaningful when "the task is made more understandable to voters by beginning with a clear decision structure that requires choice among several well-defined alternatives, which entail explicit trade-offs among objectives important to voters" (1996, 228), and the SVR does all of these.

According to McDaniels (1996), the SVR can be used in nonbinding forms as a sophisticated survey or contingent valuation method (CVM). However, we argue that it is best used as an actual referendum. When used as a referendum, it solves a key problem found in even the best-designed surveys and contingent valuations: namely, it removes hypotheticality (Boardman et al., 1996). When used as a binding referendum, voters are making decisions that have real consequences, which makes it more likely that they will engage in the hard cognitive work we seek.

The SVR cannot solve all problems with wording (Magleby, 1984) and, of course, the SVR cannot solve known voting problems such as the voting paradox, for which Arrow (1963) proved "that any voting rule that satisfies a basic set of fairness conditions may produce illogical results" (Weimer and Vining, 1999, 162). But the vagaries of voting are accepted as part of democratic and republican states. Votes have legitimacy and, in addition to resulting in better outcomes, an educative process culminating in a referendum with real consequences should have the added benefit of serving as a strengthening mechanism for democratic processes more broadly, as sought by Schneider and Ingram (1997).

THE SVR PROCESS

1. In order to use an SVR, the policy process must have moved beyond Problem Identification and Agenda Setting through Policy Formulation. To use the SVR successfully, analysts must have identified and formulated several possible alternatives that

- are expected to solve the problem, and
- involve tradeoffs in elements of value to citizens.

2. The SVR should be started by "clarifying the fundamental values (objectives) important to voters in the public decision at hand" (McDaniels, 1996, 230). This step can be accomplished through a variety of methods, including standard surveys, focus groups, or interviews of experts, special-interest groups, and other citizens. Any of the methods discussed in Chapter 10 or in this chapter may be suitable for gathering information on the fundamental values and objectives that should be considered. "These efforts should determine what objectives matter to voters in the specific decision, [and] how these objectives can best be measured. . . . Such information is crucial for structuring alternatives that are likely to be responsive to the concerns of voters [and] is also crucial for determining the kinds of information technical specialists should emphasize to document impacts of alternatives" (231). In the case of the Victoria SVR, the two criteria of most importance to voters were impacts on the ocean environment (screened sewage was piped into the ocean) and tax impacts (242).

3. The alternatives chosen for the SVR should include a range of distinct options that cover the gamut of trade-offs, and a status quo ("do nothing new") alternative should always be considered for inclusion. However, "there are obvious trade-offs between completeness and understandability in selecting the number of alternatives: The more alternatives, the harder it is for voters to make meaningful comparisons" (231). So, the different alternatives should yield different consequences, and the number of alternatives should be as few as possible while still representing the range of meaningful options. Do not include alternatives that are not feasible.

4. At some point in the process, "technical studies are required to determine the impacts of the alternatives" (231). These studies should focus on the elements that are of most concern to voters (as determined by Step 2). If technical experts disagree, referendum designers must be very careful not to let their own opinions affect how they present their information. Here, as throughout the SVR process, it is important that "communicative ethics" be maintained: Information provided during the SVR must, to the best ability of the designers, be clear, sincere, and true (Schneider and Ingram, 1997, especially 55–56).

5. Referendum designers must also be careful in designing the nature of the voting task. One important element of the referendum design is choice of the reference point, which answers the question, "Compared to what?" (McDaniels, 1996, 232). The reference point can be the status quo, or any other point useful in understanding the decision tradeoffs. Also, as illustrated by the famous case in Florida of the "butterfly ballot," clear voting choices are vital to a fair election. In the hotly contested 2000 U.S. presidential election between Al Gore (D) and George W. Bush (R), the actual physical construction of a Florida county's paper ballot apparently confused many voters; this confusion resulted in an outcome that, to many observers, lacked legitimacy (Figure 11.1 shows the infamous butterfly ballot). A complex or confusing voting task violates Tufte's rules regarding graphics, and an outcome that lacks legitimacy would be completely contrary to the intent of the SVR. The general principle here is that both the educational information and the SVR ballot itself must be clear.

6. An important element of the SVR is developing and implementing a communication program. One of the strengths of the SVR is that it is designed to educate voters about the trade-offs involved in the policy decision. Also, since (currently, at least) the SVR is novel to most voters, the communication program must include information about the SVR process itself. The SVR's communication program requires simplicity and clarity and also "referendum designers who are genuinely interested in preference elicitation" (McDaniels, 1996, 232).

- Information should be conveyed in a way that is "engaging, neutral, and understandable" (232).
- An "objectives by alternatives matrix" can provide "a compact visual structure for comparing the impacts of alternatives in any policy analysis context" (233).

7. The last step in using the SVR: Hold the referendum.

As should be obvious from this list of steps, an SVR requires significant resources. Unless the decision is both important and contentious, the SVR probably should not be used, because its costs may outweigh its benefits.

As with WalkStory (the county of Maui case discussed above), in the Victoria case residents were educated before they engaged in the decision-making task. Any of the methods described in this chapter (and others you can think of on your own) can be used in the public communication process. For the Victoria SVR, "one of many

Figure 11.1   **A Potentially Confusing Voting Task**

The confusion caused for some voters by the "butterfly" format led to a lingering sense of illegitimacy surrounding the 2000 U.S. presidential election in the state of Florida.

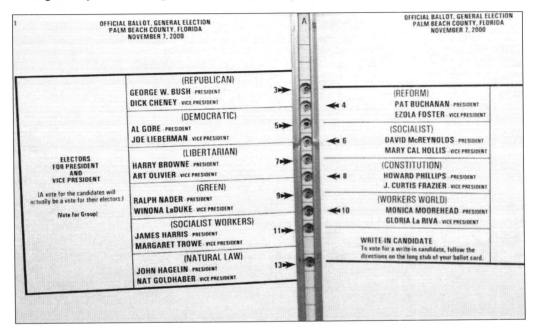

Source: Indianapolis Star, 2000. Image: Wikimedia Commons, 2000.

approaches employed to communicate information to voters was an 'objectives by alternatives' matrix" (McDaniels, 1996, 245). This approach more fully explained the different options; their costs; and their environmental, health, and land-use effects. Notice that the concept of the "objectives by alternatives" matrix is very similar to the Stabilization Wedges "Wedge Table" (excerpt shown in Case 11.4). The educational program also stressed trade-offs, noting that tax resources could be used for other projects: "For the same costs as a secondary sewage treatment plant, the region could build two hospitals, or a rapid transit system, or subsidized housing for 10,000 people" (245).

HOW DID VICTORIA'S SVR WORK OUT?

Figure 11.2 shows a copy of the actual ballot used by the Victoria Capital Regional District in its SVR. Though the SVR was held as a stand-alone election on a rainy Saturday (it is well known that turnouts are lower for stand-alone elections, for local elections, and for elections held during bad weather), 34,000 citizens voted out of 140,000 registered voters (McDaniels, 1996, 247), for a turnout of about 24 percent (standard municipal elections held a year later had a turnout of 52 percent

Figure 11.2 **An Image of the Ballot Used for the Canadian SVR**

Even though this ballot gives a choice between three options, it provides more information and presents a clearer voting task than the butterfly ballot presented in Figure 11.1. This is not to say the ballot is perfect. Think about how you might improve it without making it too complex.

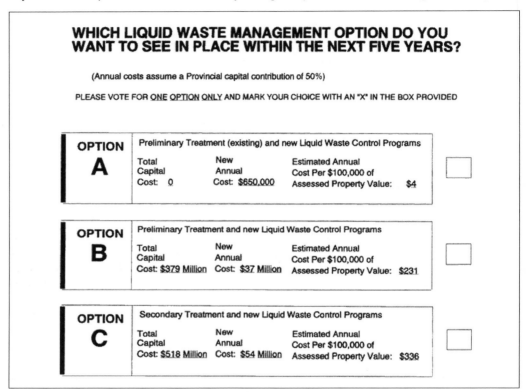

Source: McDaniels, 1996. This material is reproduced with permission of John Wiley & Sons, Inc.

[247, fn. 7]). Fifty-seven percent of those who voted chose option A, with only 21 and 22 percent voting for each of the other two. Though the vote did not end all controversy surrounding the decision, there was significant evidence that the SVR process led to more balanced media coverage and debate, and more involved and educated response by voters (247).

SVRs CAN BE USED FOR OTHER URBAN ENVIRONMENTAL POLICY ISSUES

SVRs can, of course, be used for other topics. McDaniels and Thomas (1999) used the SVR format in an experimental setting, both to assess people's attitudes toward the SVR and to gain information regarding land-use planning. The city of Richmond, British Columbia, needed to decide how to use some undeveloped land, with possibilities ranging from urban development to minimally developed parkland with wildlife habitat. Richmond had an explicit target of 6.5 acres of parkland per

1,000 persons, which it had not met. Yet, the land could also be used for housing. The four options presented included (1) using the land as a natural park with low-impact use such as hiking and bird-watching, (2) developing it as an active park (for example, with trails and sports fields), (3) developing it as a mixed-use park (some parts active and some parts low-impact), or (4) developing it as mixed residential-park use (271–272).

In the experimental setting, those registered voters sampled expressed a high degree of satisfaction with the SVR structure. The post–SVR-exercise survey asked participants to express approval on a 1-to-7 scale, with 1 expressing the greatest satisfaction. A startlingly high 112 of 200 participants chose a 1 on the scale, indicating they greatly preferred the SVR-type format to a standard referendum. Only 10 participants preferred the standard referendum to the SVR format (275–276).

CONCLUSION

This chapter is by no means a complete description of the creative ways available for gathering and disseminating policy information. And it certainly does not cover all the information you need on how to present information graphically in ways that are conducive to high-quality, democratic policymaking. Policy analysts often collaborate with others, including graphic designers. The material presented here does cover a broad range of ideas for giving information to citizens and gaining information from them. We hope it will encourage you to think about these issues both creatively and carefully. As do other chapters, here we end with a checklist, presented in Figure 11.3, of considerations for teaching—and learning from—citizens. You should use this as a starting point and then flesh out more specific questions for your particular policy context.

Figure 11.3 **Checklist for Communicating with Citizens**

For Engagement

____ Do you think creatively about ways to engage many segments of society in deliberative, cognitive work? Examples include:
- Interactive, traditional methods such as focus groups and debates
- Interactive, in-person games
- Games that are in-person and interactive but distributed by computer
- Computer games, with or without an interactive component
- Collaborative, computer-facilitated interactions such as wikis and Second Life
- Other methods/media not yet thought of!

For Graphics

____ Are you using excellent graphics to communicate key policy information, as the liquefaction maps do?
____ Are graphics confusing, like the butterfly ballot?
____ Can you reimagine concepts in ways that make complex points intuitive and salient, like the wheels of global fortune do?

Overall

____ Are you being creative, mixing and matching, and remembering that all of these methods can precede a policy legitimation event, like the SVR, that can lead to better democracy?

Notes

1. Throughout this text, images are shown in black and white, with only five pages of color images. Color enhances communication, but color increases book costs. This is our compromise between color for communication and black-and-white to save you money.

2. Fern Tiger Associates (FTA) is a strategic communications firm that works predominantly with nonprofit and public-sector organizations in the United States.

References

Alliance for Innovation. 2008. Transforming Local Government. http://transformgov.org/en/home (accessed July 23, 2011).

———. 2011. Mobile Apps for Citizens. Webinar, March 23. http://transformgov.org/en/CalendarEvent/100156/Mobile_Apps_for_Citizens.

Arrow, K. 1963. *Social Choice and Individual Values*, 2d ed. New York: Wiley. As cited in Weimer and Vining, 1999.

Bland, K. 2008. Kids can survive without video games, two Valley families find. *Arizona Republic*, September 20, E1–E4.

Boardman, A.E., P.H. Greenberg, A.R. Vining, and D.L. Weiner, 1996. *Cost-Benefit Analysis: Concepts and Practice*. Upper Saddle River, NJ: Prentice Hall.

Bourzac, K. 2008. Wheel of global fortune. *Technology Review*, January/February, M12–M15.

Davidson, R.H. 1988. What judges ought to know about lawmaking in Congress. In *Judges and Legislators: Toward Institutional Comity,* ed. R.A. Katzmann. Washington, DC: Brookings Institution.

Decision Center for a Desert City (DCDC). 2010. http://sustainability.asu.edu/research/dcdc.php (accessed September 23, 2011).

Desai, A., R.T. Greenbaum, and Y. Kim. 2009. Incorporating policy criteria in spatial analysis. *American Review of Public Administration,* 39, 1, 23–42.

ESRI. 2008. USGS soil liquefaction models reveal buildings and roads at risk. *ArcNews Online,* Summer. http://www.esri.com/news/arcnews/summer08articles/usgs-soil-liquefaction.html (accessed August 12, 2008).

Fazio, R.H., and T. Towles-Schwen. 1999. The MODE model of attitude-behavior processes. In *Dual-Process Theories in Social Psychology*, ed. S. Chaiken and Y. Trope. New York: Guilford Press.

Fern Tiger Associates (FTA). 2006. WalkStory/PlanStory: A report on the responses of participants. December. http://ferntiger.com/pdf/WalkStory_PlanStory%20_Report.pdf (accessed July 23, 2011).

Fischhoff, B., P. Slovic, and S. Lichtenstein. 1980. Knowing what you want: Measuring labile values. In *Cognitive Process in Choice and Decision Behavior*, ed. T. Wallsten. Hillsdale, NJ: Lawrence Erlbaum Associates. As cited in McDaniels, 1996.

Fischoff, B., and L.A. Cox, Jr. 1986. Conceptual framework for regulatory benefits assessment. In *Benefits Assessment: The State of the Art,* eds. J.D. Bentkover, V.T. Covello, and J. Mumpower. Boston, MA: D. Reidel Publishing.

Focus Maui Nui. 2003. *Our Islands, Our Future.* A Program of the Maui Economic Development Board, Kihei, Maui, Hawaii. Executive Summary, December 2003. http://www.focusmauinui.com/pdf/FMN_ExecSummary.pdf (accessed July 23, 2011).

Gotham Gazette. 2009. Balance! The budget game. A revised and updated version of the 2003 budget game. http://www.gothamgazette.com/games/balance2009/ (accessed July 23, 2011).

Hill, R. 2008. Personal communication with the author, September 17. At the time of communication R. Hill was the Deputy Director of the U.S. EPA Office of Civil Enforcement.

Hogarth, R.M., ed. 1982. *New Directions for Methodology of Social and Behavioral Science: Question Framing and Response Consistency.* San Francisco, CA: Jossey-Bass. As cited in McDaniels, 1996.

Hotinski, R. 2009. Stabilization wedges: A concept & game. Carbon Mitigation Initiative, Princeton Environmental Institute, Princeton University, November. http://cmi.princeton.edu/wedges/pdfs/teachers_guide.pdf (accessed March 14, 2011).

Hunting, D. 2008. Personal communication with the author, September 13. At the time of communication, D. Hunting was an analyst with the Joint Legislative Budget Committee, Arizona State Legislature.

Indystar.com. 2000. Election 2000: The presidency. *Indianapolis Star* Library Fact Files, December 14. http://www2.indystar.com/library/factfiles/gov/politics/election2000/results.html (accessed August 11, 2008).

International City/County Management Association (ICMA). 2008. Alliance for Innovation Social Media Wiki. http://icma.org/Wiki/Alliance_for_Innovation_Social_Media_Wiki (accessed August 12, 2008).

LeFever, L. 2007. Wikis in Plain English. YouTube, May 29. http://www.youtube.com/watch?v=-dnL00TdmLY (accessed August 12, 2008).

Magleby, D. 1984. *Direct Legislation: Voting on Ballot Propositions in the United States.* Baltimore, MD: Johns Hopkins University Press. As cited in McDaniels, 1996.

McDaniels, T.L. 1996. The structured value referendum: Eliciting preferences for environmental policy alternatives. *Journal of Policy Analysis and Management*, 15, 2, 227–251.

McDaniels, T.L., and K. Thomas. 1999. Eliciting preferences for land-use alternatives: A structured value referendum with approval voting. *Journal of Policy Analysis and Management*, 18, 2 (Spring), 264–280.

The MIT Joint Program on the Science and Policy of Global Change. 2011. The Greenhouse Gamble: Policy vs. No-Policy—Updated Estimates. http://globalchange.mit.edu/resources/gamble/ (accessed March 14, 2011).

Princeton University. 2009. Stabilization Wedges Slides & Graphics: Wedges PowerPoint Presentation, slides 5 and 7. Carbon Mitigation Initiative, Princeton Environmental Institute, Princeton, NJ, November. http://cmi.princeton.edu/wedges/slides.php (accessed March 14, 2011).

Schneider, A.L., and H. Ingram. 1997. *Policy Design for Democracy.* Lawrence: University Press of Kansas.

Schuman, H., and J. Scott. 1987. Problems in the use of survey questions to measure public opinion. *Science*, 236, 4804, 957–959. As cited in McDaniels, 1996.

Science and Technology Innovation Program. 2011. Budget Hero 2.0. The Woodrow Wilson International Center for Scholars. http://www.budgethero.org or http://marketplace.publicradio.org/features/budget_hero/.

Second Life. 2008a. http://secondlife.com/ (accessed August 12, 2008).

———. 2008b. What is Second Life? Education & Enterprise. http://secondlife.com/whatis/?lang=en-US#Education_&_Enterprise (accessed August 12, 2008).

———. 2008c. Real Life Government/Examples. July 17. http://wiki.secondlife.com/wiki/Real_Life_Government/Examples (accessed August 12, 2008).

Serious Games Initiative. 2002. A project of the Woodrow Wilson Center for International Scholars, Washington, DC. http://www.seriousgames.org/about2.html.

Social Impact Games. 2005. Entertaining games with non-entertainment goals (a.k.a. serious games). http://www.socialimpactgames.com/index.php (accessed July 13, 2008).

———. 2006. Public policy games. http://www.socialimpactgames.com/modules.php?op=modload&name=News&file=index&catid=13 (accessed July 13, 2008).

Tufte, E.R. 1983. *The Visual Display of Quantitative Information.* Cheshire, CT: Graphics Press.

U.S. Department of Justice. 2007. Incident Commander: A training simulation for public safety personnel. Office of Justice Programs, National Institute of Justice, July. http://www.ojp.usdoj.gov/nij/pubs-sum/217516.htm (accessed August 12, 2008).

U.S. Geological Survey (USGS). 2008. *Earthquakes Hazard Program: Liquefaction Hazard Maps—Northwestern Alameda County*, July 16. http://earthquake.usgs.gov/regional/nca/alameda/ (accessed August 12, 2008).

WaterSim n.d. Decision Center for a Desert City's WaterSim Model. http://watersim.asu.edu/ (accessed September 23, 2011).

Weimer, D.L., and A.R. Vining. 1999. *Policy Analysis: Concepts and Practice*, 3rd ed. Upper Saddle River, NJ: Prentice Hall.

Wikimedia Commons. 2000. Official ballot for the 2000 United States Presidential election, November 7, 2000, from Palm Beach County, Florida. http://commons.wikimedia.org/wiki/File:Butterfly_large.jpg.

Wikipedia. 2008. Wiki. http://en.wikipedia.org/wiki/Wiki (accessed August 12, 2008).

12 Conclusion

This book introduces an array of environmental policy tools that are applicable for administrators and analysts dealing with urban policy issues. Since one book cannot cover every issue of relevance to environmental policy, our goal has been to highlight the four themes that we think are most important for administrators and analysts. We believe that these themes provide a starting point for administrators as they think about how to manage environmental policy issues within the public sector. While the actual policy tools we have explored (such as tradable discharge permits or tax incentives) are useful, all of them must be employed within the specific context of a particular environmental policy problem facing an administrator.

Therefore, the themes that we summarize in this section of the book are written to help the administrator take a step back from the actual utilization of a specific environmental policy tool and think clearly about the "big picture" of the urban environmental challenge. While we have tried to weave these four overarching themes throughout all of the previous chapters in the book, we believe they are important enough to cover here as a concluding summary. In the following sections, therefore, we include some final comments about these four themes. In addition, we are explicit about something only implied heretofore: The urban environmental policy enterprise is not something that analysts and administrators do alone—or even just in concert with citizens. There are several other professions whose advice should be sought in this important and complex endeavor.

TAKE A HOLISTIC APPROACH TO ENVIRONMENTAL POLICY

The theme of taking a holistic approach to the management of environmental policy problems is a key topic of this book. In particular, the system model that we introduce in Chapter 1 is the anchor for our discussion throughout the book of the ecological, social, political, economic, administrative, and legal constraints associated with different types of urban environmental policy problems. The conceptual system model combining the Natural, Concretion, and Social layers, that we presented in Chapter 1 can be used by administrators and policy analysts as a framework for considering all aspects of an environmental policy issue. Before moving forward with making a decision about land-use change, for example, an administrator should consider the impacts of any decision on all of these layers of the urban system (Natural, Concretion, and Social). Also, in Chapter 5 we outline the concepts of ecosystem management and adaptive management, highlighting how these two types of scientific resource management include explicit connections between the physical and social systems.

Since the Natural layer includes the biogeophysical system within which the city exists, issues concerning this layer require careful consideration of the urban environment's physical geography, climate, plants, and animals. Therefore, the analysis of this layer by an administrator or analyst must include a scientific perspective on the urban policy problem, and, in fact, administrators may need to rely on scientific findings or advice from scientists before making policy decisions that will have direct impacts on components within the Natural layer.

On the other hand, the Concretion layer encompasses the built environment within the city, including infrastructure such as buildings, sewerage, and communication systems. The analysis of this layer by an administrator would emphasize the engineering and urban planning components of the city. Consequently, administrators can often benefit from consultation with urban planners or engineers (experts on the Concretion layer) when they make policy decisions that could have future impacts on the built environment within the city.

Finally, the Social layer includes social and political institutions within the urban environment, such as the economy, neighborhoods and their associations, religious organizations, firms, and nonprofit organizations. The governmental and policy system of the city is also included in this Social layer. The analysis of the Social layer of the urban environment should focus on policymaking mechanisms and socioeconomic dynamics within the city. If administrators or policy analysts need assistance in determining the potential impacts of policy decisions on the Social layer, they can consult with demographers, economists, other social scientists, elected officials, attorneys, and members of other city, state, or federal agencies.

It is important to reiterate that even though we present these three layers (that is, Natural, Concretion, and Social) within the urban environment in separate boxes, all three of the layers are inextricably linked; therefore, changes to one layer will automatically generate ripples of changes within the other layers. As we outlined in Chapter 5, ecosystem management is one approach that embraces the holistic management of ecological, scientific, and socioeconomic values simultaneously. Thus, our focus on this type of holistic environmental management is anchored in the historical literature on ecosystem management. We encourage administrators to explore the interactions between the Natural, Concretion, and Social layers when they think about analyzing new policies in the urban environment. Furthermore, in order to think comprehensively about this holistic perspective, urban administrators should follow up with additional readings on ecosystem management. For more information on the *science* of ecosystem management, we suggest supplemental readings by Meffe and colleagues (2002). On the other hand, for a comprehensive overview of the *social and philosophical* aspects of ecosystem management, we recommend work by Norton (2005), as well as Cortner and Moote (1998).

USE ADAPTIVE, FLEXIBLE, AND INCLUSIVE MANAGEMENT

A second overarching theme of this book is a focus on the adaptive, flexible, and inclusive management of environmental policy issues. For example, during our discussion of adaptive management in Chapter 5, we outlined how administrators could be flexible and responsive to the ecological and social aspects of environmental problems, recognizing that those might change over time, which in turn might necessitate adjustments in the ways the environmental issues are managed. A further reason to stress an adaptive and flexible approach is that the natural and ecological systems are so complex and the Law of Unintended Consequences so prevalent that even a careful and well-thought-out policy might have undesired outcomes. An adaptive and flexible management approach to environmental problems can allow administrators to respond more quickly and effectively to a variety of ecological, social, and political environmental problems within the urban environment.

Another important component of this theme is the focus on inclusive management practices that encourage a strong role for public participation and public values in urban environmental decision-making. As we have discussed, formal public participation is required for U.S. federal projects as part of the National Environmental Policy Act (NEPA) process. Even though NEPA provides a baseline for the inclusion of public values in environmental decision making, we encourage a broader view of inclusiveness—one that goes beyond just meeting NEPA requirements. Since environmental policy decisions are not made in a vacuum—or at least they are not implemented within a vacuum—the careful inclusion of public values in environmental decision-making can lead to smoother policy implementation.

We also wish to emphasize the administrator's responsibility in making sure that a broad group of the public—including citizens from a variety of income levels, racial/ethnic groups, and education levels—is involved in any engagement efforts. Without special effort, many public engagement mechanisms (such as public meetings or town halls) might not sufficiently include lower-income or minority members of the community. Therefore, we encourage administrators to be aware of the diversity of representation among the public in any engagement activities. Both for ethical and practical reasons, we also urge explicit consideration of environmental justice in decision making.

We have warned, particularly in Chapters 9, 10, and 11, that public engagement is not an easy task. Without careful planning, it can backfire. But *not* involving the public in important environmental decisions can also backfire. Above all, it is important to keep in mind that, if we accept democratic values, seeking public involvement is the right thing to do.

CONSIDER INTERACTIONS BETWEEN ENVIRONMENTAL MEDIA

A third major theme of this book is the overlap between different types of environmental media. Even though we discuss the three major environmental media— air, water, and land—in separate chapters in the book, we want to emphasize again the vital importance of considering the connections between air, water, and land in all

Figure 12.1 **Checklist for Cross-Media Issues**

Air Policy Changes

____ What ecological impacts will any changes to air policies have on land-use change, water quality, water quantity, hazardous waste emissions, and solid waste emissions?

____ What ecological impacts will any changes to air policies have on the ecosystem as a whole, as well as on animal and plant habitats?

Water Policy Changes

____ What ecological impacts will any changes to water policies have on land-use change, air quality, hazardous waste emissions, and solid waste emissions?

____ What ecological impacts will any changes to water policies have on the ecosystem as a whole, as well as on animal and plant habitats?

Land-Use Changes

____ What ecological impacts will any changes to land-use policies have on water quality, water quantity, air quality, hazardous waste emissions, and solid waste emissions?

____ What ecological impacts will any changes to land-use policies have on the ecosystem as a whole, as well as on animal and plant habitats?

environmental policies. These three elements of the natural environment are joined together in an inextricable way, so any changes in the water system can have significant impacts on air and land. Likewise, any changes to urban land use can significantly affect the quality of water and air (consider the problem of urban runoff). And so it goes across all media. The following quote emphasizes some of the changes over the past four decades in environmental policy—from a single-medium approach to a cross-media approach.

> Since 1970, important advances in environmental protection, product design, and occupational safety have been prompted by problem-, media-, and chemical-specific legislation. Our air and water are now cleaner, less pollution is being produced, and many waste sites are being restored. Yet despite such significant progress, it has become clear that the new century's problems are more complex and involve multiple environmental media and stressors: they therefore require new kinds of interdisciplinary thinking and systems solutions. . . .
>
> The U.S. is now facing many of the same stresses that confronted the Ash Council[1] in 1970, but society today needs to recognize these stresses' more complex and interrelated nature. Continued focus on media-specific problems will not solve pollution problems, but simply shift them from one medium to another (for example, from air to water). The experience of many states demonstrates that a media-based approach misses about half of the emissions of a typical facility compared to the findings of integrated permitting. Research in the Great Lakes and other major bodies of water shows that toxic pollution comes from many sources: air deposition, sediment, groundwater, and land runoff. (Fiksel et al. 2009, 8716–8717)

To increase effectiveness, environmental administrators and analysts must think outside the box of a single-medium approach to environmental policy and focus instead on linkages between air, water, and land.

Each of the environmental media chapters includes a checklist to help administrators and analysts think through specific concerns for that chapter's medium. Each of these checklists ends by encouraging thought about possible cross-medium effects.

To assist even more explicitly with cross-media urban environmental policy consideration, we include another short checklist (Figure 12.1). This list outlines some questions administrators can ask to help ensure that they are addressing cross-media policy questions. While the list does not include every question that administrators should ask themselves about cross-media pollution issues, it does provide a useful foundation of nonspecific, noncontextual questions. This checklist serves as an integrated supplement to the earlier checklists included in this book.

MAKE CONTEXTUAL AND ETHICAL USE OF POLICY TOOLS

The fourth overarching theme is a focus on the contextual and ethical use of the policy tools that we describe in various chapters. Though we have only discussed ethics explicitly in the context of environmental justice, we hope that our other discussions imply our unyielding belief in the importance of analytic integrity. We accept and urge the use of many types of evidence—including economic, ecological, engineering, and public opinion. We also urge the analyst and administrator to make the most honest representation and use of all information collected as is humanly possible.

Just as there is no single source of appropriate urban environmental policy information, so there is no single policy tool that works best in every environmental situation. Even though we have presented a wide array of policy tools, both generally and within media contexts, the administrator and analyst should think critically about the *specific* context of the environmental situation at hand and choose tools based on that critical analysis. In earlier chapters, we introduce some key questions that should be considered before choosing specific policy tools. The checklists included in those chapters serve as valuable starting points for the urban environmental professional.

While some policy tools might yield an economically efficient solution, those same tools might not yield the most ethical solution. When considering the local context of the environmental problem, the analyst should take into account issues of equity and compensation in addition to Kaldor-Hicks economic efficiency. This is particularly true in environmental justice cases. In sum, we encourage administrators and analysts to consider economic efficiency goals within the context of the larger ecological and social contexts of the problem. Furthermore, the consideration of equity issues should include a thoughtful analysis by the administrator of both intragenerational and intergenerational equity issues. While most environmental equity cases focus on equity across groups that are already born (that is, intragenerational equity), careful attention to the concepts of sustainability requires that the administrator also consider equity across generations, with an overt focus on fairness to future generations (that is, intergenerational equity).

The emphasis on future generations in the realm of sustainable development originated with the 1987 Brundtland Commission Report written by the World Commission on Environment and Development (WCED, published as *Our Common Future,* 1987). In 1983, when the WCED was formed, its goals were to (1) explore global environmental problems and develop proposals to address them, (2) encourage international cooperation on environmental issues, and (3) increase public, business, and governmental understanding about sustainable development (U.S. Environmental Protection Agency, 2011). As a result of its efforts, the commission defined sustainable development in the following way: Sustainable development is "development that meets the needs of the present without compromising the ability of future generations to meet their own needs" (WCED, 1987). The report goes on to explain an optimistic, balanced perspective on environmental protection and economic growth:

> This commission believes that people can build a future that is more prosperous, more just, and more secure. Our report is not a prediction of ever increasing environmental decay, poverty and hardship in an ever more polluted world among ever decreasing resources. We see instead the possibility for a new era of economic growth, one that must be based on policies that sustain and expand the environmental resource base. And we believe such growth to be absolutely essential to relieve the great poverty that is deepening in much of the developing world. (WCED, 1987, 18)

Despite the significant evolution of environmental policy since the 1980s (when the Brundtland Commission Report was written), environmental administrators still wrestle daily with finding the right equilibrium between environmental protection and economic growth. They also continue to face the difficult challenges of balancing issues of efficiency with issues of intergenerational and intragenerational equity, and of pairing good policy with political realities. These tough balancing acts require that environmental administrators pay attention to the social context and the ethical components of each environmental policy decision they face before choosing an environmental policy tool.

SUMMARY

When we started writing this book, we had three explicit goals. One goal was to introduce a system model of the city that would help administrators and analysts better understand how environmental policy problems are linked with natural and ecological systems, the built environment, and social systems within and outside the city. This type of holistic and comprehensive look at cities and their policy programs is particularly relevant as we see a significant increase in the number of people living in urban environments in the United States and throughout the world. A second goal of this book was to introduce the reader to a set of policy tools commonly used by policy analysts and administrators to make environmental policy decisions. The third goal was to fix attention firmly on the fact that policy must be *communicated*. The three goals, as well as the four general themes outlined earlier, provide the framework for *Urban Environmental Policy Analysis*. Our sincere hope is that this overview of existing environmental policy tools and advice on policy communication, embedded within a holistic social/scientific framework, will help you to think more critically about your role as a policymaker and analyst. The best environmental policy and management decisions always include a multifaceted and interconnected view of ecological, economic, and social sustainability.

NOTE

1. To address growing public concerns about environmental issues in the late 1960s, President Nixon required a review of the governmental efficiency of environmental policies. This review of environmental policies was led by the so-called Ash Council (which received its name because of its director, Litton Industries President Roy L. Ash). The Ash Council ultimately recommended a new environmental agency, and Nixon adopted the council's recommendation by creating the EPA.

REFERENCES

Cortner, H., and M.A. Moote. 1998. *The Politics of Ecosystem Management.* Washington, DC: Island Press.

Fiksel, J., Graedel; A.D. Hecht; D. Rejeski; G.S. Sayler; P.M. Senge; D.L. Swackhamer; T.L. Theis. 2009. EPA at 40: Bringing environmental protection into the 21st century. *Environmental Science and Technology*, 43, 23, 8716–8720.

Meffe, G., L.A. Nielson; R.L. Knight; and D.A. Schenborn. 2002. *Ecosystem Management: Adaptive, Community-Based Conservation.* Washington, DC: Island Press.

Norton, B.G. 2005. *Sustainability: A Philosophy of Adaptive Ecosystem Management.* Chicago, IL: University of Chicago Press.

U.S. Environmental Protection Agency. 2011. History of Sustainability. http://yosemite.epa.gov/r10/oi.nsf/Sustainability/History (accessed March 18, 2011).

World Commission on Environment and Development (WCED). 1987. *Our Common Future.* New York: Oxford University Press.

Index

A

Aalborg Charter (1994), xv
Aarhus Convention (1998), 233, 235, 237
Acid rain, 144–45, 153
Adaptive management
  administrative checklists, 134–36
  Concretion System, 129–30, 131–34, 136*f*
    air, 132, 135*f*
    components of, 132*t*
    land, 131, 132*t*, 135*f*
    system interaction, 131, 132–34, 135*f*
    water, 132, 135*f*
  defined, 129
  environmental policy, 287
  holistic approach, 123–24, 131–34
  informal social contract, 130–31
  mariculture, 130–31
  Natural System, 129–30, 131–34, 135*f*
    air, 132, 135*f*
    components of, 132*t*
    land, 131, 132*t*, 135*f*
    system interaction, 131, 132–34, 135*f*
    water, 131–32, 135*f*
  policy weaknesses, 130–31
  Social System, 129–30, 131–34, 136*f*
    Environmental Justice, 132–134, 135*f*
    system interaction, 131, 132–34, 135*f*
Administrative Policy Act (1946), 234–35, 236
Africa, xiv, 178, 179
Agenda Setting, 16*f*, 17
Agenda 21 (United Nations), xv, 236–37

Agricultural irrigation, 178–79
Air pollutants
  acid rain, 144–45, 153
  carbon dioxide, 142, 156–57, 164
  carbon monoxide, 142*t*, 143, 144
  criteria air pollutants, 143, 144–45
  eutrophication, 145
  ground-level ozone, 143, 145, 147, 149
  haze, 148–49 (case)
  lead, 143, 145
  list of acronyms, 142*t*
  nitrogen dioxide, 142*t*
  nitrogen oxides, 142*t*, 143, 144, 145, 152–53,
    155 (case)
  particulate matter (PM10), 142*t*, 143, 144–45
  sulfur dioxide, 142*t*, 144, 152, 153, 155 (case)
  sulfur oxides, 142*t*, 143, 144, 153
Air Pollution Control Act (1955), 143
Air quality
  adaptive management
    Concretion System, 132, 135*f*
    Natural System, 132, 135*f*
    system interaction, 131, 132–34, 135–36*f*
  Anti-Idling Campaign (Ohio), 60
  Benefit-Cost Analysis (BCA), 143
  carbon sequestration, 142
  carbon sink, 142, 164
  ecological issues, 142–45
  legislation, 133, 142*t*, 143
  media interaction, 141–42, 164–66, 287–89
  Nongovernmental Organization (NGO), 146
  policy tools, 149–59

Air quality *(continued)*
administrative checklist, 159–60*f*, 288*f*
cap-and-trade system, 151–54
carbon tax, 156–59
command-and-control regulations, 148
(case), 149, 151
emissions permit trading systems, 151–54,
155
emissions reduction credit program, 151
energy tax, 156–59
fuel tax, 154, 156–59
tax-and-refund program, 158–59
taxation, 154, 156–59
private industry groups, 146
public groups, 146
public sector groups, 146
social issues, 145–49
stakeholder groups, 146
transboundary pollution, 146–49, 150*t*
Southeast Asia, 148–49 (case)
system interaction, 9*f*, 10, 131, 132–34, 135–36*f*
vehicles, 60, 144
Alliance for Innovation, 274
American Public Media, 271
American Society for Public Administration
(ASPA), 220
American Water Resources Association, 173
American Water Works Association, 173
*An Inquiry into the Nature and Causes of the
Wealth of Nations* (Smith), 26
Argentina, 237
Arizona
Conference on Climate Change and Higher
Education, xiii
Decision Center for a Desert City (DCDC),
272–74
graywater, 174–75
Salt River Project (SRP), 40 (case)
State Implementation Plan (SIP), 133
Toxics Release Inventory Facility (TRIF), 218,
223, 224*f*
water conservation, 172, 174 (case), 175 (case),
176–77, 184
Arizona Department of Environmental Quality
(ADEQ), 133
Arizona Department of Water Resources
(ADWR), 177

Arizona State University, 165, 177, 272–73
Asbestos control (Canada), 104
ASEAN Cooperation Plan on Transboundary
Pollution, 148 (case)
Asia, 237
Asian Americans, 216–17, 218
Association for Public Policy Analysis and
Management (APPAM), 217
Association of Metropolitan Water Agencies,
173
At War with the Weather (Kunreuther), 185
Australia, 173 (case), 187 (case)
Automobiles
Anti-Idling Campaign (Ohio), 60
seat belts, 104
smog test, 144

B

Babbit, Bruce, 40 (case)
Babcock, Thomas M., 177
BBC World Service, xii-xiii
Benefit-Cost Analysis (BCA)
air quality, 143
basic components, 78–80
discussion questions/exercises, 116
double-counting, 111–12, 203–4
employment, 112–14
multiplier effects, 113–14
Environmental Justice, 216–17, 223
existence value, 110–11
externalities, 101–10
avoided health treatments, 109–10
contingent valuation method (CVM), 105,
111, 247, 249
Disability-Adjusted Life Years (DALYs),
109
epidemiology, 109
foregone activities, 109–10
health benefits, 103–9
hedonic pricing model, 102–3, 106–7, 117n3
Kaldor-Hicks Criterion, 107–8, 223
life valuation, 103–9
life-year valuation, 105–6
negative externalities, 101–2
positive externalities, 101
Quality-Adjusted Life Expectancy, 109

Benefit-Cost Analysis (BCA)
   externalities *(continued)*
      Quality-Adjusted Life Years (QALYs), 109
      shadow price, 102, 110, 247, 249
      statistical life valuation, 104–9, 117n5
   Internet websites, 116–17
   monetization, 79, 80, 84–100
      discounting, 90–100
      discount rate, 91–99
      internal rate of return, 99, 100*t*
      tennis court installation, 85–100
   performance guidelines, 115–16 (case)
   plug-in shadow price, 110
   sensitivity analysis, 114
   standing, 80–84
      criminals, 82–84
      future generations, 84, 94–95
      geopolitical boundaries, 81–82
   study guide, 116–17
   time factor, 80, 93–95
Best management practices (BMPs)
   public meetings, 239–40
   water runoff, 181–82
Blackwater, 174, 175 (case)
Botswana, 178
Bounded rationality, 241
Brownfields, 205–6
Brundtland Commission Report (1987), 289–90
Budget Hero, 271, 272–73 (case)
Buffalo hunting, 29
Bush, George W., 108, 278

C

California
   command-and-control regulations, 65
   emissions reduction program, 155 (case)
   intergovernmental agreement, 67
   Irvine Ranch Water District (IRWD), 73
   public education, 260–61 (case)
   public participation, 245, 252–53 (case)
   Russian River, 67
   State Water Project, 165
   water conservation, 179–80, 184
   West Oakland Environmental Indicators Project
      (WOEIP), 252–53 (case)
California Energy Commission, 165

Canada
   asbestos control, 104, 117n4
   emissions reduction, 68
   excess risk, 72–73
   GlobeScan, xii-xiii, 187
   salmon fishery, 67–68
Cap-and-trade system
   air quality, 151–54
   case analysis, 155
   program weaknesses, 153–54
Carbon dioxide, 142, 156–57, 164
Carbon Mitigation Initiative, 264
Carbon monoxide, 142*t*, 143, 144
Carbon sequestration, 142
Carbon sink, 142, 164
Carbon tax, 156–59
Carter, Jimmy, 40 (case)
Catchments, 184–85
Central Park (New York City), 69
Charrette, 243–44
Charter of European Cities & Towns Towards
      Sustainability (1994), xv
Chavis, Benjamin, 216
China
   Environmental Justice, 221
   public participation, 237
   water supply, 171 (case)
Citizen jury, 242–43
Citizen's Environmental Advisory Committee
      (Texas), 245
City Government Subsystem, 12*f*, 13, 15, 16*f*
Clark, Arthur C., 39, 41
Class, Environmental Justice, 217–19
Clean Air Act
   1963, 142, 143
   1970, 133, 143
Clean Air Act Amendments
   1977, 143
   1990, 143
Clean Water Act, 167–68
Clinton, Bill, 78, 79, 220
Coastlines
   coral reefs, 169 (case)
   ecological issues, 168–69, 185
   See also Oceans
Colorado
   Boulder Creek, 168

Colorado *(continued)*
  Denver, 180, 245
Command-and-control regulations
  air quality, 148 (case), 149, 151
  common pool resources (CPRs), 64, 65
Common pool resources (CPRs)
  defined, 35, 39
  goods taxonomy, 44*t*
  market failure solutions, 54–55*t*, 61–68
    command-and-control regulations, 64, 65
    congestion, 70
    elasticity, 64
    fixed-in place single government entity, 62–66
    intergovernmental agreement, 66, 67
    lobster fishing example, 63, 67
    mobile CPRs, 66–68
    multiple governments, 66
    price-elasticity, 62–63, 64
    privatization, 65
    quotas, 64, 73
    small groups, 62
    suasion/education, 65–66
    theory of fines, 62, 73
  nonexcludability, 35–37
  Ogallala Aquifer, 35–36
  policy-analytic concepts, 35–41, 44*t*
  rivalry, 35–37
  subtractability, 37
  Tragedy of the Commons, 37–41
Complement goods, 59
Complex ecosystem, 127
Concretion System
  adaptive management, 129–30, 131–34, 136*f*
    air, 132, 135*f*
    components of, 132*t*
    land, 131, 132*t*, 135*f*
    system interaction, 131, 132–34, 135*f*
    water, 132, 135*f*
  characteristics of, 9*f*, 10–11
  defined, 4
  integrated system model, 19, 20*f*, 21
  model illustration, 9*f*
  model symbolism, 7–8, 9*f*
  system interaction, 5, 9*f*, 10–11, 21, 22–23 (case), 285–86
  system model, 4, 7–11

Conference on Climate Change and Higher Education (Arizona), xiii
Congestion
  bridge example, 30
  case analysis, 31
  common pool resources (CPRs), 70
  congestion pricing, 31–32, 45–46
  marketable public/toll goods, 70
  market failure solutions, 55*t*, 70
  negative externalities, 55*t*, 70
  policy-analytic concepts, 30–33
  public goods, 30–33
  pure public good, 70
Consensus conference, 242
Contingent valuation method (CVM)
  Benefit-Cost Analysis (BCA), 105, 111, 247, 249
  survey-based approach, 247, 249
Cookbook, The (Arizona Department of Water Resources), 177
Cooper, James Fenimore, 30
Cope, Jean-Francois, 273 (case)
Cost
  congestion, 30–33
  defined, 29
  Fallacy of Sunk Costs, 46
  marginal cost, 29
  natural monopolies, 52
  opportunity costs, 85–86
  policy-analytic concepts, 29, 30–33
  Tragedy of the Commons, 38
  See also Benefit-Cost Analysis (BCA); Pricing
Criminals, 82–84
Criteria air pollutants, 143, 144–45
Crowdsourcing, 249–50
Culture
  defined, 5
  system interaction, 5, 6 (case), 7 (case)

D

Daley, Richard, 182 (case)
Dave, Anil, 14 (case)
DDT, 44
Decision Center for a Desert City (Arizona), 272–74
Declining-cost industry, 52

Demand management policy, 172–77, 180
Denmark, 233, 235, 237
Derwent River (Australia), 187 (case)
Desalination plants, 166 (case)
Direct provision
  national defense, 68
  public park, 69
  pure public goods, 68–69
Disability-Adjusted Life Years (DALYs), 109
Discount rate
  formulas, 95–98
  interest rate, 91, 95
  internal rate of return, 99, 100*t*
  monetization, 91–99
  nominal discount rate, 91, 92
  OMB Discounting Directive (2008), 91, 92–93
  project lifetime, 99, 100*t*
  real discount rate, 91, 92–93
  social rate of time preference, 93–100
  tennis court installation, 90–100
Doherty, N.A., 185
Double-counting, 111–12, 203–4
Douglas, M., 5
DPSIR Framework, 196, 197*f*
Dred Scott v. Sandford (1856), 83–84
Drought conditions
  environmental policy system model, 22–23
    (case)
  policy-analytic concepts, 48–49 (case)
Dzombak, David A., 67

E

East Asia, 13
Eco-cities, xv
Ecosystem management, 123–29
  appropriate institutional design, 128–29
  barrier solutions, 128–29
  common mistakes, 128
  complexity, 127
  defined, 124
  eight principles, 126
  holistic approach, 123–24
  incompleteness, 127–28
  Natural System, 128
  public participation, 126–27
  Social System, 128

Ecosystem management *(continued)*
  stakeholder collaboration, 124–26
  trends and principles, 124–28
  uncertainty, 127–28
Elasticity
  common pool resources (CPRs), 64
  defined, 64
  price-elasticity, 62–63, 64
Election ballots, 278–80
Electricity production, 45
Embodied cognition, 241
Emission trading regulatory systems
  air quality, 151–54, 155
  cap-and-trade system, 151–54
  case analysis, 155
  emissions reduction credit program, 151
Employment benefit-cost analysis, 112–14
  full employment, 112–13
  multiplier effects, 113–14
  reservation wage, 112
Energy and Water Integration Act (2009), 165
Energy resources
  electrical power lines, 221–22, 226n4
  geothermal power, 166 (case)
  hydroelectric dams, 165, 221
  nuclear power, 166 (case)
  solar power, 166 (case)
  thermoelectric power, 165, 166 (case), 178,
    190n2
Energy tax, 156–59
England
  congestion pricing, 31 (case), 45
  enclosure movement, 39 (case)
  Environmental Justice, 219
EnviroFone (United Arab Emirates), 165 (case)
Environmental Impact Assessment (EIA), 237
Environmental Justice
  adaptive management, 132–134, 135*f*
  analysis guidelines, 221–25
  Benefit-Cost Analysis (BCA), 216–17, 223
  class analysis, 217–19
  colocation relationship, 216–19
  compensation, 223–25
  disamenity placement, 216–19, 226n2
  environmental racism, 216–19
  government mistrust, 221–22, 227n5
  importance of, 219–21

Environmental Justice *(continued)*
  Internet websites, 226
  land usage, 205–7
  Locally Unwanted Land Uses (LULUs), 220–21
  mapping system, 223, 224*f*
  movement origins, 216
  noise pollution, 219, 221, 222 (case), 223
  Not In My Backyard (NIMBY), 221
  Not on Planet Earth (NOPE), 221
  policy debate, 215–19
  political analysis, 220–21
  power lines, 221–22, 226n4
  public participation, 225
  racial analysis, 216–19
  Toxics Release Inventory Facility (TRIF), 218, 223, 224*f*
  treatment, storage, and disposal facility (TSDF), 216
Environmental policy
  adaptive management, 287
  eco-cities, xv
  flexible management, 287
  green literature, xv, xvi*t*
  holistic approach, 123–24, 131–34, 285–86
  inclusive management, 287
  media interaction, 287–89
    administrative checklist, 288*f*
  policy-analytic perspective, xv-xvi
  policy tools, 289–90
  research overview, xvi-xviii
  urban focus, xi-xiii
  urbanization trends, xiv-xv
  See also Global urbanization
Environmental policy games. *See* Public education; *specific game*
Environmental policy system model
  characteristics of, 3–4
  Concretion System, 4, 7–11
  drought conditions example, 22–23 (case)
  integrated model, 19, 20*f*, 21
  model defined, 4, 11
  model symbolism, 7–8
    illustrated definitions, 8*f*
  Natural System, 4, 5–11
  Physical System, 4, 5–11
  Policy Process, 15–19
  purpose of, 21–23

Environmental policy system model *(continued)*
  Social System, 4, 5–7, 11, 12*f*, 13–19
  See also Concretion System; Natural System; Physical System; Policy Process; Social System
Environmental Protection Law (China, 1979), 237
Epidemiology, 109
Estuaries, 168–69
Europe
  Aalborg Charter (1994), xv
  Environmental Justice, 219
  public participation, 236–37
  See also Global urbanization; *specific country*
Eutrophication, 145
Excess risk
  market failure solutions, 55*t*, 72–73
  moral hazard, 72
Excludability
  bridge example, 33–34, 35
  continuum taxonomy, 32*f*, 34
  defined, 28
  goods typology, 29*t*, 32*f*, 33*t*, 44*t*
  legal excludability, 33–35
  marketable public/toll goods, 33–35
  physical excludability, 33–35
  policy-analytic concepts, 28–29, 32–35
  public goods, 28–29, 32–35
Executive Order 12866 (1993), 78, 79
Executive Order 12898 (1994), 220
Executive Order 13563 (2011), 234, 235*f*
Existence value
  Benefit-Cost Analysis (BCA), 110–11
  indicator species, 111
Externalities
  Benefit-Cost Analysis (BCA), 101–10
  congestion, 55*t*, 70
  defined, 41
  free riders, 43
  internalize the externality, 70, 71
  market failure solutions, 55*t*, 70–72
  negative externalities, 41–43, 44, 70–72, 101–2
  open space example, 42
  policy-analytic concepts, 41–43
  positive externalities, 41–42, 71–72, 101
  zero pollution levels, 44

F

Fairness or Efficiency (Zajac), 173
Fallacy of Sunk Costs, 46
Federal Housing Administration (FHA), 201–2 (case)
Federal Motor Vehicle Safety Standards (FMVSS), 104
Fern Tiger Associates (FTA), 266, 282n2
Fines, 62, 73
Finland, 237
Fixed-in place single government entity, 62–66
Florida, 278, 279f
Focus Maui Nui (Hawaii), 264, 266, 267 (case), 269, 270 (case)
France, 183, 219, 234, 273 (case)
Free riders, 43
Fremling, Calvin, 7 (case)
Fuel tax, 154, 156–59
Full employment
   Benefit-Cost Analysis (BCA), 112–13
   defined, 113
Future generations, 84, 94–95

G

Games. *See* Public education; *specific game*
Geographic Information Systems (GIS)
   Environmental Justice mapping, 223, 224f
   public education mapping, 260–61
   public participation mapping, 244–45, 250
Geopolitical boundaries, 81–82
Georges Bank, 35
Geothermal power, 166 (case)
Germany, 182, 219, 234
Global Institute of Sustainability (Arizona State University), 272–73
Global Refunding System (GRS), 69
Global urbanization
   air quality, 148–49 (case)
   congestion pricing, 31 (case), 45
   enclosure movement, 39 (case)
   Environmental Justice, 219, 221
   environmental policy, xi, xii-xiii, xv
   population growth, xiv
   public education, 273 (case)
   public participation, 233, 236–37

Global urbanization (*continued*)
   urbanization trends, xiv
   water supply
      agricultural irrigation, 178, 179
      desalination plants, 166
      green parking lots, 183
      green roofs, 182, 183f
      mining industry, 179 (case)
      pegged scarcity-pricing system, 173 (case)
      pollution, 6 (case), 7 (case)
      population demand, 171 (case)
      urban renewal, 14 (case), 187 (case)
   See also specific country
GlobeScan (Canada), xii-xiii, 187
Gore, Al, 278
Grace, M.F., 185
Grafton, Quentin, 173 (case)
Grand Canyon National Park, 34
Graphical public education, 258–62, 263 (case)
Graywater, 174–76
Great Lakes Basin, 66
Greece, 179 (case)
Green asphalt, 182 (case)
Greenhouse Gamble, 262, 263 (case)
Green literature, xv, xvit
Green parking lots, 183
Green roofs, 182, 183f
Ground-level ozone, 143, 145, 147, 149
Groundwater Management Act (1980), 40 (case)
Growth-management plans, 200, 202, 209–10

H

Hardin, Garrett, 37–38
Hawaii
   Focus Maui Nui, 264, 266, 267 (case), 269, 270 (case)
   mariculture development, 130, 131
   PlanStory, 264, 267, 269, 270 (case)
   WalkStory, 264, 266–67, 268 (case), 269
Haze, 148–49 (case)
Haze Technical Task Force, 148 (case)
Health benefit-cost analysis, 103–9
   avoided health treatments, 109–10
   Disability-Adjusted Life Years (DALYs), 109
   epidemiology, 109
   foregone activities, 109–10

Health benefit-cost analysis *(continued)*
  life valuation, 103–9
    Quality-Adjusted Life Expectancy, 109
    Quality-Adjusted Life Years (QALYs), 109
    statistical life valuation, 104–9, 117n5
Healthy Cities (World Health Organization), xvii
Hedonic pricing model, 102–3, 106–7, 117n3
Hispanics, 216–17, 223
Holistic approach
  adaptive management, 123–24, 131–34
  ecosystem management, 123–24
  environmental policy, 123–24, 131–34, 285–86
Home Owners Loan Corporation, 201–2 (case)
Household water usage, 170–77
Hydroelectric dams, 165, 221

I

Illinois, 182 (case)
Incident Commander, 271–72
Incomplete ecosystem, 127–28
Independent Pricing and Regulatory Tribunal
    (IPART), 173 (case)
India
  Ganesh Caturthi festival, 6 (case)
  International River Festival, 14 (case)
  public participation, 237
  urban renewal, 14 (case)
  water, 6 (case), 14 (case)
Indiana, 203
Indicator species, 111
Indonesia, 148–49 (case), 237
Informal social contract, 130–31
Information asymmetry, 52, 53, 57
Information problems
  examples, 60, 559
  information asymmetry, 52, 53, 57
  information provision, 58, 59, 60
  market failure solutions, 54t, 57–58, 59, 60
  perfect information, 57
  suasion/education, 58, 59, 60
Ingram, H., 258
Initiatives, 17
Inspection and Maintenance test
  test-and-repair program, 144
  test-only program, 144
Integrated Water Resources Management, 187, 190

Interest rate, 91, 95
Intergovernmental agreement, 66, 67
Internalize the externality, 70, 71
Internal rate of return, 99, 100t
International Association for Public Participation,
    237
Internet websites
  Benefit-Cost Analysis (BCA), 116–17
  Environmental Justice, 226
  market failure solutions, 75
  online survey, 248 (case)
  public education, 269, 271–75
  public participation, 253
  public participation methods, 248 (case), 249–
    51
  water conservation, 177, 186, 190
  Web 2.0 technology, 250–51
Invisible Hand Theorem, 26–27, 29
Irvine Ranch Water District (IRWD), California,
    73

J

Jeane, Pam, 67
*Journal of Contemporary Water Research and
    Education*, 165
Journal of the American Planning Association,
    xii

K

Kaldor-Hicks Criterion, 107–8, 223
Khatzakis, Angelos, 179 (case)
Klein, R.W., 185
Korea, 106–7
Kunreuther, H.C., 185
Kyoto Protocol, 68, 69, 156–57

L

Lakes, 168
Land
  adaptive management
    Concretion System, 131, 132t, 135f
    Natural System, 131, 132t, 135f
    system interaction, 131, 132–34, 135–36f
  DPSIR Framework, 196, 197f

Land *(continued)*
  ecological issues, 197–205
    growth-management plans, 200, 202
    land-use changes, 197–99
    monocentric city model, 200, 201–2 (case)
    urban green spaces, 202–5
    urban sprawl, 199–205
  media interaction, 141–42, 164–66, 287–89
  policy tools, 208–11
    administrative checklist, 211–12*f*, 288*f*
    growth-management plans, 200, 202, 209–10
    smart-growth theory, 209–10
    taxation, 210
    tradable development rights (TDR), 210–11
    urban green spaces, 202–5
    zoning policy, 206–7, 208–9
  social issues, 205–8
    brownfields, 205–6
    Environmental Justice, 205–7
    political institutions, 207–8
    zoning policy, 206–7
  system interaction, 9*f*, 10, 195–96
  urbanization trends, 196, 197*f*
Lawns, 173
Law of Unintended Consequences
  adaptive management, 287
  congestion pricing, 45–46
  defined, 46
Lead, 143, 145
Legal excludability, 33–35
Life valuation
  Benefit-Cost Analysis (BCA), 103–9
  Disability-Adjusted Life Years (DALYs), 109
  environmental policy, 105 (case)
  life-year valuation, 105–6
  Quality-Adjusted Life Expectancy, 109
  Quality-Adjusted Life Years (QALYs), 109
  statistical life valuation, 104–9, 117n5
Little, Val, 174 (case)
Lobster fishing, 63, 67
Locally Unwanted Land Uses (LULUs), 220–21
Los Angeles Times, 219

M

Mapping system
  Environmental Justice, 223, 224*f*

Mapping system *(continued)*
  public education, 259–61, 282n1
  public participation, 244–45
Marginal cost, 29
Mariculture (Hawaii)
  adaptive management, 130–31
  defined, 131
Marketable public/toll goods
  bridge example, 33, 34–35
  defined, 33
  excludability, 33–35
  goods taxonomy, 33*t*, 44*t*
  legal excludability, 33–35
  market failure solutions, 54*t*, 58–59, 61
    complement goods, 59
    congestion, 70
    price-elasticity, 59, 61
    substitute goods, 59
  physical excludability, 33–35
  policy-analytic concepts, 33–35, 44*t*
  rivalry, 33–35
Market failure
  defined, 27
  four types, 52
  policy-analytic concepts, 27
Market failure solutions. *See* Policy instruments
Maser, C., xvii
Massachusetts, 245
Metered water, 172
Meuse River, 168
Michel-Kerjan, E.O., 185
Mining industry, 178, 179 (case)
Minnesota, 7 (case), 14 (case)
Mississippi River
  intergovernmental agreement, 66, 67
  water quality, 7 (case), 14 (case)
Mobile Apps for Citizens, 274
Mobile common pool resources, 66–68
Monet, Claude, 183
Monetization
  Benefit-Cost Analysis (BCA), 79, 80, 84–100
  defined, 79, 80
  monopoly rent, 86
  opportunity costs, 85–86
  tennis court installation, 85–100
    benefits, 87–90, 117n1
    costs, 85–87, 88*t*

Monetization
  tennis court installation (continued)
    discounting, 90–100
    discount rate, 91–99
    net benefits, 90t, 100t, 101t
    project lifetime, 99, 100t
    streams of costs/benefits, 90–100
Monocentric city model, 200, 201–2 (case)
Monopolies, 52–53, 54t, 56
Monopoly rent, 86
Monopsony
  defined, 56–57
  market failure solutions, 54t, 56–57
Moral hazard, 72
Multiplier employment effects, 113–14
Mutual coercion mutually agreed upon, 38

N

Namibia, 178
National Ambient Air Quality Standards
    (NAAQS), 143
National Association for the Advancement of
    Colored People (NAACP), 216
National Conference on City Planning (1909), xii
National Environmental Policy Act (1969), 126–
    27, 234, 235, 287
National Research Council, 66, 67
National Science Foundation, 272–73
Native Americans, 216–17
Natural Drainage Systems (NDS), 182
Natural monopolies
  declining-cost industry, 52
  information asymmetry, 52, 53
  market failure solutions, 52–53, 54t, 56
  market power, 52–53
Natural System
  adaptive management
    air, 132, 135f
    components of, 132t
    land, 131, 132t, 135f
    system interaction, 131, 132–34, 135f
    water, 131–32, 135f
  characteristics of, 9f, 10
  defined, 4
  ecosystem management, 128
  environmental media interaction, 9f, 10

Natural System (continued)
  integrated system model, 19, 20f, 21
  model illustration, 9f
  model symbolism, 7–8, 9f
  system interaction, 5, 6 (case), 7 (case), 9f,
    10–11, 21, 22–23 (case), 285–86
  system model, 4, 5–11
Neoclassical microeconomics, 82–83
Netherlands, 182, 183f, 237
New Federalism, xi
New Jersey, 205–6
New Mexico, 245
New Public Administration, 235–36
New York City
  Central Park, 69
  metered water, 172
  public education, 271, 272–73 (case)
  public participation, 245
  zoning policy, 206
New Zealand, 156–57
Nitrogen dioxide, 142t
Nitrogen oxides, 142t, 143, 144, 145, 152–53,
    155 (case)
Noise pollution, 219, 221, 222 (case), 223
Nominal discount rate, 91, 92
Nonexcludability
  common pool resources (CPRs), 35–37
  goods typology, 29t, 32f, 33t, 44t
  policy-analytic concepts, 26, 28–33, 35–37, 44t
  pricing, 28–29
Nongovernmental Organization (NGO), 146
Nongovernmental Subsystem, 12f, 13, 15, 16f
Nonpoint source pollution, 170
Nonrivalry
  goods typology, 29t, 32f, 33t, 44t
  policy-analytic concepts, 26, 28–33, 44t
Norway, 237
Not In My Backyard (NIMBY), 221
Not on Planet Earth (NOPE), 221
Nuclear power, 166 (case)

O

Obama, Barack, 234, 235f
Oceans
  coastlines, 168–69, 185
  common pool resources (CPRs), 35

Oceans *(continued)*
  coral reefs, 169 (case)
  desalination plants, 166
  ecological issues, 166, 168–69, 185
  ocean flooding, 185
Ogallala Aquifer
  common pool resources (CPRs), 35–36
  map, 36*f*
Ohio, 60
Oleru, Ngozi, 215
Opinion survey
  bias, 249
  content, 246–47
  contingent valuation method (CVM), 247,
    249
  cost, 246
  coverage, 246
  online survey, 248 (case)
  public participation, 245–49
  sampling error, 246
  survey design, 246–49
Opportunity costs
  defined, 86
  monetization, 85–86
Oregon, 182
Other Governmental Systems, 12*f*, 14–15
Ozone
  ground-level ozone, 143, 145, 147, 149
  nonexcludability, 28–29
Ozone Transport Assessment Group (OTAG),
    147, 149

P

Pacala, Stephen, 264
Painting the Landscape (International Association
    for Public Participation), 237
Palaniappan, Meena, 252–53 (case)
Papageorgiou, Tolis, 179 (case)
Pareto efficiency, 26–27, 29, 30–31, 49n3
Particulate matter (PM10), 142*t*, 143, 144–45
PA Times, 220
Pauly, M.V., 185
Pegged scarcity-pricing system, 173 (case)
Perfect information, 57
Pfister, A.J., 177
Physical excludability, 33–35

Physical System
  integrated system model, 19, 20*f*, 21
  model illustration, 9*f*
  model symbolism, 7–8, 9*f*
  system model, 4, 5–11
  See also Concretion System; Natural System
Pioneers, The (Cooper), 30 (case)
Pittock, Jamie, 166 (case)
PlanStory (Hawaii), 264, 267, 269, 270 (case)
Plug-in shadow price, 110
Plumbing fixtures, 173–74
Point source pollution, 170
Policy-analytic concepts
  common pool resources (CPRs), 35–41, 44*t*
  congestion, 30–33
  cost, 29, 30–33
  discussion questions, 47
  drought conditions example, 48–49 (case)
  excludability, 28–29, 32–35
    legal excludability, 33–35
    physical excludability, 33–35
  externalities, 41–43
  Fallacy of Sunk Costs, 46
  free riders, 43
  goods taxonomy, 28, 29*t*, 32*f*, 44*t*
  Invisible Hand Theorem, 26–27, 29
  Law of Unintended Consequences, 45–46, 287
  marginal cost, 29
  marketable public/toll goods, 33–35, 44*t*
  market failure, 27
  nonexcludability, 26, 28–33, 35–37, 44*t*
  nonrivalry, 26, 28–33, 44*t*
  Pareto efficiency, 26–27, 29, 30–31, 49n3
  pricing, 28–29, 30–33
  private goods, 25–27, 44*t*
  public goods, 26–43, 44*t*
  pure private goods, 26–27, 29*t*, 44*t*
  pure public goods, 28–30, 44*t*
  rivalry, 26, 28–33, 35–37, 44*t*
  study guide, 47
  subtractability, 26, 37
  Tragedy of the Commons, 37–41
  zero pollution levels, 44–45
Policy-analytic perspective, xv–xvi
Policy Designs for Democracy (Schneider and
    Ingram), 258
Policy Evaluation, 16*f*, 19

Policy Formulation, 16*f*, 17–18
Policy Implementation, 16*f*, 18–19
Policy instruments
  air quality, 149–59
  for common pool resources (CPRs), 54–55*t*,
    61–68
    fixed-in place single government entity,
      62–66
    mobile CPRs, 66–68
    multiple governments, 66
    small groups, 62
  for congestion, 55*t*, 70
  discussion questions, 75
  environmental policy, 289–90
  for excess risk, 55*t*, 72–73
  for externalities, 55*t*, 70–72
  for information problems, 54*t*, 57–58, 59, 60
  Internet websites, 75
  land usage, 208–11
  for marketable public/toll goods, 54*t*, 58–59, 61
  overview, 54–55*t*
  public education, 262, 264–81
  public participation, 238–51, 252–53 (case)
  for pure private goods
    monopolies, 52–53, 54*t*, 56
    monopsony, 54*t*, 56–57
    natural monopolies, 52–53, 54*t*, 56
  for pure public goods, 55*t*, 68–69
    direct provision, 68–69
    subsidization, 68, 69
    taxation, 68
  study guide, 75
  transition management, 74–75
  water, 170–86, 187 (case)
  See also Benefit-Cost Analysis (BCA)
Policy Legitimation, 16*f*, 18
Policy Process
  Agenda Setting stage, 16*f*, 17
  City Government Subsystem, 15, 16*f*
  Governmental Subsystem, 15, 16*f*, 17–19
  initiatives, 17
  integrated system model, 19, 20*f*, 21
  model illustration, 16*f*
  Nongovernmental Subsystem, 15, 16*f*
  Policy Evaluation stage, 16*f*, 19
  Policy Formulation stage, 16*f*, 17–18
  Policy Implementation stage, 16*f*, 18–19

Policy Process *(continued)*
  Policy Legitimation stage, 16*f*, 18
  Problem Identification stage, 16*f*, 17
  propositions, 17
  referendum, 17
  system model, 15–19
Potentially Pareto Improving Criterion, 105–
  6107–8
Power lines, 221–22, 226n4
Price-elasticity
  common pool resources (CPRs), 62–63, 64
  defined, 64
  marketable public/toll goods, 59, 61
Pricing
  congestion pricing, 31–32, 45–46
  defined, 29
  hedonic pricing model, 102–3, 106–7, 117n3
  nonexcludability, 28–29
  pegged scarcity-pricing system, 173 (case)
  plug-in shadow price, 110
  policy-analytic concepts, 28–29, 30–33
  shadow price, 102, 110, 247, 249
  water pricing, 172–73
  See also Benefit-Cost Analysis (BCA); Cost
Princeton Environmental Institute, 264, 265–66
  (case), 274
Private goods
  characteristics of, 25–26
  defined, 25
  goods taxonomy, 44*t*
  policy-analytic concepts, 25–27, 44*t*
Privatization
  common pool resources (CPRs), 65
  Tragedy of the Commons, 38–39
Problem Identification, 16*f*, 17
Production water usage, 177–80
Program on International Policy Attitudes (PIPA),
  xii-xiii
Propositions, 17
Public education
  administrative checklist, 281*f*
  election ballots, 278–80
  global urbanization, 273 (case)
  graphics, 258–62, 263 (case)
    graphical excellence, 259 (case), 261
    mapping system, 259–61, 282n1
    risk presentations, 262, 263 (case)

Public education *(continued)*
  Internet websites, 269, 271–75
  online information, 274–75
  policy games, 262, 264–74
    Budget Hero, 271, 272–73 (case)
    computer games, 269, 271–74
    Focus Maui Nui (Hawaii), 264, 266, 267
      (case), 269, 270 (case)
    Incident Commander, 271–72
    in-person games, 264–69, 270 (case)
    PlanStory (Hawaii), 264, 267, 269, 270
      (case)
    Serious Games Initiative, 271
    Social Impact Games, 271
    Stabilization Wedges, 264, 265–66 (case), 274
    WalkStory (Hawaii), 264, 266–67, 268
      (case), 269
    WaterSim, 273–74
  policy tools, 262, 264–81
  structured value referendum (SVR), 275–81
Public goods
  congestion, 30–33
  defined, 26
  drought conditions, 48–49 (case)
  excludability, 28–29, 32–35
  market failure, 27
  nonexcludability, 26, 28–33, 35–37, 44*t*
  nonrivalry, 26, 28–33, 44*t*
  Pareto efficiency, 26–27, 29, 30–31, 49n3
  policy-analytic concepts, 26–43, 44*t*
  pure public goods, 28–30, 44*t*
  rivalry, 26, 28–33, 35–37, 44*t*
  summary, 43
  Valley Fever virus, 26, 49n2
Public meetings
  best practices, 239–40
  bounded rationality, 241
  embodied cognition, 241
  participation method, 239–41
Public participation
  air quality, 146
  benefits of, 238
  challenges of, 238
  charrette, 243–44
  citizen jury, 242–43
  community-based participatory research
    (CBPR), 251, 252–53 (case)

Public participation *(continued)*
  computer-based methods, 248 (case),
    249–51
  consensus conference, 242
  crowdsourcing, 249–50
  ecosystem management, 126–27
  Environmental Justice, 225
  global trends, 233, 236–37
  Google timeline (1950–2011), 236*f*
  Internet websites, 253
  legislation, 234–36
  mapping system, 244–45
  new public administration, 235–36
  online survey, 248 (case)
  opinion survey, 245–49
  policy tools, 238–51, 252–53 (case)
  public meetings, 239–41
  scenario workshop, 242
  social media, 250–51
  study circle, 243
  workshops, 241–43
Public-supply water, 177–78, 190n2
Pure private goods
  goods typology, 29*t*, 32*f*, 33*t*, 44*t*
  market failure solutions
    information asymmetry, 53
    monopolies, 52–53, 54*t*, 56
    monopsony, 54*t*, 56–57
    natural monopolies, 52–53, 54*t*, 56
  policy-analytic concepts, 26–27, 29*t*, 44*t*
Pure public goods, 28–30, 44*t*
  defined, 39
  goods typology, 29*t*, 32*f*, 33*t*, 44*t*
  market failure solutions, 55*t*, 68–69
    congestion, 70
    direct provision, 68–69
    Kyoto Protocol, 68, 69
    subsidization, 68, 69
    taxation, 68
  policy-analytic concepts, 28–30, 44*t*
Push polls, 276

Q

Quality-Adjusted Life Expectancy, 109
Quality-Adjusted Life Years (QALYs), 109
Quotas, 64, 73

R

Race, Environmental Justice, 216–19
Rainwater harvesting, 176
Real discount rate, 91, 92–93
RECLAIM (California), 155 (case)
Recreational water usage, 185–86
Referendum, 17
Regional Haze Action Plan (RHAP), 148 (case)
Rent control, 52
Reservation wage, 112
Rhine River, 168
Rio Agenda (United Nations), xv, 236–37
Risk
  excess risk, 55t, 72–73
  public education presentations, 262, 263 (case)
Risk and Culture (Douglas and Wildavsky), 5
Rivalry
  common pool resources (CPRs), 35–37
  continuum taxonomy, 32f, 34
  defined, 28
  goods typology, 29t, 32f, 33t, 44t
  marketable public/toll goods, 33–35
  policy-analytic concepts, 26, 28–33, 35–37, 44t
  public goods, 26, 28–33, 35–37, 44t
Rivers, 168
Russian River (California), 67

S

Salt River Project (Arizona), 40 (case)
Scenario workshop, 242
Schneider, A.L., 258
Schwarzenegger, Arnold, 65
Science, 37–38
Scolow, Robert, 264
Seat belts, 104
Second Life, 274–75
Sensitivity analysis, 114
Serious Games Initiative, 271
Shadow price
  Benefit-Cost Analysis (BCA), 102, 110, 247, 249
  defined, 102
  plug-in shadow price, 110
Slavery, 83–84
Slovakia, 219

Smart-growth theory, 209–10
Smith, Adam, 26
Smog test, 144
Smoking, 74–75
Social Impact Games, 271
Social media, 250–51
Social rate of time preference
  defined, 93
  discount rate, 93–100
Social System
  adaptive management, 129–30, 131–34, 136f
    Environmental Justice, 132–134, 135f
    system interaction, 131, 132–34, 135f
  characteristics of, 11, 12f, 13–15
  City Government Subsystem, 12f, 13, 15, 16f
  culture, 5, 6 (case), 7 (case)
  defined, 5
  Ecosystem management, 128
  Governmental Subsystem, 6–7, 12f, 13–14, 15, 16f, 17–19, 23n1
    case analysis, 14
  integrated system model, 19, 20f, 21
  model illustration, 12f
  model symbolism, 11, 12f, 13
  Nongovernmental Subsystem, 12f, 13, 15, 16f
  Other Governmental Systems, 12f, 14–15
  Policy Process, 15–19
  system interaction, 5, 6 (case), 7 (case), 21, 22–23 (case), 285–86
  system model, 4, 5–7, 11, 12f, 13–19
Sod houses, 182, 190n4
Solar power, 166 (case)
South Africa, 178, 237
Southeast Asia, 148–49 (case)
Stabilization Wedges, 264, 265–66 (case), 274
Stakeholders
  air quality groups, 146
  collaborative ecosystem management, 124–26
Standing
  Benefit-Cost Analysis (BCA), 80–84
  defined, 80
  exclusion, 81–82
  future generations, 84, 94–95
  geopolitical boundaries, 81–82
  inclusion, 81–82
  neoclassical microeconomics, 82–83
  political reality, 81

Standing *(continued)*
  slavery example, 83–84
State Implementation Plan
  air quality standards, 133, 141–42
  Arizona, 133
State Water Project (California), 165
Statistical life valuation, 104–9, 117n5
Stormwater runoff, 180–82
Streams, 168
Structured value referendum (SVR)
  election ballots, 278–80
  policy process, 277–79
  public education, 275–81
Study circle, 243
Suasion/education
  common pool resources (CPRs), 65–66
  defined, 58
  examples, 59, 60
  market failure solutions, 58, 59, 60
Subsidization
  externalities, 70
  Global Refunding System (GRS), 69
  Kyoto Protocol, 68, 69
  pure public goods, 68, 69
Substitute goods, 59
Subtractability, 26, 37
Sulfur dioxide, 142t, 144, 152, 153, 155 (case)
Sulfur oxides, 142t, 143, 144, 153
Summative Evaluation, 16f, 19
SustainAbility, 187
Sustainable Community Development (Maser),
  xvii
Sustainable Urban Drainage Systems (SUDS),
  182
Sweden, 237
Switzerland, 166 (case)

T

Taiwan, 237
Tanzania, 179
Tapi River (India), 6 (case)
Tax-and-refund program, 158–59
Taxation
  air quality, 154, 156–59
    advantages of, 157
    carbon tax, 156–59

Taxation
  air quality *(continued)*
    disadvantages of, 158
    energy tax, 156–59
    fuel tax, 154, 156–59
    political considerations, 157
    tax-and-refund program, 158–59
  externalities, 70
  land usage, 210
  pure public goods, 68
Test-and-repair program (vehicles), 144
Test-only program (vehicles), 144
Texas, 245
Theory of fines
  common pool resources (CPRs), 62, 73
Thermoelectric power, 165, 166 (case), 178,
  190n2
Three Gorges Dam (China), 221
Time factor
  Benefit-Cost Analysis (BCA), 80, 93–95
  social rate of time preference, 93–100
Toll goods. *See* Marketable public/toll goods
Total Maximum Daily Load (TMDL), 170
Toxics Release Inventory Facility (TRIF), 218,
  223, 224f
Toxics Release Inventory (TRI) Program, 218
Toxic Wastes and Race in the United States
  (United Church of Christ), 216, 217, 226n1
Tradable development rights (TDR), 210–11
Tragedy of the Commons
  common pool resources (CPRs), 37–41
  enclosure movement (England), 39 (case)
  examples, 37–38
  government-forced preservation, 39, 40 (case),
    41
  mutual coercion mutually agreed upon, 38
  privatization, 38–39
  solutions for, 38–41
  transaction costs, 38
Transboundary air pollution
  administrative guidelines, 150t
  air quality, 146–49, 150t
  Southeast Asia, 148–49 (case)
Transition management, 74–75
Treasury Green Book, 91–93
Treatment, storage, and disposal facility (TSDF),
  216

Tufte, E.R., 259, 261
Turf, 173
Turkey, 173
2001: A Space Odyssey (1968), 39, 41

U

Uncertain ecosystem, 127–28
United Arab Emirates, 165 (case)
United Church of Christ (UCC), 216, 217, 226n1
United Nations Agenda 21, xv, 236–37
United Nations Economic Commission for
    Europe (UNECE), 233, 235, 237
University of British Columbia, 276
Urban green spaces, 202–5
Urban heat island effect, 184
Urban sprawl, 199–205
U.S. Agency for International Development
    (USAID), 187, 190
U.S. Army Corps of Engineers, 78, 167–68
U.S. Environmental Protection Agency (EPA)
  air quality, 143, 144
  public education, 258
  State Implementation Program (Arizona), 133
  statistical life analysis, 104–5, 106–7, 108
  Toxics Release Inventory (TRI) Program, 218
  water, 167–68, 181 (case), 186
U.S. Federal Budget, 271
U.S. Federal Coastal Barrier Resources Act
    (1982), 185
U.S. Federal Emergency Management
    Administration (FEMA), 72
U.S. Fish and Wildlife Service, 220–21
U.S. General Accounting Office, 202 (case)
U.S. Geological Survey (USGS), 177–78, 259–60
U.S. National Institute of Justice, 271–72
U.S. National Park Service, 34
U.S. Office of Management and Budget (OMB),
    91–93
U.S. Public Health Service, 143
U.S. Surgeon General, 74–75

V

Valley Fever virus, 26, 49n2
Veterans Administration, 201–2 (case)
Victoria Capital Regional District, 279–80

Virginia, 181 (case)
Visual Display of Quantitative Information, The
    (Tufte), 259, 261

W

WalkStory (Hawaii), 264, 266–67, 268 (case),
    269
Washington, 182–83
Water
  adaptive management
      Concretion System, 132, 135*f*
      Natural System, 131–32, 135*f*
      system interaction, 131, 132–34, 135–36*f*
  Arizona, 172, 174 (case), 175 (case), 176–77,
      184
  Australia, 173 (case)
  carbon sink, 164
  China, 171 (case)
  conservation measures
      household usage, 171–77
      production usage, 179–80
      recreational usage, 186
      water runoff, 180–85
  coral reefs, 169 (case)
  drought conditions, 22–23 (case), 48–49 (case)
  ecological issues, 167–70
      coastlines, 168–69, 185
      estuaries, 168–69
      lakes, 168
      nonpoint source pollution, 170
      oceans, 166, 168–69, 185
      point source pollution, 170
      rivers, 168
      streams, 168
      Total Maximum Daily Load (TMDL), 170
      wetlands, 167–68
  Greece, 179 (case)
  India, 6 (case), 14 (case)
  Internet websites, 177, 186, 190
  legislation, 165, 167–68, 185
  media interaction, 141–42, 165–66
  Mississippi River, 7 (case), 14 (case)
  policy tools, 170–86, 187 (case)
      administrative checklist, 188–89*f*, 288*f*
      best management practices (BMPs), 181–82
      blackwater, 174, 175 (case)

Water
  policy tools *(continued)*
    catchments, 184–85
    community programs, 176–77
    consensus solutions, 187 (case)
    curbside landscaping, 182–83
    demand management policy, 172–77, 180
    graywater, 174–76
    green asphalt, 182 (case)
    green parking lots, 183
    green roofs, 182, 183*f*
    household conversation, 171–77
    impermeability reduction, 180–85
    insufficient water supply, 171–77
    lawns, 173
    metered water, 172
    Natural Drainage Systems (NDS), 182
    ocean flooding, 185
    pegged scarcity-pricing system, 173 (case)
    plumbing fixtures, 173–74
    production conservation, 179–80
    rainwater harvesting, 176
    recreational conservation, 186
    sod houses, 182, 190n4
    Sustainable Urban Drainage Systems
      (SUDS), 182
    urban heat island effect, 184
    water pricing, 172–73
    water runoff conservation, 180–85
    xeriscaping, 173
  social issues, 170–86
    agricultural irrigation, 178–79
    desalination plants, 166 (case)
    geothermal power, 166 (case)
    household water usage, 170–77
    hydroelectric dams, 165
    mining industry, 178, 179 (case)
    nuclear power, 166 (case)
    production usage, 177–80
    public-supply water, 177–78, 190n2
    recreational usage, 185–86
    solar power, 166 (case)
    stormwater runoff, 180–82
    thermoelectric power, 165, 166 (case), 178,
      190n2
    water runoff, 180–85

social issues *(continued)*
    Switzerland, 166 (case)
    system interaction, 9*f*, 10, 131, 132–34,
      135–36*f*, 163
    United Arab Emirates, 165 (case)
    urban renewal, 14 (case), 187 (case)
Water runoff, 180–85
WaterSim, 273–74
Web 2.0 technology, 250–51
West Oakland Environmental Indicators Project
    (WOEIP), 252–53 (case)
Wetlands, 167–68
Wikipedia, 274
Wikis, 274–75
Wildavsky, A., 5
Wired, 249
Woodrow Wilson International Center for
    Scholars, 271
Workshops
    citizen jury, 242–43
    consensus conference, 242
    public participation, 241–43
    scenario workshop, 242
    study circle, 243
World Commission on Environment and
    Development (WCED), 289–90
World Health Organization (WHO), xvii
World Public Opinion (2007), xii-xiii
World Wildlife Fund (WWF), 166 (case)

X

Xeriscaping, 173

Y

Younos, Tamim, 181 (case)
YouTube, 274

Z

Zajac, E.E., 173
Zero pollution levels, 44–45
Zoning policy, 206–7, 208–9

About the Authors

Heather E. Campbell, Chair of the Department of Politics and Policy at the Claremont Graduate University (CGU) School of Politics and Economics, does research in public policy analysis, especially environmental policy and justice. She received her BA from the University of California–San Diego, Revelle College, and her MPhil and PhD in Public Policy Analysis from Carnegie Mellon University. She has served as the editor-in-chief of the *Journal of Public Affairs Education*. Before joining CGU, she was a professor at Arizona State University and served as graduate director there.

Elizabeth A. Corley is the Lincoln Professor of Public Policy, Ethics, and Emerging Technologies and an Associate Professor in the School of Public Affairs at Arizona State University (ASU). Her research interests focus on environmental policy. She received a B.S.C.E. in Civil Engineering, an M.S.C.E. in Environmental Fluid Mechanics and Water Resources, an M.S. in Environmental Engineering, and a Ph.D. in Public Policy—all from the Georgia Institute of Technology. Before joining ASU, she held teaching and research positions at Georgia Tech, Bucknell University, and Columbia University.

Nicholas L. Cain, author of Chapter 10, is a research assistant and PhD student at Claremont Graduate University. He holds an MPA in Public Policy from Columbia University. He has contributed to many reports and publications including National Geographic's, *Atlas of the World*, 8th editon and *The World's Worker, 2004–2005*.